PREFACE

Bill Cary was the leading figure in corporate law from the early 1960's, when he assumed the chairmanship of the SEC, until his death. No one was his equal in seeing the large picture and in seeing the way the law was heading. With his passing a figure of remarkably clear vision and great moral and intellectual stature left the scene. I miss him inestimably as a friend and collaborator.

MELVIN A. EISENBERG

Berkeley, California
May, 1984

*

CASES AND MATERIALS

ON

CORPORATIONS
[ABRIDGED AND UNABRIDGED]

By

WILLIAM L. CARY
Late Dwight Professor of Law, Columbia University

and

MELVIN ARON EISENBERG
Professor of Law, University of California at Berkeley

1984 SUPPLEMENT

to

FIFTH EDITION

By

MELVIN ARON EISENBERG

Mineola, New York
THE FOUNDATION PRESS, INC.
1984

ANALYTICAL TABLE OF CONTENTS

ANALYTICAL TABLE OF CONTENTS

*

TABLE OF CASES

The principal cases are in italic type. Cases cited or discussed are in roman type. References are to pages.

*

1984 SUPPLEMENT

to

CASES AND MATERIALS

ON

CORPORATIONS

*

Chapter III

CONTROL AND MANAGEMENT OF THE CORPORATION—DISTRIBUTION OF CORPORATE POWERS, AND ACTION BY DIRECTORS AND OFFICERS

Introduction

Insert the following material at the end of the Introduction to Chapter III, at p. 140 of the unabridged edition and p. 121 of the abridged edition.

ALI, PRINCIPLES OF CORPORATE GOVERNANCE AND STRUCTURE: ANALYSIS AND RECOMMENDATIONS §§ 3.01, 3.02

(TENT. DRAFT No. 2, 1984)

§ 3.01 Management of the Corporation's Business: Powers and Functions of Senior Executives

The management of the business of a publicly held corporation [§ 1.23] should be conducted by or under the supervision of such senior executives ... as may be designated by the board of directors in accordance with the standards of the corporation [§ 1.27], and by those other officers ... and employees to whom the management function is delegated by those executives, subject to the powers and functions of the board under § 3.02 *.

§ 3.02 Powers and Functions of the Board of Directors

(a) Except as otherwise provided by statute, the board of directors of a publicly held corporation [§ 1.23] should:

(1) Elect, evaluate, and, where appropriate, dismiss the principal senior executives [§ 1.22].**

(2) Oversee the conduct of the corporation's business with a view to evaluating, on an ongoing basis, whether the corporation's re-

---

* Section 1.23 defines a publicly held corporation as "a corporation that as of the record date for its most recent annual shareholders' meeting had both 500 or more record holders ... of its equity securities ... and $3 million of total assets ...." Section 1.27 defines standard of the corporation as "a valid certificate or by-law provi-sion, or board or shareholder resolution, regulating corporate governance." (Footnote by ed.)

** Section 1.22 defines principal senior executives as "the chief executive, operating, financial, legal, and accounting officers of a corporation." (Footnote by ed.)

1

sources are being managed in a manner consistent with the principles of § 2.01 (Objective and Conduct of the Business Corporation).

(3) Review and approve corporate plans and actions that the board or the principal senior executives consider major, and changes in accounting principles and practices that the board or the principal senior executives consider material.

(4) Perform such other functions as are prescribed by law, or assigned to the board under a standard of the corporation [§ 1.27].

(b) Except as otherwise provided by statute or by a standard of the corporation, the board of directors of a publicly held corporation should also have power to:

(1) Make recommendations to shareholders.

(2) Initiate and adopt major corporate plans, commitments, and actions, and material changes in accounting principles and practices; instruct any committee, officer ..., or other employee; and review the actions of any committee, officer, or other employee.

(3) Manage the business of the corporation.

(4) Act as to all other corporate matters not requiring shareholder approval. ...

Chapter IV

CONTROL AND MANAGEMENT OF THE CORPORA-
TION—ACTION BY SHAREHOLDERS:
THE PROXY SYSTEM

SECTION 1. CONTROL IN THE PUBLIC–ISSUE
CORPORATION

(d) CORPORATE GOALS AND SOCIAL RESPONSIBILITY

Insert the following material at p. 223 of the unabridged edition, and p. 181 of the abridged edition, at the end of Chapter IV, § 1(d):

ALI, PRINCIPLES OF CORPORATE GOVERNANCE AND STRUC-
TURE: ANALYSIS AND RECOMMENDATIONS § 2.01

(TENT. DRAFT No. 2, 1984)

§ 2.01 The Objective and Conduct of the Business Corporation

A business corporation should have as its objective the conduct of business activities with a view to enhancing corporate profit and shareholder gain, except that, whether or not corporate profit and shareholder gain are thereby enhanced, the corporation, in the conduct of its business

(a) is obliged, to the same extent as a natural person, to act within the boundaries set by law,

(b) may take into account ethical considerations that are reasonably regarded as appropriate to the responsible conduct of business, and

(c) may devote a reasonable amount of resources to public welfare, humanitarian, educational, and philanthropic purposes.

SECTION 4.   PROXY CONTROL UNDER SECTION 14 OF THE SECURITIES EXCHANGE ACT OF 1934

(a) INTRODUCTION—AN OVERVIEW OF THE TWO MAJOR SECURITIES ACTS: THE DISCLOSURE PROCESS

Insert the following material at p. 275 of the unabridged edition, and p. 208 of the abridged edition, after the Note on Registration Provisions Under the 1934 Act:

SECURITIES EXCHANGE ACT

RULES 12g–1, 12g–4

Rule 12g–1. An issuer shall be exempt from the requirement to register any class of equity securities pursuant to section 12(g)(1) if on the last day of its most recent fiscal year the issuer had total assets not exceeding $3,000,000. ...

Rule 12g–4. (a) Termination of registration of a class of securities shall take effect in 90 days ... after the issuer certifies to the Commission ... that: (1) the number of holders of record of such class of securities is reduced to less than 300 persons; or (2) the number of holders of record of such class of securities is reduced to less than 500 persons and the total assets of the issuer have not exceeded $3,000,000 on the last day of each of the issuer's three most recent fiscal years ....

(b) REGULATION OF PROXIES

Substitute the following material for Proxy Rule 14a–4(a) and 4(b), at p. 280 of the unabridged edition and p. 213 of the abridged edition:

(a) The form of proxy (1) shall indicate in bold-face type whether or not the proxy is solicited on behalf of the issuer's board of directors or, if provided other than by a majority of the board of directors, shall indicate in bold-face type on whose behalf the solicitation is made; (2) shall provide a specifically designated blank space for dating the proxy card; and (3) shall identify clearly and impartially each matter or group of related matters intended to be acted upon, whether proposed by the issuer or by security holders. No reference need be made, however, to proposals as to which discretionary authority is conferred pursuant to paragraph (c) of this section.

(b)(1) Means shall be provided in the form of proxy whereby the person solicited is afforded an opportunity to specify by boxes a choice between approval or disapproval of, or abstention with respect to, each matter or group of related matters referred to therein as intended to be acted upon, other than elections to office. A proxy may confer discretionary authority with respect to matters as to which a choice is not specified by the security holder provided that the form of proxy states in bold-face type how it is intended to vote the shares represented by the proxy in each such case.

(2) A form of proxy which provides for the election of directors shall set forth the names of persons nominated for election as directors. Such form of proxy shall clearly provide any of the following means for security holders to withhold authority to vote for each nominee:

(i) a box opposite the name of each nominee which may be marked to indicate that authority to vote for such nominee is withheld; or

(ii) an instruction in bold-face type which indicates that the security holder may withhold authority to vote for any nominee by lining through or otherwise striking out the name of any nominee; or

(iii) designated blank spaces in which the shareholder may enter the names of nominees with respect to whom the shareholder chooses to withhold authority to vote; or

(iv) any other similar means, provided that clear instructions are furnished indicating how the shareholder may withhold authority to vote for any nominee.

Such form of proxy also may provide a means for the security holder to grant authority to vote for the nominees set forth, as a group, provided that there is a similar means for the security holder to withhold authority to vote for such group of nominees. Any such form of proxy which is executed by the security holder in such manner as not to withhold authority to vote for the election of any nominee shall be deemed to grant such authority, provided that the form of proxy so states in bold-face type. ...

Substitute the following material for Proxy Rule 14a–8, at pp. 283–285 of the unabridged edition, and pp. 216–218 of the abridged edition.

Rule 14a–8. Proposals of Security Holders.

(a) If any security holder of an issuer notifies the issuer of his intention to present a proposal for action at a forthcoming meeting of the issuer's security holders, the issuer shall set forth the proposal in its proxy statement and identify it in its form of proxy and provide means by which security holders can make the specification required by Rule 14a–4(b) [17 CFR 240.14a–4(b)]. Notwithstanding the foregoing, the issuer shall not be required to include the proposal in its proxy statement or form of proxy unless the security holder (hereinafter, the "proponent") has complied with the requirements of this paragraph and paragraphs (b) and (c) of this Section:

(1) *Eligibility.* (i) At the time he submits the proposal, the proponent shall be a record or beneficial owner of a least 1% or $1,000 in market value of securities entitled to be voted at the meeting and

have held such securities for at least one year, and he shall continue to own such securities through the date on which the meeting is held. If the issuer requests documentary support for a proponent's claim that he is a beneficial owner of at least $1,000 in market value of such voting securities of the issuer or that he has been a beneficial owner of the securities for one or more years, the proponent shall furnish appropriate documentation within 14 calendar days after receiving the request. In the event the issuer includes the proponent's proposal in its proxy soliciting material for the meeting and the proponent fails to comply with the requirement that he continuously hold such securities through the meeting date, the issuer shall not be required to include any proposals submitted by the proponent in its proxy material for any meeting held in the following two calendar years.

(ii) Proponents who deliver written proxy materials to holders of more than 25 percent of a class of the issuer's outstanding securities entitled to vote with respect to the same meeting of security holders will be ineligible to use the provisions of Rule 14a–8 for the inclusion of a proposal in the issuer's proxy materials. In the event the issuer includes a proponent's proposal in its proxy material and the proponent thereafter delivers written proxy materials to the holders of more than 25 percent of a class of the issuer's outstanding securities entitled to vote with respect to such meeting, the issuer shall not be required to include any proposals submitted by that proponent in its proxy soliciting materials for any meeting held in the following two calendar years.

(2) *Notice and Attendance at the Meeting.* At the time he submits a proposal, a proponent shall provide the issuer in writing with his name, address, the number of the issuer's voting securities that he holds of record or beneficially, the dates upon which he acquired such securities, and documentary support for a claim of beneficial ownership. A proposal may be presented at the meeting either by the proponent or his representative who is qualified under state law to present the proposal on the proponent's behalf at the meeting. In the event that the proponent or his representative fails, without good cause, to present the proposal for action at the meeting, the issuer shall not be required to include any proposals submitted by the proponent in its proxy soliciting material for any meeting held in the following two calendar years.

(3) *Timeliness.* The proponent shall submit his proposal sufficiently far in advance of the meeting so that it is received by the issuer within the following time periods:

(i) *Annual Meetings.* A proposal to be presented at an annual meeting shall be received at the issuer's principal executive offices not less than 120 days in advance of the date of the issuer's proxy statement released to security holders in connection with the previous year's annual meeting of security holders, except that if no annual meeting was held in the previous year or the date of the annual meeting has been changed by more than 30 calendar days from the date contemplated at the time of the previous year's proxy statement, a proposal shall be received by the issuer a reasonable time before the solicitation is made.

(ii) *Other Meetings.* A proposal to be presented at any meeting other than an annual meeting specified in paragraph (a)(3)(i) of this section shall be received a reasonable time before the solicitation is made.

NOTE: In order to curtail controversy as to the date on which a proposal was received by the issuer, it is suggested that proponents submit their proposals by Certified Mail-Return Receipt Requested.

(4) *Number of Proposals.* The proponent may submit no more than one proposal and an accompanying supporting statement for inclusion in the issuer's proxy materials for a meeting of security holders. If the proponent submits more than one proposal, or if he fails to comply with the 500 word limit mentioned in paragraph (b)(1) of this section, he shall be provided the opportunity to reduce the items submitted by him to the limits required by this rule, within 14 calendar days of notification of such limitations by the issuer.

(b)(1) *Supporting Statement.* The issuer, at the request of the proponent, shall include in its proxy statement a statement of the proponent in support of the proposal, which statement shall not include the name and address of the proponent. A proposal and its supporting statement in the aggregate shall not exceed 500 words. The supporting statement shall be furnished to the issuer at the time that the proposal is furnished, and the issuer shall not be responsible for such statement and the proposal to which it relates.

(2) *Identification of Proponent.* The proxy statement shall also include either the name and address of the proponent and the number of shares of the voting security held by the proponent or a statement that such information will be furnished by the issuer to any person, orally or in writing as requested, promptly upon the receipt of any oral or written request therefor.

(c) The issuer may omit a proposal and any statement in support thereof from its proxy statement and form of proxy under any of the following circumstances:

(1) If the proposal is, under the laws of the issuer's domicile, not a proper subject for action by security holders.

NOTE: Whether a proposal is a proper subject for action by security holders will depend on the applicable state law. Under certain states' laws, a proposal that mandates certain action by the issuer's board of directors may not be a proper subject matter for shareholder action, while a proposal recommending or requesting such action of the board may be proper under such state law.

(2) If the proposal, if implemented, would require the issuer to violate any state law or federal law of the United States, or any law of any foreign jurisdiction to which the issuer is subject, except that

this provision shall not apply with respect to any foreign law compliance with which would be violative of any state or federal law of the United States.

(3) If the proposal or the supporting statement is contrary to any of the Commission's proxy rules and regulations, including Rule 14a–9 [17 CFR 240.14a–9], which prohibits false or misleading statements in proxy soliciting materials;

(4) If the proposal relates to the redress of a personal claim or grievance against the issuer or any other person, or if it is designed to result in a benefit to the proponent or to further a personal interest, which benefit or interest is not shared with the other security holders at large;

(5) If the proposal relates to operations which account for less than 5 percent of the issuer's total assets at the end of its most recent fiscal year, and for less than 5 percent of its net earnings and gross sales for its most recent fiscal year, and is not otherwise significantly related to the issuer's business;

(6) If the proposal deals with a matter beyond the issuer's power to effectuate;

(7) If the proposal deals with a matter relating to the conduct of the ordinary business operations of the issuer;

(8) If the proposal relates to an election to office;

(9) If the proposal is counter to a proposal to be submitted by the issuer at the meeting;

(10) If the proposal has been rendered moot;

(11) If the proposal is substantially duplicative of a proposal previously submitted to the issuer by another proponent, which proposal will be included in the issuer's proxy material for the meeting;

(12) If the proposal deals with substantially the same subject matter as a prior proposal submitted to security holders in the issuer's proxy statement and form of proxy relating to any annual or special meeting of security holders held within the preceding five calendar years, it may be omitted from the issuer's proxy materials relating to any meeting of security holders held within three calendar years after the latest such previous submission:

Provided, That

(i) If the proposal was submitted at only one meeting during such preceding period, it received less than five percent of the total number of votes cast in regard thereto; or

(ii) If the proposal was submitted at only two meetings during such preceding period, it received at the time of its second submission less than eight percent of the total number of votes cast in regard thereto; or

(iii) If the prior proposal was submitted at three or more meetings during such preceding period, it received at the time of its latest submission less than 10 percent of the total number of votes cast in regard thereto; or

(13) If the proposal relates to specific amounts of cash or stock dividends.

(d) Whenever the issuer asserts, for any reason, that a proposal and any statement in support thereof received from a proponent may properly be omitted from its proxy statement and form of proxy, it shall file with the Commission, not later than 60 days prior to the date the preliminary copies of the proxy statement and form of proxy are filed pursuant to Rule 14a–6(a) [17 CFR 240.14a–6(a)], or such shorter period prior to such date as the Commission or its staff may permit, five copies of the following items: (1) the proposal; (2) any statement in support thereof as received from the proponent; (3) a statement of the reasons why the issuer deems such omission to be proper in the particular case; and (4) where such reasons are based on matters of law, a supporting opinion of counsel. The issuer shall at the same time, if it has not already done so, notify the proponent of its intention to omit the proposal from its proxy statement and form of proxy and shall forward to him a copy of the statement of reasons why the issuer deems the omission of the proposal to be proper and a copy of such supporting opinion of counsel.

(e) If the issuer intends to include in the proxy statement a statement in opposition to a proposal received from a proponent, it shall, not later than ten calendar days prior to the date the preliminary copies of the proxy statement and form of proxy are filed pursuant to Rule 14a–(6)(a), or, in the event that the proposal must be revised to be includable, not later than five calendar days after receipt by the issuer of the revised proposal promptly forward to the proponent a copy of the statement in opposition to the proposal.

In the event the proponent believes that the statement in opposition contains materially false or misleading statements within the meaning of Rule 14a–9 and the proponent wishes to bring this matter to the attention of the Commission, the proponent promptly should provide the staff with a letter setting forth the reasons for this view and at the same time promptly provide the issuer with a copy of such letter.

———

Insert the following material at p. 286 of the unabridged edition, and p. 219 of the abridged edition, following Proxy Rule 14a–12:

SAMPLE FORM OF PROXY *

UB UNIVERSAL BUSINESS CORPORATION **Proxy**

270 Universal Center, Horizon, California 91770

This Proxy is Solicited on Behalf of the Board of Directors.

The undersigned hereby appoints John Red, Mary Blue, and Lee White as Proxies, each with the power to appoint his or her substitute, and hereby authorizes them to represent and to vote, as designated below, all the shares of common stock of Universal Business held on record by the undersigned on October 23, 1980, at the annual meeting of shareholders to be held on December 20, 1980 or any adjournment thereof.

1. ELECTION OF DIRECTORS   FOR all nominees listed below ☐   WITHHOLD AUTHORITY to vote for all nominees listed below ☐

   (except as marked to the contrary below)

   (INSTRUCTION   To withhold authority to vote for any individual nominee strike a line through the nominees's name in the list below)

   J. Allen, S. Brown, J. Doe, J. Green, G. Johansen, A. Jones, M. Roe, J. Smith and M. Stanton

2. PROPOSAL TO APPROVE THE APPOINTMENT OF DOLLAR AND CENTS as the independent public accountants of the corporation

   ☐ FOR   ☐ AGAINST   ☐ ABSTAIN

3. STOCKHOLDER PROPOSAL RELATING TO FORM AND CONTENT OF POST-MEETING REPORTS:

   ☐ FOR   ☐ AGAINST   ☐ ABSTAIN

[C6891]

---

4. In their discretion the Proxies are authorized to vote upon such other business as may properly come before the meeting.

   This proxy when properly executed will be voted in the manner directed herein by the undersigned stockholder. If no direction is made, this proxy will be voted for Proposals 1, 2, and 3.

   Please sign exactly as name appears below.   When shares are held by joint tenants, both should sign.   When signing as attorney, as executor, administrator, trustee or guardian, please give full title as such. If a corporation, please sign in full corporate name by President or other authorized officer. If a partnership please sign in partnership name by authorized person.

   SAMPLE CARD A

   DATED _____ 1980

   PLEASE MARK SIGN DATE AND RETURN THE PROXY CARD PROMPTLY USING THE ENCLOSED ENVELOPE

   Signature _____

   Signature if held jointly _____

[C6892]

---

* From securities Exchange Act Release 16356 (1979).

Insert the following Note at p. 298 of the unabridged edition, and p. 228 of the abridged edition, after the Note on Implied Civil Liability Under Section 14 and Generally Under the Security Acts:

NOTE ON MERRILL LYNCH, PIERCE, FENNER & SMITH, INC. v. CURRAN

In Merrill Lynch, Pierce, Fenner & Smith, Inc. v. Curran, 456 U.S. 353, 102 S.Ct. 1825, 72 L.Ed.2d 182 (1982), the Supreme Court addressed the issue whether a private party could maintain an action for damages resulting from a violation of the Commodities Exchange Act ("CEA"). This Act had originally been adopted in 1922, and was substantially amended in 1936 and 1974. Prior to the 1974 amendments, the federal courts had recognized an implied private cause of action for violations of the Act. The Supreme Court held that an inquiry into whether a private cause of action should be implied takes on a special coloration where Congress has adopted substantial amendments to the relevant statute, while leaving intact provisions under which a private remedy had been implied:

... When federal statutes were less comprehensive, the Court applied a relatively simple test to determine the availability of an implied private remedy. If a statute was enacted for the benefit of a special class, the judiciary normally recognized a remedy for members of that class. Texas & Pacific R. Co. v. Rigsby, 241 U.S. 33, 36 S.Ct. 482, 60 L.Ed. 874 (1916). ... Under this approach, federal courts, following a common-law tradition, regarded the denial of a remedy as the exception rather than the rule. ...

In 1975 the Court unanimously decided to modify its approach to the question whether a federal statute includes a private right of action. In Cort v. Ash, 422 U.S. 66 ... (1975) ... the Court outlined criteria that primarily focused on the intent of Congress in enacting the statute under review. The increased complexity of federal legislation and the increased volume of federal litigation strongly supported the desirability of a more careful scrutiny of legislative intent than *Rigsby* had required ....

In determining whether a private cause of action is implicit in a federal statutory scheme when the statute by its terms is silent on that issue, the initial focus must be on the state of the law at the time the legislation was enacted. More precisely, we must examine Congress' perception of the law that it was shaping or reshaping. When Congress enacts new legislation, the question is whether Congress intended to create a private remedy as a supplement to the express enforcement provisions of the statute. When Congress acts in a statutory context in which an implied private remedy has already been recognized by the courts, however, the inquiry logically is different. Congress need not have intended to create a new remedy, since one already existed; the question is whether Congress intended to preserve the preexisting remedy.

The Court concluded that a private action could be maintained.

———

Insert the following material at p. 320 of the unabridged edition, and p. 250 of the abridged edition, after Securities Act Rule 175.

SECURITIES AND EXCHANGE COMMISSION
REGULATION S–K

[Projections and Security Ratings]

. . .

(b) *Commission Policy on Projections.* The Commission encourages the use in documents specified in Rule 175 ... of management's projections of future economic performance that have a reasonable basis and are presented in an appropriate format. The guidelines set forth herein represent the Commission's views on important factors to be considered in formulating and disclosing such projections.

(1) *Basis for Projections.* The Commission believes that management must have the option to present in Commission filings its good faith assessment of a registrant's future performance. Management, however, must have a reasonable basis for such an assessment. Although a history of operations or experience in projecting may be among the factors providing a basis for management's assessment, the Commission does not believe that a registrant always must have had such a history or experience in order to formulate projections with a reasonable basis. ...

(2) *Format for Projections.* In determining the appropriate format for projections included in Commission filings, consideration must be given to, among other things, the financial items to be projected, the period to be covered, and the manner of presentation to be used. Although traditionally projections have been given for three financial items generally considered to be of primary importance to investors (revenues, net income (loss) and earnings (loss) per share), projection information need not necessarily be limited to these three items. However, management should take care to assure that the choice of items projected is not susceptible of misleading inferences through selective projection of only favorable items. ... The period that appropriately may be covered by a projection depends to a large extent on the particular circumstances of the company involved. For certain companies in certain industries, a projection covering a two or three year period may be entirely reasonable. Other companies may not have a reasonable basis for projections beyond the current year. Accordingly, management should select the period most appropriate in the circumstances. In addition, management, in making a projection, should disclose what, in its opinion, is the most probable specific amount or the most reasonable range for each financial item projected based on the selected assumptions. Ranges, however, should not be so wide as to make the disclosure meaningless. Moreover, several projections based on varying assump-

tions may be judged by management to be more meaningful than a single number or range and would be permitted.

(3) *Investor Understanding* (i) When management chooses to include its projections in a Commission filing, the disclosures accompanying the projections should facilitate investor understanding of the basis for and limitations of projections. In this regard investors should be cautioned against attributing undue certainty to management's assessment .... The Commission also believes that investor understanding would be enhanced by disclosure of the assumptions which in management's opinion are most significant to the projections or are the key factors upon which the financial results of the enterprise depend and encourages disclosure of assumptions in a manner that will provide a framework for analysis of the projection.

(c) *Commission Policy on Security Ratings.* In view of the importance of security ratings ("ratings") to investors and the marketplace, the Commission permits registrants to disclose, on a voluntary basis, ratings assigned by rating organizations to classes of debt securities, convertible debt securities and preferred stock in registration statements and periodic reports. ...

... If a registrant includes in a registration statement filed under the Securities Act any ratings(s) assigned to a class of securities, it should consider including: (A) any other rating intended for public dissemination assigned to such class by a [nationally recognized statistical rating organization] that is available on the date of the initial filing of the document and that is materially different from any rating disclosed; and (B) the name of each rating organization whose rating is disclosed; each such rating organization's definition or description of the category in which it rated the class of securities; the relative rank of each rating within the assigning rating organization's overall classification system; and a statement informing investors that a security rating is not a recommendation to buy, sell or hold securities, that it may be subject to revision or withdrawal at any time by the assigning rating organization, and that each rating should be evaluated independently of any other rating. ...

Insert the following material at p. 324 in the unabridged edition, and p. 252 in the abridged edition, after the Note on SEC Proxy Rule Amendments Requiring Disclosure of Corporate Governance Information:

SECURITIES EXCHANGE ACT
PROXY RULES, SCHEDULE
14A, ITEM 6

If action is to be taken with respect to the election of directors, furnish the following information in tabular form to the extent practicable. ...

(b)(1) Furnish the information required by Item 404(a) and (c) of Regulation S–K ... .

(2) With respect to registrants other than investment companies registered under the Investment Company Act of 1940, furnish the information required by Item 404(b) of Regulation S–K. ...*

(d)(1) State whether or not the issuer has standing audit, nominating and compensation committees of the Board of Directors, or committees performing similar functions. If the issuer has such committees, however designated, identify each committee member, state the number of committee meetings held by each such committee during the last fiscal year and describe briefly the functions performed by such committees. ...

(2) If the issuer has a nominating or similar committee, state whether the committee will consider nominees recommended by shareholders and, if so, describe the procedures to be followed by shareholders in submitting such recommendations.

(e) State the total number of meetings of the board of directors (including regularly scheduled and special meetings) which were held during the last full fiscal year. Name each incumbent director who during the last full fiscal year attended fewer than 75 percent of the aggregate of (1) the total number of meetings of the board of directors (held during the period for which he has been a director) and (2) the total number of meetings held by all committees of the board on which he served (during the periods that he served).

(f) If a director has resigned or declined to stand for re-election to the board of directors since the date of the last annual meeting of shareholders because of a disagreement with the issuer on any matter relating to the issuer's operations, policies or practices, and if the director has furnished the issuer with a letter describing such disagreement and requesting that the matter be disclosed, the issuer shall state the date of resignation or declination to stand for re-election and summarize the director's description of the disagreement.

If the issuer believes that the description provided by the director is incorrect or incomplete, it may include a brief statement presenting its views of the disagreement.

(g) With respect to those classes of voting stock which participated in the election of directors at the most recent meeting at which directors were elected:

(1) state in an introductory paragraph the percentage of shares present at the meeting and voting or withholding authority to vote in the election of directors; and (2) disclose in tabular format, following such introductory paragraph, the percentage of total shares cast for and withheld from the vote for or, where applicable, cast against, each nominee, which, respectively, were voted for and withheld from the vote for, or voted against, such nominee. When groups of classes or series of classes vote together in the election of a director or directors, they shall

---

* Items 404(a), (b), and (c) of Regulation   (Footnote by ed.)
S–K are set out at pp. 15–19, infra.

be treated as a single class for the purpose of the preceding sentence. . . .

SECURITIES AND EXCHANGE COMMISSION
REGULATION S–K, ITEM 404

Item 404 (a) *Transactions with Management and Others.* Describe briefly any transaction, or series of similar transactions, since the beginning of the registrant's last fiscal year, or any currently proposed transaction, or series of similar transactions, to which the registrant or any of its subsidiaries was or is to be a party, in which the amount involved exceeds $60,000 and in which any of the following persons had, or will have, a direct or indirect material interest, naming such person and indicating the person's relationship to the registrant, the nature of such person's interest in the transaction(s), the amount of such transaction(s) and, where practicable, the amount of such person's interest in the transaction(s):

(1) Any director or executive officer of the registrant;

(2) Any nominee for election as a director;

(3) Any security holder who is known to the registrant to own of record or beneficially more than five percent of any class of the registrant's voting securities; and

(4) Any member of the immediate family of any of the foregoing persons.

Instructions to Paragraph (a) of Item 404.

1. The materiality of any interest is to be determined on the basis of the significance of the information to investors in light of all the circumstances of the particular case. The importance of the interest to the person having the interest, the relationship of the parties to the transaction with each other and the amount involved in the transactions are among the factors to be considered in determining the significance of the information to investors.

2. For purposes of paragraph (a), a person's immediate family shall include such person's spouse; parents; children; siblings; mothers and fathers-in-law; sons and daughters-in-law; and brothers and sisters-in-law. . . .

5. In describing any transaction involving the purchase or sale of assets by or to the registrant or any of its subsidiaries, otherwise than in the ordinary course of business, state the cost of the assets to the purchaser and, if acquired by the seller within two years prior to the transaction, the cost thereof to the seller. Indicate the principle followed in determining the registrant's purchase or sale price and the name of the person making such determination.

6. Information shall be furnished in answer to paragraph (a) with respect to transactions that involve remuneration from the registrant

or its subsidiaries, directly or indirectly, to any of the persons specified in paragraphs (a)(1) through (4) for services in any capacity unless the interest of such person arises solely from the ownership individually and in the aggregate of less than ten percent of any class of equity securities of another corporation furnishing the services to the registrant or its subsidiaries.

7.   No information need be given in answer to paragraph (a) as to any transactions where:

A.   The rates or charges involved in the transaction are determined by competitive bids, or the transaction involves the rendering of services as a common or contract carrier, or public utility, at rates or charges fixed in conformity with law or governmental authority. ...

8.   Paragraph (a) requires disclosure of indirect, as well as direct, material interests in transactions. A person who has a position or relationship with a firm, corporation, or other entity that engages in a transaction with the registrant or its subsidiaries may have an indirect interest in such transaction by reason of such position or relationship. Such an interest, however, shall not be deemed "material" within the meaning of paragraph (a) where:

A.   The interest arises only (i) from such person's position as a director of another corporation or organization which is a party to the transaction; or (ii) from the direct or indirect ownership by such person and all other persons specified in paragraphs (a)(1) through (4), in the aggregate, of less than a ten percent equity interest in another person (other than a partnership) which is a party to the transaction; or (iii) from both such position and ownership ... . [or]

C.   The interest of such person arises solely from the holding of an equity interest (including a limited partnership interest, but excluding a general partnership interest) or a creditor interest in another person that is a party to the transaction with the registrant or any of its subsidiaries, and the transaction is not material to such other person. ...

(b) *Certain Business Relationships.* Describe any of the following relationships regarding directors or nominees for director that exist, or have existed during the registrant's last fiscal year, indicating the identity of the entity with which the registrant has such a relationship, the name of the nominee or director affiliated with such entity and the nature of such nominee's or director's affiliation, the relationship between such entity and the registrant and the amount of the business done between the registrant and the entity during the registrant's last full fiscal year or proposed to be done during the registrant's current fiscal year:

(1) If the nominee or director is, or during the last fiscal year has been, an executive officer * of, or owns, or during the last fiscal year has owned, of record or beneficially in excess of ten percent equity interest in, any business or professional entity that has made during the registrant's last full fiscal year, or proposes to make during the registrant's current fiscal year, payments to the registrant or its subsidiaries for property or services in excess of five percent of (i) the registrant's consolidated gross revenues for its last full fiscal year, or (ii) the other entity's consolidated gross revenues for its last full fiscal year;

(2) If the nominee or director is, or during the last fiscal year has been, an executive officer of, or owns, or during the last fiscal year has owned, of record or beneficially in excess of ten percent equity interest in, any business or professional entity to which the registrant or its subsidiaries has made during the registrant's last full fiscal year, or proposes to make during the registrant's current fiscal year, payments for property or services in excess of five percent of (i) the registrant's consolidated gross revenues for its last full fiscal year, or (ii) the other entity's consolidated gross revenues for its last full fiscal year;

(3) If the nominee or director is, or during the last fiscal year has been, an executive officer of, or owns, or during the last fiscal year has owned, of record or beneficially in excess of ten percent equity interest in, any business or professional entity to which the registrant or its subsidiaries was indebted at the end of the registrant's last full fiscal year in an aggregate amount in excess of five percent of the registrant's total consolidated assets at the end of such fiscal year;

(4) If the nominee or director is, or during the last fiscal year has been, a member of, or of counsel to, a law firm that the issuer has retained during the last fiscal year or proposes to retain during the current fiscal year; *Provided, however,* that the dollar amount of fees paid to a law firm by the registrant need not be disclosed if such amount does not exceed five percent of the law firm's gross revenues for that firm's last full fiscal year;

(5) If the nominee or director is, or during the last fiscal year has been, a partner or executive officer of any investment banking firm that has performed services for the registrant, other than as a participating underwriter in a syndicate, during the last fiscal year or that the registrant proposes to perform services during the current year; *Provided, however,* that the dollar amount of compensation received by an investment banking firm need not be disclosed if such amount does not exceed five percent of the investment banking firm's consolidated gross revenues for that firm's last full fiscal year; or

---

* Rule 3b–7 under the 1934 Act provides that "The term 'executive officer,' when used with reference to a registrant, means its president, any vice-president ... in charge of a principal business unit, division or function (such as sales, administration or finance), any other officer who performs a policy making function or any other person who performs policy making functions for the registrant ...." (Footnote by ed.)

(6) Any other relationships that the registrant is aware of between the nominee or director and the registrant that are substantially similar in nature and scope to those relationships listed in paragraphs (b)(1) through (5).

Instructions to Paragraph (b) of Item 404. ...

2. In calculating payments for property and services the following may be excluded:

A. Payments where the rates or charges involved in the transaction are determined by competitive bids, or the transaction involves the rendering of services as a common contract carrier, or public utility, at rates or charges fixed in conformity with law or governmental authority ....

3. In calculating indebtedness the following may be excluded:

A. Debt securities that have been publicly offered, admitted to trading on a national securities exchange, or quoted on the automated quotation system of a registered securities association;

B. Amounts due for purchases subject to the usual trade terms ....

(c) *Indebtedness of Management.* If any of the following persons has been indebted to the registrant or its subsidiaries at any time since the beginning of the registrant's last fiscal year in an amount in excess of $60,000, indicate the name of such person, the nature of the person's relationship by reason of which such person's indebtedness is required to be described, the largest aggregate amount of indebtedness outstanding at any time during such period, the nature of the indebtedness and of the transaction in which it was incurred, the amount thereof outstanding as of the latest practicable date and the rate of interest paid or charged thereon:

(1) Any director or executive officer of the registrant;

(2) Any nominee for election as a director;

(3) Any member of the immediate family of the persons specified in paragraph (c)(1) or (2);

(4) Any corporation or organization (other than the registrant or a majority-owned subsidiary of the registrant) of which any of the persons specified in paragraphs (c)(1) or (2) is an executive officer or partner or is, directly or indirectly, the beneficial owner of ten percent or more of any class of equity securities; and

(5) Any trust or other estate in which any of the persons specified in paragraph (c)(1) or (2) has a substantial beneficial interest or as to which such person serves as a trustee or in a similar capacity.

Instructions to Paragraph (c) of Item 404.

1. For purposes of paragraph (c), the members of a person's immediate family are those persons specified in Instruction 2 to Item 404(a).

2. Exclude from the determination of the amount of indebtedness all amounts due from the particular person for purchases subject to usual trade terms, for ordinary travel and expense payments and for other transactions in the ordinary course of business. ...

SECURITIES AND EXCHANGE COMMISSION
SECURITIES ACT RELEASE NO. 6332 (1981)
[REGULATION S-K]

...

When initially adopted in 1977, Regulation S-K was intended to be the repository of standard issuer-related disclosure requirements that would be used in multiple forms to be filed under both the Securities Act and the Exchange Act. Over the three and one-half years since its adoption, the Regulation has been evolving into a centralized source of all content requirements for periodic reports and registration statements, including ... requirements addressing special circumstances and industries not uniformly applicable. The Commission has recognized that, in addition to serving as the central tool of integration through its application of standardized issuer-related disclosure provisions to both Securities Act and Exchange Act documents, Regulation S-K also can serve to simplify registrants' preparation of documents by consolidating other nonissuer-related content requirements into a single Regulation, rather than leaving registrants to sort through various regulations, forms, rules and releases to determine the requirements applicable to the content of a particular filing. ...

[As the SEC has pointed out, Regulation S-K is not self-executing: inclusion of the information specified in the Regulation is required only to the extent a form or schedule governing a document specifically directs inclusion of the information prescribed by an Item of Regulation S-K.]

Chapter V

THE SPECIAL PROBLEMS OF THE CLOSE CORPORATION AND DEVICES FOR CONTROL

SECTION 7. THE RESOLUTION OF INTRACORPORATE DISPUTES WHERE PLANNING HAS BEEN INADEQUATE OR THE PROBLEMS RESIST ADVANCE SOLUTION

(a) FIDUCIARY OBLIGATIONS OF SHAREHOLDERS IN CLOSE CORPORATIONS: UNDERSTANDINGS IMPLIED IN LAW

Insert the following case at p. 491 of the unabridged edition, and p. 367 of the abridged edition, at the end of Chapter V, Section 7(a):

SMITH [1] v. ATLANTIC PROPERTIES, INC. [2]

Appeals Court of Massachusetts, 1981.
12 Mass.App.Ct. 201, 422 N.E.2d 798.

CUTTER, JUSTICE. In December, 1951, Dr. Louis E. Wolfson agreed to purchase land in Norwood for $350,000, with an initial cash payment of $50,000 and a mortgage note of $300,000 payable in thirty-three months. Dr. Wolfson offered a quarter interest each in the land to Mr. Paul T. Smith, Mr. Abraham Zimble, and William H. Burke. Each paid to Dr. Wolfson $12,500, one quarter of the initial payment. Mr. Smith, an attorney, organized the defendant corporation (Atlantic) in 1951 to operate the real estate. Each of the four subscribers received twenty-five shares of stock. Mr. Smith included, both in the corporation's articles of organization and in its by-laws, a provision reading, "No election, appointment or resolution by the Stockholders and no election, appointment, resolution, purchase, sale, lease, contract, contribution, compensation, proceeding or act by the Board of Directors or by any officer or officers shall be valid or binding upon the corporation until effected, passed, approved or ratified by an affirmative vote of eighty (80%) per cent of the capital stock issued outstanding and entitled to vote." This

1. Lillian Zimble, executrix of the will of Abraham Zimble, and Louis Zimble [are also plaintiffs]. William H. Burke was originally a plaintiff. Prior to his death, Atlantic Properties, Inc. purchased Burke's stock in the corporation and it is now held as treasury stock. Mr. Abraham Zimble, while living, sold twelve shares to Louis Zimble.

2. Dr. Louis E. Wolfson [is also a defendant].

20

provision (hereafter referred to as the 80% provision) was included at Dr. Wolfson's request and had the effect of giving to any one of the four original shareholders a veto in corporate decisions.

Atlantic purchased the Norwood land. Some of the land and other assets were sold for about $220,000. Atlantic retained twenty-eight acres on which stood about twenty old brick or wood mill-type structures, which required expensive and constant repairs. After the first year, Atlantic became profitable and showed a profit every year prior to 1969, ranging from a low of $7,683 in 1953 to a high of $44,358 in 1954. The mortgage was paid by 1958 and Atlantic has incurred no long-term debt thereafter. Salaries of about $25,000 were paid only in 1959 and 1960. Dividends in the total amount of $10,000 each were paid in 1964 and 1970. By 1961, Atlantic had about $172,000 in retained earnings, more than half in cash.

For various reasons, which need not be stated in detail, disagreements and ill will soon arose between Dr. Wolfson, on the one hand, and the other stockholders as a group.[3] Dr. Wolfson wished to see Atlantic's earnings devoted to repairs and possibly some improvements in its existing buildings and adjacent facilities. The other stockholders desired the declaration of dividends. Dr. Wolfson fairly steadily refused to vote for any dividends. Although it was pointed out to him that failure to declare dividends might result in the imposition by the Internal Revenue Service of a penalty under the Internal Revenue Code, I.R.C. § 531 et seq. (relating to unreasonable accumulation of corporate earnings and profits), Dr. Wolfson persisted in his refusal to declare dividends. The other shareholders did agree over the years to making at least the most urgent repairs to Atlantic's buildings, but did not agree to make all repairs and improvements which were recommended in a 1962 report by an engineering firm retained by Atlantic to make a complete estimate of all repairs and improvements which might be beneficial.

The fears of an Internal Revenue Service assessment of a penalty tax were soon realized. Penalty assessments were made in 1962, 1963, and 1964. These were settled by Dr. Wolfson for $11,767.71 in taxes and interest. Despite this settlement, Dr. Wolfson continued his opposition to declaring dividends. The record does not indicate that he developed any specific and definitive schedule or plan for a series of necessary or desirable repairs and improvements to Atlantic's properties. At least none was proposed which would have had a reasonable chance of satisfying the Internal Revenue Service that expenditures for such repairs and improvements constituted "reasonable needs of the business," I.R.C. § 534(c), a term which includes (see I.R.C. § 537) "the reasonably anticipated needs of the business." Predictably, despite further warnings by Dr. Wolfson's shareholder colleagues, the Internal Revenue Service assessed further penalty taxes for the years 1965, 1966, 1967, and 1968. These taxes were upheld by the United States Tax

---

3. At least one cause of ill will on Dr. Wolfson's part may have been the refusal of the other shareholders to consent to his transferring his shares in Atlantic to the Louis E. Wolfson Foundation, a charitable foundation created by Dr. Wolfson.

Court in Atlantic Properties, Inc. v. Commissioner of Int. Rev., 62 T.C. 644 (1974), and on appeal in 519 F.2d 1233 (1st Cir. 1975). See the discussion of these opinions in Cathcart, Accumulated Earnings Tax: A Trap for the Wary, 62 A.B.A.J. 1197–1199 (1976). An examination of these decisions makes it apparent that Atlantic has incurred substantial penalty taxes and legal expense largely because of Dr. Wolfson's refusal to vote for the declaration of sufficient dividends to avoid the penalty, a refusal which was (in the Tax Court and upon appeal) attributed in some measure to a tax avoidance purpose on Dr. Wolfson's part.

On January 30, 1967, the shareholders, other than Dr. Wolfson, initiated this proceeding in the Superior Court, later supplemented to reflect developments after the original complaint. The plaintiffs sought a court determination of the dividends to be paid by Atlantic, the removal of Dr. Wolfson as a director, and an order that Atlantic be reimbursed by him for the penalty taxes assessed against it and related expenses. The case was tried before a justice of the Superior Court (jury waived) in September and October, 1979.

The trial judge made findings (but in more detail) of essentially the facts outlined above and concluded that Dr. "Wolfson's obstinate refusal to vote in favor of ... dividends was ... caused more by his dislike for other stockholders and his desire to avoid additional tax payments than ... by any genuine desire to undertake a program for improving ... [Atlantic] property." She also determined that Dr. Wolfson was liable to Atlantic for taxes and interest amounting to "$11,767.11 plus interest from the commencement of this action, plus $35,646.14 plus interest from August 11, 1975," the date of the First Circuit decision affirming the second penalty tax assessment. The latter amount includes an attorney's fee of $7,500 in the Federal tax cases. She also ordered the directors of Atlantic to declare "a reasonable dividend at the earliest practical date and reasonable dividends annually thereafter consistent with good business practice." In addition, the trial judge directed that jurisdiction of the case be retained in the Superior Court "for a period of five years to [e]nsure compliance." Judgment was entered pursuant to the trial judge's order. After the entry of judgment, Dr. Wolfson and Atlantic filed a motion for a new trial and to amend the judge's findings. This motion, after hearing, was denied, and Dr. Wolfson and Atlantic claimed an appeal from the judgment and the former from the denial of the motion. The plaintiffs (see note 1, supra) requested payment of their attorneys' fees in this proceeding and filed supporting affidavits. The motion was denied, and the plaintiffs appealed.

1. The trial judge, in deciding that Dr. Wolfson had committed a breach of his fiduciary duty to other stockholders, relied greatly on broad language in Donahue v. Rodd Electrotype Co., 367 Mass. 578, 586–597, 328 N.E.2d 505 (1975) .... Similar principles were stated in Wilkes v. Springside Nursing Home, Inc., 370 Mass. 842, 848–852, 353 N.E.2d 657 (1976), but with some modifications, mentioned in the mar-

gin,[5] of the sweeping language of the *Donahue* case. See Jessie v. Boynton, 372 Mass. 293, 304, 361 N.E.2d 1267 (1977); Hallhan v. Haltom Corp., 7 Mass.App. 68, 70–71, 385 N.E.2d 1033 (1979). See also Cain v. Cain, 3 Mass.App. 467, 473–479, 334 N.E.2d 650 (1975).

In the *Donahue* case, 367 Mass. at 593 n. 17, 328 N.E.2d 505, the court recognized that cases may arise in which, in a close corporation, majority stockholders may ask protection from a minority stockholder. Such an instance arises in the present case because Dr. Wolfson has been able to exercise a veto concerning corporate action on dividends by the 80% provision (in Atlantic's articles [of] organization and by-laws) already quoted. The 80% provision may have substantially the effect of reversing the usual roles of the majority and the minority shareholders. The minority, under that provision, becomes an ad hoc controlling interest.[6]

It does not appear to be argued that this 80% provision is not authorized by G.L. c. 156B (inserted by St.1964, c. 723, § 1). See especially § 8(*a*).* See also Seibert v. Milton Bradley Co., 380 Mass. 656, 405 N.E.2d 131 (1980). Chapter 156B was intended to provide desirable flexibility in corporate arrangements.[7] The provision is only one of several methods which have been devised to protect minority shareholders in close corporations from being oppressed by their colleagues and, if the device is used reasonably, there may be no strong public policy considerations against its use. See 1 O'Neal, Close Corporations § 4.21 (2d ed.1971 & Supp.1980). The textbook just cited contains in §§ 4.01–4,-

5. The court said (at 850–852, 353 N.E.2d 657) that it was "concerned that [the] untempered application of the strict good faith standard ... will result in the imposition of limitations on legitimate action by the *controlling group* in a close corporation which will unduly hamper its effectiveness .... The majority ... have certain rights to what has been termed 'selfish ownership' in the corporation which should be balanced against the concept of their fiduciary obligation to the minority .... [W]hen minority stockholders ... bring suit ... alleging a breach of the strict good faith duty ... we must carefully analyze the action taken by the *controlling stockholders* in the individual case. It must be asked whether the *controlling group* can demonstrate a legitimate business purpose for its action .... [T]he *controlling group* in a close corporation must have some room to maneuver in establishing the business policy of the corporation. It must have a large measure of discretion, for example, *in declaring or withholding dividends*" (emphasis supplied) and in certain other matters. "When an asserted business purpose ... is advanced by the majority, however, ... it is open to minority stockholders to demonstrate that the ... objective could have been achieved through an

alternative course ... less harmful to the minority's interest."

6. The majority shareholders, in the event of a deadlock, at least may seek dissolution of the corporation if forty percent of the voting power can be mustered, whereas a single stockholder with only twenty-five percent of the stock may not do so. See G.L. c. 156B, § 99(*b*), as amended by St. 1969, c. 392, § 23.

* M.G.L.A. c. 156B, § 8(a) provides that "Whenever, with respect to any action to be taken by the stockholders of a corporation, the articles of organization or by-laws require the vote or concurrence of the holders of all of the shares, or of any class or series thereof, or a greater proportion thereof than required by this chapter with respect to such action, the provisions of the articles of organization or by-laws shall control." (Footnote by ed.)

7. See, e.g., Hosmer, New Business Corporation Law, 1964 Ann. Survey of Mass.Law §§ 1.1–1.12: Casey, The New Business Corporation Law, 50 Mass.L.Q. (No. 3) 201 (1965); and Boston Bar Assn., Summary of Principal Changes Made by ... Chapter 156B (1964), reprinted as an appendix in Mass.Gen.Laws Ann., at 429.

30 a comprehensive discussion of the business considerations (see especially §§ 4.02, 4.03, 4.06, & 4.24) which may recommend use of such a device. See also 2 O'Neal § 8.07 (& Supp.1980 which, at 84–90, discusses the Massachusetts decisions). In the present case, Dr. Wolfson testified that he requested the inclusion of the 80% provision "in case the people [the other shareholders] whom I knew, but not very well, ganged up on me." The possibilities of shareholder disagreement on policy made the provision seem a sensible precaution.[8] A question is presented, however, concerning the extent to which such a veto power possessed by a minority stockholder may be exercised as its holder may wish, without a violation of the "fiduciary duty" referred to in the *Donahue* case, 367 Mass. at 593, 328 N.E.2d 505, as modified in the *Wilkes* case. See note 5, supra.

The decided cases in Massachusetts do little to answer this question. The most pertinent guidance is probably found in the *Wilkes* case, 370 Mass. at 849–852, 353 N.E.2d 657, ... essentially to the effect that in any judicial intervention in such a situation there must be a weighing of the business interests advanced as reasons for their action (a) by the majority or controlling group and (b) by the rival persons or group.[9] It would obviously be appropriate, before a court-ordered solution is sought or imposed, for both sides to attempt to reach a sensible solution of any incipient impasse in the interest of all concerned after consideration of all relevant circumstances. See Helms v. Duckworth, 249 F.2d 482, 485–488 (D.C.Cir.1957).

8. Dr. Wolfson himself had discovered the business opportunity which led to the formation of Atlantic, had made the initial $50,000 payment which made possible the Norwood land purchase, and had given the other shareholders an opportunity to share with him in what looked like a probably profitable enterprise. It was reasonably foreseeable that there might be differences of opinion between Dr. Wolfson, a man with substantial income likely to be in a high income tax bracket, and less affluent shareholders on such matters of policy as dividend declarations, salaries, and investment in improvements in the property. The other shareholders, two of whom were attorneys should have known that it was as open to Dr. Wolfson reasonably to exercise the veto provided to him by the 80% provision in favor of a policy of reinvestment of earnings in Atlantic's properties, which would probably avoid taxes and increase the value of the corporate assets, as it was for them (possessed of the same veto) to use reasonably their voting power in favor of a more generous dividend and salary policy.

9. The duties and quasi-fiduciary responsibilities of minority shareholders who find themselves in a position to control corporate action are discussed helpfully in Hetherington, The Minority's Duty of Loyalty in Close Corporations, 1972 Duke L.J. 921. The author recognizes (at 944) that, in disputes concerning the wisdom of a particular course of corporate action, the majority (or the ad hoc controlling minority) shareholder may be entitled to follow the course he or it thinks best.

The author concludes (at 946) with the general view: "In spite of the ... imprecision of such criteria for evaluating commercial behavior as good faith, commercial reasonableness, and unconscionability, the courts have moved toward imposing minimum requirements of fair dealing in nonfiduciary business situations. The similarly imprecise concept of fiduciary responsibility, at least as applied to majority shareholders ... has clearly promoted fair dealing within business enterprises. The majority may not exercise their corporate powers in a manner which is clearly intended to be and is in fact inimical to the corporate interest, or which is intended to deprive the minority of its pro rata share of the present or future gains accruing to the enterprise. A minority shareholder whose conduct is controlling on a particular issue should be bound by no different standard."

2. With respect to the past damage to Atlantic caused by Dr. Wolfson's refusal to vote in favor of any dividends, the trial judge was justified in finding that his conduct went beyond what was reasonable. The other stockholders shared to some extent responsibility for what occurred by failing to accept Dr. Wolfson's proposals with much sympathy, but the inaction on dividends seems the principal cause of the tax penalties. Dr. Wolfson had been warned of the dangers of an assessment under the Internal Revenue Code, I.R.C. § 531 et seq. He had refused to vote dividends in any amount adequate to minimize that danger and had failed to bring forward, within the relevant taxable years, a convincing, definitive program of appropriate improvements which could withstand scrutiny by the Internal Revenue Service. Whatever may have been the reason for Dr. Wolfson's refusal to declare dividends (and even if in any particular year he may have gained slight, if any, tax advantage from withholding dividends) we think that he recklessly ran serious and unjustified risks of precisely the penalty taxes eventually assessed, risks which were inconsistent with any reasonable interpretation of a duty of "utmost good faith and loyalty." The trial judge (despite the fact that the other shareholders helped to create the voting deadlock and despite the novelty of the situation) was justified in charging Dr. Wolfson with the out-of-pocket expenditure incurred by Atlantic for the penalty taxes and related counsel fees of the tax cases.[10]

3. The trial judge's order to the directors of Atlantic, "to declare a reasonable dividend at the earliest practical date and reasonable dividends annually thereafter," presents difficulties. It may well not be a precise, clear, and unequivocal command which (without further explanation) would justify enforcement by civil contempt proceedings. See United States Time Corp. v. G.E.M. of Boston, Inc., 345 Mass. 279, 282, 186 N.E.2d 920 (1963); United Factory Outlet, Inc. v. Jay's Stores, Inc., 361 Mass. 35, 36–39, 278 N.E.2d 716 (1972). It also fails to order the directors to exercise similar business judgment with respect to Dr. Wolfson's desire to make all appropriate repairs and improvements to Atlantic's factory properties. See the language of the Supreme Judicial Court in the *Wilkes* case, 370 Mass. at 850–852, 353 N.E.2d 657, see note 5, supra.

The somewhat ambiguous injunctive relief is made less significant by the trial judge's reservation of jurisdiction in the Superior Court, a provision which contemplates later judicial supervision. We think that such supervision should be provided now upon an expanded record. The present record does not disclose Atlantic's present financial condition or what, if anything, it has done (since the judgment under review) by way of expenditures for repairs and improvements of its properties and in respect of dividends and salaries. The judgment, of course, necessarily disregards the general judicial reluctance to interfere with a corpora-

---

10. We do not now suggest that the standard of "utmost good faith and loyalty" may require some relaxation when applied to a minority ad hoc controlling interest, created by some device, similar to the 80% provision, designed in part to protect the selfish interests of a minority shareholder. This seems to us a difficult area of the law best developed on a case by case basis. See note 4, supra.

tion's dividend policy ordinarily based upon the business judgment of its directors. See Crocker v. Waltham Watch Co., 315 Mass. 387, 402, 53 N.E.2d 230 (1944); Donahue v. Rodd Electrotype Co., 367 Mass. at 590, 328 N.E.2d 505, and authorities cited; 1 O'Neal, Close Corporations § 3.63 and 2 O'Neal § 8.08; Forced Dividends, 1 J.Corp.L. 420 (1976).

Although the reservation of jurisdiction is appropriate in this case (see Nassif v. Boston & Maine R.R., 340 Mass. 557, 566–567, 65 N.E.2d 397 [1960]; Department of Pub. Health v. Cumberland Cattle Co., 361 Mass. 817, 834, 282 N.E.2d 895 [1972]), its purpose should be stated more affirmatively. Paragraph 2 of the judgment should be revised to provide: (a) a direction that Atlantic's directors prepare promptly financial statements and copies of State and Federal income and excise tax returns for the five most recent calendar or fiscal years, and a balance sheet as of as current a date as is possible; (b) an instruction that they confer with one another with a view to stipulating a general dividend and capital improvements policy for the next ensuing three fiscal years; (c) an order that, if such a stipulation is not filed with the clerk of the Superior Court within sixty days after the receipt of the rescript in the Superior Court, a further hearing shall be held promptly (either before the court or before a special master with substantial experience in business affairs), at which there shall be received in evidence at least the financial statements and tax returns above mentioned, as well as other relevant evidence. Thereafter, the court, after due consideration of the circumstances then existing, may direct the adoption (and carrying out), if it be then deemed appropriate, of a specific dividend and capital improvements policy adequate to minimize the risk of further penalty tax assessments for the then current fiscal year of Atlantic. The court also may reserve jurisdiction to take essentially the same action for each subsequent fiscal year until the parties are able to reach for themselves an agreed program.

4. The plaintiff shareholders requested an allowance for counsel fees incurred by them in accomplishing the recovery by Atlantic from Dr. Wolfson of the amounts to be paid by him. The trial judge did not state her reasons for denying the motion for such fees. Whether to grant such an allowance was within her sound discretion. See Wilson v. Jennings, 344 Mass. 608, 621, 184 N.E.2d 642 (1962), and cases cited; Cain v. Cain, 3 Mass.App. at 479, 334 N.E.2d 650: Nolan, Equitable Remedies § 244, at 366 (1975). We perceive no abuse of discretion. She was entitled to take into account the considerations mentioned in note 8, supra, and that the controversy involved issues of business judgment and somewhat novel legal questions. See note 10, supra. She also properly could give weight to (a) the circumstance that no fraud or diversion of Atlantic's assets was engaged in by Dr. Wolfson, and (b) the portions of the evidence suggesting that the plaintiffs may have been in some measure responsible for the intensity of the bad feeling among the stockholders.

5. The judgment is affirmed so far as it (par. 1) orders payments into Atlantic's treasury by Dr. Wolfson. Paragraph 2 of the judgment is to be modified in a manner consistent with part 3 of this opinion. The trial judge's denial of the plaintiff's motion to be allowed counsel fees is affirmed. Costs of this appeal are to be paid from the assets of Atlantic.

So ordered.

Chapter VI

THE DUTIES OF DIRECTORS AND CONTROLLING SHAREHOLDERS

SECTION 1. DUTY OF CARE

(a) STATE LAW AND COMMON LAW

Insert the following case at p. 537 of the unabridged edition, and p. 394 of the abridged edition, at the end of Chapter VI, Section 1(a):

FRANCIS v. UNITED JERSEY BANK

Supreme Court of New Jersey, 1981.
87 N.J. 15, 432 A.2d 814.

POLLOCK, J. The primary issue on this appeal is whether a corporate director is personally liable in negligence for the failure to prevent the misappropriation of trust funds by other directors who were also officers and shareholders of the corporation.

Plaintiffs are trustees in bankruptcy of Pritchard & Baird Intermediaries Corp. (Pritchard & Baird), a reinsurance broker or intermediary. Defendant Lillian P. Overcash is the daughter of Lillian G. Pritchard and the executrix of her estate. At the time of her death, Mrs. Pritchard was a director and the largest single shareholder of Pritchard & Baird. Because Mrs. Pritchard died after the institution of suit but before trial, her executrix was substituted as a defendant. United Jersey Bank is joined as the administrator of the estate of Charles Pritchard, Sr., who had been president, director and majority shareholder of Pritchard & Baird.

This litigation focuses on payments made by Pritchard & Baird to Charles Pritchard, Jr. and William Pritchard, who were sons of Mr. and Mrs. Charles Pritchard, Sr., as well as officers, directors and shareholders of the corporation. Claims against Charles, Jr. and William are being pursued in bankruptcy proceedings against them.

The trial court, sitting without a jury, characterized the payments as fraudulent conveyances within N.J.S.A. 25:2–10 and entered judgment of $10,355,736.91 plus interest against the estate of Mrs. Pritchard. 162 N.J.Super. 355, 392 A.2d 1233 (Law Div.1978). The judgment includes damages from her negligence in permitting payments from the corporation of $4,391,133.21 to Charles, Jr. and $5,483,799.02 to William. The trial court also entered judgment for payments of other sums plus interest: (1) against the estate of Lillian Pritchard for $33,000 accepted by her during her lifetime; (2) against the estate of Charles Pritchard, Sr. for $189,194.17 paid to him during his lifetime and $168,454 for payment of taxes on his estate; and (3) against Lillian Overcash individually for $123,156.51 for payments to her.

The Appellate Division affirmed, but found that the payments were a conversion of trust funds, rather than fraudulent conveyances of the assets of the corporation. 171 N.J.Super. 34, 407 A.2d 1253 (1979). We granted certification limited to the issue of the liability of Lillian Pritchard as a director. 82 N.J. 285, 412 A.2d 791 (1980).

Although we accept the characterization of the payments as a conversion of trust funds, the critical question is not whether the misconduct of Charles, Jr. and William should be characterized as fraudulent conveyances or acts of conversion. Rather, the initial question is whether Mrs. Pritchard was negligent in not noticing and trying to prevent the misappropriation of funds held by the corporation in an implied trust. A further question is whether her negligence was the proximate cause of the plaintiffs' losses. Both lower courts found that she was liable in negligence for the losses cause by the wrongdoing of Charles, Jr. and William. We affirm.

I

The matrix for our decision is the customs and practices of the reinsurance industry and the role of Pritchard & Baird as a reinsurance broker. Reinsurance involves a contract under which one insurer agrees to indemnify another for loss sustained under the latter's policy of insurance. Insurance companies that insure against losses arising out of fire or other casualty seek at times to minimize their exposure by sharing risks with other insurance companies. Thus, when the face amount of a policy is comparatively large, the company may enlist one or more insurers to participate in that risk. Similarly, an insurance company's loss potential and overall exposure may be reduced by reinsuring a part of an entire class of policies (o.g., 25% of all of its fire insurance policies). The selling insurance company is known as a ceding company. The entity that assumes the obligation is designated as the reinsurer.

The reinsurance broker arranges the contract between the ceding company and the reinsurer. In accordance with industry custom before the Pritchard & Baird bankruptcy, the reinsurance contract or treaty did not specify the rights and duties of the broker. Typically, the ceding company communicates to the broker the details concerning the risk. The broker negotiates the sale of portions of the risk to the reinsurers. In most instances, the ceding company and the reinsurer do not communicate with each other, but rely upon the reinsurance broker. The ceding company pays premiums due a reinsurer to the broker, who deducts his commission and transmits the balance to the appropriate reinsurer.

When a loss occurs, a reinsurer pays money due a ceding company to the broker, who then transmits it to the ceding company.

The reinsurance business was described by an expert at trial as having "a magic aura around it of dignity and quality and integrity." A telephone call which might be confirmed by a handwritten memorandum is sufficient to create a reinsurance obligation. Though separate bank accounts are not maintained for each treaty, the industry practice is to segregate the insurance funds from the broker's general accounts. Thus, the insurance fund accounts would contain the identifiable amounts for transmittal to either the reinsurer or the ceder. The expert stated that in general three kinds of checks may be drawn on this account: checks payable to reinsurers as premiums, checks payable to ceders as loss payments and checks payable to the brokers as commissions.

Messrs. Pritchard and Baird initially operated as a partnership. Later they formed several corporate entities to carry on their brokerage activities. The proofs supporting the judgment relate only to one corporation, Pritchard & Baird Intermediaries Corp. (Pritchard & Baird), and we need consider only its activities. When incorporated under the laws of the State of New York in 1959, Pritchard & Baird had five directors: Charles Pritchard, Sr., his wife Lillian Pritchard, their son Charles Pritchard, Jr., George Baird and his wife Marjorie. William Pritchard, another son, became director in 1960. Upon its formation, Pritchard & Baird acquired all the assets and assumed all the liabilities of the Pritchard & Baird partnership. The corporation issued 200 shares of common stock. Charles Pritchard, Sr. acquired 120 shares, his sons Charles Pritchard, Jr., 15 and William 15; Mr. and Mrs. Baird owned the remaining 50. In June 1964, Baird and his wife resigned as directors and sold their stock to the corporation. From that time on the corporation operated as a close family corporation with Mr. and Mrs. Pritchard and their two sons as the only directors. After the death of Charles, Sr. in 1973, only the remaining three directors continued to operate as the board. Lillian Pritchard inherited 72 of her husband's 120 shares in Pritchard & Baird, thereby becoming the largest shareholder in the corporation with 48% of the stock.

The corporate minute books reflect only perfunctory activities by the directors, related almost exclusively to the election of officers and adoption of banking resolutions and a retirement plan. None of the minutes for any of the meetings contain a discussion of the loans to Charles, Jr. and William or of the financial condition of the corporation. Moreover, upon instructions of Charles, Jr. that financial statements were not to be circulated to anyone else, the company's statements for the fiscal years beginning February 1, 1970, were delivered only to him.

Charles Pritchard, Sr. was the chief executive and controlled the business in the years following Baird's withdrawal. Beginning in 1966, he gradually relinquished control over the operations of the corporation. In 1968, Charles, Jr. became president and William became executive vice president. Charles, Sr. apparently became ill in 1971 and during the last year and a half of his life was not involved in the affairs of the business. He continued, however, to serve as a director until his death on December 10, 1973. Notwithstanding the presence of Charles, Sr. on the board until his death in 1973, Charles, Jr. dominated the management of the corporation and the board from 1968 until the bankruptcy in 1975.

Contrary to the industry custom of segregating funds, Pritchard & Baird commingled the funds of reinsurers and ceding companies with its own funds. All monies (including commissions, premiums and loss monies) were deposited in a single account. Charles, Sr. began the practice of withdrawing funds from the commingled account in transactions identified on the corporate books as "loans." As long as Charles, Sr. controlled the corporation, the "loans" correlated with corporate profits and were repaid at the end of each year. Starting in 1970, however, Charles, Jr. and William begin to siphon ever-increasing sums from the corporation under the guise of loans. As of January 31, 1970, the "loans" to Charles, Jr. were $230,932 and to William were $207,329. At least by January 31, 1973, the annual increase in the loans exceeded annual corporate revenues. By October 1975, the year of bankruptcy, the "shareholders' loans" had metastasized to a total of $12,333,514.47.

The trial court rejected the characterization of the payments as "loans." 162 N.J.Super. at 365, 392 A.2d 1233. No corporate resolution authorized the "loans," and no note or other instrument evidenced the debt. Charles, Jr. and William paid no interest on the amounts received. The "loans" were not repaid or reduced from one year to the next; rather, they increased annually.

The designation of "shareholders' loans" on the balance sheet was an entry to account for the distribution of the premium and loss money to Charles, Sr., Charles, Jr. and William. As the trial court found, the entry was part of a "woefully inadequate and highly dangerous bookkeeping system." 162 N.J.Super. at 363, 392 A.2d 1233.

The "loans" to Charles, Jr. and William far exceeded their salaries and financial resources. If the payments to Charles, Jr. and William had been treated as dividends or compensation, then the balance sheets would have shown an excess of liabilities over assets. If the "loans" had been eliminated, the balance sheets would have depicted a corporation not only with a working capital deficit, but also with assets having a fair market value less than its liabilities. The balance sheets for 1970–1975, however, showed an excess of assets over liabilities. This result was achieved by designating the misappropriated funds as "shareholders' loans" and listing them as assets offsetting the deficits. Although the withdrawal of the funds resulted in an obligation of repayment to Pritchard & Baird, the more significant consideration is that the "loans" represented a massive misappropriation of money belonging to the clients of the corporation.

The "loans" were reflected on financial statements that were prepared annually as of January 31, the end of the corporate fiscal year. Although an outside certified public accountant prepared the 1970 financial statement, the corporation prepared only internal financial statements from 1971–1975. In all instances, the statements were simple documents, consisting of three or four 8½ × 11 inch sheets.

The statements of financial condition from 1970 forward demonstrated:

	Working Capital Deficit	Shareholders' Loans	Net Brokerage Income
1970	$ 389,022	$ 509,941	$ 807,229
1971	not available	not available	not available
1972	$ 1,684,289	$ 1,825,911	$ 1,546,263
1973	$ 3,506,460	$ 3,700,542	$ 1,736,349
1974	$ 6,939,007	$ 7,080,629	$ 876,182
1975	$10,176,419	$10,298,039	$ 551,598.

Those financial statements showed working capital deficits increasing annually in tandem with the amounts that Charles, Jr. and William withdrew as "shareholders' loans." In the last complete year of business (January 31, 1974, to January 31, 1975), "shareholders' loans" and the correlative working capital deficit increased by approximately $3,200,000.

The funding of the "loans" left the corporation with insufficient money to operate. Pritchard & Baird could defer payment on accounts payable because its clients allowed a grace period, generally 30 to 90 days, before the payment was due. During this period, Pritchard & Baird used the funds entrusted to it as a "float" to pay current accounts payable. By recourse to the funds of its clients, Pritchard & Baird not only paid its trade debts, but also funded the payments to Charles, Jr. and William. Thus, Pritchard & Baird was able to meet its obligations as they came due only through the use of clients' funds.

The pattern that emerges from these figures is the substantial increase in the monies appropriated by Charles Pritchard, Jr. and William Pritchard after their father's withdrawal from the business and the sharp decline in the profitability of the operation after his death. This led ultimately to the filing in December, 1975, of an involuntary petition in bankruptcy and the appointments of the plaintiffs as trustees in bankruptcy of Pritchard & Baird.

Mrs. Pritchard was not active in the business of Pritchard & Baird and knew virtually nothing of its corporate affairs. She briefly visited the corporate offices in Morristown on only one occasion, and she never read or obtained the annual financial statements. She was unfamiliar with the rudiments of reinsurance and made no effort to assure that the policies and practices of the corporation, particularly pertaining to the withdrawal of funds, complied with industry custom or relevant law. Although her husband had warned her that Charles, Jr. would "take the shirt off my back," Mrs. Pritchard did not pay any attention to her duties as a director or to the affairs of the corporation. 162 N.J.Super. at 370, 392 A.2d 1233.

After her husband died in December 1973, Mrs. Pritchard became incapacitated and was bedridden for a six-month period. She became listless at this time and started to drink rather heavily. Her physical condition deteriorated, and in 1978 she died. The trial court rejected testimony seeking to exonerate her because she "was old, was grief-stricken at the loss of her husband, sometimes consumed too much alcohol and was psychologically overborne by her sons." 162 N.J.Super. at 371, 392 A.2d 1233. That court found that she was competent to act and that the reason Mrs. Pritchard never knew what her sons "were doing was because she never made the slightest effort to discharge any of her responsibilities as a director of Pritchard & Baird." 162 N.J.Super. at 372, 392 A.2d 1233.

II

A preliminary matter is the determination of whether New Jersey law should apply to this case. Although Pritchard & Baird was incorporated in New York, the trial court found that New Jersey had more significant relationships to the parties and the transactions than New York. The shareholder, officers and directors were New Jersey residents. The estates of Mr. and Mrs. Pritchard are being administered in New Jersey, and the bankruptcy proceedings involving Charles, Jr., William and Pritchard & Baird are pending in New Jersey. Virtually all transactions took place in New Jersey. Although many of the creditors are located outside the state, all had contacts with Pritchard & Baird in New Jersey. Consequently, the trial court applied New Jersey law. 162 N.J.Super. at 369, 392 A.2d 1233. The parties agree that New Jersey law should apply. We are in accord.

III

Individual liability of a corporate director for acts of the corporation is a prickly problem. Generally directors are accorded broad immunity and are not insurers of corporate activities. The problem is particularly nettlesome when a third party asserts that a director, because of nonfeasance, is liable for losses caused by acts of insiders, who in this case were officers, directors and shareholders. Determination of the liability of Mrs. Pritchard requires findings that she had a duty to the clients of Pritchard & Baird, that she breached that duty and that her breach was a proximate cause of their losses.

The New Jersey Business Corporation Act, which took effect on January 1, 1969, was a comprehensive revision of the statutes relating to business corporations. One section, N.J.S.A. 14A:6–14, concerning a director's general obligation had no counterpart in the old Act. That section makes it incumbent upon directors to

discharge their duties in good faith and with that degree of diligence, care and skill which ordinarily prudent men would exercise under similar circumstances in like positions. [N.J.S.A. 14A:6–14]

This provision was based primarily on section 43 of the Model Business Corporation Act and is derived also from section 717 of the New York Business Corporation Law (L.1961, c. 855, effective September 1, 1963). Commissioners' Comments—1968 and 1972, N.J.S.A. 14A:6–14. Before the enactment of N.J.S.A. 14A:6–14, there was no express statutory authority requiring directors to act as ordinarily prudent persons under similar circumstances in like positions. Nonetheless, the requirement had been expressed in New Jersey judicial decisions.

A leading New Jersey opinion is Campbell v. Watson, 62 N.J.Eq. 396, 50 A. 120 (Ch.1901), which, like many early decisions on director liability, involved directors of a bank that had become insolvent. A receiver of the bank charged the directors with negligence that allegedly led to insolvency. In the opinion, Vice Chancellor Pitney explained that bank depositors have a right to

> rely upon the character of the directors and officers [and upon the representation] that they will perform their sworn duty to manage the affairs of the bank according to law and devote to its affairs the same diligent attention which ordinary, prudent, diligent men pay to their own affairs; and ... such diligence and attention as experience has shown it is proper and necessary that bank directors should give to that business in order to reasonably protect the bank and its creditors against loss. [Id. at 406]

Because N.J.S.A. 14A:6–14 is modeled in part upon section 717 of the New York statute, N.Y.Bus.Corp. Law § 717 (McKinney), we consider also the law of New York in interpreting the New Jersey statute. See Suter v. San Angelo Foundry & Machine Co., 81 N.J. 150, 161–162, 406 A.2d 140 (1979) (approving the propriety of examining as an interpretative aid the law of a state, the statute of which has been copied).

Prior to the enactment of section 717, the New York courts, like those of New Jersey, had espoused the principle that directors owed that degree of care that a businessman of ordinary prudence would exercise in the management of his own affairs. Kavanaugh v. Gould, 223 N.Y. 103, 105, 119 N.E. 237, 238 (Ct.App.1918); Hun v. Cary, 82 N.Y. 65, 72 (Ct.App.1880); McLear v. McLear, 265 App.Div. 556, 560, 266 App.Div. 702, 703, 40 N.Y.S.2d 432, 436 (Sup.Ct.1943), aff'd 291 N.Y. 809, 53 N.E.2d 573, 292 N.Y. 580, 54 N.E.2d 694 (Ct.App.1944); Simon v. Socony-Vacuum Oil Co., 179 Misc. 202, 203, 38 N.Y.S.2d 270, 273 (Sup.Ct.1942), aff'd 267 App.Div. 890, 47 N.Y.S.2d 589 (Sup.Ct.1944); Van Schaick v. Aron, 170 Misc. 520, 534, 10 N.Y.S.2d 550, 563 (Sup.Ct.1938). In addition to requiring that directors act honestly and in good faith, the New York courts recognized that the nature and extent of reasonable care depended upon the type of corporation, its size and financial resources. Thus, a bank director was held to stricter accountability than the director of an ordinary business.[1] Hun v. Cary, supra, 82 N.Y. at. 72; Litwin v. Allen, 25 N.Y.S.2d 667, 678 (Sup.Ct.1940).

---

1. The obligations of directors of banks involve some additional consideration because of their relationship to the public generally and depositors in particular.

In determining the limits of a director's duty, section 717 continued to recognize the individual characteristics of the corporation involved as well as the particular circumstances and corporate role of the director. Significantly, the legislative comment to section 717 states:

> The adoption of the standard prescribed by this section will allow the court to envisage the director's duty of care as a relative concept, depending on the kind of corporation involved, the particular circumstances and the corporate role of the director. [N.Y.Bus.Corp. Law § 717, comment (McKinney)]

This approach was consonant with the desire to formulate a standard that could be applied to both publicly and closely held entities. The report of the Chairman and chief counsel of the New York Joint Legislative Committee to Study Revision of Corporation Laws stated that the statute "reflects an attempt to merge the interests of public issue corporations and closely held corporations." Anderson & Lesher, The New Business Corporation Law, xxvii, reprinted in N.Y.Bus.Corp. Law §§ 1 to 800 xxv (McKinney).[2]

Underlying the pronouncements in section 717, Campbell v. Watson, supra, and N.J.S.A. 14A:6–14 is the principle that directors must discharge their duties in good faith and act as ordinarily prudent persons would under similar circumstances in like positions. Although specific duties in a given case can be determined only after consideration of all of the circumstances, the standard of ordinary care is the wellspring from which those more specific duties flow.

As a general rule, a director should acquire at least a rudimentary understanding of the business of the corporation. Accordingly, a director should become familiar with the fundamentals of the business in which the corporation is engaged. *Campbell*, supra, 62 N.J.Eq. at 416, 50 A. 120. Because directors are bound to exercise ordinary care, they cannot set up as a defense lack of the knowledge needed to exercise the requisite degree of care. If one "feels that he has not had sufficient business experience to qualify him to perform the duties of a director, he should either acquire the knowledge by inquiry, or refuse to act." Ibid.

Directors are under a continuing obligation to keep informed about the activities of the corporation. Otherwise, they may not be able to participate in the overall management of corporate affairs. Barnes v. Andrews, 298 F. 614 (S.D.N.Y.1924) (director guilty of misprision of

Statutes impose certain requirements on bank directors. For example, directors of national banks must take an oath that they will diligently and honestly administer the affairs of the bank and will not permit violation of the banking laws. Moreover, they must satisfy certain requirements such as residence, citizenship, stockholdings and not serving as an investment banker. 12 U.S.C.A. §§ 77–78. See generally R. Barnett, Responsibilities & Liabilities of Bank Directors (1980).

2. Section 717 was amended in 1977 (L.1977, c. 432, § 4, effective September 1, 1977) to provide that directors must exercise a "degree of care" in place of a "degree of diligence, care and skill." The report of the Association of the Bar of the City of New York Committee on Corporation Law states the amendment did not alter but clarified and reaffirmed existing law. Report No. 178 on S254–A and A245–A, 544.

office for not keeping himself informed about the details of corporate business); Atherton v. Anderson, 99 F.2d 883, 889–890 (6 Cir. 1938) (ignorance no defense to director liability because of director's "duty to know the facts"); *Campbell,* supra, 62 N.J.Eq. at 409, 50 A. 120 (directors "bound to acquaint themselves with ... extent ... of supervision exercised by officers"); Williams v. McKay, 46 N.J.Eq. 25, 36, 18 A. 824 (Ch.1889) (director under duty to supervise managers and practices to determine whether business methods were safe and proper). Directors may not shut their eyes to corporate misconduct, and then claim that because they did not see the misconduct, they did not have a duty to look. The sentinel asleep at his post contributes nothing to the enterprise he is charged to protect. Wilkinson v. Dodd, 42 N.J.Eq. 234, 245, 7 A. 327 (Ch.1886), aff'd 42 N.J.Eq. 647, 9 A. 685 (E. & A. 1887).

Directorial management does not require a detailed inspection of day-to-day activities, but rather a general monitoring of corporate affairs and policies. Williams v. McKay, supra, at 37, 18 A. 824. Accordingly, a director is well advised to attend board meetings regularly. Indeed, a director who is absent from a board meeting is presumed to concur in action taken on a corporate matter, unless he files a "dissent with the secretary of the corporation within a reasonable time after learning of such action." N.J.S.A. 14A:6–13 (Supp.1981–1982). Regular attendance does not mean that directors must attend every meeting, but that directors should attend meetings as a matter of practice. A director of a publicly held corporation might be expected to attend regular monthly meetings, but a director of a small, family corporation might be asked to attend only an annual meeting. The point is that one of the responsibilities of a director is to attend meetings of the board of which he or she is a member. That burden is lightened by N.J.S.A. 14A:6–7(2) (Supp.1981–1982), which permits board action without a meeting if all members of the board consent in writing.

While directors are not required to audit corporate books, they should maintain familiarity with the financial status of the corporation by a regular review of financial statements. *Campbell,* supra, 62 N.J.Eq. at 415, 50 A. 120; *Williams,* supra, 46 N.J.Eq. at 38–39, 18 A. 824; see Section of Corporation, Banking and Business Law, American Bar Association, "Corporate Director's Guidebook," 33 Bus.Law. 1595, 1608 (1978) (Guidebook); N. Lattin, The Law of Corporations 280 (2 ed. 1971). In some circumstances, directors may be charged with assuring that bookkeeping methods conform to industry custom and usage. Lippitt v. Ashley, 89 Conn. 451, 464, 94 A. 995, 1000 (Sup.Ct.1915). The extent of review, as well as the nature and frequency of financial statements, depends not only on the customs of the industry, but also on the nature of the corporation and the business in which it is engaged. Financial statements of some small corporations may be prepared internally and only on an annual basis; in a large publicly held corporation, the statements may be produced monthly or at some other regular interval. Adequate financial review normally would be more informal in a private corporation than in a publicly held corporation.

Of some relevance in this case is the circumstance that the financial records disclose the "shareholders' loans". Generally directors are immune from liability if, in good faith,

they rely upon the opinion of counsel for the corporation or upon written reports setting forth financial data concerning the corporation and prepared by an independent public accountant or certified public accountant or firm of such accountants or upon financial statements, books of account or reports of the corporation represented to them to be correct by the president, the officer of the corporation having charge of its books of account, or the person presiding at a meeting of the board. [N.J.S.A. 14A:6–14]

The review of financial statements, however, may give rise to a duty to inquire further into matters revealed by those statements. Corsicana Nat'l Bank v. Johnson, 251 U.S. 68, 71, 40 S.Ct. 82, 84, 64 L.Ed. 141 (1919); *Atherton,* supra, 99 F.2d at 890; LaMonte v. Mott, 93 N.J.Eq. 229, 239, 107 A. 462 (E. & A. 1921); see *Lippitt,* supra, 89 Conn. at 457, 94 A. at 998. Upon discovery of an illegal course of action, a director has a duty to object and, if the corporation does not correct the conduct, to resign. See Dodd v. Wilkinson, 42 N.J.Eq. 647, 651, 9 A. 685 (E. & A. 1887); Williams v. Riley, 34 N.J.Eq. 398, 401 (Ch.1881).

In certain circumstances, the fulfillment of the duty of a director may call for more than mere objection and resignation. Sometimes a director may be required to seek the advice of counsel. *Guidebook,* supra, at 1631. One New Jersey case recognized the duty of a bank director to seek counsel where doubt existed about the meaning of the bank charter. Williams v. McKay, supra, 46 N.J.Eq. at 60, 18 A. 824. The duty to seek the assistance of counsel can extend to areas other than the interpretation of corporation instruments. Modern corporate practice recognizes that on occasion a director should seek outside advice. A director may require legal advice concerning the propriety of his or her own conduct, the conduct of other officers and directors or the conduct of the corporation. In appropriate circumstances, a director would be "well advised to consult with regular corporate counsel (or his own legal adviser) at any time in which he is doubtful regarding proposed action ...." *Guidebook,* supra, at 1618. Sometimes the duty of a director may require more than consulting with outside counsel. A director may have a duty to take reasonable means to prevent illegal conduct by co-directors; in an appropriate case, this may include threat of suit. See Selheimer v. Manganese Corp., 423 Pa. 563, 572, 584, 224 A.2d 634, 640, 646 (Sup.Ct. 1966) (director exonerated when he objected, resigned, organized shareholder action group, and threatened suit).

A director is not an ornament, but an essential component of corporate governance. Consequently, a director cannot protect himself behind a paper shield bearing the motto, "dummy director." *Campbell,* supra, 62 N.J.Eq. at 443, 50 A. 120 ("The directors were not intended to be mere figure-heads without duty or responsibility"); Williams v. McKay, supra, 46 N.J.Eq. at 57–58, 18 A. 824 (director voluntarily assuming position also assumes duties of ordinary care, skill and judgment). The New

Jersey Business Corporation Act, in imposing a standard of ordinary care on all directors, confirms that dummy, figurehead and accommodation directors are anachronisms with no place in New Jersey law. See N.J.S.A. 14A:6–14. Similarly, in interpreting section 717, the New York courts have not exonerated a director who acts as an "accommodation." Barr v. Wackman, 36 N.Y.2d 371, 381, 329 N.E.2d 180, 188, 368 N.Y.S.2d 497, 507 (Ct.App.1975) (director "does not exempt himself from liability by failing to do more than passively rubber-stamp the decisions of the active managers"). See Kavanaugh v. Gould, supra, 223 N.Y. at 111–117, 119 N.E. at 240–241 (the fact that bank director never attended board meetings or acquainted himself with bank's business or methods held to be no defense, as a matter of law, to responsibility for speculative loans made by the president and acquiesced in by other directors). Thus, all directors are responsible for managing the business and affairs of the corporation. N.J.S.A. 14A:6–1 (Supp.1981–1982); 1 G. Hornstein, Corporation Law and Practice § 431 at 525 (1959).

The factors that impel expanded responsibility in the large, publicly held corporation may not be present in a small, close corporation.[3] Nonetheless, a close corporation may, because of the nature of its business, be affected with a public interest. For example, the stock of a bank may be closely held, but because of the nature of banking the directors would be subject to greater liability than those of another close corporation. Even in a small corporation, a director is held to the standard of that degree of care that an ordinarily prudent director would use under the circumstances. M. Mace, The Board of Directors of Small Corporations 83 (1948).

A director's duty of care does not exist in the abstract, but must be considered in relation to specific obligees. In general, the relationship of a corporate director to the corporation and its stockholders is that of a fiduciary. Whitfield v. Kern, 122 N.J.Eq. 332, 341, 192 A. 48 (E. & A. 1937). Shareholders have a right to expect that directors will exercise reasonable supervision and control over the policies and practices of a corporation. The institutional integrity of a corporation depends upon the proper discharge by directors of those duties.

While directors may owe a fiduciary duty to creditors also, that obligation generally has not been recognized in the absence of insolven-

---

3. Our decision is based on directorial responsibilities arising under state statutory and common law as distinguished from the Securities Act of 1933, 15 U.S.C. § 77a et seq., and the Securities Exchange Act of 1934, 15 U.S.C. § 78a et seq. Nonetheless, we recognize significant developments in directorial liability under both Acts and related rules and regulations of the Securities and Exchange Commission. For example, an outside director may be liable in negligence under section 11 of the 1933 Act for the failure to make a reasonable investigation before signing a registration statement. Escott v. Barchris Constr. Corp., 283 F.Supp. 643, 687–689 (S.D.N.Y.1968); see also Feit v. Leasco Data Processing Equip. Corp., 332 F.Supp. 544, 575–576 (E.D.N.Y. 1971) (outside director who was partner in law firm for corporation considered an insider). The Securities and Exchange Commission has made it clear that outside directors should become knowledgeable about a company's business and accounting practices so that they may make "an informed judgment of its more important affairs or the abilities and integrity of the officers." Securities Exchange Act of 1934, Release No. 11,516 (July 2, 1975). ...

cy. *Whitfield*, supra, 122 N.J.Eq. at 342, 345, 192 A. 48. With certain corporations, however, directors are [deemed] to owe a duty to creditors and other third parties even when the corporation is solvent. Although depositors of a bank are considered in some respects to be creditors, courts have recognized that directors may owe them a fiduciary duty. See Campbell, supra, 62 N.J.Eq. at 406–407, 50 A. 120. Directors of nonbanking corporations may owe a similar duty when the corporation holds funds of others in trust. Cf. McGlynn v. Schultz, 90 N.J.Super. 505, 218 A.2d 408 (Ch.Div.1966), aff'd 95 N.J.Super. 412, 231 A.2d 386 (App.Div.), certif. den. 50 N.J. 409, 235 A.2d 901 (1967) (directors who did not insist on segregating trust funds held by corporation liable to the *cestuis que trust*).

In three cases originating in New Jersey, directors who did not participate actively in the conversion of trust funds were found not liable. In each instance, the facts did not support the conclusion that the director knew or could have known of the wrongdoing even if properly attentive. *McGlynn*, supra, 90 N.J.Super. at 509, 511, 218 A.2d 408 (director from Chicago not "in a position to know the details of the corporation's business" not liable for conversions that occurred over four month period); General Films, Inc. v. Sanco Gen. Mfg. Corp., 153 N.J.Super. 369, 371, 379 A.2d 1042 (App.Div.1977), certif. den. 75 N.J. 614, 384 A.2d 843 (1978) (director and sole shareholder not liable for conversion by dominant principal, her husband, in misappropriating proceeds of single check); Ark-Tenn Distrib. Corp. v. Breidt, 209 F.2d 359, 360 (3 Cir. 1954) (president who was not active in corporation not liable for conversion of trust funds received in single transaction). To the extent that the cases support the proposition that directors are not liable unless they actively participate in the conversion of trust funds, they are disapproved.

Courts in other states have imposed liability on directors of non-banking corporations for the conversion of trust funds, even though those directors did not participate in or know of the conversion. Preston-Thomas Constr. Inc. v. Central Leasing Corp., 518 P.2d 1125 (Okl.Ct.App. 1973) (director liable for conversion of funds entrusted to corporation for acquisition of stock in another corporation); Vujacich v. Southern Commercial Co., 21 Cal.App. 439, 132 P. 80 (Dist.Ct.App.1913) (director of wholesale grocery business personally liable for conversion by corporation of worker's funds deposited for safekeeping). The distinguishing circumstances in regard to banks and other corporations holding trust funds is that the depositor or beneficiary can reasonably expect the director to act with ordinary prudence concerning the funds held in a fiduciary capacity. Thus, recognition of a duty of a director to those for whom a corporation holds funds in trust may be viewed as another application of the general rule that a director's duty is that of an ordinary prudent person under the circumstances.

The most striking circumstances affecting Mrs. Pritchard's duty as a director are the character of the reinsurance industry, the nature of the misappropriated funds and the financial condition of Pritchard & Baird.

The hallmark of the reinsurance industry has been the unqualified trust and confidence reposed by ceding companies and reinsurers in reinsurance brokers. Those companies entrust money to reinsurance intermediaries with the justifiable expectation that the funds will be transmitted to the appropriate parties. Consequently, the companies could have assumed rightfully that Mrs. Pritchard, as a director of a reinsurance brokerage corporation, would not sanction the comingling and the conversion of loss and premium funds for the personal use of the principals of Pritchard & Baird.

As a reinsurance broker, Pritchard & Baird received annually as a fiduciary millions of dollars of clients' money which it was under a duty to segregate.[4] To this extent, it resembled a bank rather than a small family business. Accordingly, Mrs. Pritchard's relationship to the clientele of Pritchard & Baird was akin to that of a director of a bank to its depositors. All parties agree that Pritchard & Baird held the misappropriated funds in an implied trust. That trust relationship gave rise to a fiduciary duty to guard the funds with fidelity and good faith. Ellsworth Dobbs, Inc. v. Johnson, 50 N.J. 528, 553, 236 A.2d 843 (1967); General Films, Inc. v. Sanco Gen. Mfg. Corp., supra, 153 N.J.Super. at 372–373, 379 A.2d 1042.

As a director of a substantial reinsurance brokerage corporation, she should have known that it received annually millions of dollars of loss and premium funds which it held in trust for ceding and reinsurance companies. Mrs. Pritchard should have obtained and read the annual statements of financial condition of Pritchard & Baird. Although she had a right to rely upon financial statements prepared in accordance with N.J.S.A. 14A:6–14, such reliance would not excuse her conduct. The reason is that those statements disclosed on their face the misappropriation of trust funds.

From those statements, she should have realized that, as of January 31, 1970, her sons were withdrawing substantial trust funds under the guise of "Shareholders' Loans." The financial statements for each fiscal year commencing with that of January 31, 1970, disclosed that the working capital deficits and the "loans" were escalating in tandem. Detecting a misappropriation of funds would not have required special expertise or extraordinary diligence; a cursory reading of the financial statements would have revealed the pillage. Thus, if Mrs. Pritchard had read the financial statements, she would have known that her sons were converting trust funds. When financial statements demonstrate that insiders are bleeding a corporation to death, a director should notice and try to stanch the flow of blood.

In summary, Mrs. Pritchard was charged with the obligation of basic knowledge and supervision of the business of Pritchard & Baird. Under

---

4. Following the Pritchard & Baird bankruptcy, New York, a reinsurance center, adopted legislation regulating reinsurance intermediaries. One statute codified the industry standard by prohibiting reinsurance intermediaries from commingling their funds with funds of their principals. N.Y. Ins. Law § 122–a(9) (McKinney Supp. 1980–1981).

the circumstances, this obligation included reading and understanding financial statements, and making reasonable attempts at detection and prevention of the illegal conduct of other officers and directors. She had a duty to protect the clients of Pritchard & Baird against policies and practices that would result in the misappropriation of money they had entrusted to the corporation. She breached that duty.

IV

Nonetheless, the negligence of Mrs. Pritchard does not result in liability unless it is a proximate cause of the loss. Kulas v. Public Serv. Elec. and Gas Co., 41 N.J. 311, 317, 196 A.2d 769 (1964). Analysis of proximate cause requires an initial determination of cause-in-fact. Causation-in-fact calls for a finding that the defendant's act or omission was a necessary antecedent of the loss, i.e., that if the defendant had observed his or her duty of care, the loss would not have occurred. Ibid., W. Prosser, Law of Torts § 41 at 238 (4 ed. 1971). Further, the plaintiff has the burden of establishing the amount of the loss or damages caused by the negligence of the defendant. H. Henn, Law of Corporations § 234 at 456 (2 ed. 1970). Thus, the plaintiff must establish not only a breach of duty, "but in addition that the performance by the director of his duty would have avoided loss, and the amount of the resulting loss." 1 Hornstein, supra, § 446 at 566.

Cases involving nonfeasance present a much more difficult causation question than those in which the director has committed an affirmative act of negligence leading to the loss. Analysis in cases of negligent omissions calls for determination of the reasonable steps a director should have taken and whether that course of action would have averted the loss.

Usually a director can absolve himself from liability by informing the other directors of the impropriety and voting for a proper course of action. Dyson, "The Director's Liability for Negligence," 40 Ind.L.J. 341, 365 (1965). Conversely, a director who votes for or concurs in certain actions may be "liable to the corporation for the benefit of its creditors or shareholders, to the extent of any injuries suffered by such persons, respectively, as a result of any such action." N.J.S.A. 14A:6–12 (Supp.1981–1982). A director who is present at a board meeting is presumed to concur in corporate action taken at the meeting unless his dissent is entered in the minutes of the meeting or filed promptly after adjournment. N.J.S.A. 14A:6–13. In many, if not most, instances an objecting director whose dissent is noted in accordance with N.J.S.A. 14A:6–13 would be absolved after attempting to persuade fellow directors to follow a different course of action. Cf. McGlynn, supra, 90 N.J.Super. at 520–521, 529, 218 A.2d 408 (receiver had no case against director who advised president that certain funds should be escrowed, wrote to executive committee to that effect, and objected at special meeting of board of directors); Selheimer v. Manganese Corp., supra, 423 Pa. at 572, 584, 224 A.2d at 640, 646 (dissenting minority director in publicly held corporation absolved because he did all he could to divert majority directors from their course of conduct by complaining to management, threatening to institute suit and organizing a stockholders' committee).

Even accepting the hypothesis that Mrs. Pritchard might not be liable if she had objected and resigned, there are two significant reasons for holding her liable. First, she did not resign until just before the bankruptcy. Consequently, there is no factual basis for the speculation that the losses would have occurred even if she had objected and resigned. Indeed, the trial court reached the opposite conclusion: "The actions of the sons were so blatantly wrongful that it is hard to see how they could have resisted any moderately firm objection to what they were doing." 162 N.J.Super. at 372, 392 A.2d 1233. Second, the nature of the reinsurance business distinguishes it from most other commercial activities in that reinsurance brokers are encumbered by fiduciary duties owed to third parties. In other corporations, a director's duty normally does not extend beyond the shareholders to third parties.

In this case, the scope of Mrs. Pritchard's duties was determined by the precarious financial condition of Pritchard & Baird, its fiduciary relationship to its clients and the implied trust in which it held their funds. Thus viewed, the scope of her duties encompassed all reasonable action to stop the continuing conversion. Her duties extended beyond mere objection and resignation to reasonable attempts to prevent the misappropriation of the trust funds. *Campbell*, supra, 62 N.J.Eq. at 427, 50 A. 120.

A leading case discussing causation where the director's liability is predicated upon a negligent failure to act is Barnes v. Andrews, 298 F. 614 (S.D.N.Y.1924). In that case the court exonerated a figurehead director who served for eight months on a board that held one meeting after his election, a meeting he was forced to miss because of the death of his mother. Writing for the court, Judge Learned Hand distinguished a director who fails to prevent general mismanagement from one such as Mrs. Pritchard who failed to stop an illegal "loan":

> When the corporate funds have been illegally lent, it is a fair inference that a protest would have stopped the loan, and that the director's neglect caused the loss. But when a business fails from general mismanagement, business incapacity, or bad judgment, how is it possible to say that a single director could have made the company successful, or how much in dollars he could have saved? [Id. at 616–617]

Pointing out the absence of proof of proximate cause between defendant's negligence and the company's insolvency, Judge Hand also wrote:

> The plaintiff must, however, go further than to show that [the director] should have been more active in his duties. This cause of action rests upon a tort, as much though it be a tort of omission as though it had rested upon a positive act. The plaintiff must accept the burden of showing that the performance of the defendant's duties

would have avoided loss, and what loss it would have avoided. [Id. at 616]

Other courts have refused to impose personal liability on negligent directors when the plaintiffs have been unable to prove that diligent execution of the directors' duties would have precluded the losses. Briggs v. Spaulding, 141 U.S. 132, 11 S.Ct. 924, 35 L.Ed. 662 (1891) (no causal relationship because discovery of defalcations could have resulted only from examination of books beyond duty of director); Hoehn v. Crews, 144 F.2d 665 (10 Cir. 1944) (failure of bank director to publish notice of liquidation of bank not proximate cause of loss to creditors who did not know at time of liquidation that they had a claim); Virginia-Carolina Chem. Co. v. Ehrich, 230 F. 1005 (E.D.S.C.1916) (close supervision of daily corporate affairs necessary to notice wrongdoing; failure to attend meetings not causally related to loss); LaMonte v. Mott, supra (director who had been in office for less than two years and had conducted only one examination held not liable); Sternberg v. Blaine, 179 Ark. 448, 17 S.W.2d 286 (Sup.Ct.1929) ("[n]o ordinary examination usually made by directors of a country bank, however careful, would have discovered" misappropriations); Holland v. American Founders Life Ins. Co., 151 Colo. 69, 376 P.2d 162 (Sup.Ct.1962) (conduct "not a contributing cause of the loss sustained because director did not neglect his duty as secretary-director"); Wallach v. Billings, 277 Ill. 218, 115 N.E. 382 (Sup.Ct.1917), cert. den. 244 U.S. 659, 37 S.Ct. 745, 61 L.Ed. 1376 (1917) (inactive director not liable because no allegation in complaint that losses caused by director negligence or that director could have prevented losses); Allied Freightways, Inc. v. Cholfin, 325 Mass. 630, 91 N.E.2d 765 (Sup.Jud.Ct.1950) (director not liable where losses resulted from general mismanagement and director, in the reasonable exercise of her duties, could not have discovered illegal payments from examination of corporate books); Hathaway v. Huntley, 284 Mass. 587, 188 N.E. 610 (Sup.Jud. Ct.1933) (negligent director not liable for bankruptcy loses caused by husband's policy of business expansion and not discernible in books by use of reasonable care and diligence); Martin v. Hardy, 251 Mich. 413, 232 N.W. 197 (Sup.Ct.1930) (six-month sale of stock below cost resulting in $37,000 loss to corporation not causally related to director negligence); Henry v. Wellington Tel. Co., 76 Ohio App. 77, 63 N.E.2d 233 (Ct.App 1945) (though directors failed to comply with formalities of statute, that failure did not result in loss).

Other courts have held directors liable for losses actively perpetrated by others because the negligent omissions of the directors were considered a necessary antecedent to the defalcations. *Atherton,* supra (directors liable for bank losses proximately caused by failure to supervise officers and to examine auditor's reports); Ringeon v. Albinson, 35 F.2d 753 (D.Minn.1929) (negligent director not excused from liability for losses that could have been prevented by supervision and prompt action); Heit v. Bixby, 276 F.Supp. 217, 231 (E.D.Mo.967) (directors liable for 40% commissions taken by co-directors because directors' "lackadaisical attitude" proximately caused the loss); Ford v. Taylor, 176 Ark. 843, 4

S.W.2d 938 (1928) (bank directors liable for losses due to misappropriations of cashier who "felt free to pursue [misconduct] without fear of detection by the directors through their failure to discharge the functions of their office"); Vujacich v. Southern Commercial Co., supra, (unless some showing of protest made, director liable for loss resulting from misappropriation of co-director); Chicago Title & Trust Co. v. Munday, 297 Ill. 555, 131 N.E. 103 (Sup.Ct.1921) (complaint states good cause of action alleging inactive directors responsible for officer's defalcations occurring as consequence of omission of directors' duty of supervision); Coddington v. Canaday, 157 Ind. 243, 61 N.E. 567 (Sup.Ct. 1901) (directors liable for losses resulting from bank insolvency due to improper supervision and concomitant acceptance of worthless notes); Bentz v. Vardaman Mfg. Co., 210 So.2d 35 (Miss.Sup.Ct.1968) (nonattendance at director meetings no relief from director liability for losses resulting from action taken at meetings); Tri-Bullion Smelting & Development Co. v. Corliss, 230 N.Y. 629, 130 N.E. 921 (Ct.App.1921) (directors liable for misappropriations by treasurer resulting from negligence of directors); Neese v. Brown, 218 Tenn. 686, 405 S.W.2d 577 (Sup.Ct.1964) (directors who abdicate control liable for losses caused by breach of trust by those left in control if due care on part of inactive directors could have avoided loss).

In assessing whether Mrs. Pritchard's conduct was a legal or proximate cause of the conversion, "[l]egal responsibility must be limited to those causes which are so closely connected with the result and of such significance that the law is justified in imposing liability." Prosser, supra, § 41 at 237. Such a judicial determination involves not only considerations of causation-in-fact and matters of policy, but also common sense and logic. Caputzal v. The Lindsay Co., 48 N.J. 69, 77–78 (1966). The act or the failure to act must be a substantial factor in producing the harm. Prosser, supra, § 41 at 240; Restatement (Second) of Torts, §§ 431, 432 (1965).

Within Pritchard & Baird, several factors contributed to the loss of the funds: comingling of corporate and client monies, conversion of funds by Charles, Jr. and William and dereliction of her duties by Mrs. Pritchard. The wrongdoing of her sons, although the immediate cause of the loss, should not excuse Mrs. Pritchard from her negligence which also was a substantial factor contributing to the loss. Restatement (Second) of Torts, supra, § 442B, comment b. Her sons knew that she, the only other director, was not reviewing their conduct; they spawned their fraud in the backwater of her neglect. Her neglect of duty contributed to the climate of corruption; her failure to act contributed to the continuation of that corruption. Consequently, her conduct was a substantial factor contributing to the loss.

Analysis of proximate cause is especially difficult in a corporate context where the allegation is that nonfeasance of a director is a proximate cause of damage to a third party. Where a case involves nonfeasance, no one can say "with absolute certainty what would have occurred if the defendant had acted otherwise." Prosser, supra, § 41 at

242. Nonetheless, where it is reasonable to conclude that the failure to act would produce a particular result and that result has followed, causation may be inferred. Ibid. We conclude that even if Mrs. Pritchard's mere objection had not stopped the depredations of her sons, her consultation with an attorney and the threat of suit would have deterred them. That conclusion flows as a matter of common sense and logic from the record. Whether in other situations a director has a duty to do more than protest and resign is best left to case-by-case determinations. In this case, we are satisfied that there was a duty to do more than object and resign. Consequently, we find that Mrs. Pritchard's negligence was a proximate cause of the misappropriations.

To conclude, by virtue of her office, Mrs. Pritchard had the power to prevent the losses sustained by the clients of Pritchard & Baird. With power comes responsibility. She had a duty to deter the depredation of the other insiders, her sons. She breached that duty and caused plaintiffs to sustain damages.

The judgment of the Appellate Division is affirmed.

For affirmance—JUSTICES SULLIVAN, PASHMAN, CLIFFORD, SCHREIBER, HANDLER and POLLOCK—6.

For reversal—none.

(b) THE BUSINESS JUDGMENT OF THE DIRECTORS

Insert the following material at p. 541 of the unabridged edition following Kamin v. American Express Co., and at p. 394 of the abridged edition at the beginning of Chapter VI, Section 1(b):

NOTE ON JOY v. NORTH

The duty-of-care area, long dormant, has come dramatically alive during the last several years. The *Francis* case is one indication of the area's new vitality. Another is Joy v. North, 692 F.2d 880 (2d Cir. 1982), cert. denied Citytrust v. Joy, ___ U.S. ___, 103 S.Ct. 1498, 75 L.Ed.2d 930 (1983). This case involved Citytrust, a wholly owned banking subsidiary of Connecticut Financial Services Corporation, both Connecticut corporations. The underlying transactions that gave rise to the complaint in this case were summarized by the court as follows:

> ... In 1967, Citytrust entered into a 20-year term lease agreement for approximately 9% of an office building which Katz was planning to build in Norwalk. Katz, then a respected developer, signed a $4 million construction mortgage for a one-and-a-half year term on January 12, 1971. Although the mortgage was written through and recorded in the name of Citytrust, Chase Manhattan Bank provided the bulk of the financing, $3.5 million, with Citytrust participating to the extent of $500,000. At this time, Katz had already borrowed, largely in unsecured form, an additional $250,000

from Citytrust to finance construction of the office building. As the building neared completion in early 1972, Katz had drawn down the full value of the $4 million mortgage. At its expiration in June, 1972, the Chase mortgage was replaced by a $4.5 million mortgage by First National City Bank, with Citytrust both issuing the mortgage and participating to the extent of $90,000. Meanwhile, Katz continued to receive unsecured loans from Citytrust. By December, 1972, that unsecured debt reached $900,000, for a total of $990,000 in Citytrust loans related to the building.

In June, 1973, with the building only half rented, the First National City mortgage was extended for a year. Katz's unsecured debt to Citytrust had by now climbed to $1,840,000. In November, in conjunction with the issuance of yet another loan to Katz, Citytrust obtained a blanket second mortgage on the building and on other Katz properties to secure what was now a total loan balance of $2,140,000. Shortly thereafter, the First National City mortgage was extended to August, 1975, and Citytrust lent Katz another $300,000. Just prior to this extension of credit, the National Bank Examiners classified the Katz loans.

In April, 1975, a refinancing plan was completed with Lincoln National Life Insurance Company providing a $6 million loan to a Katz-related partnership which had taken title to the building. The loan was secured by a first mortgage on the building and was used to consolidate Katz's debt. As a condition of the new financing, Citytrust was required to take a 30-year master lease on the still largely unrented building at a rental equaling the mortgage payments to Lincoln National, in effect guaranteeing Katz's $6 million obligation to Lincoln. In addition to undertaking the master lease, Citytrust had by now extended $2,665,000 in loans to Katz.

In May, 1975, the National Bank Examiners classified $2 million of the Katz loans as doubtful and required a charge off of $665,000. On August 18, 1976, in an apparent effort to salvage what was left of its position, Citytrust's Board of Directors authorized loans which exceeded the 10% federal statutory limit. After these loans were consummated, Katz's total indebtedness to Citytrust reached $3,545,-000. On October 20, 1976, Citytrust charged off the $2 million remaining on the second mortgage.

On June 13, 1977, the Katz-related partnership relinquished title to the building to Citytrust in exchange for a release from its obligation to Lincoln National and a release of personal guarantees previously assumed by members of the Katz family. Citytrust thus directly assumed the $6 million Lincoln National mortgage. In October, 1977, Second Nutmeg Financial purchased the building for $9,600,000 which consisted of its assumption of the $6 million Lincoln National mortgage and a $3,600,000 note to Citytrust secured by a second mortgage. There is an indication in the District Court record that an affiliate of Second Nutmeg which later acquired the building has defaulted and Citytrust once again owns it, along with the concurrent obligations. There is no indication that rental income is now adequate to meet those obligations, and we appear free to assume that the other Katz properties covered by the second mortgage are not of any significant value.

In October 1977, Dr. Joy brought a derivative suit on behalf of Connecticut financial against Citytrust and its officers and directors. The complaint alleged diversity of citizenship, breach of fiduciary duty, and violation of the National Bank Act, which limits aggregate loans to a single person or entity to 10% of a bank's combined stockholder equity and capital.

The boards of Citytrust and Connecticut Financial authorized the establishment of a Special Litigation Committee to determine whether continued prosecution of this derivative action would be in the best interests of the corporation. The Committee then rendered a report whose findings were summarized by the court as follows:

> According to the Report, Nelson L. North was Citytrust's Chief Executive Officer and Norman Schaff, Jr. was its Chief Lending Officer during the period in question. The management of Citytrust was completely dominated by North. Bank officers who did not temper themselves to his regime had a short tenure at the bank. North also exercised strong control over the activities of the Board of Directors. Board members were given neither materials nor agendas prior to meetings and requests for long range planning documents were left unanswered. North's control is illustrated by the fact that contrary to the recommendation of Citytrust's outside auditors, the bank's Audit Committee was not composed solely of outside directors but instead counted among its members Mr. North and one other officer. Minutes of the Audit Committee between 1971 and 1974 are largely incomplete.

> Mr. North apparently brought the initial proposal for the Katz loan to Citytrust. From 1971 to 1976, North's son was employed by Katz, and he apparently deemed this a sufficient conflict of interest to preclude his voting on the Katz transactions in Executive Committee meetings. This fastidiousness appears to have been limited to the formality of voting, for the Report strongly suggests that North was deeply involved in the Katz transactions, although the full degree of his involvement is left uncertain. The Report also adds that Mr. North has destroyed his records.

> Katz appears to have been experiencing financial difficulties as early as 1971. Chase Manhattan in fact opposed financing the Katz building in part because of a $1.6 million shortfall between the building cost and available lending; it was North who persuaded Chase to make the initial mortgage loan. By 1972, Katz was falling behind in its loans and by December of that year owed Citytrust $990,000 with respect to the building. The Report concludes that by then Citytrust was effectively a joint venturer with Katz in the building, sharing the risk of loss but entitled at best only to interest

and principal if things went well. There is also some indication that a portion of the unsecured advance made by Citytrust was being applied to the Chase mortgage.

Notwithstanding the increasingly evident peril in Citytrust's transactions with Katz, no appraisals of the buildings were undertaken until 1976, and no rentability study until 1974. Although Katz had suggested that a public offering would alleviate the situation, no professional review of the preliminary prospectus was undertaken. From 1972 through 1973, only one meeting of the Board of Directors or Executive Committee considered the Katz loans. The Senior Loan Committee did meet on the Katz matter late in 1972 and may have adopted a very cautious attitude toward further credit extension. Despite this, and despite the absence of Executive Committee and Board support, senior management extended almost a million dollars in loans to Katz between 1972 and 1973.

From 1973 through 1974, the number of Board meetings at which the Katz loans were considered increased to five. This is roughly contemporaneous with the recommendation of the outside auditors that a 50% special fund be set up for the Katz loans and the National Bank Examiners' classification of the total outstanding Katz indebtedness as substandard. It is, as the Report notes, "unsettling" that neither Schaff nor Citytrust's Comptroller recall being advised of the recommendation as to the special reserve. Moreover, it is not established that the Directors were advised of this recommendation.

By late 1974, the Katz loans were so clearly a problem that they were extensively considered by the Board and the Executive Committee. In fact, the Report notes that these loans were discussed at a minimum of 25 Board and Executive Committee meetings. Nevertheless, when, on August 18, 1976, the Board was presented with the request to go over the 10% limit, there was no prior mention of the issue on the agenda nor was opinion of counsel presented to the Board or even sought. Indeed, copies of the Comptroller's letter suggesting that Directors might wish to consult their personal counsel were not distributed to the Board.

The Report estimates a loss of $5.1 million to Citytrust. As stated earlier, there is an indication in the record that since the Report was issued, the new owner has defaulted and Citytrust again owns the building. If so, $5.1 million may be considerably less than the actual loss. In any event, a loss exceeding 10% of shareholder equity seems quite likely.

The court also summarized the committee's conclusions:

As to exceeding the federal statutory limit, the Committee concluded that under the compelling circumstances surrounding the vote, it is possible that no net damage to Citytrust resulted. It also concluded that even if damage did occur, the maximum recovery would be $376,000 plus interest, a sum too small in the Committee's view to justify continuance of the action.

As to the claims of breach of fiduciary duty, the Committee recommended that the suit be discontinued as to the outside defendants because there is "no reasonable possibility" that they might be found liable. As to the others, it concluded merely that

> there is a possibility that a finding of negligence could be rendered against any one or more of the senior loan officers who participated in the Katz Corporation loans. Although it is emphasized that there is no evidence whatsoever of any self-dealing or of any deliberate impropriety, there is some indication that the most prudent lending principles were not adhered to during the evolution of those loans.

Following its discussion of the Litigation Committee's Report, the court began its analysis of the case with a general discussion of the duty of care:

> While it is often stated that corporate directors and officers will be liable for negligence in carrying out their corporate duties, all seem agreed that such a statement is misleading. See generally, Lattin, Corporations, 272–75 (1971). Whereas an automobile driver who makes a mistake in judgment as to speed or distance injuring a pedestrian will likely be called upon to respond in damages, a corporate officer who makes a mistake in judgment as to economic conditions, consumer tastes or production line efficiency will rarely, if ever, be found liable for damages suffered by the corporation. See generally, Symposium, Officers' and Directors' Responsibilities and Liabilities, 27 Bus.Lawyer 1 (1971); Fever, Personal Liabilities of Corporate Officers and Directors, 28–42 (2d ed. 1974). Whatever the terminology, the fact is that liability is rarely imposed upon corporate directors or officers simply for bad judgment and this reluctance to impose liability for unsuccessful business decisions has been doctrinally labelled the business judgment rule. Although the rule has suffered under academic criticism, see, e.g., Cary, Standards of Conduct Under Common Law, Present Day Statutes and the Model Act, 27 Bus.Lawyer 61 (1972), it is not without rational basis.
>
> First, shareholders to a very real degree voluntarily undertake the risk of bad business judgment. Investors need not buy stock, for investment markets offer an array of opportunities less vulnerable to mistakes in judgment by corporate officers. Nor need investors buy stock in particular corporations. In the exercise of what is genuinely a free choice, the quality of a firm's management is often decisive and information is available from professional advisors. Since shareholders can and do select among investments partly on the basis of management, the business judgment rule merely recognizes a certain voluntariness in undertaking the risk of bad business decisions.
>
> Second, courts recognize that after-the-fact litigation is a most imperfect device to evaluate corporate business decisions. The circumstances surrounding a corporate decision are not easily reconstructed in a courtroom years later, since business imperatives often

call for quick decisions, inevitably based on less than perfect information. The entrepreneur's function is to encounter risks and to confront uncertainty, and a reasoned decision at the time made may seem a wild hunch viewed years later against a background of perfect knowledge.

Third, because potential profit often corresponds to the potential risk, it is very much in the interest of shareholders that the law not create incentives for overly cautious corporate decisions. Some opportunities offer great profits at the risk of very substantial losses, while the alternatives offer less risk of loss but also less potential profit. Shareholders can reduce the volatility [5] of risk by diversifying their holdings. In the case of the diversified shareholder, the seemingly more risky alternatives may well be the best choice since great losses in some stocks will over time be offset by even greater gains in others.[6] Given mutual funds and similar forms of diversified investment, courts need not bend over backwards to give special protection to shareholders who refuse to reduce the volatility of risk by not diversifying. A rule which penalizes the choice of seemingly riskier alternatives thus may not be in the interest of shareholders generally.

Whatever its merit, however, the business judgment rule extends only as far as the reasons which justify its existence. Thus, it does not apply in cases, e.g., in which the corporate decision lacks a business purpose, see Singer v. Magnavox, 380 A.2d 969 (Del.Supr.1977), is tainted by a conflict of interest, Globe Woolen v. Utica Gas & Electric Co., 224 N.Y. 483, 121 N.E. 378 (1918), is so egregious as to amount to a no-win decision, Litwin v. Allen, 25 N.Y.S.2d 667 (N.Y.Co.Sup.Ct.1940), or results from an obvious and prolonged failure to exercise oversight or supervision, McDonnell v. American Leduc Petroleums, Ltd., 491 F.2d 380 (2d Cir. 1974); Atherton v. Anderson, 99 F.2d 883 (6th Cir. 1938). Other examples may occur.

5. For purposes of this opinion, "volatility" is "the degree of dispersion or variation of possible outcomes." Klein, Business Organization and Finance 147 (1980).

6. Consider the choice between two investments in an example adapted from Klein, Business Organization and Finance 147–49 (1980):

INVESTMENT A

Estimated Probability of Outcome	Outcome Profit or Loss	Value
.4	+ 15	6.0
.4	+ 1	.4
.2	- 13	-2.6
1.0		3.8

INVESTMENT B

Estimated Probability of Outcome	Outcome Profit or Loss	Value
.4	+ 6	2.4
.4	+ 2	.8
.2	+ 1	.2
1.0		3.4

Next, the court turned to the legal effect of the Committee's recommendations, and concluded that Connecticut would adopt the following rule:

> ... Where a derivative suit cannot be brought without prior demand upon the directors followed by refusal, the directors' decision will stand absent a demonstration of self-interest or bad faith; but where such a demand is excused (for reasons of futility, etc.) and a derivative action is properly brought, an independent committee of directors may obtain a dismissal only if the trial court finds both (a) that the committee was independent, acted in good faith and made a reasonable investigation; and (b) that in the court's independent business judgment as to the corporation's best interest, the action should be dismissed.

Finally, the court applied that standard of review to the facts before it, and concluded that the plaintiffs had a good chance of winning a duty-of-care lawsuit:

> ... [W]e look first to potential liability generally without regard to which defendants are responsible. As to that liability, we find that plaintiff's chances of success are rather high. The loss to Citytrust resulted from decisions which put the bank in a classic "no win" situation. The Katz venture was risky and increasingly so. By continuing extensions of substantial amounts of credit the bank subjected the principal to those risks although its potential gain was no more than the interest it could have earned in less risky, more diversified loans. In a real sense, there was a low ceiling on profits but only a distant floor for losses. It is so similar to the classic case of Litwin v. Allen, supra (bank purchase of bonds with an option in the seller to repurchase at the original price, the bank thus bearing the entire risk of a drop in price with no hope of gain beyond the stipulated interest) that we cannot agree with the Committee's conclusion that only a "possibility of a finding of negligence" exists.
>
> The issue as to which defendants are responsible is less clear. The Committee concluded that there is "no reasonable possibility" of the outside defendants being found liable because they had neither information nor reasonable notice of the problems raised by the Katz transactions. We note first that members of the inside defendants may contradict that version and, if so, a possibility of liability in the outside group exists. Moreover, lack of knowledge is not necessarily a defense, if it is the result of an abdication of directional responsibility. *McDonnell*, supra; *Atherton*, supra. Directors who willingly allow others to make major decisions affecting the future of the corporation wholly without supervision or oversight may not defend

Although A is clearly "worth" more than B, it is riskier because it is more volatile. Diversification lessens the volatility by allowing investors to invest in 20 or 200 A's which will tend to guarantee a total result near the value. Shareholders are thus better off with the various firms selecting A over B, although after the fact they will complain in each case of the 2.6 loss. If the courts did not abide by the business judgment rule, they might well penalize the choice of A in each such case and thereby unknowingly injure shareholders generally by creating incentives for management always to choose B.

on their lack of knowledge, for that ignorance itself is a breach of fiduciary duty. The issue turns in large part upon how and why these defendants were left in the dark. See Graham v. Allis Chalmers Mfg. Co., 41 Del.Ch. 78, 188 A.2d 125 (1963). An individual analysis of each outside defendant's role may show that some are blameless or even that they all were justified in not acting before they did, but neither is an inexorable conclusion on the basis of the present record.

The Report concluded as to the inside defendants that there was a "possibility" of liability. This conclusion is a considerable understatement and not entirely consistent with the Report's finding as to the outside defendants. The outsiders' best defense may well be that the inside group actively concealed the Katz problem. Given the fact that exoneration of the outside defendants may show culpability of the insiders and our conclusion that the probability of liability somewhere is high, we think the exposure of the inside group is considerably more than a "possibility." Nor do we agree that "there is no evidence whatsoever" of deliberate impropriety. Not only is there the problem of North's apparently inconsistent behavior with respect to the appropriateness of his participation in the considerations of Katz transactions, but his failure to keep the Board of Directors informed may well entail more than a negligent omission.

A precise estimate of potential damages is not possible since the trier must determine at what point liability begins. We think, however, that on the present record, a trier might easily find liability extending back to early 1972 or before (assuming no statute of limitations problem), resulting in a return of several million dollars to Citytrust, or perhaps 10% or more of the shareholder equity. This far exceeds the potential cost of the litigation to the corporation. ...

Applying the analysis described above, we conclude that the probability of a substantial net return to the corporation is high. We reject, therefore, the recommendation of the Special Litigation Committee.

One judge dissented.

————

ALI, PRINCIPLES OF CORPORATE GOVERNANCE AND STRUCTURE: ANALYSIS AND RECOMMENDATIONS § 4.01

(TENT. DRAFT No. 3, 1984)

§ 4.01 Duty of Care of Directors and Officers; the Business Judgment Rule

(a) A director or officer has a duty to his corporation to perform his functions in good faith, in a manner that he reasonably believes to be in the best interests of the corporation and otherwise consistent with the principles of § 2.01, and with the care that an ordinarily prudent person would reasonably be expected to exercise in a like position and under similar circumstances.

(b) The duty of care standard set forth in Subsection (a) includes the obligation of a director or officer to make reasonable inquiry in appropriate circumstances.

(c) (1) In performing his duty and functions, a director or officer is entitled to rely on other directors or officers, employees, experts, other persons, or committees of the board in accordance with §§ 4.02–.03. (2) The board may delegate to directors, officers, employees, experts, other persons, or committees of the board the function of identifying matters requiring the attention of the board, and a director, when acting in accordance with the standards set forth in §§ 4.02–.03, is entitled to rely on the decisions, judgments, or performance of such persons or committees.

(d) A director or officer does not violate his duty under this Section with respect to the consequences of a business judgment if he:

> (1) was informed with respect to the subject of the business judgment to the extent he reasonably believed to be appropriate under the circumstances;

> (2) was not interested [§ 1.15] in the subject of the business judgment and made the judgment in good faith; and

> (3) had a rational basis for believing that the business judgment was in the best interests of the corporation.

(e) A director or officer who is subject to liability because of the breach of a duty under this Section will be held liable for damage suffered by his corporation only if the breach of a duty was the proximate cause of the damage suffered by the corporation.

*   *   *

Comment to § 4.01(d) . . . .

> *a. Comparison with present law.* There are no statutory formulations of the business judgment rule. The business judgment rule has been developed by courts and is well established in the case law. Judicial formulations of the rule have varied. The formulation of the business judgment rule set forth in § 4.01(d) is believed to be consistent with present law as it would be interpreted in most jurisdictions today, and each of the rule's basic elements (§ 4.01(d)(1)–(3)) is supported by substantial precedential authority.

> Although courts have not expressed it this way, the business judgment rule has offered a safe harbor for informed business decisions that are honestly and rationally undertaken. Section 4.01(d) articulates this safe harbor concept. The business judgment rule has often been stated as a "presumption" (with various qualifications) that directors or officers have acted properly. Confusion has been created by the numerous varying formulations of the rule and the fact that courts have often stated the rule incompletely or with

elliptical shorthand references. The relatively precise formulation of
the business judgment rule set forth in § 4.01(d) is needed to avoid
confusion and to cover the myriad of factual contexts in which
business judgment issues arise. ...

  c. Prerequisite of a conscious exercise of judgment. Section
4.01(d) affords protection only to a "business judgment." This means
that to be afforded protection a decision must have been consciously
made and judgment must, in fact, have been exercised. For efficiency reasons, corporate decisionmakers should be permitted to act
decisively and with relative freedom from a judge's or jury's subsequent second-guessing. It is desirable to encourage directors and
officers to enter new markets, develop new products, innovate, and
take other business risks.

  There is, however, no reason to provide special protection where
no business decisionmaking is to be found. If, for example, directors
failed to oversee the conduct of the corporation's business
(§ 3.02(a)(2)) by not even considering the need for an effective audit
process, and this permits an executive to abscond with corporate
funds, business judgment rule protection would be manifestly unde-
sirable. The same would be true of a situation in which a director
received but did not read basic financial information, over a period of
time, and thus allowed his corporation to be looted. Cf. DePinto v.
Provident Security Life Insurance Co., 374 F.2d 37 (9th Cir. 1967);
Francis v. United Jersey Bank, 87 N.J. 15, 432 A.2d 814 (1981). In
these and other "omission" situations, the director or officer would be
judged under § 4.01(a)–(c)'s reasonable care standards and not protected by § 4.01(d). ...

  d. Prerequisite of an informed decision. The great weight of
case law and commentator authority supports the proposition that an
informed decision (made, for example, on the basis of explanatory
information presented to the board) is a prerequisite to the legal
insulation afforded by the business judgment rule. In a much quoted
statement, the court in Casey v. Woodruff, 49 N.Y.S.2d 625, 643
(Sup.Ct.1944), observed: "When courts say that they will not interfere in matters of business judgment, it is presupposed that judgment—reasonable diligence—has in fact been exercised." See Treadway Companies, Inc. v. Care Corp., 638 F.2d 357, 384 (2d Cir. 1980)
(citing with approval the *Woodruff* statement). Professor Ballantine
concluded: "[I]t is presupposed in this 'business judgment rule' that
reasonable diligence and care have been exercised." H. Ballantine,
Law of Corporations § 63a at 161 (rev.ed.1946); see, e.g., Joy v.
North, 692 F.2d 880, 886, 896 (2d Cir. 1982), cert. denied, __ U.S. __,
103 S.Ct. 1498, 75 L.Ed.2d 930 (1983); Arsht, The Business Judgment
Rule Revisited, 8 Hofstra L.Rev. 93, 111 (1979) (The business judgment rule should not be available to directors who do "not exercise
due care to ascertain the relevant and available facts before voting").

  The informed decision prerequisite in § 4.01(d)(1) focuses on the
preparedness of a director or officer in making a business decision as

opposed to the quality of a decision itself. Fundamental to an understanding of the standard set forth in § 4.01(d) is the recognition that the extent of the information required is that which the director or officer "reasonably believed to be appropriate under the circumstances." In evaluating what is a reasonable belief in a particular situation, § 4.01(d)(1)'s "informed" requirement should be interpreted realistically and with an appreciation of the factual context in which a business judgment was made.

Some business decisions must, for example, be made under severe time pressure while others afford time for the orderly marshaling of material information. Section 4.01(d)(1) permits a director or officer to take into account the time that is realistically available in deciding the extent to which he should be informed. The time realistically available may compel risk taking, which includes the risk of not having all relevant facts concerning a proposed transaction as well as the risks related to the economic consequences of the transaction itself. A decision to accept the risk of incomplete information, so long as the director reasonably believes such informational risk taking to be appropriate under the circumstances, will be fully consistent with the application of the business judgment rule to decisions made with respect to the principal transaction. See Illustration 1 in Comment *f* to § 4.01(d).

There is, of course, no precise way to measure how much information will be required to meet the "reasonable belief" test in given circumstances. Among the factors that may have to be taken into account in judging a director's reasonable belief as to what was "appropriate under the circumstances" are: (i) the importance of the business judgment to be made; (ii) the time available for obtaining information; (iii) the costs related to obtaining information; (iv) the director's confidence in those who explored a matter and those making presentations; and (v) the state of the corporation's business at the time and the nature of competing demands for the board's attention. In general, the different backgrounds of individual directors, the distinct role each plays in the corporation, and the general value of maintaining board cohesiveness may all be relevant when determining whether a director acted "reasonably" in believing that the information he had before him was "appropriate under the circumstances."

Of course, the business or professional experience of a director may help to inform him about a decision. He may also be informed by the general views or specialized experience of colleagues. Reliance on reports, representations, statements, and opinions prepared by officers and employees of the corporation and by outside professionals and experts will often be necessary and will, in many situations, satisfy the informational requirement of § 4.01(d)(1). ... In appropriate circumstances, however, reasonable inquiry will be required. ...

e. Prerequisites of good faith and no interest. It is well settled that good faith and disinterested decisionmaking are prerequisites to entry into the business judgment rule's safe harbor. As the Second Circuit stated:

> "Once a plaintiff demonstrates that a director had an interest in the transaction at issue, the burden shifts to the director to prove that the transaction was fair and reasonable to the corporation." Treadway Companies, Inc. v. Care Corp., 638 F.2d 357, 382 (2d Cir. 1980); see Lewis v. S.L. & E., Inc., 629 F.2d 764, 769 (2d Cir. 1980) ("The business judgment rule presupposes that the directors have no conflict of interest.") ...

f. Prerequisite of a rational basis. If the requirements of § 4.01(d)(1) and (2) are met, § 4.01(d)(3) will protect a director or officer from liability for a business judgment if he "had a rational basis for believing that the business judgment was in the best interests of the corporation." This "rational basis" test is the basis of the legal insulation provided by Subsection (d)'s formulation of the business judgment rule. See, e.g., Panter v. Marshall Field & Co., 646 F.2d 271, 293 (7th Cir. 1981) (courts will not disturb a business judgment if "any rational business purpose can be attributed" to a director's decision); Sinclair Oil Corp. v. Levien, 280 A.2d 717, 720 (Del.Sup.Ct.1971) ("rational business purpose" test).

There have been varying approaches taken in the cases and by commentators as to the proper standard for judicial review of business judgments. Some courts have stated that a director's or officer's business judgment must be "reasonable" to be upheld. See, e.g., Meyers v. Moody, 693 F.2d 1196 (5th Cir. 1982); McDonnell v. American Leduc Petroleums, Limited, 491 F.2d 380, 384 (2d Cir. 1974) (the Court, applying California law, concluded that the "business judgment rule protects only reasonable acts of a director or officer"). Similarly, the *Corporate Director's Guidebook* (p. 1604) speaks of the business judgment rule applying only to a director who acts "with a reasonable basis for believing that the action was in the lawful and legitimate furtherance of the corporation's purposes."

Other courts (in a few cases usually involving the termination of derivative suits) have wholly omitted reference to "rational basis" or "reasonableness" in setting forth their business judgment criteria and have simply said that a director's or officer's judgment would be upheld if made by disinterested directors, in an informed manner, and in good faith. Both a "reasonableness" test and the "good faith alone" approach have been rejected in § 4.01(d).

Sound public policy dictates that directors and officers be given greater protection than courts and commentators using a "reasonableness" test would afford. Indeed, some courts and commentators even when using a "reasonableness" test have expressly indicated that they do not intend that business judgments be given the rigorous review that the word "reasonable" may be read to imply. In Cramer

v. General Telephone & Electronics Corp., 582 F.2d 259, 275 (3d Cir. 1978), cert. denied, 439 U.S. 1129, 99 S.Ct. 1048, 59 L.Ed.2d 90 (1979), for example, the Court used the word reasonable, but concluded that directors' judgments must be "so unwise or unreasonable as to fall outside the permissible bounds of the directors' sound discretion" before the business judgment rule would become inapplicable. See *Corporate Director's Guidebook* (p. 1604).

The "rational basis" standard set forth in § 4.01(d)(3) is intended to afford directors and officers wide latitude when making business decisions that meet the other prerequisites of Subsection (d). The approach taken in Subsection (d)(3) is consistent with the large majority of business judgment cases and with sound public policy. Many courts have used words like "reckless disregard" or "recklessness" to convey a similar sense of the wide latitude that directors or officers should be afforded. See Reporter's Note 4 to § 4.01(d). Delaware case law has been summarized as follows:

> "[A] court will interfere with the discretion vested in the board of directors upon a finding that the judgment of the directors was arbitrary, resulted from a reckless disregard of the corporation's and its stockholders' best interests, or is simply so removed from the realm of reason that it cannot be sustained." Arsht & Hinsey, Codified Standard—Same Harbor But Charted Channel: A Response, 35 Bus.Law. ix, xxii (1980).

On the other hand, courts that have articulated only a "good faith" test provide too much legal insulation for directors and officers. There is no reason to insulate an objectively irrational business decision—one so removed from the realm of reason that it should not be sustained—solely on the basis that it was made in subjective good faith. The weight of authority and wise public policy favor barring from § 4.01(d)'s safe harbor directors and officers who do not have a rational basis for believing that their business judgments are in the best interests of the corporation. See Reporter's Note hereto.

In general, it should be noted that if circumstances change so that a decision that was once a proper business judgment would, if made again in the current context, lack a rational basis, then the protection of the business judgment rule would not be available to a repetition of the same decision. Similarly, if circumstances change and a director or officer knows, or should know, of these changed circumstances and if he is still in a position to change or modify a prior decision, then the protection of the business judgment rule would not be available if he makes a judgment not to change course and this judgment lacks a rational basis. In general, under § 4.01(a)–(c), directors and officers have continuing obligations to act in a manner that they reasonably believe to be in the best interests of the corporation and to use reasonable care.

Insert the following case and note at p. 552 of the unabridged edition, and p. 405 of the abridged edition, after Auerbach v. Bennett:

ZAPATA CORP. v. MALDONADO

Supreme Court of Delaware, 1981.
430 A.2d 779.

Before DUFFY, QUILLEN and HORSEY, JJ.

QUILLEN, JUSTICE. This is an interlocutory appeal from an order entered on April 9, 1980, by the Court of Chancery denying appellant-defendant Zapata Corporation's (Zapata) alternative motions to dismiss the complaint or for summary judgment. The issue to be addressed has reached this Court by way of a rather convoluted path.

In June, 1975, William Maldonado, a stockholder of Zapata, instituted a derivative action in the Court of Chancery on behalf of Zapata against ten officers and/or directors of Zapata, alleging, essentially, breaches of fiduciary duty. Maldonado did not first demand that the board bring this action, stating instead such demand's futility because all directors were named as defendants and allegedly participated in the acts specified.[1] In June, 1977, Maldonado commenced an action in the United States District Court for the Southern District of New York against the same defendants, save one, alleging federal security law violations as well as the same common law claims made previously in the Court of Chancery.

By June, 1979, four of the defendant-directors were no longer on the board, and the remaining directors appointed two new outside directors to the board. The board then created an "Independent Investigation Committee" (Committee), composed solely of the two new directors, to investigate Maldonado's actions . . . and to determine whether the corporation should continue any or all of the litigation. The Committee's determination was stated to be "final, . . . not . . . subject to review by the Board of Directors and . . . in all respects . . . binding upon the Corporation."

Following an investigation, the Committee concluded, in September, 1979, that each action should "be dismissed forthwith as their continued maintenance is inimical to the Company's best interests . . . ." Consequently, Zapata moved for dismissal or summary judgment . . . .

On March 18, 1980, the Court of Chancery, in a reported opinion, the basis for the order of April 9, 1980, denied Zapata's motions, holding that Delaware law does not sanction this means of dismissal. More specifically, it held that the "business judgment" rule is not a grant of authority to dismiss derivative actions and that a stockholder has an individual

---

1. Court of Chancery Rule 23.1 states in part: "The complaint shall also allege with particularity the efforts, if any, made by the plaintiff to obtain the action he desires from the directors or comparable authority and the reasons for his failure to obtain the action or for not making the effort."

right to maintain derivative actions in certain instances. Maldonado v. Flynn, Del.Ch., 413 A.2d 1251 (1980) (herein *Maldonado*). Pursuant to the provisions of Supreme Court Rule 42, Zapata filed an interlocutory appeal with this Court shortly thereafter. ... *

... As the Vice Chancellor noted, 413 A.2d at 1257, "it is the law of the State of incorporation which determines whether the directors have this power of dismissal, Burks v. Lasker, 441 U.S. 471, 99 S.Ct. 1831, 60 L.Ed.2d 404 (1979)". We limit our review in this interlocutory appeal to whether the Committee has the power to cause the present action to be dismissed.

We begin with an examination of the carefully considered opinion of the Vice Chancellor which states, in part, that the "business judgment" rule does not confer power "to a corporate board of directors to terminate a derivative suit", 413 A.2d at 1257. His conclusion is particularly pertinent because several federal courts, applying Delaware law, have held that the business judgment rule enables boards (or their committees) to terminate derivative suits, decisions now in conflict with the holding below.[1]

As the term is most commonly used, and given the disposition below, we can understand the Vice Chancellor's comment that "the business judgment rule is irrelevant to the question of whether the Committee has the authority to compel the dismissal of this suit." 413 A.2d at 1257. Corporations, existing because of legislative grace, possess authority as granted by the legislature. Directors of Delaware corporations derive their managerial decision making power, which encompasses decisions whether to initiate, or refrain from entering, litigation, from 8 Del.C. § 141(a). This statute is the fount of directorial powers. The "business judgment" rule is a judicial creation that presumes propriety, under certain circumstances, in a board's decision. Viewed defensively, it does not create authority. In this sense the "business judgment" rule is not relevant in corporate decision making until after a decision is made. It is generally used as a defense to an attack on the decision's soundness. The board's managerial decision making power, however, comes from § 141(a). The judicial creation and legislative grant are related because the "business judgment" rule evolved to give recognition and deference to directors' business expertise when exercising their managerial power under § 141(a).

---

* Maldonado had also filed federal actions in the Southern District of Texas and the Southern District of New York. The former court denied Zapata's motion to dismiss, in an opinion consistent with that of Delaware Chancery. The latter court granted Zapata's motion, however, on the ground that, as it interpreted Delaware law, the committee had authority under the business judgment rule to require termination of the action. Maldonado's appeal of that decision to the Second Circuit was ordered stayed pending the decision of the Delaware Supreme Court on the appeal from Delaware Chancery. (Footnote by ed.)

4. Abbey v. Control Data Corp., 8th Cir., 603 F.2d 724 (1979), cert. denied, 444 U.S. 1017, 100 S.Ct. 670, 62 L.Ed.2d 647 (1980); Lewis v. Adams, N.D.Okl., No. 77–266C (November 15, 1979); Siegal v. Merrick, S.D.N.Y., 84 F.R.D. 106 (1979); and, of course, Maldonado v. Flynn, S.D.N.Y., 485 F.Supp. 274 (1980). See also Abramowitz v. Posner, S.D.N.Y., 513 F.Supp. 120 (1981) which specifically rejected the result reached by the Vice Chancellor in this case.

In the case before us, although the corporation's decision to move to dismiss or for summary judgment was, literally, a decision resulting from an exercise of the directors' (as delegated to the Committee) business judgment, the question of "business judgment", in a defensive sense, would not become relevant until and unless the decision to seek termination of the derivative lawsuit was attacked as improper. ... This question was not reached by the Vice Chancellor because he determined that the stockholder had an individual right to maintain this derivative action. ...

Thus, the focus in this case is on the power to speak for the corporation as to whether the lawsuit should be continued or terminated. As we see it, this issue in the current appellate posture of this case has three aspects: the conclusions of the Court below concerning the continuing right of a stockholder to maintain a derivative action; the corporate power under Delaware law of an authorized board committee to cause dismissal of litigation instituted for the benefit of the corporation; and the role of the Court of Chancery in resolving conflicts between the stockholder and the committee.

Accordingly, we turn first to the Court of Chancery's conclusions concerning the right of a plaintiff stockholder in a derivative action. We find that its determination that a stockholder, once demand is made and refused, possesses an independent, individual right to continue a derivative suit for breaches of fiduciary duty over objection by the corporation, *Maldonado*, 413 A.2d at 1262–63, as an absolute rule, is erroneous. ...

... McKee v. Rogers, Del.Ch., 156 A. 191 (1931), stated "as a general rule" that "a stockholder cannot be permitted ... to invade the discretionary field committed to the judgment of the directors and sue in the corporation's behalf when the managing body refuses. This rule is a well settled one." 156 A. at 193.

The *McKee* rule, of course, should not be read so broadly that the board's refusal will be determinative in every instance. Board members, owing a well-established fiduciary duty to the corporation, will not be allowed to cause a derivative suit to be dismissed when it would be a breach of their fiduciary duty.[8] Generally disputes pertaining to control of the suit arise in two contexts.

Consistent with the purpose of requiring a demand, a board decision to cause a derivative suit to be dismissed as detrimental to the company, after demand has been made and refused, will be respected unless it was wrongful.[10] ... A claim of a wrongful decision not to sue is thus the

---

8. Compare Baker v. Bankers' Mortgage Co., Del.Ch., 129 A. 775, 776–77 (1925). ... In *Baker*, Chancellor Wolcott posed a rhetorical question that is entirely consistent with the result we reach today: "[W]hy should not a stockholder, if the managing body absolutely refuses to act, be permitted to assert on behalf of himself and other stockholders a complaint, not against matters lying in sound discretion and honest judgment, but against frauds perpetrated by an officer in clear breach of his trust?" 129 A. at 777. [Footnote transposed by ed.]

10. In other words, when stockholders, after making demand and having their suit rejected, attack the board's decision as improper, the board's decision falls under the "business judgment" rule and will be respected if the requirements of the rule are

first exception and the first context of dispute. Absent a wrongful refusal, the stockholder in such a situation simply lacks legal managerial power. ...

But it cannot be implied that, absent a wrongful board refusal, a stockholder can never have an individual right to initiate an action. For, as is stated in *McKee*, a "well settled" exception exists to the general rule.

> "[A] stockholder may sue in equity in his derivative right to assert a cause of action in behalf of the corporation, *without prior demand* upon the directors to sue, when it is apparent that a demand would be futile, that the officers are under an influence that sterilizes discretion and could not be proper persons to conduct the litigation."

156 A. at 193 (emphasis added). This exception, the second context for dispute, is consistent with the Court of Chancery's statement below, that "[t]he stockholders' individual right to bring the action does not ripen, however, ... unless he can show a demand to be futile." *Maldonado*, 413 A.2d at 1262.[11]

These comments in *McKee* and in the opinion below make obvious sense. A demand, when required and refused (if not wrongful), terminates a stockholder's legal ability to initiate a derivative action. But where demand is properly excused, the stockholder does possess the ability to initiate the action on his corporation's behalf.

These conclusions, however, do not determine the question before us. Rather, they merely bring us to the question to be decided. It is here that we part company with the Court below. Derivative suits enforce corporate rights and any recovery obtained goes to the corporation. ... We see no inherent reason why the "two phases" of a derivative suit, the stockholder's suit to compel the corporation to sue and the corporation's suit, ... should automatically result in the placement in the hands of the litigating stockholder [of] sole control of the corporate right throughout the litigation. To the contrary, it seems to us that such an inflexible rule would recognize the interest of one person or group to the exclusion of all others within the corporate entity. Thus, we reject the view of the Vice Chancellor as to the first aspect of the issue on appeal.

The question to be decided becomes: When, if at all, should an authorized board committee be permitted to cause litigation, properly initiated by a derivative stockholder in his own right, to be dismissed? As noted above, a board has the power to choose not to pursue litigation when demand is made upon it, so long as the decision is not wrongful. If the board determines that a suit would be detrimental to the company, the board's determination prevails. Even when demand is excusable, circumstances may arise when continuation of the litigation would not be

met. ... That situation should be distinguished from the instant case, where demand was not made, and the *power* of the board to seek a dismissal, due to disqualification, presents a threshold issue. ... We recognize that the two contexts can overlap in practice.

11. These statements are consistent with Rule 23.1's "reasons for ... failure" to make demand. ...

in the corporation's best interests. Our inquiry is whether, under such circumstances, there is a permissible procedure under § 141(a) by which a corporation can rid itself of detrimental litigation. If there is not, a single stockholder in an extreme case might control the destiny of the entire corporation. This concern was bluntly expressed by the Ninth Circuit in Lewis v. Anderson, 9th Cir., 615 F.2d 778, 783 (1979), cert. denied, 449 U.S. 869, 101 S.Ct. 206, 66 L.Ed.2d 89 (1980): "To allow one shareholder to incapacitate an entire board of directors merely by leveling charges against them gives too much leverage to dissident shareholders." But, when examining the means, including the committee mechanism examined in this case, potentials for abuse must be recognized. This takes us to the second and third aspects of the issue on appeal.

Before we pass to equitable considerations as to the mechanism at issue here, it must be clear that an independent committee possesses the corporate power to seek the termination of a derivative suit. Section 141(c) allows a board to delegate all of its authority to a committee. Accordingly, a committee with properly delegated authority would have the power to move for dismissal or summary judgment if the entire board did.

Even though demand was not made in this case and the initial decision of whether to litigate was not placed before the board, Zapata's board, it seems to us, retained all of its corporate power concerning litigation decisions. If Maldonado had made demand on the board in this case, it could have refused to bring suit. Maldonado could then have asserted that the decision not to sue was wrongful and, if correct, would have been allowed to maintain the suit. The board, however, never would have lost its statutory managerial authority. The demand requirement itself evidences that the managerial power is retained by the board. When a derivative plaintiff is allowed to bring suit after a wrongful refusal, the board's authority to choose whether to pursue the litigation is not challenged although its conclusion—reached through the exercise of that authority—is not respected since it is wrongful. Similarly, Rule 23.1, by excusing demand in certain instances, does not strip the board of its corporate power. It merely saves the plaintiff the expense and delay of making a futile demand resulting in a probable tainted exercise of that authority in a refusal by the board or in giving control of litigation to the opposing side. But the board entity remains empowered under § 141(a) to make decisions regarding corporate litigation. The problem is one of member disqualification, not the absence of power in the board.

The corporate power inquiry then focuses on whether the board, tainted by the self-interest of a majority of its members, can legally delegate its authority to a committee of two disinterested directors. We find our statute clearly requires an affirmative answer to this question. As has been noted, under an express provision of the statute, § 141(c), a committee can exercise all of the authority of the board to the extent provided in the resolution of the board. Moreover, at least by analogy to our statutory section on interested directors, 8 Del.C. § 141, it seems clear that the Delaware statute is designed to permit disinterested directors to act for the board.[14] Compare Puma v. Marriott, Del.Ch., 283 A.2d 693, 695–96 (1971).

We do not think that the interest taint of the board majority is per se a legal bar to the delegation of the board's power to an independent committee composed of disinterested board members. The committee can properly act for the corporation to move to dismiss derivative litigation that is believed to be detrimental to the corporation's best interest.

Our focus now switches to the Court of Chancery which is faced with a stockholder assertion that a derivative suit, properly instituted, should continue for the benefit of the corporation and a corporate assertion, properly made by a board committee acting with board authority, that the same derivative suit should be dismissed as inimical to the best interests of the corporation.

At the risk of stating the obvious, the problem is relatively simple. If, on the one hand, corporations can consistently wrest bona fide derivative actions away from well-meaning derivative plaintiffs through the use of the committee mechanism, the derivative suit will lose much, if not all, of its generally recognized effectiveness as an intra-corporate means of policing boards of directors. See Dent, supra note 5, 75 Nw.U.L.Rev. at 96 & n. 3, 144 & n. 241. If, on the other hand, corporations are unable to rid themselves of meritless or harmful litigation and strike suits, the derivative action, created to benefit the corporation, will produce the opposite, unintended result. For a discussion of strike suits, see Dent, supra, 75 Nw.U.L.Rev. at 137. See also Cramer v. General Telephone & Electronics Corp., 3d Cir., 582 F.2d 259, 275 (1978), cert. denied, 439 U.S. 1129, 99 S.Ct. 1048, 59 L.Ed.2d 90 (1979). It thus appears desirable to us to find a balancing point where bona fide stockholder power to bring corporation causes of action cannot be unfairly trampled on by the board of directors, but the corporation can rid itself of detrimental litigation.

As we noted, the question has been treated by other courts as one of the "business judgment" of the board committee. If a "committee, composed of independent and disinterested directors, conducted a proper review of the matters before it, considered a variety of factors and reached, in good faith, a business judgment that [the] action was not in the best interest of [the corporation]", the action must be dismissed. See, e.g., Maldonado v. Flynn, supra, 485 F.Supp. at 282, 286. The issues become solely independence, good faith, and reasonable investigation. The ultimate conclusion of the committee, under that view, is not subject to judicial review.

We are not satisfied, however, that acceptance of the "business judgment" rationale at this stage of derivative litigation is a proper balancing point. While we admit an analogy with a normal case respecting board judgment, it seems to us that there is sufficient risk in the

14. [The court quoted Del. § 144.]

realities of a situation like the one presented in this case to justify caution beyond adherence to the theory of business judgment.

The context here is a suit against directors where demand on the board is excused. We think some tribute must be paid to the fact that the lawsuit was properly initiated. It is not a board refusal case. Moreover, this complaint was filed in June of 1975 and, while the parties undoubtedly would take differing views on the degree of litigation activity, we have to be concerned about the creation of an "Independent Investigation Committee" four years later, after the election of two new outside directors. Situations could develop where such motions could be filed after years of vigorous litigation for reasons unconnected with the merits of the lawsuit.

Moreover, notwithstanding our conviction that Delaware law entrusts the corporate power to a properly authorized committee, we must be mindful that directors are passing judgment on fellow directors in the same corporation and fellow directors, in this instance, who designated them to serve both as directors and committee members. The question naturally arises whether a "there but for the grace of God go I" empathy might not play a role. And the further question arises whether inquiry as to independence, good faith and reasonable investigation is sufficient safeguard against abuse, perhaps subconscious abuse.

There is another line of exploration besides the factual context of this litigation which we find helpful. The nature of this motion finds no ready pigeonhole, as perhaps illustrated by its being set forth in the alternative. It is perhaps best considered as a hybrid summary judgment motion for dismissal because the stockholder plaintiff's standing to maintain the suit has been lost. But it does not fit neatly into a category described in Rule 12(b) of the Court of Chancery Rules nor does it correspond directly with Rule 56 since the question of genuine issues of fact on the merits of the stockholder's claim are not reached.

It seems to us that there are two other procedural analogies that are helpful in addition to reference to Rules 12 and 56. There is some analogy to a settlement in that there is a request to terminate litigation without a judicial determination of the merits. See Perrine v. Pennroad Corp., Del. Super., 47 A.2d 479, 487 (1946). "In determining whether or not to approve a proposed settlement of a derivative stockholders' action [when directors are on both sides of the transaction], the Court of Chancery is called upon to exercise its own business judgment." Neponsit Investment Co. v. Abramson, Del.Super., 405 A.2d 97, 100 (1979) and cases therein cited. In this case, the litigating stockholder plaintiff facing dismissal of a lawsuit properly commenced ought, in our judgment, to have sufficient status for strict Court review.

Finally, if the committee is in effect given status to speak for the corporation as the plaintiff in interest, then it seems to us there is an analogy to Court of Chancery Rule 41(a)(2) where the plaintiff seeks a dismissal after an answer. Certainly, the position of record of the litigating stockholder is adverse to the position advocated by the corporation in the motion to dismiss. Accordingly, there is perhaps some wisdom to be gained by the direction in Rule 41(a)(2) that "an action shall not be dismissed at the plaintiff's instance save upon order of the Court and upon such terms and conditions as the Court deems proper."

Whether the Court of Chancery will be persuaded by the exercise of a committee power resulting in a summary motion for dismissal of a derivative action, where a demand has not been initially made, should rest, in our judgment, in the independent discretion of the Court of Chancery. We thus steer a middle course between those cases which yield to the independent business judgment of a board committee and this case as determined below which would yield to unbridled plaintiff stockholder control. In pursuit of the course, we recognize that "[t]he final substantive judgment whether a particular lawsuit should be maintained requires a balance of many factors—ethical, commercial, promotional, public relations, employee relations, fiscal as well as legal." Maldonado v. Flynn, supra, 485 F.Supp. at 285. But we are content that such factors are not "beyond the judicial reach" of the Court of Chancery which regularly and competently deals with fiduciary relationships, disposition of trust property, approval of settlements and scores of similar problems. We recognize the danger of judicial overreaching but the alternatives seem to us to be outweighed by the fresh view of a judicial outsider. Moreover, if we failed to balance all the interests involved, we would in the name of practicality and judicial economy foreclose a judicial decision on the merits. At this point, we are not convinced that is necessary or desirable.

After an objective and thorough investigation of a derivative suit, an independent committee may cause its corporation to file a pretrial motion to dismiss in the Court of Chancery. The basis of the motion is the best interests of the corporation, as determined by the committee. The motion should include a thorough written record of the investigation and its findings and recommendations. Under appropriate court supervision, akin to proceedings on summary judgment, each side should have an opportunity to make a record on the motion. As to the limited issues presented by the motion noted below, the moving party should be prepared to meet the normal burden under Rule 56 that there is no genuine issue as to any material fact and that the moving party is entitled to dismiss as a matter of law.[15] The Court should apply a two-step test to the motion.

First, the Court should inquire into the independence and good faith of the committee and the bases supporting its conclusions. Limited discovery may be ordered to facilitate such inquiries. The corporation should have the burden of proving independence, good faith and a reasonable investigation, rather than presuming independence, good

---

15. We do not foreclose a discretionary trial of factual issues but that issue is not presented in this appeal. See Lewis v. Anderson, supra, 615 F.2d at 780. Nor do we foreclose the possibility that other motions may proceed or be joined with such a pretrial summary judgment motion to dismiss, e.g., a partial motion for summary judgment on the merits.

faith and reasonableness.[17] If the Court determines that the committee is not independent or has not shown reasonable bases for its conclusions, or, if the Court is not satisfied for other reasons relating to the process, including but not limited to the good faith of the committee, the Court shall deny the corporation's motion. If, however, the Court is satisfied under Rule 56 standards that the committee was independent and showed reasonable bases for good faith findings and recommendations, the Court may proceed, in its discretion, to the next step.

The second step provides, we believe, the essential key in striking the balance between legitimate corporate claims as expressed in a derivative stockholder suit and a corporation's best interests as expressed by an independent investigating committee. The Court should determine, applying its own independent business judgment, whether the motion should be granted.[18] This means, of course, that instances could arise where a committee can establish its independence and sound bases for its good faith decisions and still have the corporation's motion denied. The second step is intended to thwart instances where corporate actions meet the criteria of step one, but the result does not appear to satisfy its spirit, or where corporate actions would simply prematurely terminate a stockholder grievance deserving of further consideration in the corporation's interest. The Court of Chancery of course must carefully consider and weigh how compelling the corporate interest in dismissal is when faced with a non-frivolous lawsuit. The Court of Chancery should, when appropriate, give special consideration to matters of law and public policy in addition to the corporation's best interests.

If the Court's independent business judgment is satisfied, the Court may proceed to grant the motion, subject, of course, to any equitable terms or conditions the Court finds necessary or desirable.

The interlocutory order of the Court of Chancery is reversed and the cause is remanded for further proceedings consistent with this opinion.

NOTE ON MILLER v. TRIBUNE SYNDICATE, INC.

Miller was a shareholder in Register and Tribune Syndicate, Inc. In September 1979, Miller brought a derivative action in federal court alleging that Register had sold its stock at fraudulently low prices and for grossly inadequate consideration to key employees, including all of the corporation's four directors, who were made defendants. In December, the board expanded its number to six, elected two new directors, and

---

17. Compare Auerbach v. Bennett, 47 N.Y.2d 619, 419 N.Y.S.2d 920, 928–29, 393 N.E.2d 994 (1979). Our approach here is analogous to and consistent with the Delaware approach to "interested director" transactions, where the directors, once the transaction is attacked, have the burden of establishing its "intrinsic fairness" to a court's careful scrutiny. See, e.g., Sterling v. Mayflower Hotel Corp., Del.Supr., 93 A.2d 107 (1952).

18. This step shares some of the same spirit and philosophy of the statement by the Vice Chancellor: "Under our system of law, courts and not litigants should decide the merits of litigation." 413 A.2d at 1263.

established an "Independent Litigation Committee" consisting of the two new directors. The committee was authorized to "determine whether the corporation or anyone acting on the corporation's behalf shall undertake or continue any litigation against one or more of the present or former Directors ... or against anyone else in respect of" the matters referred to in Miller's action, and was delegated all the powers and authority of the board in connection with its investigation and determination.

In May 1982, the litigation committee filed a report which concluded that that there was no justification for any further expenditures for continuing the lawsuit. Register then filed a motion for a summary judgment on the ground that the committee had determined that the litigation was not in Register's best interests. The federal district court thereupon issued the following certified question to the Iowa Supreme Court:

> Under the law of the State of Iowa, may the Board of Directors of [an Iowa] corporation ... acting through directors who are named as defendants in a derivative action ... (1) appoint a Special Litigation Committee composed of two directors who were not serving as directors at the time of the incidents in question, and (2) confer upon such committee the power to (a) investigate the merits of such derivative action, (b) determine in good faith whether in its business judgment, the best interest of the corporation would be served by the prosecution, dismissal or settlement of such action, and (c) bind the corporation to its decision?

The Iowa Supreme Court answered, no.

> ... Elements commonly required to be shown in the use of the business judgment rule in derivative actions include: (1) whether the special litigation committee appointed by the board of directors is endowed with the requisite corporate power to bind the corporation to its recommendation of dismissal; and (2) whether it has been demonstrated that the special litigation committee was disinterested, independent, acted in good faith, and that the bases for its conclusions were sufficient based upon reasonable investigative techniques. ...

> Consideration of the certified question within the context of the reasons which the federal court stated in support of its decision to certify, suggests that only the element of delegation of power is involved [in the certified question].... We find no hint in either the language of the certified question or the circumstances which prompted it that we are being asked to express any views on the scope of judicial review to be applied to the committee's decision. ...

> [We believe that an Iowa corporation,] acting through independent directors,[2] [may] appoint a special litigation committee and confer upon such committee the power to investigate the merits of a derivative action ... and determine in good faith whether, in the business

---

2. The words "independent directors" as used in this opinion refer to those directors [who are completely free from any dual relationship which prevents an unprejudiced exercise of judgment].

judgment of the committee the best interest of the corporation would be served by the prosecution, dismissal or settlement of the derivative action. . . .

In the absence of the special litigation committee device, it would not be possible for the business judgment rule to be invoked at the instance of a board of directors if the majority of the board are alleged to be involved in the self-dealing. . . . It is tacitly, if not expressly, conceded by the defendant corporation and the defendant directors in the present case that the board itself could not seek dismissal of the action against the majority of its own members by invoking the business judgment rule. The question which naturally arises is whether, given this circumstance, the board has the power to delegate to a committee the authority to do that which it may not do itself.

The litigation committee device has alarmed many commentators, who argue the trend of the decisions toward liberality in litigation committee powers is wrong and that the powers should be more circumscribed. . . .

The central theme of these concerns has been focused on the "structural bias" approach, which suggests that it is unrealistic to assume that the members of independent committees are free from personal, financial or moral influences which flow from the directors who appoint them. The argument is made that this is all the more so where, as in the present federal derivative action, the members of the special committee are fellow directors. . . .

Director disqualification based on structural bias was explored in Clark v. Lomas & Nettleton Financial Corp., 625 F.2d 49, 52–54 (5th Cir. 1980). There the court held that seemingly independent directors were disqualified from settling a derivative action when a majority of the board was elected by a stockholder who was a defendant in the suit. In so ruling, the court stated:

> Jack Booth [the principal shareholder and a defendant in the case] wielded power to strip them not only of directorates, but of officers and consulting positions as well. Nor can we ignore the possibility of "structural bias" in this case.

Clark, 625 F.2d at 53. The issue in the present case involves the potential for structural bias of the litigation committee appointed by directors who are defendants in the action, whereas *Clark* involved the structural bias of directors appointed by a controlling stockholder who was a defendant. Despite this distinction we conclude that the applicable principles are similar. We believe that the potential for structural bias on the part of a litigation committee appointed by directors who are parties to derivative actions is sufficiently great and sufficiently difficult of precise proof in an individual case to require the adoption of a prophylactic rule. We conclude that we should prevent the potential for structural bias in some case by effectively limiting the powers of such directors in all cases.

In this case of first impression in this jurisdiction we hold that directors of Iowa corporations ... who are parties to a derivative action may not confer upon a special committee of the type described in the certified question the power to bind the corporation as to its conduct of the litigation.[3] We accordingly answer the certified question in the negative.

This decision does not render an Iowa corporation powerless to utilize the litigation committee device when a majority of its directors are parties to the action. Under Iowa law, equity has broad powers to make appointments to enable corporate functions to be carried out. See Rowen v. LeMars Mutual Insurance Co., 230 N.W.2d 905, 916 (Iowa 1975) (court appointment of separate counsel for corporations); Holi Rest, Inc. v. Treloar, 217 N.W.2d 517, 527 (Iowa 1974) (court appointment of fiscal agent for corporation). Consistent with these decisions, we conclude that a corporation may apply to the court for appointment of a "special panel" to make an investigation and report on the pursuit or dismissal of a stockholder derivative action, which panel may be invested for these purposes with the powers of the board of directors.

Miller v. Register & Tribune Syndicate, Inc., 336 N.W.2d 709 (Iowa 1983).

SECTION 2. DUTY OF LOYALTY

(b) CORPORATE OPPORTUNITIES AND OTHER DUTIES TO THE CORPORATION

---

(1) Conflict of Interest Statutes

Insert the following case, and the extract from ALI, Principles of Corporate Governance, at p. 606 of the unabridged edition, and p. 453 of the abridged edition, at the end of Chapter VI, Section 2(b)(1):

ARONOFF v. ALBANESE

Supreme Court of New York, Appellate Division, Second Department, 1982.
85 A.D.2d 3, 446 N.Y.S.2d 368.

Before DAMIANI, J. P., LAZER, COHALAN and BRACKEN, JJ.

3. Because a majority of the directors in the present case are defendants in the derivative action, we answer the certified question based solely on this basis for disqualification. Notwithstanding this limitation on our holding, wherever we have used the term "independent directors" in our discussion (except as we have referred to that term as defined in other source material) we have intended to encompass directors completely free from any dual relationship which prevents an unprejudiced exercise of judgment.

PER CURIAM.   Plaintiffs, stockholders of defendant Hospital Building Corporation (HBC), commenced this derivative action to recover lost profits of HBC as a result of certain transactions with the individual defendants, who are directors of HBC and also partners of Pelham Bay General Hospital (PBGH) which leases a hospital from HBC. The first transaction involved the rent paid by PBGH to HBC. The rent was $30,000 monthly from 1962 until January, 1975, when it was increased to $36,000 per month. In July, 1976 the monthly rent was reduced to $20,000 due to PBGH's cash flow problems (caused by delay in Medicare reimbursement). In May, 1977 the rent was increased to $30,000 per month. The 10 months of reduced rent caused a loss of $160,000 to HBC. The other transactions which are the subject of objection by the shareholders include the purchase, with HBC funds, of certain permanent and semi-permanent equipment for the hospital totaling approximately $600,000, and the installation of an Intensive Care Unit (replacing its Obstetrics Unit) and a central air conditioning system in 1976–1977, which unit and air conditioning system cost $214,000. While the leases prior to 1975 were silent on the matter, a 1975 lease modification provided that the landlord would be responsible for major repairs or replacements of installed chattels, fixtures and equipment for a complete hospital. In 1977, a further modification provided that the purchase of additional chattels, fixtures and equipment would be accompanied by a corresponding net increase in rent.

To all of this, the individual defendants asserted the defense of ratification on the basis that a majority of HBC stockholders, at a December 15, 1977 meeting, approved the mentioned transaction. Subsequently, Special Term granted said defendants' motion for summary judgment dismissing the complaint and plaintiffs have appealed.

The issue on appeal is whether the questioned transactions can be effectively ratified by the stockholders—that is, whether they are void or merely voidable. The courts have drawn a distinction between transactions which are only voidable at the option of the corporation and transactions which are void. Voidable transactions can be ratified by a majority vote of the stockholders, but a void act is not subject to ratification (Quintal v. Kellner, 264 N.Y. 32, 189 N.E. 770; Pollitz v. Wabash R.R. Co., 207 N.Y. 113, 100 N.E. 721; Continental Securities Co. v. Belmont, 206 N.Y. 7, 99 N.E. 138). Further, it is settled law that waste or a gift of corporate assets are void acts and cannot be ratified by a majority of stockholders (Meredith v. Camp Hill Estates, 77 A.D.2d 649, 430 N.Y.S.2d 383; see Diamond v. Davis, Sup., 38 N.Y.S.2d 103, affd. 265 App.Div. 919, 39 N.Y.S.2d 412, affd. 292 N.Y. 552, 54 N.E.2d 683; see, also, Selman v. Allen, Sup., 121 N.Y.S.2d 142; 2 Fletcher, Cyclopedia of Corporations [Perm.ed.], § 764). The rationale for the rule is that "[a]n unconscionable deal between directors personally and the corporation they represent could not become conscionable merely because most of the stockholders were either indifferent or actually in sympathy with the directors' scheme" (Gottlieb v. Heyden Chem. Corp., 33 Del.Ch. 82, 91, 90 A.2d 660, 665).

The essence of a claim of gift is lack of consideration and the essence of waste is the diversion of corporate assets for improper or unnecessary purposes (Michelson v. Duncan, 407 A.2d 211, 217 [Del.]). In Amdur v. Meyer, 15 A.D.2d 425, 430, 224 N.Y.S.2d 440, the court held that certain stock options were not a gift, since "the corporation might reasonably expect benefit to flow to the corporation." Also, a clearly inadequate consideration invokes the same principles as the absence of consideration (see Gottlieb v. McKee, 34 Del.Ch. 537, 107 A.2d 240). In Pollitz v. Wabash R.R. Co., 207 N.Y. 113, 100 N.E. 721, supra, the director improperly applied assets to his own use (through issuance of stock without consideration). Other examples of unratifiable acts include the use of corporate funds to discharge personal obligations (Quintal v. Kellner, 264 N.Y. 32, 189 N.E. 770, supra), distribution of surplus earnings under guise of additional salaries to directors and officers (Godley v. Crandall & Godley Co., 212 N.Y. 121, 105 N.E. 818), transfer of assets without consideration (Meredith v. Camp Hill Estates, 77 A.D.2d 649, 430 N.Y.S.2d 383, supra), use of corporate property given to a foreign corporation without consideration (Boaz v. Sterlingworth Ry. Supply Co., 68 App.Div. 1, 73 N.Y.S. 1039), payment of a false claim (Continental Securities Co. v. Belmont, 206 N.Y. 7, 99 N.E. 138, supra), and payment of excessive investment fees to directors (Saxe v. Brady, 40 Del.Ch. 474, 184 A.2d 602). The directors would be liable for every form of waste of assets regardless of whether it was intentional or negligent (see Rapoport v. Schneider, 29 N.Y.2d 396, 328 N.Y.S.2d 431, 278 N.E.2d 642).

The existence of benefit to the corporation, in turn, is generally committed to the sound business judgment of the directors (see Auerbach v. Bennett, 47 N.Y.2d 619, 419 N.Y.S.2d 920, 393 N.E.2d 994; Amdur v. Meyer, 15 A.D.2d 425, 224 N.Y.S.2d 440, supra; Cohen v. Ayers, 596 F.2d 733 [CCA 7th Cir., applying New York law]). The objecting stockholder must demonstrate that no person of ordinary sound business judgment would say that the corporation received fair benefit (Id.; Michelson v. Duncan, 407 A.2d 211, 224, supra). If ordinary businessmen might differ on the sufficiency of consideration received by the corporation, the courts will uphold the transaction (see Saxe v. Brady, supra). The motives or personal benefit to the directors is also a relevant concern. The objecting stockholders must show that the directors must have acted with an intent to serve some outside interest, regardless of the consequence (see Gamble v. Queens County Water Co., 123 N.Y. 91, 25 N.E. 201). If there is a great disparity in values between the assets expended and the benefits received, the courts will infer that the directors are guilty of improper motives, or at least recklessly indifferent to the stockholders' interests (see Alcott v. Hyman, 42 Del.Ch. 233, 208 A.2d 501).

The determination of whether or not there has been a gift of corporate assets is largely a question of fact (see Gottlieb v. McKee, 34 Del.Ch. 537, 107 A.2d 240, supra). The existence of ratification makes the objecting stockholders' burden more difficult since ratification shifts the burden of proof to the opponents of the transactions (see Cohen v. Ayers, 596 F.2d 733, supra; Kerbs v. California Eastern Airways, 33 Del.Ch. 69, 90 A.2d 652). On the other hand, compliance with section 713 of the Business Corporation Law does not automatically validate any transaction (see Rapoport v. Schneider, 29 N.Y.2d 396, 328 N.Y.S.2d 431, 278 N.E.2d 642, supra; Remillard Brick Co. v. Remillard-Dandini Co., 109 Cal.App.2d 405, 241 P.2d 66 [section 713 of the Business Corporation Law is derived from section 820 of the California General Corporations Law]; see, also, 76 Colum.L.Rev. 1156; 41 Fordham L.Rev. 639).

Turning to the instant case, although plaintiffs never alleged "gift" or "waste" in their complaint, the omission does not bar a consideration of the gift or waste claims. Under liberal rules of pleading, plaintiffs' assertions of unreasonable transactions—which benefited the individual defendants personally—should be sufficient to put them on notice of plaintiffs' theory (see CPLR 3013; Foley v. D'Agostino, 21 A.D.2d 60, 248 N.Y.S.2d 121; Siegel, New York Practice, § 208). "A claimant need not necessarily expressly aver 'gift' or 'waste' in order to make out a claim on these theories [s]o long as claimant alleges facts in his description of a series of events from which a gift or waste may reasonably be inferred" (Michelson v. Duncan, 407 A.2d 211, 217, supra). Since the complaint gives sufficient notice of the events out of which plaintiffs' grievances arise, it can be construed as relying on a theory of "gift", a transaction which cannot be ratified by a majority of the stockholders. Thus, Special Term erroneously concluded that plaintiffs did not raise the theory.

While the individual defendants may ultimately prevail after trial, it cannot be said, as a matter of law, that a person of ordinary business judgment would say that HBC received fair consideration. On the rent reduction claim, the individual defendants allege that the cash flow problems of PBGH were to blame. In addition, there is a factual issue as to whether the purchase of hospital equipment with HBC funds benefited the corporation and the argument of the individual defendants that the purchases were necessary for the future of the hospital merely makes the question a factual issue for determination at trial. Furthermore, the purchase apparently violated the lease because the lease did not obligate HBC to buy equipment. Once the lease was modified to provide for such purchases, with a corresponding rent increase, the lease apparently was violated again, since no increase in rent was given. In this particular case, the ratification of actions by the majority of stockholders of HBC, together with the then existing financial condition of PBGH, emphasize that any benefit to HBC is a triable issue of fact. Finally, plaintiffs should be given the opportunity to obtain additional information through discovery since the facts are particularly within the knowledge of the individual defendants (see Limmer v. Medallion Group, 75 A.D.2d 299, 428 N.Y.S.2d 961).

In sum, plaintiffs have demonstrated factual issues with respect to the alleged void acts constituting gift and waste so as to defeat summary judgment.

Judgment of the Supreme Court, Westchester County (MARBACH, J.)., entered November 28, 1980, reversed, on the law, with $50 costs and disbursements, and motion for summary judgment denied.

ALI, PRINCIPLES OF CORPORATE GOVERNANCE AND STRUCTURE: ANALYSIS AND RECOMMENDATIONS §§ 1.15, 1.19, 1.25, 1.27, 1.30, 5.01, 5.03, 5.04, 5.05, 5.06, 5.08

(TENT. DRAFT No. 3, 1984)

§ 1.15 Interested

(1) A director ... is "interested" in a transaction if:

(a) the director or officer is a party to the transaction, or

(b) the director or officer or an associate [§ 5.01] of the director or officer has a pecuniary interest in the transaction, or the director or officer has a financial or familial relationship to a party to the transaction, that is sufficiently substantial that it would reasonably be expected to affect the director's or officer's judgment with respect to the transaction in a manner adverse to the corporation.

(2) A shareholder is interested in a transaction if either the shareholder or, to his knowledge, an associate of the shareholder, is a party to the transaction.

§ 1.19 Officer

"Officer" means (1) the chief executive, operating, financial, legal, and accounting officers of a corporation; (2) to the extent not encompassed by the foregoing, the chairman of the board of directors (unless the chairman neither performs a policymaking function other than as a director, nor receives a material amount of compensation in excess of director's fees), president, treasurer, secretary, and controller, and a vice-president who is in charge of a principal business unit, division, or function (such as sales, administration, or finance) or performs a major policymaking function for the corporation; or (3) any other individual designated as an officer of the corporation.

§ 1.25 Senior Executives

"Senior executives" means the officers described in §§ 1.19(1) and (2).

§ 1.27 Standard of the Corporation

"Standard of the corporation" means a valid certificate or by-law provision, or board or shareholder resolution, regulating corporate governance.

§ 1.30 Waste of Corporate Assets

A "waste of corporate assets" means a transaction whose terms are such that no person of ordinary sound business judgment would say that the consideration received by the corporation was a fair exchange for what was given by the corporation.

§ 5.01   Associate

(a) An "associate" means:

(1) A spouse, child, parent, or sibling of a director ... or of a senior executive [§ 1.25] or of a shareholder, or

(2) Any person ... for whom a director, senior executive, or shareholder has financial responsibility, or with whom he has a business relationship that is sufficiently substantial that it would reasonably be expected to affect his judgment with respect to the transaction in question in a manner adverse to the corporation.

(b) Notwithstanding § 5.01(a)(2), a business organization ... is not an associate of a director, senior executive, or shareholder by virtue of the fact that the director, senior executive or shareholder is a principal manager ... of such business organization. A business organization in which a director, senior executive, or dominating shareholder is the beneficial or record holder of not more than 10 percent of any class of equity interest ... is presumed not to be an associate. A business organization in which a director, senior executive or dominating share-holder is the beneficial or record holder (other than in a custodial capacity) of more than 10 percent of any class of equity interest is presumed to be an associate by reason of such holding unless the value of the interest to him is sufficiently insubstantial that it would not reasonably be expected to affect his judgment with respect to the particular transaction in a manner adverse to the corporation.

§ 5.03   Material Fact

A fact is "material" if there is a substantial likelihood that a reasonable person would consider it important under the circumstances in determining his course of action.

§ 5.04   Action By Disinterested Directors

A provision that gives a specified effect to action by disinterested directors requires the affirmative votes of a majority of the directors on the board or an appropriate committee who are not interested [§ 1.15] in the transaction in question.

§ 5.05   Action by Disinterested Shareholders

A provision that gives a specified effect to action by disinterested shareholders requires approval of the proposal by a majority of the votes cast by shareholders who are not interested [§ 1.15] in the transaction in question.

§ 5.06   Effect of Standard of the Corporation

(a) A transaction or conduct subject to Part V [Duty of Loyalty] shall be treated as if it has been authorized by action of disinterested directors [§ 5.04] if the transaction or conduct is of a type permitted by the terms of a standard of the corporation [§ 1.27] that has been authorized by action of disinterested directors [§ 5.04].

(b) A transaction or conduct subject to Part V shall be treated as if it has been authorized or ratified by action of disinterested shareholders [§ 5.05] if the transaction or conduct is of a type permitted by the terms of a standard of the corporation [§ 1.27] that has been authorized or ratified by action of disinterested shareholders [§ 5.05].

§ 5.08 Transactions with the Corporation

(a) *General Rule:*

A director or senior executive [§ 1.25] who enters into a transaction with the corporation (other than a transaction involving the payment of compensation ...), or whose associate [§ 5.01] enters into a transaction with the corporation, violates the duty of loyalty owed to the corporation if:

(1) Disclosure of the material facts [§ 5.03] known to the director or senior executive concerning the particular transaction and his conflict of interest has not been made to the corporate decisionmaker ... who authorizes or ratifies the transaction (unless the corporate decisionmaker is otherwise aware of such material facts); or

(2) (A) In the case of a transaction that was authorized by disinterested directors [§ 5.04] following such disclosure, the directors could not reasonably have believed the transaction to be fair to the corporation;

(B) In the case of a transaction that was authorized or ratified by disinterested shareholders [§ 5.05] following such disclosure, the transaction constituted a waste of corporate assets [§ 1.30]; or

(C) In the case of a transaction that was not authorized or ratified in the manner contemplated in § 5.08(a)(2)(A) or (B), or permitted by the terms of a standard of the corporation [§ 1.27] adopted in accordance with § 5.06, the transaction was not fair to the corporation.

(b) *Burden of Proof:*

In any proceeding to challenge a transaction that is subject to § 5.08 the challenging party has the burden of proof, except that if the transaction was not authorized or ratified in the manner contemplated in § 5.08(a)(2)(A) or (B) or permitted by the terms of a standard of the corporation [§ 1.27] adopted in accordance with § 5.06, the director or senior executive has the burden of proving that the transaction was fair to the corporation. If a good faith attempt has been made to achieve the disclosure contemplated by § 5.08(a)(1) in connection with authorization of a transaction, the burden of proof remains on the challenging party even if the disclosure is incomplete, so long as the transaction is ratified by disinterested directors or shareholders after the disclosure required by § 5.08(a)(1) has been made.

(c) *Remedies:*

If the party challenging the transaction prevails because the transaction fails to comply with § 5.08(a), the transaction is (A) unenforceable against the corporation, and (B) ground for appropriate relief, including damages, rescission and restitutionary relief, or other equitable relief. ... Relief for failure to comply with § 5.08(a)(1) is not available if, at any time before the corporation obtains relief, the transaction is ratified, following the disclosure required by § 5.08(a)(1), by the board of directors, the shareholders, or the corporate decisionmaker who initially authorized the transaction or his successor.

Comment:

a. Comparison with existing law. Corporation statutes in many states seek to regulate transactions between directors and the corporation, and may literally be read to preclude judicial inquiry into the fairness of a transaction that has been approved by disinterested directors or shareholders following proper disclosure. Section 5.08 does not take this approach, but instead recommends a construction of these statutes which permits limited review of the fairness of a transaction even where there is disinterested approval. Section 5.08 provides a newly formulated standard that requires a challenging party to show that disinterested directors could not reasonably have believed the transaction to be fair to the corporation or, in the case of approval by disinterested shareholders, that the transaction constituted a waste of corporate assets. Section 5.08 also permits a transaction to be set aside even if it falls within a range of fairness if the appropriate disclosure has not been made.

Conflict-of-interest transactions have generally been approached in state corporation statutes in terms of the voidability of transactions and the effect of approval by disinterested directors or shareholders, rather than imposing an affirmative duty of loyalty. This may reflect the evolution of the law in this area from a rule which originally permitted all transactions with directors to be set aside without regard to fairness and a tendency to leave the development of affirmative duties of loyalty to the case law. Thirty-eight states have adopted "safe harbor" statutes governing transactions between directors and the corporation. Thirty-five of these statutes by their terms preclude attack on a transaction which has been approved by disinterested directors or by shareholders following disclosure. Twenty-two of these statutes require disclosure only of the director's interest in the transaction. Sixteen explicitly require disclosure of both the conflict of interest and the material facts concerning the transaction.

In the limited number of instances where the issue has been squarely raised, some courts have said that failure to make full disclosure of material facts is one factor to be considered in determining the fairness of the transaction. Others, however, have expressed the view (recommended by § 5.08) that failure to make full disclosure affords an independent basis for the corporation to avoid the transaction. This latter position finds support in the Restatements of Agency, Contracts, Torts, and Restitution to the extent that the relationship between a director or senior executive and the corporation is viewed as a relationship of trust and confidence. ...

The "safe harbor" statutes generally draw no distinction between the effect of disinterested directors' and shareholders' approval and many do not explicitly require that shareholder approval be by vote of disinterested shareholders. All but four of these statutes (Alabama, California, Connecticut, and Kentucky) may literally be read to preclude judicial inquiry into the fairness of a transaction that has been approved by disinterested directors or shareholders following proper disclosure. However, cases interpreting these statutes have not squarely taken this position, and indeed seem to reject the literal interpretation and permit judicial inquiry, although such statutes are also susceptible to a more qualified interpretation. The Alabama, Connecticut, and Kentucky statutes expressly permit judicial inquiry into fairness even when there has been approval by disinterested directors or shareholders. The California statute permits judicial review of fairness where the transaction has been approved by disinterested directors, but precludes such review where a transaction has been approved by disinterested shareholders. ...

Fourteen "safe harbor" statutes require that approval of a transaction by directors or shareholders be "in good faith." This good faith requirement may permit courts in these states to engage in a more intense scrutiny of transactions than would otherwise be permitted by the literal terms of the statutes. ...

Comment to § 5.08(a)(1):

A director or senior executive should not deal with the corporation as a stranger on the basis of caveat emptor. He owes a duty to the corporation not only to avoid misleading it by misstatements or omissions, but to disclose affirmatively the material facts concerning a transaction in which he has a personal interest. Section 5.08(a)(1) accordingly requires that the director or senior executive disclose to the appropriate corporate decisionmaker the material facts known to the director or senior executive concerning both the transaction and the director's or senior executive's conflict of interest. The director or senior executive is intended to be treated as having a relation of "trust and confidence" with the corporation, so as to require disclosure of "material matters," as contemplated in Restatement, Second, Torts § 551(2)(a), rather than treated as a stranger to the corporation with the more limited duty of disclosure of "facts basic to the transaction" contemplated in Restatement, Second, Torts § 551(2)(e). Compare Comments *e, f* and *k*, Restatement, Second, Torts § 551. The duty of one who occupies a relationship of trust and confidence to disclose material facts is also recognized in other Restatements. See Restatement, Second, Contracts § 161, Comment *f*; Restatement,

Second, Agency § 390; and Restatement of Restitution § 191, Comment on Clause (b). While the director or senior executive is not obligated under § 5.08 to volunteer that he is realizing a profit in a sale to the corporation or the amount of the profit, or the maximum amount he is willing to pay in a purchase from the corporation, the corporate decisionmaker may in a particular case find it appropriate to seek such information. If the director or senior executive declines to furnish it, the transaction may still be approved, but the corporate decisionmaker should be particularly careful that the consideration paid or received by the corporation is fair.

Section 5.08(a)(2)(A) and (B) contemplate that the disclosure required by § 5.08(a)(1) will be made to the board of directors or board committee or shareholders who approve the transaction, as the corporate decisionmakers. The director or senior executive need not rely on § 5.08(a)(2)(A) or (B), and in such case the disclosure required by § 5.08(a)(1) may be made to a corporate decisionmaker below the level of the board of directors, such as a subordinate officer. However, in such case the burden will be on the director or senior executive to prove the fairness of the transaction to the corporation where he does not seek disinterested board of directors or shareholder approval. See § 5.08(a)(2)(C).

By permitting the corporation to rescind a transaction when there has not been the full disclosure required by § 5.08(a)(1) (absent ratification), § 5.08(c)(1) reaches a result similar to that reached in State ex rel. Hayes Oyster Co. v. Keypoint Oyster Co., 64 Wn.2d 375, 391 P.2d 979 (1964). The importance of disclosure as a separate aspect of the duty of loyalty to the corporation was also recently recognized as an aspect of "fair dealing" by the Supreme Court of Delaware in Weinberger v. UOP, Inc., 457 A.2d 701 (Del.1983).

Ratification of a transaction, after the disclosure of previously omitted facts, may be effected at any time, even after a complaint has been filed attacking the transaction, since § 5.08(a)(1) is intended simply to permit the corporation to avoid a transaction where there has been inadequate disclosure.

Illustrations:

1. A, a director of X Corporation, following disclosure and authorization of the transaction in advance by disinterested directors as contemplated in §§ 5.08(a)(1) and 5.08(a)(2)(A), purchases a surplus parcel of land owned by X Corporation at its fair market value at the time of A's purchase. Six months later, Y, a third party, decides to build a sizeable shopping center on the property adjoining the land purchased by A, resulting in a substantial increase in its value. The transaction satisfies § 5.08(a), even though judged in hindsight, X Corporation could now sell the property for a substantially higher price. If, however, A knew of Y's plans at the time he purchased the land from X Corporation and failed to disclose that fact to X Corpora-

tion, A will have violated § 5.08(a)(1), even though the transaction is otherwise fair.

2. X Corporation is seeking a new headquarters building. D, a vice president of X Corporation, owns all the stock of R Corporation, which owns an office building. D causes a real estate agent to offer R Corporation's building to X Corporation, but does not disclose his ownership of R Corporation. X Corporation's board of directors agrees to purchase the building for a fair price. Two weeks later, X Corporation learns of D's interest in R Corporation. D will have violated § 5.08(a)(1).

3. The facts being otherwise as stated in Illustration 2, X Corporation's board ratifies the acquisition after it learns of D's interest in R Corporation. X Corporation cannot thereafter seek rescission of the transaction with R Corporation.

4. The facts being otherwise as stated in Illustration 2, D discloses to X Corporation, prior to the acquisition, his interest in R Corporation. D fails to disclose, however, that to his knowledge the State Highway Department has formally decided to run a highway through the property on which R Corporation's building stands, and to condemn the building under its power of eminent domain. The price paid by X Corporation is fair even taking the proposed condemnation into account, since the condemnation award is likely to equal or exceed the price. Two weeks after the acquisition, X Corporation learns of the Highway Department's decision. D will have violated § 5.08(a)(1).

5. The facts being otherwise as stated in Illustration 4, X Corporation's board ratifies the acquisition after it learns of the Highway Department's decision. X Corporation cannot thereafter seek rescission of the transaction with R Corporation.

Comment to § 5.08(a)(2):

In addition to the disclosure of material facts required by § 5.08(a)(1), § 5.08(a)(2) requires that a transaction must also meet one of the standards of "fairness" provided in §§ 5.08(a)(2)(A), (B) or (C), or in §§ 5.14(a)(1)(B) or 5.14(a)(2) if the director or senior executive is also a dominating shareholder. "Fairness" of a transaction is analyzed in § 5.08 in terms of two elements: (1) the character of judicial scrutiny to be applied (i.e., whether the directors could not reasonably have believed the transaction to be fair to the corporation, whether the transaction constituted a waste of corporate assets, or whether the transaction was not fair to the corporation), and (2) the burden of proof placed on the person seeking to discharge or uphold the transaction. Each of these elements will vary, depending upon the nature of disinterested approval, if any, which the transaction has received, following the disclosure required by § 5.08(a)(1).

In situations to which § 5.08 applies, the courts are generally reviewing conflict of interest transactions with directors and senior

executives which need not be entered into, rather than the usual
types of transactions with third parties which call for the exercise of
business judgment. Accordingly, while according due deference to
the judgment of disinterested directors or shareholders when approving § 5.08 transactions, the focus of judicial inquiry under § 5.08(a)(2)
is on the fairness of the transaction, rather than, for example, on
whether there is any rational basis for the decision, as is the case
when analyzing directors' actions under the business judgment rule.

Comment to § 5.08(a)(2)(A):

If a transaction has been authorized in advance by disinterested
directors, the burden of proof will be on the party challenging the
transaction under § 5.02(a)(2)(A), but a somewhat more intense level
of judicial scrutiny than the rational basis test required under the
business judgment rule (and a somewhat less intense level of scrutiny
than that required if there has been no disinterested director or
shareholder approval) is to be applied—namely, whether the directors
who approved the transaction could not reasonably have believed the
transaction to be fair. The test of fairness as so formulated is
intended to set forth an objective standard which adopts the concept
of an arm's-length bargain to the extent that such a concept can be
applied. It seeks to establish a "range of reasonableness" within
which conflict-of-interest transactions may be sustained. Cf. Clark v.
Lomas & Nettleton Financial Corp., 625 F.2d 49, 54 (5th Cir.1980),
cert. denied, 450 U.S. 1029, 101 S.Ct. 1738, 68 L.Ed.2d 224 (1981).
Accordingly, a person attacking a transaction approved by disinterested directors with the burden of showing that it is unfair must show
that a corporate decisionmaker could not reasonably have believed the
transaction to be fair to the corporation, and will not prevail if the
transaction is within the range of reasonableness. Although the test
of fairness as so formulated is intended to set forth an objective
standard, it assumes that the directors in fact believe in good faith
that the transaction is fair to the corporation.

Illustration:

6. A, a senior executive of X Corporation, enters into a
contract to lease to X Corporation automobiles that A purchases
from Y Corporation. A discloses to the board of directors of X
Corporation that X Corporation may lease the automobiles directly
from Y Corporation at a substantial savings and without any
added burden. Even if the directors of X Corporation are disinterested and authorize execution of the contract in advance, after
such disclosure, the contract cannot be found to be fair to X
Corporation, since (in the absence of other facts) the directors
could not reasonably have believed the transaction to be fair to X
Corporation.

Section 5.08(a)(2)(A) contemplates that (unless a standard of the
corporation [§ 1.27] adopted in accordance with § 5.06 permits a
transaction) the director or senior executive before entering into a

transaction with the corporation will normally secure the advance authorization of disinterested directors to whom full disclosure has been made of the matters required by § 5.08(a)(1). Section 5.08(a)(2)(A) reflects the policy that where a director or senior executive, or his associate, deals with the corporation, such a transaction should as a matter of course come to the attention of the board of directors or a committee of the board. Where this procedure is not followed, the transaction will not automatically be invalidated, but under § 5.08(a)(2)(C) the burden will be placed upon the director or senior executive to prove the fairness of the transaction to the corporation unless disinterested shareholder authorization or ratification is obtained.

Where ratification of a conflict-of-interest transaction is sought after it has been entered into by the corporation, there is less likelihood that the corporation will be able to negotiate more favorable terms. Furthermore, the requirement of advance approval serves to encourage disclosure of conflict of interest transactions. Accordingly, failure to obtain advance authorization of the transaction by the board of directors or a board committee will result in the burden being placed on the director or senior executive to sustain the fairness of the transaction to the corporation, and obtaining board ratification of the transaction will not shift this burden of proof. ...

Comment to § 5.08(b):

Section 5.08(b) places on the party attacking a transaction the burden of coming forward with evidence and the ultimate burden of proof as to all elements of the case, except where, because of failure to obtain disinterested director or shareholder approval or failure to act under a standard of the corporation adopted in accordance with § 5.06, the director or senior executive has the burden of proving fairness. See § 5.08(a)(2)(C). Where the facts are peculiarly within the knowledge of the director or senior executive, the court will have the discretion of placing the burden on him of coming forward with evidence, with the ultimate burden of persuasion remaining on the party attacking the transaction. See Schreiber v. Pennzoil Co., 419 A.2d 952 (Del.Ch.1980).

(e) EXECUTIVE COMPENSATION

Insert the following case at p. 663 of the unabridged edition, after the Note on Corporate Aspects of Stock Options, and at p. 483 of the abridged edition, at the end of Section (e)(2):

MICHELSON v. DUNCAN

Supreme Court of Delaware, 1979.
407 A.2d 211.

Before HERRMANN, C.J., QUILLEN and HORSEY, JJ.

HORSEY, Justice:

Plaintiff appeals the Court of Chancery's grant of summary judgment in a derivative shareholder's suit brought to set aside stock options granted by the defendants, officers and directors of Household Finance Corporation (hereafter, "HFC") to key employees, including themselves. The source of the controversy between the parties is action taken by the directors in 1971–1974 to modify the Company's 1966 stock option plan (sometimes hereafter, "the Plan") and their issuance of stock options under the Plan as modified. The principal issue on appeal is whether a 1977 non-unanimous shareholder ratification of the earlier modifications of the Plan and of the options granted under the modified Plan entitled defendants to a grant of summary judgment.

For the reasons hereafter stated, we affirm in part and reverse in part the holdings of the Vice Chancellor. More specifically, we hold (1) that the Complaint states a claim for gift or waste of corporate assets; (2) that such claim was not waived or conceded by plaintiff before the court below; (3) that ratification cured or overcame attack on the options granted under the Plan as modified on the ground of lack of director authority but does not dispose of the claim of gift or waste; and (4) as to the latter, trial is required as to the issue of existence and adequacy of consideration for the grant of the new or modified options, but shareholder ratification shifts the burden of proof of failure or inadequacy of consideration from defendants to plaintiff.

The relevant facts are lengthy but are set out in detail in the opinion below, Michelson v. Duncan, Del.Ch., 386 A.2d 1144 (1978) and need not be repeated here, except those that are pertinent to this decision.

In 1966, the Board of Directors of HFC authorized a stock option plan whereby certain key employees, including a number of the directors, were granted options to purchase stock in HFC following a two year waiting period after grant. Purchases under the non-tax qualified portion of the 1966 plan, with which we are concerned, were to be made at 90% of the market price at the time of grant. A grant limit of 5,000 shares per year per optionee, later raised to 15,000 shares, was imposed. The options could be exercised at a rate of 10% a year after the second year with the final 30% exercisable following the ninth anniversary of the grant. The Plan was described in proxy materials, but not set out in toto, and was overwhelmingly approved by the shareholders at their 1966 annual meeting.

The transactions in question relate to conduct of the Board of Directors from 1971 to 1974. In 1971 and again in 1973 the Board, acting on the recommendation of the Compensation Committee,* amended the rate of exercise limit to increase that limit from 10% per year to

---

* The Compensation Committee was established under the 1966 Plan and was composed of non-employee directors. Under the terms of the Plan they were charged with selecting employees eligible for the option plan, determining the number of shares to be granted and fixing the terms for exercising each option. Moreover, the Plan provided that the Compensation Committee could recommend to the Board to waive the exercise limitation for selected optionees.

33⅓% following each of the second, third and fourth anniversaries of a grant. The net effect of this modification was to reduce the minimum time necessary to exercise an entire option from nine years to four years.

In 1974, following a dramatic decline in the market price of HFC stock, the Board of Directors in order to restore incentive to exercise the options, developed and adopted a plan (sometimes hereafter referred to as "the Amended Plan") whereby the existing options would be cancelled and new options issued in their place at the current lower market price. The exercise price of the new options was some $7.00 to $18.00 below the price of the old options. At the same meeting of the directors, 304,900 old options were exchanged for new options and 25,000 new options were issued without exchange. During the next year an additional 71,800 options were granted without exchange.

The Complaint attacks the options granted after December 31, 1973, and specifically the exchange options granted in April, 1974 on essentially two grounds: (1) lack of authority of the Board of Directors to grant the options as modified without prior shareholder approval; and (2) the options issued were void for lack of consideration.

More specifically, plaintiff claims that the Board lacked authority: to grant options in excess of 15,000 shares per optionee per 12 month period; to reduce the option purchase price below that provided under the 1966 plan; to increase the yearly percentage limit of options exercisable; and to exceed the total number of shares available for option under the 1966 Plan. The Complaint seeks (a) cancellation of all the options issued to all optionees, including defendants; (b) an accounting by the individual defendants for all profits realized by them under any options received; and (c) recovery from the individual defendants of all losses and damages sustained by HFC.

Admitting generally the amendments to the 1966 Plan but claiming that they were not contrary to the Plan, defendants, shortly after answer and before any extensive discovery had been undertaken by plaintiff or defendants, moved for summary judgment. In their opening brief filed with their motion, defendants argued: (1) that the cancellation of existing stock options in exchange for the issuance of new stock options at reduced prices is permissible under Delaware law as stated in Dann v. Chrysler Corp., Del.Ch., 41 Del.Ch. 438, 198 A.2d 185 (1963); aff'd sub nom. Hoffman v. Dann, Del.Supr., 205 A.2d 343 (1964), cert. denied 380 U.S. 973, 85 S.Ct. 1332, 14 L.Ed.2d 269 (1965); (2) that there was consideration for the new grants in that the optionee-employees were induced to remain with the corporation for an additional two years; and (3) that the grant of the new options in exchange for the old was not in violation of the terms of the 1966 Plan.

Plaintiff countered with a cross-motion for summary judgment asserting a contrary position; but in his opening brief below, plaintiff did not argue lack of consideration for the options granted or that they represented gifts or waste of corporate assets. Instead, plaintiff limited his argument to alleged lack of director authority.

Defendants then proceeded to obtain from the shareholders of HFC at its upcoming 1977 annual meeting a ratification that was less than unanimous of the actions of the directors complained of in this lawsuit concerning the Amended Plan and stock options issued thereunder by the directors over the period 1971–1974. More or less simultaneously with this shareholder action, defendants filed their reply brief in support of summary judgment, referred to the recently accomplished shareholder ratification and argued that such shareholder action constituted a complete defense to the instant action and in particular to plaintiff's claim of lack of shareholder authority for the Amended Plan and options issued thereunder. Defendants argued that the director action was, at most, voidable, rather than void, and as such, any alleged defect that was the subject of the Complaint was curable by shareholder ratification. Defendants added that plaintiff had, in his briefing of the cross summary judgment motions, abandoned any claim of gift or waste of corporate assets which might have constituted a non-ratifiable action.

Plaintiff responded by supplemental memorandum that the HFC shareholder ratification action had injected a new fact element into the litigation not present at time of filing of his answering brief; that he had not abandoned his claim that the new options were granted without consideration and constituted gifts or waste of corporate assets; and plaintiff proceeded to argue that non-unanimous shareholder ratification was not a legal defense to a claim of gift or waste of corporate assets, even if it were a defense to his claim of lack of shareholder authority.

The Vice-Chancellor, following oral argument, granted summary judgment on defendants' motion and denied summary judgment on plaintiff's cross-motion. The Vice-Chancellor stated that while he would have been required to deny defendants summary judgment had plaintiff alleged gift or waste of corporate assets and presented sufficient evidence in support of such claim, he concluded that plaintiff had failed to plead, or, if pleaded, had later abandoned any claim that the Amended Plan and options granted thereunder amounted to gift or waste of corporate assets. He then found the 1977 shareholder ratification of the directors' 1971–1974 actions to have been fair and complete and thus, the ratification to be "intrinsically valid." The Vice-Chancellor further found no evidence of breach of fiduciary duty by the directors in delegating authority to grant options to the compensation Committee of the Board; and the Vice-Chancellor concluded that the 1977 shareholder ratification cured all remaining challenges to the acts of the defendants-directors. It is that decision which is appealed by plaintiff, A. Elihu Michelson.

I

Michelson contends that the Court's initial error was its ruling that plaintiff had not alleged a claim of gift or waste of corporate assets. We agree. Paragraph 17 of the Complaint fairly clearly asserts two separate and distinct claims: *first*, that the Board's modifications of the option Plan were invalid because contrary to and not authorized under the terms of the 1966 Plan; and *second*, that the "new" options granted in and subsequent to 1974 were without consideration.

By subparagraph 17(a) through (f) and (h) of the Complaint, plaintiff alleged that the directors lacked the authority to modify the 1966 Plan and that the shareholders had not approved the directors' action. By subparagraph 17(g), plaintiff alleged, that the "new" options granted in and subsequent to 1974 were without consideration.

By subparagraph 17(a) through (f) and (h) of the Complaint, plaintiff alleged that the directors lacked the authority to modify the 1966 Plan and that the shareholders had not approved the directors' action. By subparagraph 17(g), plaintiff alleged, "There was no consideration for the grant of the options." By paragraphs 19 and 20 of the Complaint, plaintiff asserted: that there was "no consideration" for the extension of the period during which options could be exercised ..."; that the cancellation of the outstanding options in exchange for the "new" options enabled "the optionees to acquire HFC's shares at grossly inadequate prices in violation of the terms of the 1966 Plan"; and that modifications of the option price and extension of the "period during which said options could be exercised" were "granted for no consideration and solely in order to enrich the optionees, and particularly said optionees who were officers and directors of HFC."

In view of these averments of the Complaint, the Vice-Chancellor's conclusion that plaintiff had not alleged a claim of gift or waste of corporate assets is not supported by the record. While the Complaint does not use the words "gift or waste", the averments that the options were granted for "no consideration" is tantamount to an allegation of gift or waste of assets. The essence of a claim of gift is lack of consideration. The essence of a claim of waste of corporate assets is the diversion of corporate assets for improper or unnecessary purposes. Although directors are given wide latitude in making business judgments, they are bound to act out of fidelity and honesty in their roles as fiduciaries. See, e.g., Warshaw v. Calhoun, Del.Supr., 43 Del Ch 148, 221 A.2d 487 (1966); 19 Am.Jur.2d, *Corporations*, § 1145 et seq. And they may not, simply because of their position, "by way of excessive salaries and other devices, oust the minority of a fair return upon its investment." Baker v. Cohn, N.Y.Supr., 42 N.Y.S.2d 159 at 166 (1942). It is common sense that a transfer for no consideration amounts to a gift or waste of corporate assets. ...

[The court then held that the plaintiff had not waived or abandoned this claim; that the ratification was sufficient to cure any invalidity of the Plan's amendments based on the contention that the 1971–1974 director action was contrary to the terms of the 1966 Plan; but that the ratification did not dispose of plaintiff's claim that there was no consideration for the option grants and that they constituted gifts or waste of corporate assets.]

IV

This brings us to the final question, namely, whether Michelson presented sufficient evidence as to gift or waste to preclude summary judgment in defendants' favor.

Defendants make essentially two arguments in support of their position that there is no triable issue as to gift or waste. *First,* they contend plaintiff has failed to establish any material issue of fact relating to the question of adequacy of consideration for the cancellation of the old options in exchange for grant of the new options. *Second,* defendants claim that there is sufficiency of consideration as a matter of law by application of the pertinent facts to Delaware statute law, 8 *Del.C.* § 157,[4] and decisional law under Hoffman v. Dann, supra. We will now take up each of these arguments.

A.

Defendants contend that under Gottlieb v. Heyden, supra, and Kaufman v. Schoenberg, Del.Ch., 33 Del.Ch. 211, 91 A.2d 786 (1952), shareholder ratification shifted the burden of proof of lack of consideration to plaintiff. Since plaintiff has failed to offer any evidence thereof, defendants claim that summary judgment below should be affirmed.

Plaintiff does not agree that there is insufficient evidence in the record of gift or waste of assets to raise a triable issue of fact. Plaintiff states this evidence includes the following director action: across the board, indiscriminate modifications of the 1966 Plan; lowering the exercise prices; accelerating the exercise rates; and the granting of new options in 1974 with no parity of services rendered to value of options granted.

Delaware decisional law supports plaintiff's position. Claims of gift or waste of corporate assets are seldom subject to disposition by summary judgment; and when there are genuine issues of fact as to the existence of consideration, a full hearing is required regardless of shareholder ratification. See Kerbs v. California Eastern Airways, supra; Gottlieb v. Heyden Chemical Corp., supra. "The determination of whether or not there has been in any given situation a gift of corporate assets does not rest upon any hard and fast rule. It is largely a question of fact." Gottlieb v. McKee, Del.Ch., 34 Del.Ch. 537, 107 A.2d 240 at 243

---

4. 8 *Del.C.* § 157 provides in pertinent part:

"*§ 157. Rights and options respecting stock.*

Subject to any provisions in the certificate of incorporation, every corporation may create and issue ... rights or options entitling the holders thereof to purchase from the corporation any shares of its capital stock ....

"The terms upon which ... such shares may be purchased from the corporation upon the exercise of any such right or option, shall be such as shall be stated in the certificate of incorporation, or in a resolution adopted by the board of directors .... In the absence of actual fraud in the transaction, the judgment of the directors as to the consideration for the issuance of such rights or options and the sufficiency thereof shall be conclusive."

(1954). In Saxe v. Brady, Del.Ch., 40 Del.Ch. 474, 184 A.2d 602 (1962), Chancellor Seitz stated, "Where waste of corporate assets is alleged, the court, notwithstanding independent stockholder ratification, must examine the facts of the situation." (184 A.2d at 610). In *Heyden*, this Court stated:

> An important question, which is not yet answered, is whether these services and these options can sensibly be deemed to be the subject of a fair exchange. This is obviously not a mere question of law. An issue of fact is raised, as to which, as yet, no evidence has been taken." 33 Del.Ch. 177, 91 A.2d 57 at 59.

Similarly, in Gottlieb v. McKee, supra, the Court of Chancery, finding affidavits insufficient and otherwise inadequate for determination of an issue of gift or waste of assets, denied summary judgment for defendants as to a corporate opportunity claim and held a full hearing was required, notwithstanding shareholder ratification. See also Gamble v. Penn Valley Crude Oil Corp., Del.Ch., 34 Del.Ch. 359, 104 A.2d 257 (1954), cross-motions for summary judgment as to right of plaintiff to exercise and receive stock options were denied on the state of the record, the Court stating, "Vital facts are either lacking or in conflict and it would therefore be inappropriate to attempt either to assume them or to evaluate them on cross-motions for summary judgment." 104 A.2d at 263.

While, of course, each case must be determined on its own facts, the above cases indicate a strong disfavor for summary judgment in stock option claims where waste of corporate assets is alleged. Here, Michelson has, by his Complaint and affidavit of his attorney, raised material issues of fact as to the existence of consideration for grant of options, thus making summary judgment inappropriate on the issue of waste of corporate assets.

B.

Defendants alternatively argue that 8 Del.C. § 157 rules out any fact issue by making any consideration sufficient as a matter of law, relying on the following language of that section: "In the absence of actual fraud in the transaction, the judgment of the directors as to the consideration for the issuance of such rights or options and the sufficiency thereof shall be conclusive." The meaning of the quoted sentence is clear. However, defendant goes too far in his reliance on this section. Implicit in that section is the existence of some consideration, and assuming that fact begs the question at issue in a challenge of wasting corporate assets. See *Kerbs*, supra; Frankel v. Donovan, Del.Ch., 35 Del.Ch. 433, 120 A.2d 311 (1956).

Section 157 was intended to protect directors' business judgment in consideration inuring to the corporation in exchange for creating and issuing stock options. However, to assert that there was no consideration for the cancellation of the existing options in exchange for new options—as asserted here—is far different from asserting that there was inadequate consideration for doing so. Whether or not § 157 disposes of an inadequacy of consideration claim is not the issue before us. Here, the contention is made that there was no consideration received by HFC from the grant of the new or exchange options in 1974. We do not read § 157 as intended to erect a legal barrier to any claim for relief as to an alleged gift or waste of corporate assets in the issuance of stock options where the claim asserted is one of absolute failure of consideration.

Defendants also claim that under Hoffman v. Dann, supra, the grant of options by disinterested directors and ratification by stockholders precludes any attack on the option plan. Defendant's reliance on this case is misplaced. It is important to note that *Hoffman* arose in the context of approval of a contested settlement. The standard for approval of a settlement is significantly different from that used for grant of summary judgment. In response to the challenge of wasting corporate assets, in *Hoffman* this Court found that there was not a "probability of substantial recovery" by the challenging shareholders. The question we must resolve here is not the likelihood of success, but rather whether or not there is a material issue of fact in question. *Hoffman* should not be interpreted as contradicting the well-established rule that non-unanimous shareholder approval cannot cure an act of waste of corporate assets. *Kerbs*, supra.

Reinforcing our conclusion that the case should be remanded for further proceedings is plaintiff's contention that there has not been an adequate time provided for discovery; that discovery has not included any depositions or extensive interrogatories to date; and that since the pendency of the motion for summary judgment, all further discovery has been stayed. Though this has been with the consent of the parties, it would be inappropriate at this stage of the case for plaintiff's right to discovery to be said to have been foreclosed.

C.

We further hold, as the Vice-Chancellor ruled, that shareholder ratification shifted the burden of proof of want or inadequacy of consideration for the grant of the options from defendants to plaintiff. See Gottlieb v. Heyden Chemical Corporation, supra, and Kaufman v. Schoenberg, supra. In *Gottlieb*, this Court stated that ". . . [T]he entire atmosphere is freshened and a new set of rules invoked where formal approval has been given by a majority of independent, fully informed stockholders. . . ." 91 A.2d at 59.

Similarly, in *Kaufman*, the Chancellor stated that in the absence of independent stockholder ratification, interested directors have the burden of showing that the consideration to be received for the grant of options represented a "fair exchange", but the burden shifts where there has been shareholder ratification:

> "Where there has been independent stockholder ratification of interested director action, the objecting stockholder has the burden of

showing that no person of ordinary sound business judgment would say that the consideration received for the options was a fair exchange for the options granted." 91 A.2d 791.

See also Fidanque v. American Maracaibo Co., Del.Ch., 33 Del.Ch. 262, 92 A.2d 311 (1952), stating:

"Even in cases, such as a case involving interlocking directorates, where the burden is upon the directors to prove the validity of their action and their good faith, a stockholder ratification shifts the burden of proof to the objector. Gottlieb v. Heyden Chemical Co., supra." 92 A.2d at 321.

. . .

Affirmed in part and reversed in part.

SECTION 3. TRANSACTIONS IN SHARES OF THE CORPORATION BY DIRECTORS AND CONTROLLING OR "INSIDE" SHAREHOLDERS

(b) THE DEVELOPMENT OF FEDERAL CORPORATION LAW; RELATING PRIMARILY TO INSIDERS

(1) Section 10(b) of the Securities Exchange Act of 1934

B. The Liability of Insiders

CHIARELLA v. UNITED STATES

In light of the recent decision in Dirks v. Securities and Exchange Commission, infra, Chiarella v. United States, which now appears in Section 3(b)(1)(D) (at p. 755 of the unabridged edition and p. 543 of the abridged edition), should instead be read and considered at the end of Section 3(b)(1)(C), at p. 839 of the unabridged edition and p. 592 of the abridged edition.

Insert the following case at p. 796 of the unabridged edition, and p. 564 of the abridged edition, at the end of Section 3(b)(1)(B):

HERMAN & MacLEAN v. HUDDLESTON

Supreme Court of the United States, 1983.
459 U.S. 375, 103 S.Ct. 683, 74 L.Ed.2d 548.

JUSTICE MARSHALL delivered the opinion of the Court.

These consolidated cases raise two unresolved questions concerning Section 10(b) of the Securities Exchange Act of 1934, 15 U.S.C. § 78j(b). The first is whether purchasers of registered securities who allege they were defrauded by misrepresentations in a registration statement may maintain an action under Section 10(b) notwithstanding the express remedy for misstatements and omissions in registration statements provided by Section 11 of the Securities Act of 1933, 15 U.S.C. § 77k. The second question is whether persons seeking recovery under Section 10(b) must prove their cause of action by clear and convincing evidence rather than by a preponderance of the evidence.

I

In 1969 Texas International Speedway, Inc. ("TIS"), filed a registration statement and prospectus with the Securities and Exchange Commission offering a total of $4,398,900 in securities to the public. The proceeds of the sale were to be used to finance the construction of an automobile speedway. The entire issue was sold on the offering date, October 30, 1969. TIS did not meet with success, however, and the corporation filed a petition for bankruptcy on November 30, 1970.

In 1972 plaintiffs Huddleston and Bradley instituted a class action in the United States District Court ... on behalf of themselves and other purchasers of TIS securities. The complaint alleged violations of Section 10(b) of the Securities Exchange Act of 1934 ("the 1934 Act") and SEC Rule 10b–5 promulgated thereunder, 17 CFR 240.10b–5.[2] Plaintiffs sued most of the participants in the offering, including the accounting firm, Herman & MacLean, which had issued an opinion concerning certain financial statements and a pro forma balance sheet[3] that were contained in the registration statement and prospectus. Plaintiffs claimed that the defendants had engaged in a fraudulent scheme to misrepresent or conceal material facts regarding the financial condition of TIS, including the costs incurred in building the speedway.

After a three-week trial, the District Judge submitted the case to the jury on special interrogatories relating to liability. The judge instructed the jury that liability could be found only if the defendants acted with scienter.[4] The judge also instructed the jury to determine whether

---

2. Plaintiffs also alleged violations of, *inter alia*, Section 17(a) of the Securities Act of 1933, 15 U.S.C. § 77q(a). We have previously reserved decision on whether Section 17(a) affords a private remedy, International Brotherhood of Teamsters v. Daniel, 439 U.S. 551, 557, n. 9, 99 S.Ct. 790, 795, n. 9, 58 L.Ed.2d 808 (1979), and we do so once again. Plaintiffs have abandoned their Section 17(a) claim, Brief, at 4, n. 6, and the Court of Appeals did not address the existence of a separate cause of action under Section 17(a). Accordingly, there is no need for us to decide the issue.

3. A pro forma balance sheet is one prepared on the basis of assumptions as to future events.

4. The judge stated that reckless behavior could satisfy the scienter requirement. While this instruction reflects the prevailing view of the courts of appeals that have addressed the issue, see McLean v. Alexander, 599 F.2d 1190, 1197, and n. 12 (CA3 1979) (collecting cases), we have explicitly left open the question whether recklessness satisfies the scienter requirement. Ernst & Ernst v. Hochfelder, 425 U.S. 185, 194, n. 12, 96 S.Ct. 1375, 1381 n. 12, 47 L.Ed.2d 668 (1976).

plaintiffs had proven their cause of action by a preponderance of the evidence. After the jury rendered a verdict in favor of the plaintiffs on the submitted issues, the judge concluded that Herman & MacLean and others had violated Section 10(b) and Rule 10b–5 by making fraudulent misrepresentations in the TIS registration statement.[5] The court then determined the amount of damages and entered judgment for the plaintiffs.

On appeal, the United States Court of Appeals for the Fifth Circuit held that a cause of action may be maintained under Section 10(b) of the 1934 Act for fraudulent misrepresentations and omissions even when that conduct might also be actionable under Section 11 of the Securities Act of 1933 ("the 1933 Act"). Huddleston v. Herman & MacLean, 640 F.2d 534, 540–543 (1981). However, the Court of Appeals disagreed with the District Court as to the appropriate standard of proof for an action under Section 10(b), concluding that a plaintiff must prove his case by "clear and convincing" evidence. Id., at 545–546. The Court of Appeals reversed the District Court's judgment on other grounds and remanded the case for a new trial. Id., at 547–550, 560.

We granted certiorari to consider whether an implied cause of action under Section 10(b) of the 1934 Act will lie for conduct subject to an express civil remedy under the 1933 Act, an issue we have previously reserved, and to decide the standard of proof applicable to actions under Section 10(b).[7] 456 U.S. 914, 102 S.Ct. 1766, 72 L.Ed.2d 173 (1982). We now affirm the court of appeals' holding that plaintiffs could maintain an action under Section 10(b) of the 1934 Act, but we reverse as to the applicable standard of proof.

II

The Securities Act of 1933 and the Securities Exchange Act of 1934 "constitute interrelated components of the federal regulatory scheme

5. The trial court also found that Herman & MacLean had aided and abetted violations of Section 10(b). While several courts of appeals have permitted aider and abettor liability, see IIT, An International Investment Trust v. Cornfeld, 619 F.2d 909, 922 (CA2 1980) (collecting cases), we specifically reserved this issue in Ernst & Ernst v. Hochfelder, supra, 425 U.S., at 191–192, n. 7, 96 S.Ct., at 1380, n. 7. Cf. Merrill Lynch, Pierce, Fenner & Smith v. Curran, 456 U.S. 353, 394–395, 102 S.Ct. 1825, 1847–48, 72 L.Ed.2d 182 (1982) (discussing liability for participants in a conspiracy under analogous Commodity Exchange Act provision).

[In *Merrill Lynch*, the Court stated:

Having concluded that [commodity] exchanges can be held accountable for breaching their statutory duties to enforce their own rules prohibiting price manipulation, it necessarily follows that those persons who are participants in a conspiracy to manipulate the market in violation of those rules are also subject to suit by futures traders who can prove injury from these violations. As we said regarding the analogous Rule 10b–5, "privity of dealing or even personal contact between potential defendant and potential plaintiff is the exception and not the rule." Blue Chip Stamps v. Manor Drug Stores, 421 U.S., at 745, 95 S.Ct. at 1929. Because there is no indication of legislative intent that privity should be an element of the implied remedy under the CEA, we are not prepared to fashion such a limitation.

456 U.S. at 394–395, 102 S.Ct. at 1847] (Material in brackets added by ed.)

7. The Fifth Circuit's adoption of a clear-and-convincing-evidence standard in a private action under Section 10(b) appears to be unprecedented. ... Other courts have employed a preponderance-of-the-evidence standard in private actions under the securities laws. ...

governing transactions in securities." Ernst & Ernst v. Hochfelder, 425 U.S. 185, 206 (1976). The Acts created several express private rights of action,[8] one of which is contained in Section 11 of the 1933 Act. In addition to the private actions created explicitly by the 1933 and 1934 Acts, federal courts have implied private remedies under other provisions of the two laws.[9] Most significantly for present purposes, a private right of action under Section 10(b) of the 1934 Act and Rule 10b–5 has been consistently recognized for more than 35 years.[10] The existence of this implied remedy is simply beyond peradventure.

The issue in this case is whether a party should be barred from invoking this established remedy for fraud because the allegedly fraudulent conduct would apparently also provide the basis for a damage action under Section 11 of the 1933 Act.[11] The resolution of this issue turns on the fact that the two provisions involve distinct causes of action and were intended to address different types of wrongdoing.

Section 11 of the 1933 Act allows purchasers of a registered security to sue certain enumerated parties in a registered offering when false or misleading information is included in a registration statement. The section was designed to assure compliance with the disclosure provisions of the Act by imposing a stringent standard of liability [12] on the parties

---

8. Securities Act, §§ 11, 12, 15, 15 U.S.C. §§ 77k, 77*l*, 77o; Securities Exchange Act, §§ 9, 16, 18, 15 U.S.C. §§ 78i, 78p, 78r.

9. See, e.g., J.I. Case Co. v. Borak, 377 U.S. 426, 84 S.Ct. 1556, 12 L.Ed.2d 423 (1964) (Section 14(a) of the Securities Exchange Act); Dan River, Inc. v. Unitex Ltd., 624 F.2d 1216 (CA4 1980), cert. denied, 449 U.S. 1101, 101 S.Ct. 896, 66 L.Ed.2d 827 (1981) (Section 13 of the Securities Exchange Act); Kirshner v. United States, 603 F.2d 234, 241 (CA2 1978), cert. denied, 442 U.S. 909, 99 S.Ct. 2821, 61 L.Ed.2d 274 (1979) (Section 17(a) of the Securities Act). But see, e.g., Touche Ross & Co. v. Redington, 442 U.S. 560, 99 S.Ct. 2479, 61 L.Ed.2d 82 (1979) (no implied private right of action under Section 17(a) of the Securities Exchange Act); Piper v. Chris-Craft Industries, Inc., 430 U.S. 1, 97 S.Ct. 926, 51 L.Ed.2d 124 (1977) (defeated tender offeror has no implied private right of action under Section 14(e) of the Securities Exchange Act).

10. The right of action was first recognized in Kardon v. National Gypsum Co., 69 F.Supp. 512 (ED Pa.1946). ... By 1969, the existence of a private cause of action had been recognized by ten of the eleven courts of appeals. See VI L. Loss, Securities Regulation 3871–3873 (2d ed. Supp. 1969) (collecting cases). When the question

whether an implied cause of action can be brought under Section 10(b) and Rule 10b–5 was first considered in this Court, we confirmed the existence of such a cause of action without extended discussion. See Superintendent of Insurance v. Bankers Life & Cas. Co., 404 U.S. 6, 13, n. 9, 92 S.Ct. 165, 169, n. 9, 30 L.Ed.2d 128 (1971). We have since repeatedly reaffirmed that "the existence of a private cause of action for violations of the statute and the Rule is now well established." Ernst & Ernst v. Hochfelder, supra, 425 U.S., at 196, 96 S.Ct., at 1382 (citing prior cases).

11. The Court of Appeals noted that the plaintiffs "apparently did have a Section 11 remedy." 640 F.2d, at 541, n. 5. While accurate as to the two other defendants, this conclusion may be open to question with respect to Herman & MacLean. Accountants are liable under Section 11 only for those matters which purport to have been prepared or certified by them. 15 U.S.C. § 77k(a)(4). Herman & MacLean contends that it did not "expertise" at least some of the materials that were the subject of the lawsuit, Tr. of Oral Arg. at 6–8, which if true could preclude a Section 11 remedy with respect to these materials.

12. See H.R.Rep.No.85, 73d Cong., 1st Sess. 9 (1933) (Section 11 creates "correspondingly heavier legal liability" in line with responsibility to the public).

who play a direct role in a registered offering.[13] If a plaintiff purchased a security issued pursuant to a registration statement, he need only show a material misstatement or omission to establish his *prima facie* case. Liability against the issuer of a security is virtually absolute,[14] even for innocent misstatements. Other defendants bear the burden of demonstrating due diligence. See 15 U.S.C. § 77k(b).

Although limited in scope, Section 11 places a relatively minimal burden on a plaintiff. In contrast, Section 10(b) is a "catchall" antifraud provision, but it requires a plaintiff to carry a heavier burden to establish a cause of action. While a Section 11 action must be brought by a purchaser of a registered security, must be based on misstatements or omissions in a registration statement, and can only be brought against certain parties, a Section 10(b) action can be brought by a purchaser or seller of "*any* security" against "*any* person" who has used "*any* manipulative or deceptive device or contrivance*" in connection with the purchase or sale of a security. 15 U.S.C. § 78j (emphasis added). However, a Section 10(b) plaintiff carries a heavier burden than a Section 11 plaintiff. Most significantly, he must prove that the defendant acted with scienter, i.e., with intent to deceive, manipulate, or defraud.[16]

Since Section 11 and Section 10(b) address different types of wrongdoing, we see no reason to carve out an exception to Section 10(b) for fraud occurring in a registration statement just because the same conduct may also be actionable under Section 11.[17] Exempting such conduct from liability under Section 10(b) would conflict with the basic purpose of the 1933 Act: to provide greater protection to purchasers of registered securities. It would be anomalous indeed if the special protection afforded to purchasers in a registered offering by the 1933 Act were deemed to deprive such purchasers of the protections against manipulation and deception that Section 10(b) makes available to all persons who deal in securities.

While some conduct actionable under Section 11 may also be actionable under Section 10(b), it is hardly a novel proposition that the Securities Exchange Act and the Securities Act "prohibit some of the same conduct." United States v. Naftalin, 441 U.S. 768, 778, 99 S.Ct. 2077, 2084, 60 L.Ed.2d 624 (1979) (applying Section 17(a) of the 1933 Act to conduct also prohibited by Section 10(b) of the 1934 Act in an action by the SEC). " 'The fact that there may well be some overlap is neither

---

13. A Section 11 action can be brought only against the issuer, its directors or partners, underwriters, and accountants who are named as having prepared or certified the registration statement. See 15 U.S.C. § 77k(a). At the same time, Sections 3 and 4 of the 1933 Act exclude a wide variety of securities (such as those issued by the government and certain banks) and transactions (such as private ones and certain small offerings) from the registration requirement. § 77c and d.

14. See Feit v. Leasco Data Processing Equipment Corp., 332 F.Supp. 544, 575 (EDNY 1971); R. Jennings & H. Marsh, Securities Regulation 828–829 (1977).

16. See Ernst & Ernst v. Hochfelder, supra, 425 U.S., at 193, 96 S.Ct., at 1380.

17. Cf. Mills v. Electric Auto-Lite, 396 U.S. 375, 390–391, 90 S.Ct. 616, 624, 24 L.Ed.2d 593 (1970) (existence of express provisions for recovery of attorneys' fees in §§ 9(e) and 18(a) of the 1934 Act does not preclude award of attorneys' fees under § 14(a) of the Act).

unusual nor unfortunate.'" Ibid., quoting SEC v. National Securities, Inc., 393 U.S. 453, 468, 89 S.Ct. 564, 572, 21 L.Ed.2d 668 (1969). In savings clauses included in the 1933 and 1934 Acts, Congress rejected the notion that the express remedies of the securities laws would preempt all other rights of action. Section 16 of the 1933 Act states unequivocally that "[t]he rights and remedies provided by this subchapter shall be in addition to any and all other rights and remedies that may exist at law or in equity." 15 U.S.C. § 77p. Section 28(a) of the 1934 Act contains a parallel provision. 15 U.S.C. § 78bb(a). These provisions confirm that the remedies in each Act were to be supplemented by "any and all" additional remedies.

This conclusion is reinforced by our reasoning in Ernst & Ernst v. Hochfelder, supra, which held that actions under Section 10(b) require proof of scienter and do not encompass negligent conduct. In so holding, we noted that each of the express civil remedies in the 1933 Act allowing recovery for negligent conduct is subject to procedural restrictions not applicable to a Section 10(b) action.[18] 425 U.S., at 208–210. We emphasized that extension of Section 10(b) to negligent conduct would have allowed causes of action for negligence under the express remedies to be brought instead under Section 10(b), "thereby nullify[ing] the effectiveness of the carefully drawn procedural restrictions on these express actions." Id., at 210 (footnote omitted). In reasoning that scienter should be required in Section 10(b) actions in order to avoid circumvention of the procedural restrictions surrounding the express remedies, we necessarily assumed that the express remedies were not exclusive. Otherwise there would have been no danger of nullification. Conversely, because the added burden of proving scienter attaches to suits under Section 10(b), invocation of the Section 10(b) remedy will not "nullify" the procedural restrictions that apply to the express remedies.[19]

This cumulative construction of the remedies under the 1933 and 1934 Acts is also supported by the fact that, when Congress comprehensively revised the securities laws in 1975, a consistent line of judicial decisions had permitted plaintiffs to sue under Section 10(b) regardless of the availability of express remedies. In 1975 Congress enacted the "most substantial and significant revision of this country's Federal securities laws since the passage of the Securities Exchange Act in 1934." ... When Congress acted, federal courts had consistently and routinely permitted a plaintiff to proceed under Section 10(b) even where express remedies under Section 11 or other provisions were available. In light of this well-established judicial interpretation, Congress' decision to leave

---

18. For example, a plaintiff in a Section 11 action may be required to post a bond for costs, 15 U.S.C. § 77k(e), and the statute of limitations is only one year, § 77m. In contrast, Section 10(b) contains no provision requiring plaintiffs to post security for costs. Also, courts look to the most analogous statute of limitations of the forum state, which is usually longer than the period provided for Section 11 actions. See Ernst & Ernst v. Hochfelder, supra, 425 U.S., at 210, n. 29, 96 S.Ct., at 1389, n. 29.

19. See Fischman v. Raytheon Mfg. Co., 188 F.2d 783, 786–787 (CA2 1951); A. Bromberg & L. Lowenfels, Securities Fraud & Commodities Fraud § 2.4(403), at 2:179–2:180 (1982).

Section 10(b) intact suggests that Congress ratified the cumulative nature of the Section 10(b) action. See Merrill Lynch, Pierce, Fenner & Smith, Inc. v. Curran, 456 U.S. 353, 381–382, 102 S.Ct. 1825, 1841, 72 L.Ed.2d 182 (1982); Lorillard v. Pons, 434 U.S. 575, 580–581, 98 S.Ct. 866, 870, 55 L.Ed.2d 40 (1978).

A cumulative construction of the securities laws also furthers their broad remedial purposes. In enacting the 1934 Act, Congress stated that its purpose was "to impose requirements necessary to make [securities] regulation and control reasonably complete and effective." 15 U.S.C. § 78b. In furtherance of that objective, Section 10(b) makes it unlawful to use "*any* manipulative or deceptive device or contrivance" in connection with the purchase or sale of any security. The effectiveness of the broad proscription against fraud in Section 10(b) would be undermined if its scope were restricted by the existence of an express remedy under Section 11.[22] Yet we have repeatedly recognized that securities laws combating fraud should be construed "not technically and restrictively, but flexibly to effectuate [their] remedial purposes." SEC v. Capital Gains Research Bureau, 375 U.S. 180, 195, 84 S.Ct. 275, 284, 11 L.Ed.2d 237 (1963). ... We therefore reject an interpretation of the securities laws that displaces an action under Section 10(b). ...

Accordingly, we hold that the availability of an express remedy under Section 11 of the 1933 Act does not preclude defrauded purchasers of registered securities from maintaining an action under Section 10(b) of the 1934 Act. To this extent the judgment of the court of appeals is affirmed.

III

In a typical civil suit for money damages, plaintiffs must prove their case by a preponderance of the evidence. Similarly, in an action by the SEC to establish fraud under Section 17(a) of the Securities Act, 15 U.S.C. § 77q(a), we have held that proof by a preponderance of the evidence suffices to establish liability. SEC v. C.M. Joiner Leasing Corp., 320 U.S. 344, 355, 64 S.Ct. 120, 125, 88 L.Ed. 88 (1943). "Where ... proof is offered in a civil action, as here, a preponderance of the evidence will establish the case ...." Ibid. The same standard applies in administrative proceedings before the SEC and has been consistently employed by the lower courts in private actions under the securities laws.

---

22. Moreover, certain individuals who play a part in preparing the registration statement generally cannot be reached by a Section 11 action. These include corporate officers other than those specified in 15 U.S.C. § 77k(a), lawyers not acting as "experts," and accountants with respect to parts of a registration statement which they are not named as having prepared or certified. If, as Herman & MacLean argues, purchasers in registered offerings were required to rely solely on Section 11, they would have no recourse against such individuals even if the excluded parties engaged in fraudulent conduct while participating in the registration statement. The exempted individuals would be immune from federal liability for fraudulent conduct even though Section 10(b) extends to "any person" who engages in fraud in connection with a purchase or sale of securities.

The Court of Appeals nonetheless held that plaintiffs in a Section 10(b) suit must establish their case by clear and convincing evidence. The Court of Appeals relied primarily on the traditional use of a higher burden of proof in civil fraud actions at common law. 640 F.2d, at 545–546. Reference to common law practices can be misleading, however, since the historical considerations underlying the imposition of a higher standard of proof have questionable pertinence here.[27] ... Moreover, the antifraud provisions of the securities laws are not coextensive with common law doctrines of fraud. Indeed, an important purpose of the federal securities statutes was to rectify perceived deficiencies in the available common law protections by establishing higher standards of conduct in the securities industry. ... We therefore find reference to the common law in this instance unavailing.

Where Congress has not prescribed the appropriate standard of proof and the Constitution does not dictate a particular standard, we must prescribe one. See Steadman v. SEC, 450 U.S. 91, 95, 101 S.Ct. 999, 1004, 67 L.Ed.2d 69 (1981). ... In doing so, we are mindful that a standard of proof "serves to allocate the risk of error between the litigants and to indicate the relative importance attached to the ultimate decision." ... [I]n SEC v. C.M. Joiner Leasing Corp., 320 U.S., at 355, 64 S.Ct., at 125, we held that a preponderance of the evidence suffices to establish fraud under Section 17(a) of the 1933 Act.

A preponderance-of-the-evidence standard allows both parties to "share the risk of error in roughly equal fashion." Addington v. Texas, 421 U.S., at 423, 99 S.Ct., at 1808. Any other standard expresses a preference for one side's interests. The balance of interests in this case warrants use of the preponderance standard. On the one hand, the defendants face the risk of opprobrium that may result from a finding of fraudulent conduct, but this risk is identical to that in an action under Section 17(a), which is governed by the preponderance-of-the-evidence standard. The interests of defendants in a securities case do not differ qualitatively from the interests of defendants sued for violations of other federal statutes such as the antitrust or civil rights laws, for which proof by a preponderance of the evidence suffices. On the other hand, the interests of plaintiffs in such suits are significant. Defrauded investors are among the very individuals Congress sought to protect in the securities laws. If they prove that it is more likely than not that they were defrauded, they should recover.

We therefore decline to depart from the preponderance-of-the-evidence standard generally applicable in civil actions.[30] Accordingly, the

---

27. A higher standard of proof apparently arose in courts of equity when the chancellor faced claims that were unenforceable at law because of the Statute of Wills, the Statute of Frauds, or the parol evidence rule. ... Concerned that claims would be fabricated, the chancery courts imposed a more demanding standard of proof. The higher standard subsequently received wide acceptance in equity proceedings to set aside presumptively valid written instruments on account of fraud. ...

30. The Court of Appeals also noted that the proof of scienter required in fraud cases is often a matter of inference from circumstantial evidence. If anything, the difficulty of proving the defendant's state of mind supports a lower standard of proof. In any

Court of Appeals' decision as to the appropriate standard of proof is reversed.

IV

The judgment of the Court of Appeals is affirmed in part and reversed in part and otherwise remanded for proceedings consistent with this opinion.

It is so ordered.

JUSTICE POWELL took no part in the decision of these cases.

C. Inroads Upon Expansive Interpretation

Insert, at p. 808 of the unabridged edition, and p. 568 of the abridged edition, following the Note on Blue Chip Stamps v. Manor Drug Stores, a cross-reference to the Note on Rubin v. United States, infra, p. 132.

CHIARELLA v. UNITED STATES

Read Chiarella v. United States at the end of Chapter VI, Section 3(b)(1)(C) (p. 839 of the unabridged edition and p. 592 of the abridged edition). (This case begins at p. 755 of the unabridged edition and p. 543 of the abridged edition.)

Insert the following case after Chiarella:

DIRKS v. SECURITIES AND EXCHANGE COMMISSION

Supreme Court of the United States, 1983.
___ U.S. ___, 103 S.Ct. 3255, 77 L.Ed.2d 911.

JUSTICE POWELL delivered the opinion of the Court.

Petitioner Raymond Dirks received material nonpublic information from "insiders" of a corporation with which he had no connection. He disclosed this information to investors who relied on it in trading in the shares of the corporation. The question is whether Dirks violated the antifraud provisions of the federal securities laws by this disclosure.

I

In 1973, Dirks was an officer of a New York broker-dealer firm who specialized in providing investment analysis of insurance company securities to institutional investors. On March 6, Dirks received information

---

event, we have noted elsewhere that circumstantial evidence can be more than sufficient. Michalic v. Cleveland Tankers, Inc., 364 U.S. 325, 330, 81 S.Ct. 6, 10, 5 L.Ed.2d 20 (1960). See TSC Industries, Inc. v. Northway, Inc., 426 U.S. 438, 463, and n. 24, 96 S.Ct. 2126, 2139, and n. 24, 48 L.Ed.2d 757 (1976).

from Ronald Secrist, a former officer of Equity Funding of America. Secrist alleged that the assets of Equity Funding, a diversified corporation primarily engaged in selling life insurance and mutual funds, were vastly overstated as the result of fraudulent corporate practices. Secrist also stated that various regulatory agencies had failed to act on similar charges made by Equity Funding employees. He urged Dirks to verify the fraud and disclose it publicly.

Dirks decided to investigate the allegations. He visited Equity Funding's headquarters in Los Angeles and interviewed several officers and employees of the corporation. The senior management denied any wrongdoing, but certain corporation employees corroborated the charges of fraud. Neither Dirks nor his firm owned or traded any Equity Funding stock, but throughout his investigation he openly discussed the information he had obtained with a number of clients and investors. Some of these persons sold their holdings of Equity Funding securities, including five investment advisers who liquidated holdings of more than $16 million.[2]

While Dirks was in Los Angeles, he was in touch regularly with William Blundell, the Wall Street Journal's Los Angeles bureau chief. Dirks urged Blundell to write a story on the fraud allegations. Blundell did not believe, however, that such a massive fraud could go undetected and declined to write the story. He feared that publishing such damaging hearsay might be libelous.

During the two-week period in which Dirks pursued his investigation and spread word of Secrist's charges, the price of Equity Funding stock fell from $26 per share to less than $15 per share. This led the New York Stock Exchange to halt trading on March 27. Shortly thereafter California insurance authorities impounded Equity Funding's records and uncovered evidence of the fraud. Only then did the Securities and Exchange Commission (SEC) file a complaint against Equity Funding[3] and only then, on April 2, did the Wall Street Journal publish a front-page story based largely on information assembled by Dirks. Equity Funding immediately went into receivership.[4]

---

2. Dirks received from his firm a salary plus a commission for securities transactions above a certain amount that his clients directed through his firm. See 21 S.E.C. Docket, at 1402, n. 3. But "[i]t is not clear how many of those with whom Dirks spoke promised to direct some brokerage business through [Dirks' firm] to compensate Dirks, or how many actually did so." 220 U.S.App. D.C., at 316, 681 F.2d, at 831. The Boston Company Institutional Investors, Inc., promised Dirks about $25,000 in commissions, but it is unclear whether Boston actually generated any brokerage business for his firm. See App. 199, 204–205; 21 S.E.C. Docket, at 1404, n. 10; 220 U.S.App.D.C., at 316, n. 5, 681 F.2d, at 831, n. 5.

3. As early as 1971, the SEC had received allegations of fraudulent accounting practices at Equity Funding. Moreover, on March 9, 1973, an official of the California Insurance Department informed the SEC's regional office in Los Angeles of Secrist's charges of fraud. Dirks himself voluntarily presented his information at the SEC's regional office beginning on March 27.

4. A federal grand jury in Los Angeles subsequently returned a 105-count indictment against 22 persons, including many of Equity Funding's officers and directors. All defendants were found guilty of one or more counts, either by a plea of guilty or a conviction after trial. See Brief for Petitioner 15; App. 149–153.

The SEC began an investigation into Dirks' role in the exposure of the fraud. After a hearing by an administrative law judge, the SEC found that Dirks had aided and abetted violations of § 17(a) of the Securities Act of 1933, 15 U.S.C. § 77q(a), § 10(b) of the Securities Exchange Act of 1934, 15 U.S.C. § 78j(b), and SEC Rule 10b-5, 17 CFR § 240.10b-5 (1982), by repeating the allegations of fraud to members of the investment community who later sold their Equity Funding stock. The SEC concluded: "Where 'tippees'—regardless of their motivation or occupation—come into possession of material 'information that they know is confidential and know or should know came from a corporate insider,' they must either publicly disclose that information or refrain from trading." 21 S.E.C. Docket 1401, 1407 (1981) (footnote omitted) (quoting Chiarella v. United States, 445 U.S. 222, 230 n. 12, 100 S.Ct. 1108, 1115 n. 12, 63 L.Ed.2d 348 (1980)). Recognizing, however, that Dirks "played an important role in bringing [Equity Funding's] massive fraud to light," 21 S.E.C. Docket, at 1412,[8] the SEC only censured him.[9]

Dirks sought review in the Court of Appeals for the District of Columbia Circuit. The court entered judgment against Dirks "for the reasons stated by the Commission in its opinion." App. to Pet. for Cert. C-2. Judge Wright, a member of the panel, subsequently issued an opinion. Judge Robb concurred in the result and Judge Tamm dissented; neither filed a separate opinion. Judge Wright believed that "the obligations of corporate fiduciaries pass to all those to whom they disclose their information before it has been disseminated to the public at large." 220 U.S.App.D.C. 309, 324, 681 F.2d 824, 839 (1982). Alternatively, Judge Wright concluded that, as an employee of a broker-dealer, Dirks had violated "obligations to the SEC and to the public completely independent of any obligations he acquired" as a result of receiving the information. Id., at 325, 681 F.2d, at 840.

In view of the importance to the SEC and to the securities industry of the question presented by this case, we granted a writ of certiorari. 459 U.S. 1014, 103 S.Ct. 371, 74 L.Ed.2d 506 (1982). We now reverse.

II

In the seminal case of In re Cady, Roberts & Co., 40 S.E.C. 907 (1961), the SEC recognized that the common law in some jurisdictions imposes

---

8. Justice Blackmun's dissenting opinion minimizes the role Dirks played in making public the Equity Funding fraud. ... The dissent would rewrite the history of Dirks' extensive investigative efforts. See, e.g., 21 S.E.C., at 1412 ("It is clear that Dirks played an important role in bringing [Equity Funding's] massive fraud to light, and it is also true that he reported the fraud allegation to [Equity Funding's] auditors and sought to have the information published in the Wall Street Journal."); 681 F.2d, at 829 (Wright, J.) ("Largely thanks to Dirks one of the most infamous frauds in recent mem-

ory was uncovered and exposed, while the record shows that the SEC repeatedly missed opportunities to investigate Equity Funding.").

9. Section 15 of the Securities Exchange Act, 15 U.S.C. § 78o(b)(4)(E), provides that the SEC may impose certain sanctions, including censure, on any person associated with a registered broker-dealer who has "willfully aided [or] abetted" any violation of the federal securities laws. See 15 U.S.C. § 78ff(a) (providing criminal penalties).

on "corporate 'insiders,' particularly officers, directors, or controlling stockholders" an "affirmative duty of disclosure ... when dealing in securities." Id., at 911, and n. 13.[10] The SEC found that not only did breach of this common-law duty also establish the elements of a Rule 10b—5 violation,[11] but that individuals other than corporate insiders could be obligated either to disclose material nonpublic information[12] before trading or to abstain from trading altogether. Id., at 912. In *Chiarella*, we accepted the two elements set out in *Cady, Roberts* for establishing a Rule 10b–5 violation: "(i) the existence of a relationship affording access to inside information intended to be available only for a corporate purpose, and (ii) the unfairness of allowing a corporate insider to take advantage of that information by trading without disclosure." 445 U.S., at 227, 100 S.Ct. at 1114. In examining whether Chiarella had an obligation to disclose or abstain, the Court found that there is no general duty to disclose before trading on material nonpublic information,[13] and held that "a duty to disclose under § 10(b) does not arise from the mere possession of nonpublic market information." Id., at 235, 100 S.Ct., at 1118. Such a duty arises rather from the existence of a fiduciary relationship. See id., at 227–235, 100 S.Ct., at 1114–1118.

Not "all breaches of fiduciary duty in connection with a securities transaction," however, come within the ambit of Rule 10b–5. Santa Fe Industries, Inc. v. Green, 430 U.S. 462, 472, 97 S.Ct. 1292, 1300, 51 L.Ed.2d 480 (1977). There must also be "manipulation or deception." Id., at 473, 97 S.Ct., at 1300. In an inside-trading case this fraud derives from the "inherent unfairness involved where one takes advantage" of "information intended to be available only for a corporate purpose and not for the personal benefit of anyone." In re Merrill Lynch, Pierce, Fenner & Smith, Inc., 43 S.E.C. 933, 936 (1968). Thus, an insider will be liable under Rule 10b–5 for inside trading only where he fails to disclose

---

10. The duty that insiders owe to the corporation's shareholders not to trade on inside information differs from the common-law duty that officers and directors also have to the corporation itself not to mismanage corporate assets, of which confidential information is one. See 3 Fletcher Cyclopedia of the Laws of Private Corporations §§ 848, 900 (1975 ed. and Supp. 1982); 3A Fletcher §§ 1168.1, 1168.2. In holding that breaches of this duty to shareholders violated the Securities Exchange Act, the *Cady, Roberts* Commission recognized, and we agree, that "[a] significant purpose of the Exchange Act was to eliminate the idea that use of inside information for personal advantage was a normal emolument of corporate office." See 40 S.E.C., at 912, n. 15.

11. Rule 10b–5 is generally the most inclusive of the three provisions on which the SEC rested its decision in this case, and we will refer to it when we note the statutory basis for the SEC's inside-trading rules.

12. The SEC views the disclosure duty as requiring more than disclosure to purchasers or sellers: "Proper and adequate disclosure of significant corporate developments can only be effected by a public release through the appropriate public media, designed to achieve a broad dissemination to the investing public generally and without favoring any special person or group." In re Faberge, Inc., 45 S.E.C. 249, 256 (1973).

13. See 445 U.S., at 233, 100 S.Ct., at 1117; id., at 237, 100 S.Ct., at 1119 (Stevens, J., concurring); id., at 238–239, 100 S.Ct., at 1119–1120 (Brennan, J., concurring in the judgment); id., at 239–240, 100 S.Ct., at 1120 (Burger, C.J., dissenting). Cf. id., at 252, n. 2, 100 S.Ct., at 1126, n. 2 (Blackmun, J., dissenting) (recognizing that there is no obligation to disclose material nonpublic information obtained through the exercise of "diligence or acumen" and "honest means," as opposed to "stealth").

material nonpublic information before trading on it and thus makes "secret profits." *Cady, Roberts*, 40 S.E.C., at 916, n. 31.

III

We were explicit in *Chiarella* in saying that there can be no duty to disclose where the person who has traded on inside information "was not [the corporation's] agent, . . . was not a fiduciary, [or] was not a person in whom the sellers [of the securities] had placed their trust and confidence." 445 U.S., at 232, 100 S.Ct., at 1116. Not to require such a fiduciary relationship, we recognized, would "depar[t] radically from the established doctrine that duty arises from a specific relationship between two parties" and would amount to "recognizing a general duty between all participants in market transactions to forgo actions based on material, nonpublic information." Id., at 232, 233, 100 S.Ct., at 1116, 1117. This requirement of a specific relationship between the shareholders and the individual trading on inside information has created analytical difficulties for the SEC and courts in policing tippees who trade on inside information. Unlike insiders who have independent fiduciary duties to both the corporation and its shareholders, the typical tippee has no such relationships.[14] In view of this absence, it has been unclear how a tippee acquires the *Cady, Roberts* duty to refrain from trading on inside information.

A

The SEC's position, as stated in its opinion in this case, is that a tippee "inherits" the *Cady, Roberts* obligation to shareholders whenever he receives inside information from an insider:

"In tipping potential traders, Dirks breached a duty which he had assumed as a result of knowingly receiving confidential information from [Equity Funding] insiders. Tippees such as Dirks who receive non-public material information from insiders become 'subject to the same duty as [the] insiders.' Shapiro v. Merrill Lynch, Pierce, Fenner

14. Under certain circumstances, such as where corporate information is revealed legitimately to an underwriter, accountant, lawyer, or consultant working for the corporation, these outsiders may become fiduciaries of the shareholders. The basis for recognizing this fiduciary duty is not simply that such persons acquired nonpublic corporate information, but rather that they have entered into a special confidential relationship in the conduct of the business of the enterprise and are given access to information solely for corporate purposes. See SEC v. Monarch Fund, 608 F.2d 938, 942 (CA2 1979); In re Investors Management Co., 44 S.E.C. 633, 645 (1971); In re Van Alystne, Noel & Co., 43 S.E.C. 1080, 1084–

1085 (1969); In re Merrill Lynch, Pierce, Fenner & Smith, Inc., 43 S.E.C. 933, 937 (1968); Cady, Roberts, 40 S.E.C., at 912. When such a person breaches his fiduciary relationship, he may be treated more properly as a tipper than a tippee. See Shapiro v. Merrill Lynch, Pierce, Fenner & Smith, Inc., 495 F.2d 228, 237 (CA2 1974) (investment banker had access to material information when working on a proposed public offering for the corporation). For such a duty to be imposed, however, the corporation must expect the outsider to keep the disclosed nonpublic information confidential, and the relationship at least must imply such a duty.

& Smith, Inc. [495 F.2d 228, 237 (CA2 1974) (quoting Ross v. Licht, 263 F.Supp. 395, 410 (SDNY 1967))]. Such a tippee breaches the fiduciary duty which he assumes from the insider when the tippee knowingly transmits the information to someone who will probably trade on the basis hereof.... Presumably, Dirks' informants were entitled to disclose the [Equity Funding] fraud in order to bring it to light and its perpetrators to justice. However, Dirks—standing in their shoes—committed a breach of the fiduciary duty which he had assumed in dealing with them, when he passed the information on to traders." 21 S.E.C. Docket, at 1410, n. 42.

This view differs little from the view that we rejected as inconsistent with congressional intent in *Chiarella*. In that case, the Court of Appeals agreed with the SEC and affirmed Chiarella's conviction, holding that " '[a]nyone —corporate insider or not—who regularly receives material nonpublic information may not use that information to trade in securities without incurring an affirmative duty to disclose.' " United States v. Chiarella, 588 F.2d 1358, 1365 (CA2 1978) (emphasis in original). Here, the SEC maintains that anyone who knowingly receives nonpublic material information from an insider has a fiduciary duty to disclose before trading.[15]

In effect, the SEC's theory of tippee liability in both cases appears rooted in the idea that the antifraud provisions required equal information among all traders. This conflicts with the principle set forth in *Chiarella* that only some persons, under some circumstances, will be barred from trading while in possession of material nonpublic information.[16] Judge Wright correctly read our opinion in *Chiarella* as repudiat-

---

15. Apparently, the SEC believes this case differs from *Chiarella* in that Dirks' receipt of inside information from Secrist, an insider, carried Secrist's duties with it, while Chiarella received the information without the direct involvement of an insider and thus inherited no duty to disclose or abstain. The SEC fails to explain, however, why the receipt of nonpublic information from an insider automatically carries with it the fiduciary duty of the insider. As we emphasized in *Chiarella*, mere possession of nonpublic information does not give rise to a duty to disclose or abstain; only a specific relationship does that. And we do not believe that the mere receipt of information from an insider creates such a special relationship between the tippee and the corporation's shareholders.

Apparently recognizing the weakness of its argument in light of *Chiarella*, the SEC attempts to distinguish that case factually as involving not "inside" information, but rather "market" information, i.e., "information generated within the company relating to its assets or earnings." Brief for Respondent 23. This Court drew no such distinction in *Chiarella* and, as The Chief Jus-

tice noted, "[i]t is clear that § 10(b) and Rule 10b–5 by their terms and by their history make no such distinction." 445 U.S., at 241, n. 1 (dissenting opinion). See ALI Fed.Sec. Code § 1603, Comment (2)(j) (Proposed Official Draft 1978).

16. In *Chiarella*, we noted that formulation of an absolute equal information rule "should not be undertaken absent some explicit evidence of congressional intent." 445 U.S., at 233, 100 S.Ct., at 1117. Rather than adopting such a radical view of securities trading, Congress has expressly exempted many market professionals from the general statutory prohibition set forth in § 11(a)(1) of the Securities Exchange Act, 15 U.S.C. § 78k(a)(1), against members of a national securities exchange trading for their own account. See id., at 233, n. 16, 100 S.Ct., at 1117, n. 16. We observed in *Chiarella* that "[t]he exception is based upon Congress' recognition that [market professionals] contribute to a fair and orderly marketplace at the same time they exploit the informational advantage that comes from their possession of [nonpublic information]." Ibid.

ing any notion that all traders must enjoy equal information before trading: "[T]he 'information' theory is rejected. Because the disclose-or-refrain duty is extraordinary, it attaches only when a party has legal obligations other than a mere duty to comply with the general antifraud proscriptions in the federal securities laws." 220 U.S.App.D.C., at 322, 681 F.2d at 837. See *Chiarella*, 445 U.S., at 235, n. 20, 100 S.Ct., at 1118, n. 20. We reaffirm today that "[a] duty [to disclose] arises from the relationship between parties . . . and not merely from one's ability to acquire information because of his position in the market." 445 U.S., at 232–233, n. 14, 100 S.Ct., at 1116–1117, n. 14.

Imposing a duty to disclose or abstain solely because a person knowingly receives material nonpublic information from an insider and trades on it could have an inhibiting influence on the role of market analysts, which the SEC itself recognizes is necessary to the preservation of a healthy market.[17] It is commonplace for analysts to "ferret out and analyze information," 21 S.E.C., at 1406,[18] and this often is done by meeting with and questioning corporate officers and others who are insiders. And information that the analysts obtain normally may be the basis for judgments as to the market worth of a corporation's securities. The analyst's judgment in this respect is made available in market letters or otherwise to clients of the firm. It is the nature of this type of information, and indeed of the markets themselves, that such information cannot be made simultaneously available to all of the corporation's stockholders or the public generally.

B

The conclusion that recipients of inside information do not invariably acquire a duty to disclose or abstain does not mean that such tippees

17. The SEC expressly recognized that "[t]he value to the entire market of [analysts'] efforts cannot be gainsaid; market efficiency in pricing is significantly enhanced by [their] initiatives to ferret out and analyze information, and thus the analyst's work redounds to the benefit of all investors." 21 S.E.C., at 1406. The SEC asserts that analysts remain free to obtain from management corporate information for purposes of "filling in the 'interstices in analysis'. . . ." Brief for Respondent 42 (quoting *Investors Management Co.*, 44 S.E.C., at 646). But this rule is inherently imprecise, and imprecision prevents parties from ordering their actions in accord with legal requirements. Unless the parties have some guidance as to where the line is between permissible and impermissible disclosures and uses, neither corporate insiders nor analysts can be sure when the line is crossed. Cf. *Adler v. Klawans*, 267 F.2d 840, 845 (CA2 1959) (Burger, J., sitting by designation.)

18. On its facts, this case is the unusual one. Dirks is an analyst in a broker-dealer firm, and he did interview management in the course of his investigation. He uncovered, however, startling information that required no analysis or exercise of judgment as to its market relevance. Nonetheless, the principle at issue here extends beyond these facts. The SEC's rule—applicable without regard to any breach by an insider—could have serious ramifications on reporting by analysts of investment views.

Despite the unusualness of Dirks' "find," the central role that he played in uncovering the fraud at Equity Funding, and that analysts in general can play in revealing information that corporations may have reason to withhold from the public, is an important one. Dirks' careful investigation brought to light a massive fraud at the corporation. And until the Equity Funding fraud was exposed, the information in the trading market was grossly inaccurate. But for Dirks' efforts, the fraud might well have gone undetected longer. See n. 8, supra.

always are free to trade on the information. The need for a ban on some tippee trading is clear. Not only are insiders forbidden by their fiduciary relationship from personally using undisclosed corporate information to their advantage, but they may not give such information to an outsider for the same improper purpose of exploiting the information for their personal gain. See 15 U.S.C. § 78t(b) (making it unlawful to do indirectly "by means of any other person" any act made unlawful by the federal securities laws). Similarly, the transactions of those who knowingly participate with the fiduciary in such a breach are "as forbidden" as transactions "on behalf of the trustee himself." Mosser v. Darrow, 341 U.S. 267, 272, 71 S.Ct. 680, 683, 95 L.Ed. 927 (1951). See Jackson v. Smith, 254 U.S. 586, 589, 41 S.Ct. 200, 202, 65 L.Ed. 418 (1921); Jackson v. Ludeling, 88 U.S. 616, 631–632, 22 L.Ed. 492 (1874). As the Court explained in *Mosser*, a contrary rule "would open up opportunities for devious dealings in the name of the others that the trustee could not conduct in his own." 341 U.S., at 271, 71 S.Ct., at 682. See SEC v. Texas Gulf Sulphur Co., 446 F.2d 1301, 1308 (CA2), cert. denied, 404 U.S. 1005, 92 S.Ct. 561, 30 L.Ed.2d 558 (1971). Thus, the tippee's duty to disclose or abstain is derivative from that of the insider's duty. See Tr. of Oral Arg. 38. Cf. *Chiarella*, 445 U.S.,at 246, n. 1, 100 S.Ct., at 1122, n. 1 (Blackmun, J., dissenting). As we noted in *Chiarella*, "[t]he tippee's obligation has been viewed as arising from his role as a participant after the fact in the insider's breach of a fiduciary duty." 445 U.S., at 230, n. 12, 100 S.Ct., at 1115, n. 12.

Thus, some tippees must assume an insider's duty to the shareholders not because they receive inside information, but rather because it has been made available to them *improperly*.[19] And for Rule 10b–5 purposes, the insider's disclosure is improper only where it would violate his *Cady, Roberts* duty. Thus, a tippee assumes a fiduciary duty to the shareholders of a corporation not to trade on material nonpublic information only when the insider has breached his fiduciary duty to the shareholders by disclosing the information to the tippee and the tippee knows or should know that there has been a breach.[20] As Commissioner

19. The SEC itself has recognized that tippee liability properly is imposed only in circumstances where the tippee knows, or has reason to know, that the insider has disclosed improperly inside corporate information. In *Investors Management Co.*, supra, the SEC stated that one element of tippee liability is that the tippee knew or had reason to know "that [the information] was non-public and had been obtained *improperly* by selective revelation or otherwise." 44 S.E.C., at 641 (emphasis added). Commissioner Smith read this test to mean that a tippee can be held liable only if he received information in breach of an insider's duty not to disclose it. Id., at 650 (concurring in the result).

20. Professor Loss has linked tippee liability to the concept in the law of restitution that " '[w]here a fiduciary in violation of his duty to the beneficiary communicates confidential information to a third person, the third person, if he had notice of the violation of duty, holds upon a constructive trust for the beneficiary any profit which he makes through the use of such information.' " 3 L. Loss, Securities Regulation 1451 (2d ed. 1961) (quoting Restatement of Restitution § 201(2) (1937)). Other authorities likewise have expressed the view that tippee liability exists only where there has been a breach of trust by an insider of which the tippee had knowledge. See, e.g., Ross v. Licht, 263 F.Supp. 395, 410 (SDNY 1967); A. Jacobs, The Impact of Rule 10b–5,

Smith perceptively observed in *Investors Management Co.*: "[T]ippee responsibility must be related back to insider responsibility by a necessary finding that the tippee knew the information was given to him in breach of a duty by a person having a special relationship to the issuer not to disclose the information ...." 44 S.E.C., at 651 (concurring in the result). Tipping thus properly is viewed only as a means of indirectly violating the *Cady, Roberts* disclose-or-abstain rule.[21]

C

In determining whether a tippee is under an obligation to disclose or abstain, it thus is necessary to determine whether the insider's "tip" constituted a breach of the insider's fiduciary duty. All disclosures of confidential corporate information are not inconsistent with the duty insiders owe to shareholders. In contrast to the extraordinary facts of this case, the more typical situation in which there will be a question whether disclosure violates the insider's *Cady, Roberts* duty is when insiders disclose information to analysts. See n. 16, supra. In some situations, the insider will act consistently with his fiduciary duty to shareholders, and yet release of the information may affect the market. For example, it may not be clear—either to the corporate insider or to the recipient analyst—whether the information will be viewed as material nonpublic information. Corporate officials may mistakenly think the information already has been disclosed or that it is not material enough to affect the market. Whether disclosure is a breach of duty therefore depends in large part on the purpose of the disclosure. This standard

§ 167, at 7–4 (1975) ("[T]he better view is that a tipper must know or have reason to know the information is nonpublic and was improperly obtained."); Fleischer, Mundheim & Murphy, An Initial Inquiry Into the Responsibility to Disclose Market Information, 121 U.Pa.L.Rev. 798, 818, n. 76 (1973) ("The extension of rule 10b–5 restrictions to tippees of corporate insiders can best be justified on the theory that they are participating in the insider's breach of his fiduciary duty."). Cf. Restatement (Second) of Agency § 312, comment c (1958) ("A person who, with notice that an agent is thereby violating his duty to his principal, receives confidential information from the agent, may be [deemed] ... a constructive trustee.").

21. We do not suggest that knowingly trading on inside information is ever "socially desirable or even that it is devoid of moral considerations." Dooley, Enforcement of Insider Trading Restrictions, 66 Va.L.Rev. 1, 55 (1980). Nor do we imply an absence of responsibility to disclose promptly indications of illegal actions by a corporation to the proper authorities—typically the SEC and exchange authorities in cases involving securities. Depending on the circumstances, and even where permitted by law, one's trading of material nonpublic information is behavior that may fall below ethical standards of conduct. But in a statutory area of the law such as securities regulation, where legal principles of general application must be applied, there may be "significant distinctions between actual legal obligations and ethical ideals." SEC, Report of the Special Study of Securities Markets, H. R. Doc. No. 95, 88th Cong., 1st Sess., pt. 1, pp. 237–238 (1963). The SEC recognizes this. At oral argument, the following exchange took place:

"Question: So, it would not have satisfied his obligation under the law to go to the SEC first?

"[SEC's counsel]: That is correct. That an insider has to observe what has come to be known as the abstain or disclosure rule. Either the information has to be disclosed to the market if it is inside information ... or the insider must abstain." Tr. of Oral Arg. 27.

Thus, it is clear that Rule 10b–5 does not impose any obligation simply to tell the SEC about the fraud before trading.

was identified by the SEC itself in *Cady, Roberts*: a purpose of the securities laws was to eliminate " use of inside information for personal advantage." 40 S.E.C., at 912, n. 15. See n. 10, supra. Thus, the test is whether the insider personally will benefit, directly or indirectly, from his disclosure. Absent some personal gain, there has been no breach of duty to stockholders. And absent a breach by the insider, there is no derivative breach.[22] As Commissioner Smith stated in *Investors Management Co.* "It is important in this type of case to focus on policing insiders and what they do ... rather than on policing information *per se* and its possession. ..." 44 S.E.C., at 648 (concurring in the result).

The SEC argues that, if inside-trading liability does not exist when the information is transmitted for a proper purpose but is used for trading, it would be a rare situation when the parties could not fabricate some ostensibly legitimate business justification for transmitting the information. We think the SEC is unduly concerned. In determining whether the insider's purpose in making a particular disclosure is fraudulent, the SEC and the courts are not required to read the parties' minds. Scienter in some cases is relevant in determining whether the tipper has violated his *Cady, Roberts* duty.[23] But to determine whether the disclosure itself "deceive[s], manipulate[s], or defraud[s]" shareholders, Aaron v. SEC, 446 U.S. 680, 686, 100 S.Ct. 1945, 1950, 64 L.Ed.2d 611 (1980), the initial inquiry is whether there has been a breach of duty by the insider. This requires courts to focus on objective criteria, i.e., whether the insider receives a direct or indirect personal benefit from the disclosure, such as a pecuniary gain or a reputational benefit that will translate into future earnings. Cf. 40 S.E.C., at 912, n. 15; Brudney, Insiders, Outsid-

---

22. An example of a case turning on the court's determination that the disclosure did not impose any fiduciary duties on the recipient of the inside information is Walton v. Morgan Stanley & Co., 623 F.2d 796 (CA2 1980). There, the defendant investment banking firm, representing one of its own corporate clients, investigated another corporation that was a possible target of a takeover bid by its client. In the course of negotiations the investment banking firm was given, on a confidential basis, unpublished material information. Subsequently, after the proposed takeover was abandoned, the firm was charged with relying on the information when it traded in the target corporation's stock. For purposes of the decision, it was assumed that the firm knew the information was confidential, but that it had been received in arm's-length negotiations. See id., at 798. In the absence of any fiduciary relationship, the Court of Appeals found no basis for imposing tippee liability on the investment firm. See id., at 799.

23. *Scienter*—"a mental state embracing intent to deceive, manipulate, or defraud," Ernst & Ernst v. Hochfelder, 425 U.S. 185, 193, n. 12, 96 S.Ct. 1375, 1380, n.

12, 47 L.Ed.2d 668 (1976)—is an independent element of a Rule 10b–5 violation. See Aaron v.SEC, 446 U.S. 680, 695, 100 S.Ct. 1945, 1954, 64 L.Ed.2d 611 (1980). Contrary to the dissent's suggestion, see post, at p. 7, n. 10, motivation is not irrelevant to the issue of *scienter*. It is not enough that an insider's conduct results in harm to investors; rather, a violation may be found only where there is "intentional or willful conduct designed to deceive or defraud investors by controlling or artificially affecting the price of securities." *Ernst & Ernst v. Hochfelder*, supra, at 199, 100 S.Ct., at 1383. The issue in this case, however, is not whether Secrist or Dirks acted with *scienter*, but rather whether there was any deceptive or fraudulent conduct at all, i.e., whether Secrist's disclosure constituted a breach of his fiduciary duty and thereby caused injury to shareholders. See n. 27, infra. Only if there was such a breach did Dirks, a tippee, acquire a fiduciary duty to disclose or abstain. [References in the opinion to internal page numbers are based on the advance slip opinion, which was the only opinion available when this Supplement went to press.—Ed.]

ers, and Informational Advantages Under the Federal Securities Laws, 93 Harv.L.Rev. 324, 348 (1979) ("The theory ...is that the insider, by giving the information out selectively, is in effect selling the information to its recipient for cash, reciprocal information, or other things of value for himself ..."). There are objective facts and circumstances that often justify such an inference. For example, there may be a relationship between the insider and the recipient that suggests a *quid pro quo* from the latter, or an intention to benefit the particular recipient. The elements of fiduciary duty and exploitation of nonpublic information also exist when an insider makes a gift of confidential information to a trading relative or friend. The tip and trade resemble trading by the insider himself followed by a gift of the profits to the recipient.

Determining whether an insider personally benefits from a particular disclosure, a question of fact, will not always be easy for courts. But it is essential, we think, to have a guiding principle for those whose daily activities must be limited and instructed by the SEC's inside-trading rules, and we believe that there must be a breach of the insider's fiduciary duty before the tippee inherits the duty to disclose or abstain. In contrast, the rule adopted by the SEC in this case would have no limiting principle.[24]

IV

Under the inside-trading and tipping rules set forth above, we find that there was no actionable violation by Dirks.[25] It is undisputed that Dirks himself was a stranger to Equity Funding, with no pre-existing fiduciary duty to its shareholders.[26] He took no action, directly or

---

24. Without legal limitations, market participants are forced to rely on the reasonableness of the SEC's litigation strategy, but that can be hazardous, as the facts of this case make plain. Following the SEC's filing of the *Texas Gulf Sulphur* action, Commissioner (and later Chairman) Budge spoke of the various implications of applying Rule 10b–5 in inside-trading cases:

"Turning to the realm of possible defendants in the present and potential civil actions, the Commission certainly does not contemplate suing every person who may have come across inside information. In the Texas Gulf action neither tippees nor persons in the vast rank and file of employees have been named as defendants. In my view, the Commission in future cases normally should not join rank and file employees or persons outside the company *such as an analyst or reporter* who learns of inside information." Speech of Hamer Budge to the New York Regional Group of the American Society of Corporate Secretaries, Inc. (Nov. 18, 1965) (emphasis added), reprinted in Budge, The Texas Gulf Sulphur Case—

What It Is and What It Isn't, Corp. Secretary No. 127, at 6 (Dec. 17, 1965).

25. Dirks contends that he was not a "tippee" because the information he received constituted unverified allegations of fraud that were denied by management and were not "material facts" under the securities laws that required disclosure before trading. He also argues that the information he received was not truly "inside" information, i.e., intended for a confidential corporate purpose, but was merely evidence of a crime. The Solicitor General agrees. See Brief for United States as *Amicus Curiae* 22. We need not decide, however, whether the information constituted "material facts," or whether information concerning corporate crime is properly characterized as "inside information." For purposes of deciding this case, we assume the correctness of the SEC's findings, accepted by the Court of Appeals, that petitioner was a tippee of material inside information.

26. Judge Wright found that Dirks acquired a fiduciary duty by virtue of his position as an employee of a broker-dealer.

indirectly, that induced the shareholders or officers of Equity Funding to repose trust or confidence in him. There was no expectation by Dirks' sources that he would keep their information in confidence. Nor did Dirks misappropriate or illegally obtain the information about Equity Funding. Unless the insiders breached their *Cady, Roberts* duty to shareholders in disclosing the nonpublic information to Dirks, he breached no duty when he passed it on to investors as well as to the Wall Street Journal.

It is clear that neither Secrist nor the other Equity Funding employees violated their *Cady, Roberts* duty to the corporation's shareholders by providing information to Dirks.[27] The tippers received no monetary

See 220 U.S.App.D.C., at 325–327, 681 F.2d, at 840–842. The SEC, however, did not consider Judge Wright's novel theory in its decision, nor did it present that theory to the Court of Appeals. The SEC also has not argued Judge Wright's theory in this Court. See Brief for Respondent 21, n. 27. The merits of such a duty are therefore not before the Court. See SEC v. Chenery Corp., 332 U.S. 194, 196–197, 67 S.Ct. 1575, 1577, 91 L.Ed. 1995 (1947).

27. In this Court, the SEC appears to contend that an insider invariably violates a fiduciary duty to the corporation's shareholders by transmitting nonpublic corporate information to an outsider when he has reason to believe that the outsider may use it to the disadvantage of the shareholders. "Thus, regardless of any ultimate motive to bring to public attention the derelictions at Equity Funding, Secrist breached his duty to Equity Funding shareholders." Brief for Respondent 31. This perceived "duty" differs markedly from the one that the SEC identified in *Cady, Roberts* and that has been the basis for federal tippee-trading rules to date. In fact, the SEC did not charge Secrist with any wrongdoing, and we do not understand the SEC to have relied on any theory of a breach of duty by Secrist in finding that Dirks breached his duty to Equity Funding's shareholders. See App. 250 (decision of administrative law judge) ("One who knows himself to be a beneficiary of non-public, selectively disclosed inside information must fully disclose or refrain from trading."); SEC's Reply to Notice of Supplemental Authority before the SEC 4 ("If Secrist was acting properly, Dirks inherited a duty to [Equity Funding]'s shareholders to refrain from improper private use of the information."); Brief on behalf of the SEC in the Court of Appeals, at 47–50; id., at 51 ("[K]nowing possession of inside information by any person imposes a duty to abstain or disclose."); id., at 52–54; id., at 55 ("[T]his obligation arises not from the manner in which such information

is acquired. ..."); 220 U.S.App.D.C., at 322–323, 681 F.2d, at 838 (Wright, J.).

The dissent argues that "Secrist violated his duty to Equity Funding shareholders by transmitting material nonpublic information to Dirks with the intention that Dirks would cause his clients to trade on that information." Post, at 12. By perceiving a breach of fiduciary duty whenever inside information is intentionally disclosed to securities traders, the dissenting opinion effectively would achieve the same result as the SEC's theory below, i.e., mere possession of inside information while trading would be viewed as a Rule 10b–5 violation. But *Chiarella* made it explicitly clear there is no general duty to forgo market transactions "based on material, nonpublic information." 445 U.S., at 233, 100 S.Ct., at 1117. Such a duty would "depar[t] radically from the established doctrine that duty arises from a specific relationship between two parties." Ibid. See p. 7, supra.

Moreover, to constitute a violation of Rule 10b–5, there must be fraud. See Ernst & Ernst v. Hochfelder, 425 U.S. 185, 199, 96 S.Ct. 1375, 1383, 47 L.Ed.2d 668 (1976) (statutory words "manipulative," "device," and "contrivance ... connot[e] intentional or willful conduct designed to *deceive or defraud* investors by controlling or artificially affecting the price of securities") (emphasis added). There is no evidence that Secrist's disclosure was intended to or did in fact "deceive or defraud" anyone. Secrist certainly intended to convey relevant information that management was unlawfully concealing, and—so far as the record shows—he believed that persuading Dirks to investigate was the best way to disclose the fraud. Other efforts had proved fruitless. Under any objective standard, Secrist received no direct or indirect personal benefit from the disclosure.

The dissenting opinion focuses on shareholder "losses," "injury," and "damages," but in many cases there may be no clear or personal benefit for revealing Equity Funding's secrets, nor was their purpose to make a gift of valuable information to Dirks. As the facts of this case clearly indicate, the tippers were motivated by a desire to expose the fraud. See supra, at 1–2. In the absence of a breach of duty to shareholders by the insiders, there was no derivative breach by Dirks. See n. 20, supra. Dirks therefore could not have been "a participant after the fact in [an] insider's breach of a fiduciary duty." *Chiarella*, 445 U.S., at 230, n. 12, 100 S.Ct., at 1115, n. 12.

V

We conclude that Dirks, in the circumstances of this case, had no duty to abstain from use of the inside information that he obtained. The judgment of the Court of Appeals therefore is reversed.

JUSTICE BLACKMUN, with whom JUSTICE BRENNAN and JUSTICE MARSHALL join, dissenting.

The Court today takes still another step to limit the protections provided investors by § 10(b) of the Securities Exchange Act of 1934.[1] See Chiarella v. United States, 445 U.S. 222, 246, 100 S.Ct. 1108, 1123, 63 L.Ed.2d 348 (1980) (dissenting opinion). The device employed in this case engrafts a special motivational requirement on the fiduciary duty doctrine. This innovation excuses a knowing and intentional violation of an insider's duty to shareholders if the insider does not act from a motive of personal gain. Even on the extraordinary facts of this case, such an innovation is not justified.

I

As the Court recognizes, ... the facts here are unusual. After a meeting with Ronald Secrist, a former Equity Funding employee, on

causal connection between inside trading and outsiders' losses. In one sense, as market values fluctuate and investors act on inevitably incomplete or incorrect information, there always are winners and losers; but those who have "lost" have not necessarily been defrauded. On the other hand, inside trading for personal gain is fraudulent, and is a violation of the federal securities laws. See Dooley, supra, at 39–41, 70. Thus, there is little legal significance to the dissent's argument that Secrist and Dirks created new "victims" by disclosing the information to persons who traded. In fact, they prevented the fraud from continuing and victimizing many more investors.

1. See, e.g., Blue Chip Stamps v. Manor Drug Stores, 421 U.S. 723, 95 S.Ct. 1917, 44 L.Ed.2d 539 (1975); Ernst & Ernst v. Hochfelder, 425 U.S. 185, 96 S.Ct. 1375, 47 L.Ed.2d 668 (1976); Piper v. Chris-Craft Industries, Inc., 430 U.S. 1, 97 S.Ct. 926, 51 L.Ed.2d 124 (1977); Chiarella v. United States, 445 U.S. 222, 100 S.Ct. 1108, 63 L.Ed.2d 348 (1980); Aaron v. SEC, 446 U.S. 680, 100 S.Ct. 1945, 64 L.Ed.2d 611 (1980). This trend frustrates the congressional intent that the securities laws be interpreted flexibly to protect investors, see Affiliated Ute Citizens v. United States, 406 U.S. 128, 151, 92 S.Ct. 1456, 1471, 31 L.Ed.2d 741 (1972); SEC v. Capital Gains Research Bureau, Inc., 375 U.S. 180, 186, 84 S.Ct. 275, 279, 11 L.Ed.2d 237 (1963), and to regulate deceptive practices "detrimental to the interests of the investor," S.Rep. No. 792, 73d Cong., 2 Sess., 18 (1934); see H.R.Rep. No. 1383, 73d Cong., 2d Sess., 10 (1934). Moreover, the Court continues to refuse to accord to SEC administrative decisions the deference it normally gives to an agency's interpretation of its own statute. See, e.g., Blum v. Bacon, 457 U.S. 132, 102 S.Ct. 2355, 72 L.Ed.2d 728 (1982).

March 7, 1973, App. 226, petitioner Raymond Dirks found himself in possession of material nonpublic information of massive fraud within the company.[2] In the Court's words, "[h]e uncovered ... startling information that required no analysis or exercise of judgment as to its market relevance." Ante, at 11, n. 17. In disclosing that information to Dirks, Secrist intended that Dirks would disseminate the information to his clients, those clients would unload their Equity Funding securities on the market, and the price would fall precipitously, thereby triggering a reaction from the authorities. App. 16, 25, 27.

Dirks complied with his informant's wishes. Instead of reporting that information to the Securities and Exchange Commission (SEC or Commission) or to other regulatory agencies, Dirks began to disseminate the information to his clients and undertook his own investigation.[3] One of his first steps was to direct his associates at Delafield Childs to draw up a list of Delafield clients holding Equity Funding securities. On March 12, eight days before Dirks flew to Los Angeles to investigate Secrist's story, he reported the full allegations to Boston Company Institutional Investors, Inc., which on March 15 and 16 sold approximately $1.2 million of Equity securities.[4] See id., at 199. As he gathered more information, he selectively disclosed it to his clients. To those holding Equity Funding securities he gave the "hard" story—all the allegations; others received the "soft" story—a recitation of vague factors that might reflect adversely on Equity Funding's management. See id., at 211, n. 24.

Dirks' attempts to disseminate the information to nonclients were feeble, at best. On March 12, he left a message for Herbert Lawson, the San Francisco bureau chief of The Wall Street Journal. Not until March 19 and 20 did he call Lawson again, and outline the situation. William Blundell, a Journal investigative reporter based in Los Angeles, got in

2. Unknown to Dirks, Secrist also told his story to New York insurance regulators the same day. App. 23. They immediately assured themselves that Equity Funding's New York subsidiary had sufficient assets to cover its outstanding policies and then passed on the information to California regulators who in turn informed Illinois regulators. Illinois investigators, later joined by California officials, conducted a surprise audit to Equity Funding's Illinois subsidiary, id., at 87–88, to find $22 million of the subsidiary's assets missing. On March 30, these authorities seized control of the Illinois subsidiary. Id., at 271.

3. In the same administrative proceeding at issue here, the Administrative Law Judge (ALJ) found that Dirks' clients—five institutional investment advisors—violated § 17(a) of the Securities Act of 1933, 15 U.S.C. § 77q(a), § 10(b) of the Securities Exchange Act of 1934, 15 U.S.C. § 78j(b), and Rule 10b–5, 17 CFR § 240.10b–5, by trading on Dirks' tips. App. 297. All the

clients were censured, except Dreyfus Corporation. The ALJ found that Dreyfus had made significant efforts to disclose the information to Goldman, Sachs, the purchaser of its securities. App. 299, 301. None of Dirks' clients appealed these determinations. App. to Pet. for Cert. B–2, n. 1.

4. The Court's implicit suggestion that Dirks did not gain by this selective dissemination of advice, ante, at 2, n. 2, is inaccurate. The ALJ found that because of Dirks' information, Boston Company Institutional Investors, Inc., directed business to Delafield Childs that generated approximately $25,000 in commissions. App. 199, 204–205. While it is true that the exact economic benefit gained by Delafield Childs due to Dirks' activities is unknowable because of the structure of compensation in the securities market, there can be no doubt that Delafield and Dirks gained both monetary rewards and enhanced reputations for "looking after" their clients.

touch with Dirks about his March 20 telephone call. On March 21, Dirks met with Blundell in Los Angeles. Blundell began his own investigation, relying in part on Dirks' contacts, and on March 23 telephoned Stanley Sporkin, the SEC's Deputy Director of Enforcement. On March 26, the next business day, Sporkin and his staff interviewed Blundell and asked to see Dirks the following morning. Trading was halted by the New York Stock Exchange at about the same time Dirks was talking to Los Angeles SEC personnel. The next day, March 28, the SEC suspended trading in Equity Funding securities. By that time, Dirks' clients had unloaded close to $15 million of Equity Funding stock and the price had plummeted from $26 to $15. The effect of Dirks' selective dissemination of Secrist's information was that Dirks' clients were able to shift the losses that were inevitable due to the Equity Funding fraud from themselves to uninformed market participants.

II

A

No one questions that Secrist himself could not trade on his inside information to the disadvantage of uninformed shareholders and purchasers of Equity Funding securities. See Brief for United States as *Amicus Curiae* 19, n. 12. Unlike the printer in *Chiarella*, Secrist stood in a fiduciary relationship with these shareholders. As the Court states, ante, at 5, corporate insiders had an affirmative duty of disclosure when trading with shareholders of the corporation. See *Chiarella*, 445 U.S., at 227, 100 S.Ct. at 1114. This duty extends as well to purchasers of the corporation's securities. Id., at 227, n. 8, 100 S.Ct., at 1114, n. 8, citing Gratz v. Claughton, 187 F.2d 46, 49 (CA2), cert. denied, 341 U.S. 920, 71 S.Ct. 741, 95 L.Ed. 1353 (1951).

The Court also acknowledges that Secrist could not do by proxy what he was prohibited from doing personally. Ante, at 12; Mosser v. Darrow, 341 U.S. 267, 272, 71 S.Ct. 680, 685, 95 L.Ed. 927 (1951). But this is precisely what Secrist did. Secrist used Dirks to disseminate information to Dirks' clients, who in turn dumped stock on unknowing purchasers Secrist thus intended Dirks to injure the purchasers of Equity Funding securities to whom Secrist had a duty to disclose. Accepting the Court's view of tippee liability,[5] it appears that Dirks' knowledge of this breach makes him liable as a participant in the breach after the fact. Ante, at 12, 19; *Chiarella*, 445 U.S., at 230, n. 12, 100 S.Ct., at 1115, n. 12.

B

The Court holds, however, that Dirks is not liable because Secrist did not violate his duty; according to the Court, this is so because Secrist did

---

5. I interpret the Court's opinion to impose liability on tippees like Dirks when the tippee knows or has reason to know that the information is material and nonpublic and was obtained through a breach of duty by selective revelation or otherwise. See In re Investors Management Co., 44 S.E.C. 633, 641 (1971).

not have the improper purpose of personal gain. Ante, at 15–16, 18–19. In so doing, the Court imposes a new, subjective limitation on the scope of the duty owed by insiders to shareholders. The novelty of this limitation is reflected in the Court's lack of support for it.[6]

The insider's duty is owed directly to the corporation's shareholders.[7] See Langevoort, Insider Trading and the Fiduciary Principle: A Post-*Chiarella* Restatement, 70 Calif.L.Rev. 1, 5 (1982); 3A W. Fletcher, Private Corporations § 1168.2, pp. 288–289 (1975). As *Chiarella* recognized, it is based on the relationship of trust and confidence between the insider and the shareholder. 445 U.S., at 228. That relationship assures the shareholder that the insider may not take actions that will harm him unfairly.[8] The affirmative duty of disclosure protects against this injury. See Pepper v. Litton, 308 U.S. 295, 307, n. 15, 60 S.Ct. 238, 243, n. 15, 84 L.Ed. 281 (1939); Strong v. Rapide, 213 U.S. 419, 431–434, 29 S.Ct. 521, 525, 53 L.Ed. 853 (1909); see also *Chiarella*, 445 U.S., at 228, n. 10, 100 S.Ct., at 1113, n. 10; cf. *Pepper*, 308 U.S., at 307, 60 S.Ct., at 243 (fiduciary obligation to corporation exists for corporation's protection).

C

The fact that the insider himself does not benefit from the breach does not eradicate the shareholder's injury.[9] Cf. Restatement (Second)

---

6. The Court cites only a footnote in a SEC decision and Professor Brudney to support its rule. Ante, at 15–16. The footnote, however, merely identifies one result the securities laws are intended to prevent. It does not define the nature of the duty itself. See n. 9, infra. Professor Brudney's quoted statement appears in the context of his assertion that the duty of insiders to disclose prior to trading with shareholders is in large part a mechanism to correct the information available to noninsiders. Professor Brudney simply recognizes that the most common motive for breaching this duty is personal gain; he does not state, however, that the duty prevents only personal aggrandizement. Insiders, Outsiders, and Informational Advantages Under the Federal Securities Laws, 93 Harv.L.Rev. 322, 345–348 (1979). Surely, the Court does not now adopt Professor Brudney's access-to-information theory, a close cousin to the equality-of-information theory it accuses the SEC of harboring. See ante, at 8–10.

7. The Court correctly distinguishes this duty from the duty of an insider to the corporation not to mismanage corporate affairs or to misappropriate corporate assets. Ante, at 5, n. 9. That duty also can be breached when the insider trades in corporate securities on the basis of inside information. Although a shareholder suing in the name of the corporation can recover for the corporation damages for any injury the insider causes by the breach of this distinct duty, Diamond v. Oreamuno, 24 N.Y.2d 494, 498, 301 N.Y.S.2d 78, 80, 248 N.E.2d 910,

912 (1969); see Thomas v. Roblins Industries, Inc., 520 F.2d 1393, 1397 (CA3 1975), insider trading generally does not injure the corporation itself. See Langevoort, Insider Trading and the Fiduciary Principle: A Post-*Chiarella* Restatement, 70 Calif.L. Rev. 1, 2, n. 5, 28, n. 111 (1982).

8. As it did in *Chiarella*, 445 U.S., at 226–229, 100 S.Ct., at 1113–1115, the Court adopts the *Cady, Roberts* formulation of the duty. Ante, at 5–6.

"Analytically, the obligation rests on two principal elements; first, the existence of a relationship giving access, directly or indirectly, to information intended to be available only for a corporate purpose and not for the personal benefit of anyone, and second, the inherent unfairness involved where a party takes advantage of such information knowing it is unavailable to those with whom he is dealing." In re Cady, Roberts & Co., 40 S.E.C. 907, 912 (1961) (footnote omitted).

The first element—on which *Chiarella*'s holding rests—establishes the type of relationship that must exist between the parties before a duty to disclose is present. The second—not addressed by *Chiarella*—identifies the harm that the duty protects against: the inherent unfairness to the shareholder caused when an insider trades with him on the basis of undisclosed inside information.

9. Without doubt, breaches of the insider's duty occur most often when an insider

of Trusts § 205, Comments c and d (1959) (trustee liable for acts causing diminution of value of trust); 3 A. Scott on Trusts § 205, p. 1665 (1967) (trustee liable for any losses to trust caused by his breach). It makes no difference to the shareholder whether the corporate insider gained or intended to gain personally from the transaction; the shareholder still has lost because of the insider's misuse of nonpublic information. The duty is addressed not to the insider's motives,[10] but to his actions and their consequences on the shareholder. Personal gain is not an element of the breach of this duty.[11]

This conclusion is borne out by the Court's decision in Mosser v. Darrow, 341 U.S. 267, 71 S.Ct. 680, 95 L.Ed. 927 (1951). There, the Court faced an analogous situation: a reorganization trustee engaged two

seeks personal aggrandizement at the expense of shareholders. Because of this, descriptions of the duty to disclose are often coupled with statements that the duty prevents unjust enrichment. See, e.g., In re Cady, Roberts & Co., 40 S.E.C. 907, 912, n. 15 (1961); Langevoort, 70 Calif.L.Rev., at 19. Private gain is certainly a strong motivation for breaching the duty.

It is, however, not an element of the breach of this duty. The reference to personal gain in *Cady, Roberts* for example, is appended to the first element underlying the duty which requires that an insider have a special relationship to corporate information that he cannot appropriate for his own benefit. See n. 8, supra. It does not limit the second element which addresses the injury to the shareholder and is at issue here. See ibid. In fact, *Cady, Roberts* describes the duty more precisely in a later footnote: "In the circumstances, [the insider's] relationship to his customers was such that he would have a duty not to take a position adverse to them, not to take secret profits at their expense, not to misrepresent facts to them, and in general to place their interests ahead of his own." 40 S.E.C., at 916, n. 31. This statement makes clear that enrichment of the insider himself is simply one of the results the duty attempts to prevent.

10. Of course, an insider is not liable in a Rule 10b–5 administrative action unless he has the requisite scienter. Aaron v. SEC, 446 U.S. 680, 691, 100 S.Ct. 1945, 1952, 64 L.Ed.2d 611 (1980). He must know or intend that his conduct violate his duty. Secrist obviously knew and intended that Dirks would cause trading on the inside information and that Equity Funding shareholders would be harmed. The scienter requirement addresses the intent necessary to support liability; it does not address the motives behind the intent.

11. The Court seems concerned that this case bears on insiders' contacts with analysts for valid corporate reasons. Ante, at 10–11. It also fears that insiders may not be able to determine whether the information transmitted is material or nonpublic. Id., at 14–15. When the disclosure is to an investment banker or some other adviser, however, there is normally no breach because the insider does not have scienter: he does not intend that the inside information be used for trading purposes to the disadvantage of shareholders. Moreover, if the insider in good faith does not believe that the information is material or nonpublic, he also lacks the necessary scienter. Ernst & Ernst v. Hochfelder, 425 U.S. 185, 197, 96 S.Ct. 1375, 1382–1383, 47 L.Ed.2d 668 (1976). In fact, the scienter requirement functions in part to protect good faith errors of this type. Id., at 211, n. 31, 96 S.Ct., at 1389, n. 31.

Should the adviser receiving the information use it to trade, it may breach a separate contractual or other duty to the corporation not to misuse the information. Absent such an arrangement, however, the adviser is not barred by Rule 10b–5 from trading on that information if it believes that the insider has not breached any duty to his shareholders. See Walton v. Morgan Stanley & Co., 623 F.2d 796, 798–799 (CA2 1980).

The situation here, of course, is radically different. Ante, at 11, n. 17 (Dirks received information requiring no analysis "as to its market relevance"). Secrist divulged the information for the precise purpose of causing Dirks' clients to trade on it. I fail to understand how imposing liability on Dirks will affect legitimate insider-analyst contacts.

employee-promoters of subsidiaries of the companies being reorganized to provide services that the trustee considered to be essential to the successful operation of the trust. In order to secure their services, the trustee expressly agreed with the employees that they could continue to trade in the securities of the subsidiaries. The employees then turned their inside position into substantial profits at the expense both of the trust and of other holders of the companies' securities.

The Court acknowledged that the trustee neither intended to nor did in actual fact benefit from this arrangement; his motives were completely selfless and devoted to the companies. 341 U.S., at 275, 71 S.Ct., at 684. The Court, nevertheless, found the trustee liable to the estate for the activities of the employees he authorized.[12] The Court described the trustee's defalcation as "a willful and deliberate setting up of an interest in employees adverse to that of the trust." Id., at 272. The breach did not depend on the trustee's personal gain, and his motives in violating his duty were irrelevant; like Secrist, the trustee intended that others would abuse the inside information for their personal gain. Cf. Dodge v. Ford Motor Co., 204 Mich. 459, 506–509, 170 N.W. 668, 684–685 (1919) (Henry Ford's philanthropic motives did not permit him to set Ford Motor Company dividend policies to benefit public at expense of shareholders).

As *Mosser* demonstrates, the breach consists in taking action disadvantageous to the person to whom one owes a duty. In this case, Secrist owed a duty to purchasers of Equity Funding shares. The Court's addition of the bad purpose element to a breach of fiduciary duty claim is flatly inconsistent with the principle of *Mosser*. I do not join this limitation of the scope of an insider's fiduciary duty to shareholders.[13]

III

12. The duty involved in *Mosser* was the duty to the corporation in trust not to misappropriate its assets. This duty, of course, differs from the duty to shareholders involved in this case. See n. 7, supra. Trustees are also subject to a higher standard of care than scienter. 3 A. Scott on Trusts § 201, p. 1650 (1967). In addition, strict trustees are bound not to trade in securities at all. See Langevoort, 70 Calif. L.Rev., at 2, n. 5. These differences, however, are irrelevant to the principle of *Mosser* that the motive of personal gain is not essential to a trustee's liability. In *Mosser*, as here, personal gain accrued to the tippees. See 341 U.S., at 273, 71 S.Ct. at 683.

13. Although I disagree in principle with the Court's requirement of an improper motive, I also note that the requirement adds to the administrative and judicial burden in Rule 10b–5 cases. Assuming the validity of the requirement, the SEC's approach—a violation occurs when the insider knows that the tippee will trade with the information, Brief for SEC 31—can be seen as a presumption that the insider gains from the tipping. The Court now requires a case-by-case determination, thus prohibiting such a presumption.

The Court acknowledges the burdens and difficulties of this approach, but asserts that a principle is needed to guide market participants. Ante, at 16. I fail to see how the Court's rule has any practical advantage over the SEC's presumption. The Court's approach is particularly difficult to administer when the insider is not directly enriched monetarily by the trading he induces. For example, the Court does not explain why the benefit Secrist obtained—the good feeling of exposing a fraud and his enhanced reputation—is any different from the benefit to an insider who gives the information as a gift to a friend or relative. Under the Court's somewhat cynical view, gifts involve personal gain. See ibid. Secrist surely gave Dirks a gift of the commissions Dirks made on the deal in order to induce him to disseminate the information. The distinction between pure altruism and self-interest has puzzled philosophers for centuries; there is no reason to believe that courts and administrative law judges will have an easier time with it.

The improper purpose requirement not only has no basis in law, but it rests implicitly on a policy that I cannot accept. The Court justifies Secrist's and Dirks' action because the general benefit derived from the violation of Secrist's duty to shareholders outweighed the harm caused to those shareholders, see Heller, *Chiarella*, SEC Rule 14e–3 and *Dirks*: "Fairness" versus Economic Theory, 37 Bus. Lawyer 517, 550 (1982); Easterbrook, Insider Trading, Secret Agents, Evidentiary Privileges, and the Production of Information, 1981 S.Ct.Rev. 309, 338—in other words, because the end justified the means. Under this view, the benefit conferred on society by Secrist's and Dirks' activities may be paid for with the losses caused to shareholders trading with Dirks' clients.[14]

Although Secrist's general motive to expose the Equity Funding fraud was laudable, the means he chose were not. Moreover, even assuming that Dirks played a substantial role in exposing the fraud,[15] he and his clients should not profit from the information they obtained from Secrist. Misprision of a felony long has been against public policy. Branzburg v. Hayes, 408 U.S. 665, 696–697, 92 S.Ct. 2646, 2664, 33 L.Ed.2d 626 (1972); see 18 U.S.C. § 4. A person cannot condition his transmission of information of a crime on a financial award. As a citizen, Dirks had at least an ethical obligation to report the information to the proper authorities. See ante, at 13, n. 20. The Court's holding is deficient in policy terms not because it fails to create a legal norm out of that ethical norm, see ibid., but because it actually rewards Dirks for his aiding and abetting.

Dirks and Secrist were under a duty to disclose the information or to refrain from trading on it.[16] I agree that disclosure in this case would have been difficult. Ante, at 13, n. 20. I also recognize that the SEC seemingly has been less than helpful in its view of the nature of the disclosure necessary to satisfy the disclose-or-refrain duty. The Commis-

---

14. This position seems little different from the theory that insider trading should be permitted because it brings relevant information to the market. See H. Manne, Insider Trading and the Stock Market 59–76, 111–146 (1966); Manne, Insider Trading and the Law Professors, 23 Vand.L.Rev 547, 565–576 (1970). The Court also seems to embrace a variant of that extreme theory, which postulates that insider trading causes no harm at all to those who purchase from the insider. Ante, at 18, n. 27. Both the theory and its variant sit at the opposite end of the theoretical spectrum from the much maligned equality-of-information theory, and never have been adopted by Congress or ratified by this Court. See Langevoort, 70 Calif.L.Rev., at 1 and n. 1. The theory rejects the existence of any enforceable principle of fairness between market participants.

15. The Court uncritically accepts Dirks' own view of his role in uncovering the Equi-

ty Funding fraud. See ante, at 11, n. 17. It ignores the fact that Secrist gave the same information at the same time to state insurance regulators, who proceeded to expose massive fraud in a major Equity Funding subsidiary. The fraud surfaced before Dirks ever spoke to the SEC.

16. Secrist did pass on his information to regulatory authorities. His good but misguided motive may be the reason the SEC did not join him in the administrative proceedings against Dirks and his clients. The fact that the SEC, in an exercise of prosecutorial discretion, did not charge Secrist under Rule 10b–5 says nothing about the applicable law. Cf. ante, at 18, n. 25 (suggesting otherwise). Nor does the fact that the SEC took an unsupportable legal position in proceedings below indicate that neither Secrist nor Dirks is liable under any theory. Cf. ibid. (same).

sion tells persons with inside information that they cannot trade on that information unless they disclose; it refuses, however, to tell them how to disclose. See In re Faberge, Inc., 45 S.E.C. 249, 256 (1973) (disclosure requires public release through public media designed to reach investing public generally). This seems to be a less than sensible policy, which it is incumbent on the Commission to correct. The Court, however, has no authority to remedy the problem by opening a hole in the congressionally mandated prohibition on insider trading, thus rewarding such trading.

IV

In my view, Secrist violated his duty to Equity Funding shareholders by transmitting material nonpublic information to Dirks with the intention that Dirks would cause his clients to trade on that information. Dirks, therefore, was under a duty to make the information publicly available or to refrain from actions that he knew would lead to trading. Because Dirks caused his clients to trade, he violated § 10(b) and Rule 10b–5. Any other result is a disservice to this country's attempt to provide fair and efficient capital markets. I dissent.

Chapter VII

SHAREHOLDERS' DERIVATIVE AND
CLASS ACTIONS

SECTION 1. DERIVATIVE ACTIONS

(a) INTRODUCTION

*Insert the following new Model Act provision at p. 886 of the unabridged
edition, and p. 632 of the abridged edition, following N.Y. § 626.*

Model Act § 49. Provisions Relating to Actions by Shareholders

No action shall be brought in this State by a shareholder in the right
of a domestic or foreign corporation unless (1) the plaintiff was a
shareholder of record or the beneficial owner of shares held by a
nominee or the holder of voting trust certificates at the time of the
transaction of which he complains, or his shares or his beneficial ownership of shares held by a nominee or voting trust certificates thereafter
devolved upon him by operation of law from a person who was a holder
of record at such time; (2) the complaint be verified; and (3) the
complaint alleges with particularity the efforts, if any, made by the
plaintiff to obtain the action he desires from the directors and the
reasons for his failure to obtain the action he desires or for not making
the effort. If the corporation undertakes an investigation upon receipt
of a demand by plaintiff for action, or following commencement of suit,
the court may stay any action commenced as the circumstances reasonably require.

In any action hereafter instituted in the right of any domestic or
foreign corporation by the person or persons described in the above
paragraph, the court having jurisdiction, upon final judgment and a
finding that the action was brought without reasonable cause, may
require the plaintiff or plaintiffs to pay to the parties named as defendant the reasonable expenses, including fees of attorneys, incurred by
them in the defense of such action.

An action authorized by this section shall not be discontinued, com-
promised or settled without approval by the court having jurisdiction of
the action. If the court determines that the interest of the shareholders
or of any class thereof will be substantially affected by the discontin-
uance, compromise or settlement, the court may direct that notice, by

117

publication or otherwise, be given to the shareholders or any class thereof whose interests it determines will be so affected.

(n) THE ROLE OF CORPORATE COUNSEL

Insert the following material at p. 997 of the unabridged edition, and p. 710 of the abridged edition, after the Background Note on Garner v. Wolfinbarger:

NOTE ON UPJOHN v. UNITED STATES

In Upjohn Co. v. United States, 449 U.S. 383, 101 S.Ct. 677, 66 L.Ed.2d 584 (1981), Upjohn's independent accountant discovered that an Upjohn subsidiary had made improper payments to secure foreign government business. After consultation among Upjohn's general counsel, outside counsel, and chairman of the board, it was decided that the company would conduct an internal investigation of "questionable payments." As part of this investigation the attorneys prepared a letter containing a questionnaire which was sent to "All Foreign General and Area Managers" over the chairman's signature. Subsequently, the Internal Revenue Service issued a summons demanding production of certain records, including the questionnaires. The Supreme Court held that the questionnaires were protected from disclosure by the attorney-client privilege:

> ... As we stated last term ... "The lawyer-client privilege rests on the need for the advocate and counselor to know all that relates to the client's reasons for seeking representation if the professional mission is to be carried out." ...

> The Court of Appeals ... considered the application of the privilege in the corporate context to present a "different problem," since the client was an inanimate entity and "only the senior management, guiding and integrating the several operations, ... can be said to possess an identity analogous to the corporation as a whole." 600 F.2d, at 1226. The first case to articulate the so-called "control group test" ... reflected a similar conceptual approach:

>> "Keeping in mind that the question is, Is it the corporation which is seeking the lawyer's advice when the asserted privileged communication is made?, the most satisfactory solution, I think, is that if the employee making the communication, of whatever rank he may be, is in a position to control or even to take a substantial part in a decision about any action which the corporation may take upon the advice of the attorney, ... then, in effect, *he is (or personifies) the corporation* when he makes his disclosure to the lawyer and the privilege would apply." (Emphasis supplied.)

Such a view, we think, overlooks the fact that the privilege exists to protect not only the giving of professional advice to those who can act on it but also the giving of information to the lawyer to enable him to give sound and informed advice. ...

In the case of the individual client the provider of information and the person who acts on the lawyer's advice are one and the same. In the corporate context, however, it will frequently be employees beyond the control group as defined by the court below—"officers and agents ... responsible for directing [the company's] actions in response to legal advice"—who will possess the information needed by the corporation's lawyers. ...

The control group test adopted by the court below thus frustrates the very purpose of the privilege by discouraging the communication of relevant information by employees of the client to attorneys seeking to render legal advice to the client corporation. The attorney's advice will also frequently be more significant to noncontrol group members than to those who officially sanction the advice, and the control group test makes it more difficult to convey full and frank legal advice to the employees who will put into effect the client corporation's policy. ...

The narrow scope given the attorney-client privilege by the court below not only makes it difficult for corporate attorneys to formulate sound advice when their client is faced with a specific legal problem but also threatens to limit the valuable efforts of corporate counsel to ensure their client's compliance with the law. ...

The Court of Appeals declined to extend the attorney-client privilege beyond the limits of the control group test for fear that doing so would entail severe burdens on discovery and create a broad "zone of silence" over corporate affairs. Application of the attorney-client privilege to communications such as those involved here, however, puts the adversary in no worse position than if the communications had never taken place. ... Here the Government was free to question the employees who communicated with Thomas and outside counsel.

Chief Justice Burger, concurring, stated:

... Because of the great importance of the issue, in my view the Court should make clear now that, as a general rule, a communication is privileged at least when, as here, an employee or former employee speaks at the direction of the management with an attorney regarding conduct or proposed conduct within the scope of employment. The attorney must be one authorized by the management to inquire into the subject and must be seeking information to assist counsel in performing any of the following functions: (a) evaluating whether the employee's conduct has bound or would bind the corporation; (b) assessing the legal consequences, if any, of that conduct; or (c) formulating appropriate legal responses to actions that have been or may be taken by others with regard to that conduct. ... Other communications between employees and corporate counsel may indeed be privileged   ...   but the need for certainty does not compel us now to prescribe all the details of the privilege in this case.

NOTE ON ABA MODEL RULES OF PROFESSIONAL CONDUCT, RULE 1.13

Over the last several years, the ABA has been reviewing its rules of professional conduct. A proposed revision of the rule governing lawyers for organizations was significantly amended by the ABA's House of Delegates in February 1983, in contemplation of a final vote in August 1983. The rule as proposed by the ABA's Commission on Evaluation of Professional Standards, and as amended by the House of Delegates, is as follows:

RULE 1.13   Organization as the Client

[As Proposed]

(a) A lawyer employed or retained to represent an organization represents the organization as distinct from its directors, officers, employees, members, shareholders or other constituents.

(b) If a lawyer for an organization knows that an officer, employee or other person associated with the organization is engaged in action, intends to act or refuses to act in a manner related to the representation that is a violation of a legal obligation to the organization, or a violation of law which reasonably might be imputed to the organization, and is likely to result in substantial injury to the organization, the lawyer shall proceed as is reasonably necessary in the best interest of the organization. In determining how to proceed, the lawyer shall give due consideration to the seriousness of the violation and its consequences, the scope and nature of the lawyer's representation, the responsibility in the organization and the apparent motivation of the person involved, the policies of the organization concerning such matters and any other relevant considerations. Any measures taken shall be designed to minimize disruption of the organization and the risk of revealing information relating to the representation to persons outside the organization. Such measures may include among others:

(1) asking reconsideration of the matter;

(2) advising that a separate legal opinion on the matter be sought for presentation to appropriate authority in the organization; and

(3) referring the matter to higher authority in the organization, including, if warranted by the seriousness of the matter, referral to the highest authority that can act on behalf of the organization as determined by applicable law.*

---

* It was apparently stated in the debate   that "the highest authority that can act on

(c) When the organization's highest authority insists upon action, or refuses to take action, that is clearly a violation of a legal obligation to the organization, or a violation of law which reasonably might be imputed to the organization, and is likely to result in substantial injury to the organization, the lawyer may take further remedial action that the lawyer reasonably believes to be in the best interest of the organization. Such action may include revealing information otherwise protected by Rule 1.6 only if the lawyer reasonably believes that:

(1) the highest authority in the organization has acted to further the personal or financial interests of members of that authority which are in conflict with the interests of the organization; and

(2) revealing the information is necessary in the best interest of the organization.

(d) In dealing with an organization's directors, officers, employees, members, shareholders or other constituents, a lawyer shall explain the identity of the client when the lawyer believes that such explanation is necessary to avoid misunderstandings on their part.

(e) A lawyer representing an organization may also represent any of its directors, officers, employees, members, shareholders or other constituents, subject to the provisions of Rule 1.7. If the organization's consent to the dual representation is required by Rule 1.7, the consent shall be given by an appropriate official of the organization other than the individual who is to be represented or by the shareholders.

[As Revised]

(a) A lawyer employed or retained by an organization represents the organization, including its directors, officers, employees, members, shareholders or other constituents, as a group, except where the interests of any one or more of the group may be adverse to the organization's interest.

(b) (no change)

(c) If, despite the lawyer's efforts in accordance with paragraph (b), the highest authority that can act on behalf of the organization insists upon action, or a refusal to act, that is clearly a violation of law and is likely to result in substantial injury to the organization, the lawyer may resign in accordance with Rule 1.16.

(d) In dealing with an organization's directors, officers, employees, members, shareholders or other constituents, a lawyer shall

behalf of the organization as determined by applicable law" was not intended as a reference to the body of shareholders. (Footnotes by ed.)

explain the identity of the client when it is apparent that the organization's interests are adverse to those of the constituents with whom the lawyer is dealing.

(e) (no change)

Chapter VIII

FINANCING THE CORPORATION

SECTION 8.   THE PUBLIC ISSUE OF SECURITIES, THE
SECURITIES ACT OF 1933 AND THE
DISCLOSURE REQUIREMENTS

(c) THE SECURITIES ACT OF 1933

*Insert the following new Section, (c)(5), at p. 1194 of the unabridged edition,
and p. 787 of the abridged edition, following Chapter VIII, Section 8(c)(4):*

(5) Integration of the Securities Laws

SECURITIES AND EXCHANGE COMMISSION
SECURITIES ACT RELEASE NO. 6235 (1980)
[REGISTRATION FORMS]

. . .

SUMMARY: The Commission is publishing for comment three proposed new forms to be used to register offerings of securities under the
Securities Act of 1933.   This action represents another major step in the
Commission's efforts to integrate the disclosure systems under the
various federal securities laws and to simplify and streamline the disclosure requirements imposed under those systems.   The three new forms
proposed today would constitute the basic disclosure document format
for most Securities Act registration, with different levels of disclosure
and delivery requirements applicable for different levels of companies
registering offerings of securities.   . . .

I.   Integration

The Commission's integration program involves a comprehensive evaluation of the disclosure policies and procedures underlying the Securities
Act of 1933 and the Securities Exchange Act of 1934 with a view toward
integrating the information systems under those Acts so that investors
and the marketplace are provided meaningful, nonduplicative information
periodically and when securities are sold to the public, while the costs of
compliance for public companies are decreased.

The shape of the program will be influenced by the answers to two
fundamental questions:

(1) What information is material to investment decisions in the context of public offerings of securities; and

(2) Under what circumstances and in what form should such material information be disseminated and made available by companies making public offerings of securities to the various participants in the capital market system?

The task of identifying what information is material to investment and voting decisions is a continuing one in the field of securities regulation. Integration, as a concept, involves a conclusion as to equivalency between transactional (Securities Act) and periodic (Exchange Act) reporting. If a subject matter is material information (other than a description of the transaction itself), then it will be material both in the distribution of securities and to the trading markets. Moreover, requirements governing the description of such subject matters should be the same for both purposes. As an example, if a management's discussion of the financial statements is important for transactions involving distributions, then it would also be equally important for an informed trading market. Thus, both prospectuses and periodic reports should take this information into account. Also, the requirements for its content should be essentially the same. This principle of equivalency has led to the development and expansion of Regulation S–K, a technical device designed to state in one place uniform requirements which both Securities Act and Exchange Act items incorporate by reference. ...

Integration consists, however, of more than just the notion of equivalency of reportable material information under both Acts. It involves answers to the second question posed above: Under what circumstances and to whom should this information be made available? Equivalency alone might be read to suggest that all the information contained, for example, in a Form 10–K should also be reiterated in all prospectuses.

However, the concept of integration also proceeds from the observation that information is regularly being furnished to the market through periodic reports under the Exchange Act. This information is evaluated by professional analysts and other sophisticated users, is available to the financial press and is obtainable by any other person who seeks it for free or at nominal cost. To the extent that the market accordingly acts efficiently, and this information is adequately reflected in the price of a registrant's outstanding securities, there seems little need to reiterate this information in a prospectus in the context of a distribution. The fact of market availability of information for sophisticated users also allows the exploration of other values in addition to cost reductions afforded through non-duplication: in particular, readability and effective communication in specific contexts. ...

A. *Background* ...

1. *The Law*

The Securities Act and the Exchange Act were enacted as separate legislation and in response to different needs. The Securities Act was intended to prevent frauds in the sale of securities by providing full and fair disclosure in the context of public offerings of securities. The Exchange Act was enacted to regulate brokers and dealers and securities markets. The disclosure framework of the Exchange Act contemplated in 1934 pertained primarily to classes of securities traded on stock exchanges. While both statutes were designed to provide disclosure to investors and the marketplace, the framework of the Securities Act was transaction oriented, i.e., the focus was upon the public offering of securities by any company. The framework of the Exchange Act was status oriented, i.e, the focus was upon issuers with a class of securities listed and traded on an exchange. Also, the two frameworks operated independently. Information required in the Securities Act context was not modified because of the existence of Exchange Act reporting and was only triggered by public offerings at varying times.

While the disparate orientations of the two statutes still exist, the gap between the disclosure frameworks has significantly narrowed since 1934. In 1936, Section 15(d) was added to the Exchange Act to provide that under certain circumstances the continuous reporting system would apply to unlisted companies with respect to classes of their securities for which a registration statement had become effective under the Securities Act. Thus, Section 15(d) expanded investor protection under the Exchange Act to the over-the-counter market, but only on a fragmentary basis.

The disparity between Exchange Act disclosure requirements for listed and unlisted classes of securities was not resolved until the passage of the Securities Acts Amendments of 1964 which brought many more companies into the continuous reporting system of the Exchange Act. With the passage of Section 15(d) and the 1964 amendments, all issuers of a certain size and issuers with certain characteristics selling securities to the public pursuant to an effective registration statement were subjected to the registration and reporting obligations of the Exchange Act. It is estimated that over 9,000 companies are now required to file periodic reports under the Exchange Act.

These amendments not only closed a gap under the Exchange Act, but also narrowed the gap between the disclosure framework under the Securities Act—information concerning the issuer and the transaction given only in the context of the public offering—and that under the Exchange Act—continuous disclosure about the issuer. Milton Cohen, a principal advocate of the concept of integration, opined that the disclosure frameworks under the Acts would have been quite different—and perhaps more congruent—if they "had been enacted in opposite order, or had been enacted as a single, integrated statute—that is, if the starting point had been a statutory scheme of continuous disclosures covering issuers of actively traded securities and the question of special disclosure in connection with public offerings had then been faced in this setting." In large part, the Commission's efforts will attempt to redress this legislative anomaly by establishing an integrated system of disclosure which will provide investor protection both in public offerings and in the securities markets, at a minimum burden to public companies.

2. *Nature of the Securities Markets*

The basic issues relating to Securities Act disclosure, i.e., the type of information that should be available and the dissemination of that information, must also be considered in light of the composition of today's markets. The participants in the markets, and therefore the users of the information made available to the markets, are varied and have correspondingly varied needs. They include the professional analyst, the institutional investor, the financial press, and the individual investor.

The professional analysts, widespread throughout the country, constantly digest and synthesize market and company-specific information. These professionals use, and often implore the Commission to require, increasingly complex and sophisticated information. The influx of institutional investors, and their financial advisors, also contributes to the constituency for technical but important statistical data. To a large extent, these professionals act as essential conduits in the flow of information to the ordinary investor and as intermediaries acting on behalf of participants in collective investment media.

In addition, this country has a uniquely active and responsive financial press which facilitates the broad dissemination of highly timely and material company-oriented information to a vast readership. The information needs of the individual investor must be considered in this context, recognizing that information reaches the individual investor through both direct and indirect routes.

It is incumbent upon the Commission to consider the entire community of users of company information in developing the proposed system and its model information package and to maintain a balance between the needs of the more and less sophisticated users. ...

SECURITIES AND EXCHANGE COMMISSION
RELEASE NO. 6331 (1981)
[REGISTRATION FORMS]

...

SUMMARY: The Commission is republishing for public comment three proposed forms to be used to register offerings of securities under the Securities Act of 1933. The three proposed forms would constitute the basic framework for registration statements under the Securities Act, with different levels of disclosure and delivery requirements applicable for different levels of companies registering offerings of securities. Republication of these and related proposals is intended to afford the public an opportunity to consider in a comprehensive manner the various elements of the Commission's integrated disclosure system. This action is a significant part of the Commission's program to integrate the disclosure systems under the various Federal securities laws and to simplify and improve the disclosure requirements imposed under these systems. ...

...

II. Overview

Under the proposed registration statement framework, registrants would be classified into three categories: (1) companies which are widely followed by professional analysts; (2) companies which have been subject to the periodic reporting system of the Exchange Act for three or more years, but which are not widely followed; and (3) companies which have been in the Exchange Act reporting system for less than three years. The first category would be eligible to use proposed Form S 3, which relies on incorporation by reference of Exchange Act reports and contains minimal disclosure in the prospectus. This form is predicated on the Commission's belief that the market operates efficiently for these companies, i.e., that the disclosure in Exchange Act reports and other communications by the registrant, such as press releases, has already been disseminated and accounted for by the market place. The second category would be eligible for Form S-2, which represents a combination of incorporation by reference of Exchange Act reports and presentation in the prospectus or in an annual report to security holders of certain information. The third category would use Form S-1, which requires complete disclosure of information in the prospectus and does not permit incorporation by reference. ...

... [T]he proposed framework markedly reduces or eliminates ... criteria relating to the "quality" of the registrant, and premises eligibility generally on dissemination of information in the market place, as represented by the length and nature of compliance by the company with the reporting requirements of the Exchange Act, and, with respect to proposed Form S-3, on the registrant's float.

The Commission believes that the standards of Exchange Act experience and float are more appropriate than the quality of the registrant in determining the type and amount of disclosure which is set forth in the prospectus delivered to investors. In the Commission's view, the "quality" of the registrant indicia, such as net income, are more appropriately disclosure matters, rather than criteria for eligibility to use a form. Thus, the eligibility criteria are designed to recognize the realities of the marketplace by matching a registrant to the form which will furnish investors with the appropriate disclosure for delivery in the prospectus.

Proposed Form S-3 recognizes the applicability of the efficient market theory to the registration statement framework with respect to those registrants which usually provide high quality corporate reports, including Exchange Act reports, and whose corporate information is broadly disseminated, because such companies are widely followed by professional analysts and investors in the market place. Because these registrants are widely followed, the disclosure set forth in the prospectus may appropriately be limited, without the loss of investor protection, to information concerning the offering and material facts which have not been disclosed previously. The abbreviated disclosure is made possible by the use of incorporation by reference of the registrant's Exchange Act information into the prospectus. Because of the abbreviated disclosure, the utility of proposed Form S–3 is limited to widely followed companies. ... The proposed float requirement is designed to correlate the use of abbreviated Form S–3 to widely followed registrants.

... [P]roposed Form S–2 is designed for improved readability by streamlining disclosure requirements and allowing certain disclosure obligations to be satisfied either through the delivery of the annual report to security holders or by presentation of comparable updated information in the prospectus. More specifically, the financial statements, management's discussion and analysis and the brief business description required by proposed Form S–2 are identical to those already presented in the annual report to security holders. ...

Finally, proposed Form S–1 ... would be used to register securities when no other form is authorized or prescribed and would be used by companies in the Exchange Act reporting system for less than three years, such as new issuers. To ensure that adequate information concerning these registrants is readily available to investors, proposed Form S–1 requires delivery of a more lengthy and comprehensive prospectus than either proposed Form S–2 or Form S–3. ...

III. Synopsis ...

A. *Eligibility Rules for Use of Forms S–3, S–2 and S–1* ...

1. *Form S–3*

The eligibility requirements for use of Form S–3 are broken down into two classifications, "Registrant Requirements" and "Transaction Requirements." A registrant first must meet the Registrant Requirements (which are identical for Forms S–3 and S–2) and then must meet at least one of the Transaction Requirements before it can use Form S–3.

a. *Registrant Requirements*

The first three Registrant Requirements are quite similar to those in existing Form S–7. The first requires that the registrant be organized under the laws of the United States, its various states or territories, and have its principal business operations located there. The second requires that the registrant have a class of securities registered pursuant to Section 12(b) or 12(g) of the Exchange Act or be required to file reports pursuant to Section 15(d) of that Act. The third requires that the registrant have filed all the information required by Sections 13, 14 or 15(d) of the Exchange Act for at least 36 months and have been timely in such filings for the preceding 12 months. These requirements are necessary because the operation of an efficient market for a security depends on such information being made public promptly and its inclu-

sion in filings made under the Exchange Act helps ensure its accuracy.
...

b. *Transaction Requirements*

...   If a registrant, which meets the eligibility requirements, meets
the conditions of any one of the Transaction Requirements, it may use
Form S–3 for the covered transaction.

i. *Primary and Secondary Offerings*

The first requirement proposes that, in order to use Form S–3 for
primary and secondary offerings, an issuer must have a minimum of
$150 million in aggregate value of voting stock held by non-affiliates
(hereinafter referred to as "float"). This test was designed to make the
Form available for such offerings only to those issuers which are
actively and widely followed in the securities markets. ...

ii. *Investment Grade Debt Securities*

Under the second Transaction Requirement any registrant which
meets the Registrant Requirements, even one which does not meet the
float criteria, would be able to register certain high grade non-convertible debt securities, defined as "investment grade debt securities," on
Form S–3. This proposal reflects ...   the Commission's position that
with respect to offerings of high quality debt issues a detailed prospectus is unnecessary since such securities are generally purchased on the
basis of interest rates and security ratings. ...

The proposed Form would define an "investment grade debt security"
as a non-convertible debt security which, at the time the registration
statement becomes effective, is rated in one of the top four corporate
bond categories by at least one nationally recognized statistical rating
organization. The proposed use of the top four categories is consistent
with the Commission's current use of securities ratings and with the
categories used by the rating organizations themselves, i.e., Standard &
Poor's Corporation, Moody's Investor Service and Fitch Investors Service, Inc. ...

2. *Form S–2*

As mentioned above, the Registrant Requirements of Form S–3 also
constitute virtually the entire eligibility requirements for the use of
Form S–2 .... The Commission believes that the streamlined nature of
the Form S–2 prospectus, while much more complete than that of Form
S–3, still should be supplemented by the availability of a complete and
current three year series of Exchange Act reports. Accordingly, it has
retained the Exchange Act eligibility criteria which also are used for
Form S–3. ...

3. *Form S–1*

. . . [T]his more comprehensive form must be used by first time filers and others who have only been filing reports for a short period of time. . . .

c. *Disclosure Provisions*

In proposed Forms S–1, S–2 and S–3, the Commission has developed a Securities Act registration system which identifies the information material to investment decisions in the context of all public offerings and then determines in what form and to whom issuers must disseminate such information. The material information will be required to be part of all Securities Act registration statements, regardless of the form used, through incorporation by reference in some cases. Differences among the forms primarily involve dissemination, i.e., the extent to which the required information must be presented in the prospectus, or may be presented in other documents delivered with the prospectus and incorporated by reference, or may be simply incorporated by reference from information contained in the Exchange Act continuous reporting system.

Generally, it is the issuer-oriented part of the information material to a public offering, as opposed to the transaction-specific information, which, depending on the form available, may be satisfied otherwise than through full prospectus presentation. This information includes the basic package of information about the issuer which the Commission believes is material to investment decisions in all contexts and thus is also required to be presented in annual reports to the Commission on Form 10–K and in annual reports to security holders. Information about the offering will not have been reported on in any other disclosure document or otherwise have been publicly disseminated and thus will be required to be presented in all cases. . . .

2. *Incorporation by Reference*

The technique of incorporation by reference of Exchange Act disclosure documents is central to the integrated Securities Act registration system represented by proposed Forms S–1, S–2 and S–3. Proposed Form S–3 relies on incorporation by reference to replace prospectus presentation of information about the issuer of the securities being registered. Proposed Form S–2 uses incorporation by reference to allow streamlining of the prospectus presentation of issuer-specific information. Proposed Form S–1 uses no incorporation by reference and instead requires full disclosure about the issuer of the securities to be presented in the prospectus. . . .

3. *Disclosure Requirements by Form*

a. *Form S–3*

Proposed Form S–3 provides the shortest form for Securities Act registration. The prospectus would be required to present [certain] items calling for information about the offering. . . .

Information concerning the registrant would be incorporated by reference from Exchange Act reports, which would be available to investors on request. The documents required to be incorporated are the latest annual report on Form 10–K and all other reports filed pursuant to Section 13(a) or 15(d) of the Exchange Act since the end of the fiscal year covered by the Form 10–K, including all Section 13(d) or 15(d) reports filed subsequent to effectiveness of the registration statement and prior to termination of the offering. Unless there has been a material change in the registrant's affairs which has not been reported in an Exchange Act filing, the prospectus would not be required to present any information concerning the registrant. ...

b. *Form S–2*

Proposed Form S–2 provides a simplified form for registration by certain registrants. While it requires delivery of information about the registrant in addition to delivery of the same information about the offering as required by Form S–3, proposed Form S–2 significantly streamlines the registrant-specific disclosure by making the required level of disclosure delivered to investors that of the annual report to security holders pursuant to Rule 14a–3 rather than that of the annual report on Form 10 K. Required information about the registrant includes the basic information package components (market price and dividend data, selected financial data, financial statements and management's discussion and analysis) and such other items (brief descriptions of business, segments, supplementary financial information) as are required to be included in the annual report to security holders pursuant to Rule 14a–3. Moreover, registrants are granted the option of providing this information either by presenting it in the prospectus or by delivering the latest annual report to security holders along with the prospectus. Finally, the registrant's latest annual report on Form 10–K and periodic reports on Form 10–Q and Form 8–K must be incorporated by reference into the prospectus, and made available upon request, to round out the information provided about the registrant. ...

If the Form S–2 registrant elects the alternative of delivering its annual report, it must incorporate certain information in that document by reference and describe in the prospectus any material changes in its affairs since the end of the latest fiscal year reported in the delivered annual report. In addition, it must provide updating information but may avoid duplication of previously reported quarterly information because updating may be accomplished by any one of three means: (1) including in the prospectus such financial and other information as would be required to be reported in a report on Form 10–Q; (2) delivering a copy of the latest Form 10–Q with the prospectus and annual report; (3) delivering a copy of the latest informal quarterly report to shareholders if such report contained the same required information. ...

c. *Form S–1*

Proposed Form S–1 presents a simple format. Full disclosure of all material information about the offering and the registrant is required to be presented in the prospectus itself. No incorporation by reference to any Exchange Act documents is allowed. Proposed Form S–1 looks entirely to Regulation S–K for its non-financial substantive disclosure provisions. First, like proposed Forms S–2 and S–3, proposed Form S–1 requires prospectus presentation of the offering-oriented items of § 229.500 of Regulation S–K and the description of securities (proposed Item 202 of Regulation S–K). In addition, the proposed Form S–1 prospectus must include the same information about the registrant as is required to be reported in an annual report on Form 10–K. This information includes, in addition to the basic information package with respect to the registrant, the full Regulation S–K descriptions of business, properties and legal proceedings as well as the Regulation S–K disclosures with respect to management and security holders.   ...

NOTE ON REGISTRATION FORMS

As adopted, Forms S–1 and S–2 reflected no major changes from the proposal in Release No. 33–6331. Form S–3, however, was revised in several important respects. The Commission adopted the proposed $150-million-float and high-grade-debt tests, but added two others: (i) the issuance of securities by companies with a $100 million float and 3 million share annual trading volume, and (ii) the issuance of high-grade non-convertible preferred. See Securities Act Release No. 6383 (1982).

(e) COVERAGE OF THE ACT: DEFINITIONS

---

(2) Note: What Is a Sale?

Insert the following Note at p. 1206 of the unabridged edition, after Note, What is a Sale?:

NOTE ON RUBIN v. UNITED STATES

In Rubin v. United States, 449 U.S. 424, 101 S.Ct. 698, 66 L.Ed.2d 633 (1981), the Supreme Court held that a pledge of securities was an "offer" or "sale" within § 17(a) of the Securities Act of 1933 (from whose language Rule 10b–5 was drawn). The court first quoted § 2(3) of the 1933 Act:

"The term 'sale' or 'sell' shall include every contract of sale *or disposition* of a security *or interest in a security*, for value. The term ... 'offer' shall include every *attempt or offer to dispose of,* or solicitation of an offer to buy, a security *or interest in a security*, for value." (Emphasis added by the Court.)

It concluded:

... Obtaining a loan secured by a pledge of shares of stock unmistakably involves a "disposition of [an] interest in a security, for value." Although pledges transfer less than absolute title, the interest thus transferred nonetheless is an "interest in a security." The pledges contemplated a self-executing procedure under a power that could, at the option of the pledgee (the bank) in the event of a default, vest absolute title and ownership. Bankers Trust parted with substantial consideration—specifically, a total of $475,000—and obtained the inchoate but valuable interest under the pledges and concomitant powers. It is not essential under the terms of the Act that full title pass to a transferee for the transaction to be an "offer" or a "sale." See, e.g., United States v. Gentile, 530 F.2d 461, 466 (CA2), cert. denied, 426 U.S. 936, 96 S.Ct. 2651, 49 L.Ed.2d 388 (1976).

. . . Treating pledges as included among "offers" and "sales" comports with the purpose of the Act and specifically, with that of § 17(a). We frequently have observed that these provisions were enacted to protect against fraud and promote the free flow of information in the public dissemination of securities. E.g., United States v. Naftalin, 441 U.S. 768, 774, 99 S.Ct. 2077, 2082, 60 L.Ed.2d 624 (1979); Ernst & Ernst v. Hochfelder . . . . The economic considerations and realities present when a lender parts with value and accepts securities as collateral security for a loan are similar in important respect to the risk an investor undertakes when purchasing shares. Both are relying on the value of the securities themselves, and both must be able to depend on the representations made by the transferor of the securities, regardless of whether the transferor passes full title or only a conditional and defeasible interest to secure repayment of a loan.

Prior to *Rubin,* the same issue arose under Rule 10b-5, and the cases were in conflict. The definition of "sale" in the 1934 Act, contained in § 3(a)(14), is comparable but not identical to the definition in § 2(3) of the 1933 Act:

(14) The terms "sale" or "sell" each include any contract to sell or otherwise dispose of.

(h) EXEMPTED TRANSACTIONS: NON–PUBLIC OFFERINGS; SECTION 4(2) AND RULE 146

Delete the material at pp. 1243–1252 of the unabridged edition, and insert the following material in its place:

SECURITIES ACT

§§ 3(b), 4(6)

Section 3. . . . Except as hereinafter expressly provided, the provisions of this title shall not apply to any of the following classes of securities:

. . .

(b) The Commission may from time to time by its rules and regulations, and subject to such terms and conditions as may be prescribed therein, add any class of securities to the securities exempted as provided in this section, if it finds that the enforcement of this title with respect to such securities is not necessary in the public interest and for the protection of investors by reason of the small amount involved or the limited character of the public offering; but no issue of securities shall be exempted under this subsection where the aggregate amount at which such issue is offered to the public exceeds $5,000,000.

Section 4. The provisions of Section 5 shall not apply to—

. . .

(6) transactions involving offers or sales by an issuer solely to one or more accredited investors, if the aggregate offering price of an issue of securities offered in reliance on this paragraph does not exceed the amount allowed under section 3(b) of this title, if there is no advertising or public solicitation in connection with the transaction by the issuer or anyone acting on the issuer's behalf, and if the issuer files such notice with the Commission as the Commission shall prescribe.

SECURITIES ACT § 2(15) AND RULE 215

Section 2. When used in this title . . .

(15) The term "accredited investor" shall mean—

(i) a bank . . .; an insurance company . . .; an investment company registered under the Investment Company Act of 1940 . . .; [certain other institutional investors]; or

(ii) any person who, on the basis of such factors as financial sophistication, net worth, knowledge, and experience in financial matters, or amount of assets under management qualifies as an accredited investor under rules and regulations which the Commission shall prescribe.

Rule 215. The term "accredited investor" as used in section 2(15)(ii) of the Securities Act of 1933 . . . shall include the following persons: . . .

(c) Any organization described in Section 501(c)(3) of the Internal Revenue Code with total assets in excess of $5,000,000;

(d) Any director, executive officer, or general partner of the issuer of the securities being offered or sold . . .;

(e) Any person who purchases at least $150,000 of the securities being offered, where the purchaser's total purchase price does not exceed 20 percent of the purchaser's net worth at the time of sale, or joint net worth with that person's spouse, for [cash, marketable securities, or certain other consideration];

(f) Any natural person whose individual net worth, or joint net worth with that person's spouse, at the time of his purchase exceeds $1,000,000;

(g) Any natural person who had an individual income in excess of $200,000 in each of the two most recent years and who reasonably expects an income in excess of $200,000 in the current year ....

SECURITIES AND EXCHANGE COMMISSION
SECURITIES ACT RELEASE NO. 6389 (1982)
[REGULATION D]

. . .

SUMMARY: The Commission announces the adoption of a new regulation governing certain offers and sales of securities without registration under the Securities Act of 1933 and a uniform notice of sales form to be used for all offerings under the regulation. The regulation replaces three exemptions and four forms, all of which are being rescinded. The new regulation is designed to simplify and clarify existing exemptions, to expand their availability, and to achieve uniformity between federal and state exemptions in order to facilitate capital formation consistent with the protection of investors. ...

I. Background

Regulation D is the product of the Commission's evaluation of the impact of its rules and regulations on the ability of small businesses to raise capital. This study has revealed a particular concern that the registration requirements and the exemptive scheme of the Securities Act impose disproportionate restraints on small issuers. ...

Coincident with the Commission's small business program, Congress enacted the Small Business Investment Incentive Act of 1980 (the "Incentive Act") [94 Stat. 2275 (codified in scattered sections of 15 U.S.C.)]. The Incentive Act included three changes to the Securities Act: the addition of an exemption in Section 4(6) for offers and sales solely to accredited investors, the increase in the ceiling of Section 3(b) from $2,000,000 to $5,000,000, and the addition of Section 19(c) which, among other things, authorized "the development of a uniform exemption from registration for small issuers which can be agreed upon among several States or between the States and the Federal Government." ...

II. Discussion

A. *Overview*

Regulation D is a series of six rules, designated Rules 501–506, that establishes three exemptions from the registration requirements of the Securities Act and replaces exemptions that currently exist under Rules 146, 240, and 242. The regulation is designed to simplify existing rules and regulations, to eliminate any unnecessary restrictions that those rules and regulations place on issuers, particularly small businesses, and to achieve uniformity between state and federal exemptions in order to facilitate capital formation consistent with the protection of investors.

Rules 501–503 set forth definitions, terms, and conditions that apply generally throughout the regulation. ...

B. *Rule 501—Definitions and Terms Used in Regulation D* ...

[Two of the most important definitions under Rule 501 are "accredited investor" and "purchaser representative." The term "accredited investor" is defined to include, essentially, those persons covered by § 2(15) of the Securities Act and Rule 215, supra. The term "purchaser representative" is defined to mean a person who lacks defined ties to the issuer, has "such knowledge and experience in financial and business matters that he is capable of evaluating ... the merits and risks of the prospective investment," and is "acknowledged by the purchaser in writing, during the course of the transaction, to be his purchaser representative in connection with evaluating the merits and risks of the prospective investment."]

C. *Rule 502—General Conditions to Be Met*

Rule 502 sets forth general conditions that relate to all offerings under Rules 504 through 506. These cover guidelines for determining whether separate offers and sales constitute part of the same offering under principles of integration, requirements as to specific disclosure requirements in Regulation D offerings, and limitations on the manner of conducting the offering and on the resale of securities acquired in the offering. ...

1. *Integration.* Rule 502(a) provides that all sales that are part of the same Regulation D offering must be integrated. The rule provides a safe harbor for all offers and sales that take place at least six months before the start of or six months after the termination of the Regulation D offering, so long as there are no offers and sales, excluding those to employee benefit plans, of the same securities within either of these six-month periods. ...

2. *Information Requirements.* Rule 502(b) provides when and what type of disclosure must be furnished in Regulation D offerings. If an issuer sells securities under Rule 504 or only to accredited investors, then Regulation D does not mandate any specific disclosure. If securities are sold under Rule 505 or 506 to any investors that are not accredited, then Rule 502(b)(1)(ii) requires delivery of the information specified in Rule 502(b)(2) to all purchasers. The type of information to be furnished varies depending on the size of the offering and the nature of the issuer. ...

The specific disclosure requirements are as follows.

a. Non-reporting companies. Disclosure requirements for companies that are not subject to the reporting obligations of the Exchange Act are set forth in Rule 502(b)(2)(i). These requirements are keyed to the size of the offering.

In offerings up to $5,000,000 an issuer must provide the same kind of information as required in Part I of Form S–18, or, for an issuer that is not qualified to use Form S–18, the same kind of information as required in Part I of a registration form available to the issuer.[21] The issuer need only provide two years of financial statements and only the most recent year need be audited. For issuers that are not limited partnership, only a balance sheet dated within 120 days of the offering must be audited if obtaining an audit of the other financial statements would constitute an unreasonable effort or expense. Limited partnerships may furnish tax basis financial statements if the basic requirements are an unreasonable effort or expense.

For offerings over $5,000,000 issuers must furnish the same kind of information as specified in Part I of an available form of registration. Where the audited financials cannot be obtained without unreasonable effort or expense, the issuer is given options similar to those in offerings up to $5,000,000. ...

b. *Reporting companies.* Companies that are subject to Exchange Act reporting obligations must furnish the same kind of disclosure regardless of the size of the offering. These issuers, however, have an option as to the form that this disclosure may take. Under Rule 502(b)(2)(ii)(A), a reporting company may provide its most recent annual report to shareholders, assuming it is in accordance with Rule 14a–3 or 14c–3 [17 CFR 240.14a–3 or 240.14c–3] under the Exchange Act, the definitive proxy statement filed in connection with that annual report, and, if requested in writing, the most recent Form 10–K [17 CFR 249.310]. Alternatively, those issuers may elect under Rule 502(b)(2)(ii)(B) to provide the information contained in the most recent of its Form 10–K or a Form S–1 [17 CFR 239.11] registration statement under the Securities Act or a Form 10 [17 CFR 249.10] registration statement under the Exchange Act. Although the requirement under subparagraph (B) refers to specific forms, it does not mandate delivery of the actual reference documents. An issuer, for instance, may choose to prepare and deliver a separate document that contains the necessary information.

Regardless of the issuer's choice of disclosure in subparagraph (A) or (B), Rule 502(b)(2)(ii)(C) requires the basic information to be supplemented by information contained in certain Exchange Act reports filed after the distribution or filing of the report or registration statement in question. Further, the issuer must provide certain information regarding the offering and any material charges in the issuer's affairs that are not disclosed in the basic documents. ...

3. *Manner of Offering.* Rule 502(c) prohibits the use of general solicitation or general advertising in connection with Regulation D offerings, except in certain cases under Rule 504. ...

---

21. Currently, Form S–18 is available for an offering up to $5,000,000 but not for an issuer that, among other things, is sub- ject to Exchange Act reporting obligations. ...

4. *Limitations on Resale.* Securities acquired in a Regulation D offering, with the exception of certain offerings under Rule 504, have the status of securities acquired in a transaction under Section 4(2) of the Securities Act. As further provided in Rule 502(d), the issuer shall exercise reasonable care to assure that purchasers of securities are not underwriters, which reasonable care will include certain inquiry as to investment purpose, disclosure of resale limitations and placement of a legend on the certificate. ...

D. *Rule 503—Filings of Notice of Sales.*

The Commission is adopting a uniform notice of sales form for use in offerings under both Regulation D and Section 4(6) of the Securities Act. ...

Rule 503 sets forth the filing requirements for Form D. The notice is due 15 days after the first sale of securities in an offering under Regulation D. Subsequent notices are due every six months after first sale and 30 days after the last sale. ...

E. *Rule 504—Exemption for Offers and Sales Not Exceeding $500,000*

Rule 504, which replaces Rule 240, provides an exemption under Section 3(b) of the Securities Act for certain offers and sales not exceeding an aggregate offering price of $500,000. ... Proceeds from securities sold within the preceding 12 months in all transactions exempt under Section 3(b) [29] or in violation of Section 5(a) of the Securities Act must be included in computing the aggregate offering price under Rule 504. The exemption is not available to investment companies or issuers subject to Exchange Act reporting obligations.[*] Commissions or similar transaction related remuneration may be paid.

... [T]he exemption under Rule 504 does not mandate specific disclosure requirements. However, the issuer remains subject to the antifraud and civil liability provisions of the federal securities laws and must also comply with state requirements.

Offers and sales under Rule 504 must be made in accordance with all the general terms and conditions in Rules 501 through 503. However, if the entire offering is made exclusively in states that require registration and the delivery of a disclosure document, and if the offering is in compliance with those requirements, then the general limitations on the manner of offering and on resale will not apply. ...

F. *Rule 505—Exemption for Offers and Sales Not*

---

29. Exemptions under Section 3(b) include ... Regulation A, and Rules 504 and 505 of Regulation D. ...

[*] Reporting companies are excluded from Rule 504 because "it is the Commission's intention that the proposed rule be used to facilitate the capital formation needs of the small start-up company seeking venture capital, and not seasoned issuers for which information is readily available by means of Exchange Act documents." Securities Act Release No. 6339 (1981). (Footnote by ed.)

Exceeding $5,000,000

Rule 505 replaces Rule 242. The rule provides an exemption under Section 3(b) of the Securities Act for offers and sales to no more than 35 purchasers that are not accredited [and an unlimited number of investors who are accredited] where the aggregate offering price over 12 months does not exceed $5,000,000. As with Rule 504, the aggregate offering price includes proceeds from offers and sales under Section 3(b) or in violation of Section 5(a) of the Securities Act. ...

Rule 505 is available to any issuer that is not an investment company. ...

G. *Rule 506—Exemption for Offers and Sales Without Regard to Dollar Amount*

Rule 506 relates to transactions that are deemed to be exempt under Section 4(2) of the Securities Act. [Rule 506 is available to all issuers, without a dollar ceiling, for offerings sold to not more than 35 purchasers, other than accredited investors. To qualify under the Rule, however, an issuer must make a determination that each purchaser meets certain standards of sophistication. Specifically, the Rule requires that "[t]he issuer shall reasonably believe immediately prior to making any sale that each purchaser who is not an accredited investor either alone or with his purchaser representative(s) has such knowledge and experience in financial and business matters that he is capable of evaluating the merits and risks of the prospective investment."] ...

Comparative Chart of Securities Act Limited Offering Exemptions **

Comparison Item	Rule 504	Rule 505	Rule 506	Section 4(6)
Aggregate Offering Price Limitation	$500,000	$5,000,000 (12 mos.)	Unlimited	$5,000,000
Number of Investors	Unlimited	35 plus unlimited accredited		Unlimited accredited only
Investor Qualification	None required	Accredited or none required	Purchaser must be sophisticated (alone or with representative) Accredited presumed to be qualified	Accredited
Commissions	Permitted	Permitted		Permitted
Limitations on Manner of Offering	No general solicitation unless registered in states that require delivery of a	No general solicitation permitted		No general solicitation permitted

** Adapted from Securities Act Release   No. 6389 (footnote by ed.)

Comparison Item	Rule 504	Rule 505	Rule 506	Section 4(6)
	disclosure document.			
Limitations on Resale	Restricted unless registered in states that require delivery of a disclosure document	Restricted		Restricted
Issuer Qualifications	No reporting or investment companies	No investment companies or issuers disqualified under Regulation A	None	None
Notice of Sales	Form D required as a condition of exemption—5 copies filed with Commission 15 days after first sale, every 6 months after first sale, 30 days after last sale			Form 4(6) required as condition of exemption —5 copies filed with Commission 10 days after first sale, every 6 months after first sale, 10 days after completion
Information Requirements	No information specified	1. If purchased solely by accredited, no information specified 2. If purchased by non-accredited, a. non-reporting companies must furnish i. offerings up to $5,000,000—information in Part I of Form S–18 or available registration, 2 yr. financials, 1 year audited—if undue effort or expense, issuers other than limited partnerships only balance sheet as of 120 days before offering must be audited—if limited partnership and undue effort or expense, financials may be tax basis ii. offerings over $5,000,000—information in Part I of available registration—if undue effort or expense, issuers other than limited partnerships only balance sheet as of 120 days before offering must be audited—if limited partnership and undue effort or expense, financials may be tax basis		No information specified

Comparison Item	Rule 504	Rule 505	Rule 506	Section 4(6)

b. reporting companies must furnish

    i. Rule 14a–3 annual report to shareholders, definitive proxy statement and 10–K, if requested, plus subsequent reports and other updating information or

    ii. information in most recent Form S–1 or Form 10 or Form 10–K plus subsequent reports and other updating information

c. Issuers must make available prior to sale

    i. exhibits

    ii. written information given to accredited investors

    iii. opportunity to ask questions and receive answers

(k) THE REGISTRATION PROCESS

Insert the following material at p. 1286 of the unabridged edition, at the end of Chapter VIII, Section 8(k):

(2) Forms S–1, S–2, S–3

[See pp. 126–132, supra.]

(3) Shelf Registration

SECURITIES ACT RULE 415
[SHELF REGISTRATION]

Delayed or Continuous Offering and Sale of Securities.

(a) Securities may be registered for an offering to be made on a continuous or delayed basis in the future, provided that—

(1) The registration statement pertains to:

(i) Securities in an amount which, at the time the registration statement becomes effective, is reasonably expected to be offered and sold within two years from the initial effective date of the registration statement by or on behalf of the registrant, a subsidiary of the registrant or a person of which the registrant is a subsidiary; or

(ii) Securities which are to be offered or sold solely by or on behalf of a person or persons other than the registrant, a subsidiary of the registrant or a person of which the registrant is a subsidiary; or

(iii) Securities which are to be offered and sold pursuant to a dividend or interest reinvestment plan or an employee benefit plan of the registrant; or

(iv) Securities which are to be issued upon the exercise of outstanding options, warrants or rights; or

(v) Securities which are to be issued upon conversion of other outstanding securities; or

(vi) Securities which are pledged as collateral. ...

(2) The registrant furnishes the undertakings required by Item 512(a) of Regulation S–K.*

(3) In the case of a registration statement pertaining to an at the market offering of equity securities by or on behalf of the registrant: (i) The registrant must meet the registrant requirements and the applicable transaction requirements of Form S–3 ... (ii) where voting stock is registered, the amount of securities registered for such purposes must not exceed 10% of the aggregate market value of the registrant's outstanding voting stock held by non-affiliates of the registrant (calculated as of a date within 60 days prior to the date of filing); (iii) the securities must be sold through an underwriter or underwriters, acting as principal(s) or as agent(s) for the registrant; and (iv) the underwriter or underwriters must be named in the prospectus which is part of the registration statement. As used in this paragraph, the term "at the market offering" means an offering of securities into an existing trading market for outstanding shares of the same class at other than a fixed price on or through the

---

* Item 512(a) of Regulation S–K provides that in the case of a Rule 415 offering, the registrant shall include the following undertaking:

(1) To file, during any period in which offers or sales are being made, a post-effective amendment to this registration statement:

(i) To include any prospectus required by section 10(a)(3) of the Securities Act of 1933;

(ii) To reflect in the prospectus any facts or events arising after the effective date of the registration statement (or the most recent post-effective amendment thereof) which, individually or in the aggregate, represent a fundamental change in the information set forth in the registration statement;

(iii) To include any material information with respect to the plan of distribution not previously disclosed in the registration statement or any material change to such information in the regis-

tration statement, including (but not limited to) any addition or deletion of a managing underwriter;

Provided, however, that paragraphs (a)(1)(i) and (a)(1)(ii) do not apply if the registration statement is on Form S–3 [or] Form S–8 and the information required to be included in a post-effective amendment by those paragraphs is contained in periodic reports filed by the registrant pursuant to section 13 or section 15(d) of the Securities Exchange Act of 1934 that are incorporated by reference in the registration statement.

(2) That, for the purpose of determining any liability under the Securities Act of 1933, each such post-effective amendment shall be deemed to be a new registration statement relating to the securities offered therein, and the offering of such securities at that time shall be deemed to be the initial bona fide offering thereof.

(Footnote by ed.)

facilities of a national securities exchange or to or through a market maker otherwise than on an exchange. ...**

SECURITIES AND EXCHANGE COMMISSION
RELEASE NO. 6276 (1981)
[SHELF REGISTRATION]

. . .

The last sentence of Section 6(a) of the Securities Act provides: "A registration statement shall be deemed effective only as to the securities specified therein as proposed to be offered." ... [The Commission has interpreted] that sentence to prohibit the registration of securities for a delayed or postponed offering, commonly referred to as "shelf" offering or registration.

In the absence of any specific legislative comment upon the meaning of the last sentence of Section 6(a) of the Securities Act, as enacted by Congress in 1933, early opinions of the Commission and its staff interpreted the provision as requiring that a registration statement be effective only as to those securities proposed to be offered "in the proximate future" .... This general prohibition against shelf registration was designed to effectuate the clear policy underlying the last sentence of Section 6(a) that "the registration statements and prospectuses on which they rely, so far as is reasonably possible, provide current information." This interpretation was, in turn, premised upon the assumption that the registration of securities which are to be offered at "some remote future time" gives "the appearance of a registered status" without providing its true substance—accurate and current information.

In practice, the Commission has never adhered to such an absolute prohibition [and] .... such registration has been permitted for several types of offerings ....

After substantial experience with [several] types of shelf registration, the Commission is not aware of major abuses that have harmed investors. In addition, the integration of the Securities Act and Exchange Act disclosure systems provides an increasingly efficient basis for updating disclosure in securities offerings. Shelf registrations can utilize integration effectively thereby facilitating the development of important new capital raising techniques. Accordingly, the Commission believes that a restrictive policy on shelf registration is not appropriate or necessary for the protection of investors. The Commission is proposing ... that its stated prohibition of shelf registration be replaced with proposed Rule [415] ....

** Rule 415 was adopted by the SEC in March 1982 on an experimental basis, to be effective until December 1982. In September 1982, the SEC extended the effectiveness of Rule 415 to December 1983. See Securities Act Releases Nos. 6383, 6423 (1982). (Footnote by ed.)

SECURITIES AND EXCHANGE COMMISSION
RELEASE NO. 6383 (1982)
[SHELF REGISTRATION]

. . .

Rule 415 permits shelf registration of "at the market offerings" of equity securities directly by or on behalf of the registrant. Because such offerings raise concerns for the public and for the marketplace, the Shelf Release proposed the imposition of two conditions. First, the Commission proposed that those securities must be sold through an underwriter or underwriters, acting as principal(s) or agent(s) for the registrant, and that such underwriter(s) must be named in the prospectus which is part of the registration statement. Second, the Commission proposed to define an "at the market offering" as an offering of securities into an existing trading market for outstanding shares of the same class of securities at other than a fixed price on or through the facilities of a national securities exchange or to a market maker otherwise than on an exchange.

A number of commentators agreed with the Commission that it should impose conditions upon the availability of shelf registration for an at the market offering. The Commission has determined to adopt the conditions proposed and to adopt two further conditions: (1) that the registrant must meet the registrant requirements and applicable transaction requirements of Form S–3 and (2) that the amount of securities registered must not exceed ten percent of the registrant's non-affiliate float. The Commission is conditioning primary equity offerings at the market on Form S–3 availability and is limiting such offerings to ten percent of a registrant's float in view of the experimental nature of the temporary rule.

The Commission is adopting the requirement for a named underwriter because it believes that the direct involvement of an underwriter can provide a desirable discipline upon such offerings of equity securities into an existing trading market and that the presence of an underwriter helps to ensure that accurate and current disclosure is made to investors in the prospectus and that the prospectus delivery requirements of the Securities Act are met. . . .

Chapter IX

CORPORATE DISTRIBUTIONS

SECTION 1. DIVIDENDS

(h) THE CALIFORNIA STATUTE AND THE PROPOSED REVISION OF THE MODEL ACT

Insert the following material at p. 1399 of the unabridged edition, and p. 831 of the abridged edition, at the end of the Note on the Proposed New Model Act Dividend Test:

The proposed revision of Model Act § 45 has been adopted by the ABA's Committee on Corporation Law.

Chapter X

ORGANIC CHANGES: COMBINATIONS, RECAPITALIZATIONS, AND CHARTER AMENDMENTS

SECTION 1. CORPORATE COMBINATIONS

(c) THE APPRAISAL REMEDY

Following the cross-reference to Piemonte v. New Boston Garden Corp. at p. 1453 of the unabridged edition and p. 849 of the abridged edition, insert a cross-reference to pp. 161–164 of Weinberger v. UOP, infra.

Insert the following Note at p. 1453 of the unabridged edition, and p. 849 of the abridged edition, before the extract from Eisenberg, The Structure of the Corporation:

NOTE ON THE NEW YORK APPRAISAL STATUTE

In 1982, New York enacted a statute making a sweeping reform of its appraisal provisions, N.Y. Laws, ch. 202. The statute provides, in pertinent part:

Section 1. Legislative declaration. A shareholder's right to dissent from certain corporate actions and to receive payment of fair value for his shares is a basic right of share ownership and, except where the corporate action is unlawful or fraudulent as to the shareholder, it is exclusive. Consequently, it is important that the right be made effective. Procedures for the exercise of the right should be as simple as possible, and dissenting shareholders should be entitled to receive payment for their shares on an expedited basis. Resolution, without judicial proceedings, of disagreements between dissenting shareholders and the corporation regarding fair value should be encouraged. Courts should determine fair value by reference to the nature and effects of the transaction giving rise to the shareholder's right to dissent, to the concepts and methods then customary in the relevant securities and financial markets and to all other relevant factors. The case law interpretation of fair value has not always reflected the reality of corporate business combinations. These transactions involve the sale of the corporation as a whole, and the corporation's value as an entirety may be substantially in excess of the actual or hypothetical market price for shares trading among investors. Thus, experience has demonstrated that large premiums over market price are commonplace in mergers and in asset acquisitions. In cases where the transaction involves a restructuring of the shareholders' relative interests in the corporation by amendment of the certificate of incorporation, courts may find it appropriate to determine only the fair value of the dissenters' shares rather than the value of the corporation as a whole, employing traditional valuation concepts.

. . .

Section 8. [Section 623 of the Business Corporation Law] is amended to read as follows:

(g) Within fifteen days after the expiration of the period within which shareholders may file their notices of election to dissent, or within fifteen days after the proposed corporate action is consummated, whichever is later . . . the corporation . . . shall make a written offer by registered mail to each shareholder who has filed such notice of election to pay for his shares at a specified price which the corporation considers to be their fair value. . . . If the corporate action has been consummated, such offer shall . . . be accompanied by . . . advance payment to each such shareholder who has submitted the certificates representing his shares to the corporation . . . of an amount equal to eighty percent of the amount of such offer. . . . Every advance payment . . . shall include advice to the shareholder to the effect that acceptance of such payment does not constitute a waiver of any dissenters' rights. . . .

(h) The following procedure shall apply if the corporation fails to make such offer within such period of fifteen days, or if it makes the offer and any dissenting shareholder or shareholders fail to agree with it within the period of thirty days thereafter upon the price to be paid for their shares: . . .

(4) The court shall . . . fix the value of the shares, which, for the purposes of this section, shall be the fair value as of the close of business on the day prior to the shareholders' authorization date. . . . In fixing the fair value of the shares, the court shall consider the nature of the transaction giving rise to the shareholder's right to receive payment for shares and its effects on the corporation and its shareholders, the concepts and methods then customary in the relevant securities and financial markets for determining fair value of shares of a corporation engaging in a similar transaction under comparable circumstances and all other relevant factors.* The court shall determine the fair value of the shares without a jury and without referral to an appraiser or referee. Upon application by the corporation or by any shareholder who is a party to the proceeding, the court may, in its discre-

---

* The new statute drops a provision in the prior statute that in fixing value the court should exclude "any appreciation or depreciation directly induced by" the corporate action dissented from. (Footnote by ed.)

tion, permit pretrial disclosure, including, but not limited to, disclosure of any expert's reports relating to the fair value of the shares whether or not intended for use at the trial in the proceeding. ...

(6) The final order shall include an allowance for interest at such rate as the court finds to be equitable, from the date the corporate action was consummated to the date of payment. In determining the rate of interest, the court shall consider all relevant factors, including the rate of interest which the corporation would have had to pay to borrow money during the pendency of the proceeding. If the court finds that the refusal of any shareholder to accept the corporate offer of payment for his shares was arbitrary, vexatious or otherwise not in good faith, no interest shall be allowed to him.

(k) FREEZEOUTS

Insert the following case at p. 1552 of the unabridged edition, after Roland International Corp. v. Najjar, and p. 898 of the abridged edition, after the Background Note on Singer and Tanzer:

WEINBERGER v. UOP, INC.

Supreme Court of Delaware, 1983.
457 A.2d 701.

This post-trial appeal was reheard en banc from a decision of the Court of Chancery. It was brought by the class action plaintiff below, a former shareholder of UOP, Inc., who challenged the elimination of UOP's minority shareholders by a cash-out merger between UOP and its majority owner, The Signal Companies, Inc.[2] Originally, the defendants in this action were Signal, UOP, certain officers and directors of those companies, and UOP's investment banker, Lehman Brothers Kuhn Loeb, Inc.[3] The present Chancellor held that the terms of the merger were fair to the plaintiff and the other minority shareholders of UOP. Accordingly, he entered judgment in favor of the defendants.

Numerous points were raised by the parties, but we address only the following questions presented by the trial court's opinion:

(1) The plaintiff's duty to plead sufficient facts demonstrating the unfairness of the challenged merger;

(2) The burden of proof upon the parties where the merger has been approved by the purportedly informed vote of a majority of the minority shareholders;

---

2. For the opinion of the trial court see Weinberger v. UOP, Inc., Del.Ch., 426 A.2d 1333 (1981).
3. Shortly before the last oral argument, the plaintiff dismissed Lehman Brothers

from the action. Thus, we do not deal with the issues raised by the plaintiff's claims against this defendant.

(3) The fairness of the merger in terms of adequacy of the defendants' disclosures to the minority shareholders;

(4) The fairness of the merger in terms of adequacy of the price paid for the minority shares and the remedy appropriate to that issue; and

(5) The continued force and effect of Singer v. Magnavox Co., Del.Supr., 380 A.2d 969, 980 (1977), and its progeny.

In ruling for the defendants, the Chancellor re-stated his earlier conclusion that the plaintiff in a suit challenging a cash-out merger must allege specific acts of fraud, misrepresentation, or other items of misconduct to demonstrate the unfairness of the merger terms to the minority.[4] We approve this rule and affirm it.

The Chancellor also held that even though the ultimate burden of proof is on the majority shareholder to show by a preponderance of the evidence that the transaction is fair, it is first the burden of the plaintiff attacking the merger to demonstrate some basis for invoking the fairness obligation. We agree with that principle. However, where corporate action has been approved by an informed vote of a majority of the minority shareholders, we conclude that the burden entirely shifts to the plaintiff to show that the transaction was unfair to the minority. See, e.g., Michelson v. Duncan, Del.Supr., 407 A.2d 211, 224 (1979). But in all this, the burden clearly remains on those relying on the vote to show that they completely disclosed all material facts relevant to the transaction.

Here, the record does not support a conclusion that the minority stockholder vote was an informed one. Material information, necessary to acquaint those shareholders with the bargaining positions of Signal and UOP, was withheld under circumstances amounting to a breach of fiduciary duty. We therefore conclude that this merger does not meet the test of fairness, at least as we address that concept, and no burden thus shifted to the plaintiff by reason of the minority shareholder vote. Accordingly, we reverse and remand for further proceedings consistent herewith.

In considering the nature of the remedy available under our law to minority shareholders in a cash-out merger, we believe that it is, and hereafter should be, an appraisal under 8 Del.C. § 262 as hereinafter construed. We therefore overrule Lynch v. Vickers Energy Corp., Del.Supr., 429 A.2d 497 (1981) (*Lynch II*) to the extent that it purports to limit a stockholder's monetary relief to a specific damage formula. See *Lynch II*, 429 A.2d at 507–08 (McNeilly & Quillen, JJ., dissenting). But to give full effect to section 262 within the framework of the General Corporation Law we adopt a more liberal, less rigid and stylized, approach to the valuation process than has heretofore been permitted by our courts. While the present state of these proceedings does not admit the plaintiff to the appraisal remedy per se, the practical effect of the remedy we do grant him will be co-extensive with the liberalized valua-

---

4. In a pre-trial ruling the Chancellor ordered the complaint dismissed for failure to state a cause of action. See Weinberger v. UOP, Inc., Del.Ch., 409 A.2d 1262 (1979).

tion and appraisal methods we herein approve for cases coming after this decision.

Our treatment of these matters has necessarily led us to a reconsideration of the business purpose rule announced in the trilogy of Singer v. Magnavox Co., supra; Tanzer v. International General Industries, Inc., Del.Supr., 379 A.2d 1121 (1977); and Roland International Corp. v. Najjar, Del.Supr., 407 A.2d 1032 (1979). For the reasons hereafter set forth we consider that the business purpose requirement of these cases is no longer the law of Delaware.

I.

The facts found by the trial court, pertinent to the issues before us, are supported by the record, and we draw from them as set out in the Chancellor's opinion.[5]

Signal is a diversified, technically based company operating through various subsidiaries. Its stock is publicly traded on the New York, Philadelphia and Pacific Stock Exchanges. UOP, formerly known as Universal Oil Products Company, was a diversified industrial company engaged in various lines of business, including petroleum and petrochemical services and related products, construction, fabricated metal products, transportation equipment products, chemicals and plastics, and other products and services including land development, lumber products and waste disposal. Its stock was publicly held and listed on the New York Stock Exchange.

In 1974 Signal sold one of its wholly-owned subsidiaries for $420,000,-000 in cash. See Gimbel v. Signal Companies, Inc., Del.Ch., 316 A.2d 599, aff'd, Del.Supr., 316 A.2d 619 (1974). While looking to invest this cash surplus, Signal became interested in UOP as a possible acquisition. Friendly negotiations ensued, and Signal proposed to acquire a controlling interest in UOP at a price of $19 per share. UOP's representatives sought $25 per share. In the arm's length bargaining that followed, an understanding was reached whereby Signal agreed to purchase from UOP 1,500,000 shares of UOP's authorized but unissued stock at $21 per share.

This purchase was contingent upon Signal making a successful cash tender offer for 4,300,000 publicly held shares of UOP, also at a price of $21 per share. This combined method of acquisition permitted Signal to acquire 5,800,000 shares of stock, representing 50.5% of UOP's outstanding shares. The UOP board of directors advised the company's shareholders that it had no objection to Signal's tender offer at that price. Immediately before the announcement of the tender offer, UOP's common stock had been trading on the New York Stock Exchange at a fraction under $14 per share.

The negotiations between Signal and UOP occurred during April 1975, and the resulting tender offer was greatly oversubscribed. How-

5. Weinberger v. UOP, Inc., Del.Ch., 426 A.2d 1333, 1335–40 (1981).

ever, Signal limited its total purchase of the tendered shares so that, when coupled with the stock bought from UOP, it had achieved its goal of becoming a 50.5% shareholder of UOP.

Although UOP's board consisted of thirteen directors, Signal nominated and elected only six. Of these, five were either directors or employees of Signal. The sixth, a partner in the banking firm of Lazard Freres & Co., had been one of Signal's representatives in the negotiations and bargaining with UOP concerning the tender offer and purchase price of the UOP shares.

However, the president and chief executive officer of UOP retired during 1975, and Signal caused him to be replaced by James V. Crawford, a long-time employee and senior executive vice president of one of Signal's wholly-owned subsidiaries. Crawford succeeded his predecessor on UOP's board of directors and also was made a director of Signal.

By the end of 1977 Signal basically was unsuccessful in finding other suitable investment candidates for its excess cash, and by February 1978 considered that it had no other realistic acquisitions available to it on a friendly basis. Once again its attention turned to UOP.

The trial court found that at the instigation of certain Signal management personnel, including William W. Walkup, its board chairman, and Forrest N. Shumway, its president, a feasibility study was made concerning the possible acquisition of the balance of UOP's outstanding shares. This study was performed by two Signal officers, Charles S. Arledge, vice president (director of planning), and Andrew J. Chitiea, senior vice president (chief financial officer). Messrs. Walkup, Shumway, Arledge and Chitiea were all directors of UOP in addition to their membership on the Signal board.

Arledge and Chitiea concluded that it would be a good investment for Signal to acquire the remaining 49.5% of UOP shares at any price up to $24 each. Their report was discussed between Walkup and Shumway who, along with Arledge, Chitiea and Brewster L. Arms, internal counsel for Signal, constituted Signal's senior management. In particular, they talked about the proper price to be paid if the acquisition was pursued, purportedly keeping in mind that as UOP's majority shareholder, Signal owed a fiduciary responsibility to both its own stockholders as well as to UOP's minority. It was ultimately agreed that a meeting of Signal's Executive Committee would be called to propose that Signal acquire the remaining outstanding stock of UOP through a cash-out merger in the range of $20 to $21 per share.

The Executive Committee meeting was set for February 28, 1978. As a courtesy, UOP's President, Crawford, was invited to attend, although he was not a member of Signal's executive committee. On his arrival, and prior to the meeting, Crawford was asked to meet privately with Walkup and Shumway. He was then told of Signal's plan to acquire full ownership of UOP and was asked for his reaction to the proposed price range of $20 to $21 per share. Crawford said he thought such a price would be "generous", and that it was certainly one which should be

submitted to UOP's minority shareholders for their ultimate consideration. He stated, however, that Signal's 100% ownership could cause
internal problems at UOP. He believed that employees would have to be
given some assurance of their future place in a fully-owned Signal
subsidiary. Otherwise, he feared the departure of essential personnel.
Also, many of UOP's key employees had stock option incentive programs
which would be wiped out by a merger. Crawford therefore urged that
some adjustment would have to be made, such as providing a comparable
incentive in Signals' shares, if after the merger he was to maintain his
quality of personnel and efficiency at UOP.

Thus, Crawford voiced no objection to the $20 to $21 price range, nor
did he suggest that Signal should consider paying more than $21 per
share for the minority interests. Later, at the Executive Committee
meeting the same factors were discussed, with Crawford repeating the
position he earlier took with Walkup and Shumway. Also considered
was the 1975 tender offer and the fact that it had been greatly oversubscribed at $21 per share. For many reasons, Signal's management
concluded that the acquisition of UOP's minority shares provided the
solution to a number of its business problems.

Thus, it was the consensus that a price of $20 to $21 per share would
be fair to both Signal and the minority shareholders of UOP. Signal's
executive committee authorized its management "to negotiate" with
UOP "for a cash acquisition of the minority ownership in UOP, Inc., with
the intention of presenting a proposal to [Signal's] board of directors
. . . on March 6, 1978". Immediately after this February 28, 1978
meeting, Signal issued a press release stating:

> The Signal Companies, Inc. and UOP, Inc. are conducting negotia-
> tions for the acquisition for cash by Signal of the 49.5 per cent of
> UOP which it does not presently own, announced Forrest N. Shum-
> way, president and chief executive officer of Signal, and James V.
> Crawford, UOP president.

> Price and other terms of the proposed transaction have not yet
> been finalized and would be subject to approval of the boards of
> directors of Signal and UOP, scheduled to meet early next week, the
> stockholders of UOP and certain federal agencies.

The announcement also referred to the fact that the closing price of
UOP's common stock on that day was $14.50 per share.

Two days later, on March 2, 1978, Signal issued a second press
release stating that its management would recommend a price in the
range of $20 to $21 per share for UOP's 49.5% minority interest. This
announcement referred to Signal's earlier statement that "negotiations"
were being conducted for the acquisition of the minority shares.

Between Tuesday, February 28, 1978 and Monday, March 6, 1978, a
total of four business days, Crawford spoke by telephone with all of
UOP's non-Signal, i.e., outside, directors. Also during that period, Crawford retained Lehman Brothers to render a fairness opinion as to the
price offered the minority for its stock. He gave two reasons for this

choice.   First, the time schedule between the announcement and the board meetings was short (by then only three business days) and since Lehman Brothers had been acting as UOP's investment banker for many years, Crawford felt that it would be in the best position to respond on such brief notice.   Second, James W. Glanville, a long-time director of UOP and a partner in Lehman Brothers, had acted as a financial advisor to UOP for many years.   Crawford believed that Glanville's familiarity with UOP, as a member of its board, would also be of assistance in enabling Lehman Brothers to render a fairness opinion within the existing time constraints.

Crawford telephoned Glanville, who gave his assurance that Lehman Brothers had no conflicts that would prevent it from accepting the task. Glanville's immediate personal reaction was that a price of $20 to $21 would certainly be fair, since it represented almost a 50% premium over UOP's market price.   Glanville sought a $250,000 fee for Lehman Brothers' services, but Crawford thought this too much.   After further discussions Glanville finally agreed that Lehman Brothers would render its fairness opinion for $150,000.

During this period Crawford also had several telephone contacts with Signal officials.   In only one of them, however, was the price of the shares discussed.   In a conversation with Walkup, Crawford advised that as a result of his communications with UOP's non-Signal directors, it was his feeling that the price would have to be the top of the proposed range, or $21 per share, if the approval of UOP's outside directors was to be obtained.   But again, he did not seek any price higher than $21.

Glanville assembled a three-man Lehman Brothers team to do the work on the fairness opinion.   These persons examined relevant documents and information concerning UOP, including its annual reports and its Securities and Exchange Commission filings from 1973 through 1976, as well as its audited financial statements for 1977, its interim reports to shareholders, and its recent and historical market prices and trading volumes.   In addition, on Friday, March, 3, 1978, two members of the Lehman Brothers team flew to UOP's headquarters in Des Plaines, Illinois, to perform a "due diligence" visit, during the course of which they interviewed Crawford as well as UOP's general counsel, its chief financial officer, and other key executives and personnel.

As a result, the Lehman Brothers team concluded that "the price of either $20 or $21 would be a fair price for the remaining shares of UOP". They telephoned this impression to Glanville, who was spending the weekend in Vermont.

On Monday morning, March 6, 1978, Glanville and the senior member of the Lehman Brothers team flew to Des Plaines to attend the scheduled UOP directors meeting.   Glanville looked over the assembled information during the flight.   The two had with them the draft of a "fairness opinion letter" in which the price had been left blank.   Either during or immediately prior to the directors' meeting, the two-page "fairness opinion letter" was typed in final form and the price of $21 per share was inserted.

On March 6, 1978, both the Signal and UOP boards were convened to consider the proposed merger. Telephone communications were maintained between the two meetings. Walkup, Signal's board chairman, and also a UOP director, attended UOP's meeting with Crawford in order to present Signal's position and answer any questions that UOP's non-Signal directors might have. Arledge and Chitiea, along with Signal's other designees on UOP's board, participated by conference telephone. All of UOP's outside directors attended the meeting either in person or by conference telephone.

First, Signal's board unanimously adopted a resolution authorizing Signal to propose to UOP a cash merger of $21 per share as outlined in a certain merger agreement and other supporting documents. This proposal required that the merger be approved by a majority of UOP's outstanding minority shares voting at the stockholders meeting at which the merger would be considered, and that the minority shares voting in favor of the merger, when coupled with Signal's 50.5% interest would have to comprise at least two-thirds of all UOP shares. Otherwise the proposed merger would be deemed disapproved.

UOP's board then considered the proposal. Copies of the agreement were delivered to the directors in attendance, and other copies had been forwarded earlier to the directors participating by telephone. They also had before them UOP financial data for 1974–1977, UOP's most recent financial statements, market price information, and budget projections for 1978. In addition they had Lehman Brothers' hurriedly prepared fairness opinion letter finding the price of $21 to be fair. Glanville, the Lehman Brothers partner, and UOP director, commented on the information that had gone into preparation of the letter.

Signal also suggests that the Arledge-Chitiea feasibility study, indicating that a price of up to $24 per share would be a "good investment" for Signal, was discussed at the UOP directors' meeting. The Chancellor made no such finding, and our independent review of the record, detailed infra, satisfies us by a preponderance of the evidence that there was no discussion of this document at UOP's board meeting. Furthermore, it is clear beyond peradventure that nothing in that report was ever disclosed to UOP's minority shareholders prior to their approval of the merger.

After consideration of Signal's proposal, Walkup and Crawford left the meeting to permit a free and uninhibited exchange between UOP's non-Signal directors. Upon their return a resolution to accept Signal's offer was then proposed and adopted. While Signal's men on UOP's board participated in various aspects of the meeting they abstained from voting. However, the minutes show that each of them "if voting would have voted yes".

On March 7, 1978, UOP sent a letter to its shareholders advising them of the action taken by UOP's board with respect to Signal's offer. This document pointed out, among other things, that on February 28, 1978 "both companies had announced negotiations were being conducted."

Despite the swift board action of the two companies, the merger was not submitted to UOP's shareholders until their annual meeting on May 26, 1978. In the notice of that meeting and proxy statement sent to shareholders in May, UOP's management and board urged that the merger be approved. The proxy statement also advised:

> The price was determined after *discussions* between James V. Crawford, a director of Signal and Chief Executive Officer of UOP, and officers of Signal which took place during meetings on February 28, 1978, and in the course of several subsequent telephone conversations. (Emphasis added.)

In the original draft of the proxy statement the word "negotiations" had been used rather than "discussions". However, when the Securities and Exchange Commission sought details of the "negotiations" as part of its review of these materials, the term was deleted and the word "discussions" was substituted. The proxy statement indicated that the vote of UOP's board in approving the merger had been unanimous. It also advised the shareholders that Lehman Brothers had given its opinion that the merger price of $21 per share was fair to UOP's minority. However, it did not disclose the hurried method by which this conclusion was reached.

As of the record date for UOP's annual meeting, there were 11,488,-302 shares of UOP common stock outstanding, 5,688,302 of which were owned by the minority. At the meeting only 56%, or 3,208,652, of the minority shares were voted. Of these, 2,953,812, or 51.9% of the total minority, voted for the merger, and 254,840 voted against it. When Signal's stock was added to the minority shares voting in favor, a total of 76.2% of UOP's outstanding shares approved the merger while only 2.2% opposed it.

By its terms the merger became effective on May 26, 1978, and each share of UOP's stock held by the minority was automatically converted into a right to receive $21 cash.

II.

A.

A primary issue mandating reversal is the preparation by two UOP directors, Arledge and Chitiea, of their feasibility study for the exclusive use and benefit of Signal. This document was of obvious significance to both Signal and UOP. Using UOP data, it described the advantages to Signal of ousting the minority at a price range of $21–$24 per share. Mr. Arledge, one of the authors, outlined the benefits to Signal:[6]

Purpose of the Merger

6. The parentheses indicate certain handwritten comments of Mr. Arledge.

(1) Provides an outstanding investment opportunity for Signal—(Better than any recent acquisition we have seen.)

(2) Increases Signal's earnings.

(3) Facilitates the flow of resources between Signal and its subsidiaries—(Big factor—works both ways.)

(4) Provides cost savings potential for Signal and UOP.

(5) Improves the percentage of Signal's 'operating earnings' as opposed to 'holding company earnings'.

(6) Simplifies the understanding of Signal.

(7) Facilitates technological exchange among Signal's subsidiaries.

(8) Eliminates potential conflicts of interest.

Having written those words, solely for the use of Signal, it is clear from the record that neither Arledge nor Chitiea shared this report with their fellow directors of UOP. We are satisfied that no one else did either. This conduct hardly meets the fiduciary standards applicable to such a transaction. While Mr. Walkup, Signal's chairman of the board and a UOP director, attended the March 6, 1978 UOP board meeting and testified at trial that he had discussed the Arledge-Chitiea report with the UOP directors at this meeting, the record does not support this assertion. Perhaps it is the result of some confusion on Mr. Walkup's part. In any event Mr.Shumway, Signal's president, testified that he made sure the Signal outside directors had this report prior to the March 6, 1978 Signal board meeting, but he did not testify that the Arledge-Chitiea report was also sent to UOP's outside directors.

Mr. Crawford, UOP's president, could not recall that any documents, other than a draft of the merger agreement, were sent to UOP's directors before the March 6, 1978 UOP meeting. Mr. Chitiea, an author of the report, testified that it was made available to Signal's directors, but to his knowledge it was not circulated to the outside directors of UOP. He specifically testified that he "didn't share" that information with the outside directors of UOP with whom he served.

None of UOP's outside directors who testified stated that they had seen this document. The minutes of the UOP board meeting do not identify the Arledge-Chitiea report as having been delivered to UOP's outside directors. This is particularly significant since the minutes describe in considerable detail the materials that actually were distributed. While these minutes recite Mr. Walkup's presentation of the Signal offer, they do not mention the Arledge-Chitiea report or any disclosure that Signal considered a price of up to $24 to be a good investment. If Mr. Walkup had in fact provided such important information to UOP's outside directors, it is logical to assume that these carefully drafted minutes would disclose it. The post-trial briefs of Signal and UOP contain a thorough description of the documents purportedly available to their boards at the March 6, 1978, meetings. Although the Arledge-Chitiea report is specifically identified as being available to the Signal directors, there is no mention of it being among the documents submitted to the UOP board. Even when queried at a prior oral argument before this Court, counsel for Signal did not claim that the Arledge-Chitiea report had been disclosed to UOP's outside directors. Instead, he chose to belittle its contents. This was the same approach taken before us at the last oral argument.

Actually, it appears that a three-page summary of figures was given to all UOP directors. Its first page is identical to one page of the Arledge-Chitiea report, but this dealt with nothing more than a justification of the $21 price. Significantly, the contents of this three-page summary are what the minutes reflect Mr. Walkup told the UOP board. However, nothing contained in either the minutes or this three-page summary reflects Signal's study regarding the $24 price.

The Arledge-Chitiea report speaks for itself in supporting the Chancellor's finding that a price of up to $24 was a "good investment" for Signal. It shows that a return on the investment at $21 would be 15.7% versus 15.5% at $24 per share. This was a difference of only two-tenths of one percent, while it meant over $17,000,000 to the minority. Under such circumstances, paying UOP's minority shareholders $24 would have had relatively little long-term effect on Signal, and the Chancellor's findings concerning the benefit to Signal, even at a price of $24, were obviously correct. Levitt v. Bouvier, Del.Supr., 287 A.2d 671, 673 (1972).

Certainly, this was a matter of material significance to UOP and its shareholders. Since the study was prepared by two UOP directors, using UOP information for the exclusive benefit of Signal, and nothing whatever was done to disclose it to the outside UOP directors or the minority shareholders, a question of breach of fiduciary duty arises. This problem occurs because there were common Signal-UOP directors participating, at least to some extent, in the UOP board's decision-making processes without full disclosure of the conflicts they faced.[7]

B.

In assessing this situation, the Court of Chancery was required to: examine what information defendants had and to measure it against what they gave to the minority stockholders, in a context in which "complete candor" is required. In other words, the limited function of the Court was to determine whether defendants had disclosed all

---

7. Although perfection is not possible, or expected, the result here could have been entirely different if UOP had appointed an independent negotiating committee of its outside directors to deal with Signal at arm's length. See, e.g., Harriman v. E.I. duPont de Nemours & Co., 411 F.Supp. 133 (D.Del.1975). Since fairness in this context can be equated to conduct by a theoretical, wholly independent, board of directors acting upon the matter before them, it is unfortunate that this course apparently was

neither considered nor pursued. Johnston v. Greene, Del.Supr., 121 A.2d 919, 925 (1956). Particularly in a parent-subsidiary context, a showing that the action taken was as though each of the contending parties had in fact exerted its bargaining power against the other at arm's length is strong evidence that the transaction meets the test of fairness. Getty Oil Co. v. Skelly Oil Co., Del.Supr., 267 A.2d 883, 886 (1970); Puma v. Marriott, Del.Ch., 283 A.2d 693, 696 (1971).

information in their possession germane to the transaction in issue. And by "germane" we mean, for present purposes, information such as a reasonable shareholder would consider important in deciding whether to sell or retain stock.

. . .

. . . Completeness, not adequacy, is both the norm and the mandate under present circumstances.

Lynch v. Vickers Energy Corp., Del.Supr., 383 A.2d 278, 281 (1977) (*Lynch I*). This is merely stating in another way the long-existing principle of Delaware law that these Signal designated directors on UOP's board still owed UOP and its shareholders an uncompromising duty of loyalty. The classic language of Guth v. Loft, Inc., Del.Supr., 5 A.2d 503, 510 (1939), requires no embellishment:

A public policy, existing through the years, and derived from a profound knowledge of human characteristics and motives, has established a rule that demands of a corporate officer or director, peremptorily and inexorably, the most scrupulous observance of his duty, not only affirmatively to protect the interests of the corporation committed to his charge, but also to refrain from doing anything that would work injury to the corporation, or to deprive it of profit or advantage which his skill and ability might properly bring to it, or to enable it to make in the reasonable and lawful exercise of its powers. The rule that requires an undivided and unselfish loyalty to the corporation demands that there shall be no conflict between duty and self-interest.

Given the absence of any attempt to structure this transaction on an arm's length basis, Signal cannot escape the effects of the conflicts it faced, particularly when its designees on UOP's board did not totally abstain from participation in the matter. There is no "safe harbor" for such divided loyalties in Delaware. When directors of a Delaware corporation are on both sides of a transaction, they are required to demonstrate their utmost good faith and the most scrupulous inherent fairness of the bargain. Gottlieb v. Heyden Chemical Corp., Del.Supr., 91 A.2d 57, 57–58 (1952). The requirement of fairness is unflinching in its demand that where one stands on both sides of a transaction, he has the burden of establishing its entire fairness, sufficient to pass the test of careful scrutiny by the courts. Sterling v. Mayflower Hotel Corp., Del.Supr., 93 A.2d 107, 110 (1952); Bastian v. Bourns, Inc., Del.Ch., 256 A.2d 680, 681 (1969), aff'd, Del.Supr., 278 A.2d 467 (1970); David J. Greene & Co. v. Dunhill International Inc., Del.Ch., 249 A.2d 427, 431 (1968).

There is no dilution of this obligation where one holds dual or multiple directorships, as in a parent-subsidiary context. Levien v. Sinclair Oil Corp., Del.Ch., 261 A.2d 911, 915 (1969). Thus, individuals who act in a dual capacity as directors of two corporations, one of whom is parent and the other subsidiary, owe the same duty of good management to both corporations, and in the absence of an independent negotiating structure (see note 7, supra), or the directors' total abstention from any participation in the matter, this duty is to be exercised in light of what is best for both companies. Warshaw v. Calhoun, Del.Supr., 221 A.2d 487, 492 (1966). The record demonstrates that Signal has not met this obligation.

C.

The concept of fairness has two basic aspects: fair dealing and fair price. The former embraces questions of when the transaction was timed, how it was initiated, structured, negotiated, disclosed to the directors, and how the approvals of the directors and the stockholders were obtained. The latter aspect of fairness relates to the economic and financial considerations of the proposed merger, including all relevant factors: assets, market value, earnings, future prospects, and any other elements that affect the intrinsic or inherent value of a company's stock. Moore, The "Interested" Director or Officer Transaction, 4 Del.J.Corp.L. 674, 676 (1979); Nathan & Shapiro, Legal Standard of Fairness of Merger Terms Under Delaware Law, 2 Del.J.Corp.L. 44, 46–47 (1977). See Tri-Continental Corp. v. Battye, Del.Supr., 74 A.2d 71, 72 (1950); 8 Del.C. § 262(h). However, the test for fairness is not a bifurcated one as between fair dealing and price. All aspects of the issue must be examined as a whole since the question is one of entire fairness. However, in a non-fraudulent transaction we recognize that price may be the preponderant consideration outweighing other features of the merger. Here, we address the two basic aspects of fairness separately because we find reversible error as to both.

D.

Part of fair dealing is the obvious duty of candor required by *Lynch I*, supra. Moreover, one possessing superior knowledge may not mislead any stockholder by use of corporate information to which the latter is not privy. Lank v. Steiner, Del.Supr., 224 A.2d 242, 244 (1966). Delaware has long imposed this duty even upon persons who are not corporate officers or directors, but who nonetheless are privy to matters of interest or significance to their company. Brophy v. Cities Service Co., Del.Ch., 70 A.2d 5, 7 (1949). With the well-established Delaware law on the subject, and the Court of Chancery's findings of fact here, it is inevitable that the obvious conflicts posed by Arledge and Chitiea's preparation of their "feasibility study", derived from UOP information, for the sole use and benefit of Signal, cannot pass muster.

The Arledge-Chitiea report is but one aspect of the element of fair dealing. How did this merger evolve? It is clear that it was entirely initiated by Signal. The serious time constraints under which the principals acted were all set by Signal. It had not found a suitable outlet for its excess cash and considered UOP a desirable investment, particularly since it was now in a position to acquire the whole company for itself. For whatever reasons, and they were only Signal's, the entire transaction was presented to and approved by UOP's board within four business days. Standing alone, this is not necessarily indicative of any lack of fairness by a majority shareholder. It was what occurred, or more properly, what did not occur, during this brief period that makes the time constraints imposed by Signal relevant to the issue of fairness.

The structure of the transaction, again, was Signal's doing. So far as negotiations were concerned, it is clear that they were modest at best. Crawford, Signal's man at UOP, never really talked price with Signal, except to accede to its management's statements on the subject, and to convey to Signal the UOP outside directors' view that as between the $20-$21 range under consideration, it would have to be $21. The latter is not a surprising outcome, but hardly arm's length negotiations. Only the protection of benefits for UOP's key employees and the issue of Lehman Brothers' fee approached any concept of bargaining.

As we have noted, the matter of disclosure to the UOP directors was wholly flawed by the conflicts of interest raised by the Arledge-Chitiea report. All of those conflicts were resolved by Signal in its own favor without divulging any aspect of them to UOP.

This cannot but undermine a conclusion that this merger meets any reasonable test of fairness. The outside UOP directors lacked one material piece of information generated by two of their colleagues, but shared only with Signal. True, the UOP board had the Lehman Brothers' fairness opinion, but that firm has been blamed by the plaintiff for the hurried task it performed, when more properly the responsibility for this lies with Signal. There was no disclosure of the circumstances surrounding the rather cursory preparation of the Lehman Brothers' fairness opinion. Instead, the impression was given UOP's minority that a careful study had been made, when in fact speed was the hallmark, and Mr. Glanville, Lehman's partner in charge of the matter, and also a UOP director, having spent the weekend in Vermont, brought a draft of the "fairness opinion letter" to the UOP directors' meeting on March 6, 1978 with the price left blank. We can only conclude from the record that the rush imposed on Lehman Brothers by Signal's timetable contributed to the difficulties under which this investment banking firm attempted to perform its responsibilities. Yet, none of this was disclosed to UOP's minority.

Finally, the minority stockholders were denied the critical information that Signal considered a price of $24 to be a good investment. Since this would have meant over $17,000,000 more to the minority, we cannot conclude that the shareholder vote was an informed one. Under the circumstances, an approval by a majority of the minority was meaningless. *Lynch I*, 383 A.2d at 279, 281; Cahall v. Lofland, Del.Ch., 114 A. 224 (1921).

Given these particulars and the Delaware law on the subject, the record does not establish that this transaction satisfies any reasonable concept of fair dealing, and the Chancellor's findings in that regard must be reversed.

E.

Turning to the matter of price, plaintiff also challenges its fairness. His evidence was that on the date the merger was approved the stock was worth at least $26 per share. In support, he offered the testimony of a chartered investment analyst who used two basic approaches to valuation: a comparative analysis of the premium paid over market in ten other tender offer-merger combinations, and a discounted cash flow analysis.

In this breach of fiduciary duty case, the Chancellor perceived that the approach to valuation was the same as that in an appraisal proceeding. Consistent with precedent, he rejected plaintiff's method of proof and accepted defendants' evidence of value as being in accord with practice under prior case law. This means that the so-called "Delaware block" or weighted average method was employed wherein the elements of value, i.e., assets, market price, earnings, etc., were assigned a particular weight and the resulting amounts added to determine the value per share. This procedure has been in use for decades. See In re General Realty & Utilities Corp., Del.Ch., 52 A.2d 6, 14–15 (1947). However, to the extent it excludes other generally accepted techniques used in the financial community and the courts, it is now clearly outmoded. It is time we recognize this in appraisal and other stock valuation proceedings and bring our law current on the subject.

While the Chancellor rejected plaintiff's discounted cash flow method of valuing UOP's stock, as not corresponding with "either logic or the existing law" (426 A.2d at 1360), it is significant that this was essentially the focus, i.e., earnings potential of UOP, of Messrs. Arledge and Chitiea in their evaluation of the merger. Accordingly, the standard "Delaware block" or weighted average method of valuation, formerly employed in appraisal and other stock valuation cases, shall no longer exclusively control such proceedings. We believe that a more liberal approach must include proof of value by any techniques or methods which are generally considered acceptable in the financial community and otherwise admissible in court, subject only to our interpretation of 8 Del.C. § 262(h), infra. . . . This will obviate the very structured and mechanistic procedure that has heretofore governed such matters. See Jacques Coe & Co. v. Minneapolis-Moline Co., Del.Ch. 75 A.2d 244, 247 (1950); Tri-Continental Corp. v. Battye, Del.Ch., 66 A.2d 910, 917–18 (1949); In re General Realty and Utilities Corp., supra.

Fair price obviously requires consideration of all relevant factors involving the value of a company. This has long been the law of Delaware as stated in *Tri-Continental Corp.*, 74 A.2d at 72:

The basic concept of value under the appraisal statute is that the stockholder is entitled to be paid for that which has been taken from him, viz., his proportionate interest in a going concern. By value of the stockholder's proportionate interest in the corporate enterprise is meant the true or intrinsic value of his stock which has been taken by the merger. In determining what figure represents this true or intrinsic value, the appraiser and the courts must take into consideration all factors and elements which reasonably might enter into the fixing of value. Thus, market value, asset value, dividends, earning prospects, the nature of the enterprise and any other facts which were known or which could be ascertained as of the date of merger and which throw any light on *future prospects* of the merged corporation are not only pertinent to an inquiry as to the value of the dissenting stockholders' interest but *must be considered* by the agency fixing the value. (Emphasis added.)

This is not only in accord with the realities of present day affairs, but it is thoroughly consonant with the purpose and intent of our statutory law. Under 8 Del.C. § 262(h), the Court of Chancery:

shall appraise the shares, determining their *fair* value exclusive of any element of value arising from the accomplishment or expectation of the merger, together with a fair rate of interest, if any, to be paid upon the amount determined to be the *fair* value. In determining such *fair* value, the Court shall take into account *all relevant factors* . . . (Emphasis added)

See also Bell v. Kirby Lumber Corp., Del.Supr., 413 A.2d 137, 150–51 (1980) (Quillen, J., concurring).

It is significant that section 262 now mandates the determination of "fair" value based upon "all relevant factors". Only the speculative elements of value that may arise from the "accomplishment or expectation" of the merger are excluded. We take this to be a very narrow exception to the appraisal process, designed to eliminate use of *pro forma* data and projections of a speculative variety relating to the completion of a merger. But elements of future value, including the nature of the enterprise, which are known or susceptible of proof as of the date of the merger and not the product of speculation, may be considered. When the trial court deems it appropriate, fair value also includes any damages, resulting from the taking, which the stockholders sustain as a class. If that was not the case, then the obligation to consider "all relevant factors" in the valuation process would be eroded. We are supported in this view not only by *Tri-Continental Corp.*, 74 A.2d at 72, but also by the evolutionary amendments to section 262.

Prior to an amendment in 1976, the earlier relevant provision of section 262 stated:

(f) The appraiser shall determine the value of the stock of the stockholders . . . . The Court shall by its decree determine the value of the stock of the stockholders entitled to payment therefor . . .

The first references to "fair" value occurred in a 1976 amendment to section 262(f), which provided:

(f) . . . the Court shall appraise the shares, determining their fair value exclusively of any element of value arising from the accomplishment or expectation of the merger. . . .

It was not until the 1981 amendment to section 262 that the reference to "fair value" was repeatedly emphasized and the statutory mandate that the Court "take into account all relevant factors" appeared [section 262(h)]. Clearly, there is a legislative intent to fully compensate shareholders for whatever their loss may be, subject only to the narrow limitation that one can not take speculative effects of the merger into account.

Although the Chancellor received the plaintiff's evidence, his opinion indicates that the use of it was precluded because of past Delaware practice. While we do not suggest a monetary result one way or the other, we do think the plaintiff's evidence should be part of the factual mix and weighed as such. Until the $21 price is measured on remand by the valuation standards mandated by Delaware law, there can be no finding at the present stage of these proceedings that the price is fair. Given the lack of any candid disclosure of the material facts surrounding establishment of the $21 price, the majority of the minority vote, approving the merger, is meaningless.

The plaintiff has not sought an appraisal, but rescissory damages of the type contemplated by Lynch v. Vickers Energy Corp., Del.Supr., 429 A.2d 497, 505–06 (1981) (*Lynch II*). In view of the approach to valuation that we announce today, we see no basis in our law for *Lynch II*'s exclusive monetary formula for relief. On remand the plaintiff will be permitted to test the fairness of the $21 price by the standards we herein establish, in conformity with the principle applicable to an appraisal— that fair value be determined by taking "into account all relevant factors" [see 8 Del.C. § 262(h), supra]. In our view this includes the elements of rescissory damages if the Chancellor considers them susceptible of proof and a remedy appropriate to all the issues of fairness before him. To the extent that *Lynch II*, 429 A.2d at 505–06, purports to limit the Chancellor's discretion to a single remedial formula for monetary damages in a cash-out merger, it is overruled.

While a plaintiff's monetary remedy ordinarily should be confined to the more liberalized appraisal proceeding herein established, we do not intend any limitation on the historic powers of the Chancellor to grant such other relief as the facts of a particular case may dictate. The appraisal remedy we approve may not be adequate in certain cases, particularly where fraud, misrepresentation, self-dealing, deliberate waste of corporate assets, or gross and palpable overreaching are involved. Cole v. National Cash Credit Association, Del.Ch., 156 A. 183, 187 (1931). Under such circumstances, the Chancellor's powers are complete to fashion any form of equitable and monetary relief as may be appropriate, including rescissory damages. Since it is apparent that this long completed transaction is too involved to undo, and in view of the Chancellor's discretion, the award, if any, should be in the form of monetary damages based upon entire fairness standards, i.e., fair dealing and fair price.

Obviously, there are other litigants, like the plaintiff, who abjured an appraisal and whose rights to challenge the element of fair value must be preserved.[8] Accordingly, the quasi-appraisal remedy we grant the plaintiff here will apply only to: (1) this case; (2) any case now pending on appeal to this Court; (3) any case now pending in the Court of Chancery which has not yet been appealed but which may be eligible for direct appeal to this Court; (4) any case challenging a cash-out merger, the effective date of which is on or before February 1, 1983; and (5) any proposed merger to be presented at a shareholders' meeting, the notification of which is mailed to the stockholders on or before February 23, 1983. Thereafter, the provisions of 8 Del.C. § 262, as herein construed, respecting the scope of an appraisal and the means for perfecting the same, shall govern the financial remedy available to minority shareholders in a cash-out merger. Thus, we return to the well established principles of Stauffer v. Standard Brands, Inc., Del.Supr., 187 A.2d 78 (1962) and David J. Greene & Co. v. Schenley Industries, Inc., Del.Ch., 281 A.2d 30 (1971), mandating a stockholder's recourse to the basic remedy of an appraisal.

III.

Finally, we address the matter of business purpose. The defendants contend that the purpose of this merger was not a proper subject of inquiry by the trial court. The plaintiff says that no valid purpose existed—the entire transaction was a mere subterfuge designed to eliminate the minority. The Chancellor ruled otherwise, but in so doing he clearly circumscribed the thrust and effect of *Singer*. Weinberger v. UOP, 426 A.2d at 1342–43, 1348–50. This has led to the thoroughly sound observation that the business purpose test "may be ... virtually interpreted out of existence, as it was in *Weinberger*".[9]

The requirement of a business purpose is new to our law of mergers and was a departure from prior case law. See Stauffer v. Standard Brands, Inc., supra; David J. Greene & Co. v. Schenley Industries, Inc., supra.

In view of the fairness test which has long been applicable to parent-subsidiary mergers, Sterling v. Mayflower Hotel Corp., Del.Supr., 93 A.2d 107, 109–10 (1952), the expanded appraisal remedy now available to shareholders, and the broad discretion of the Chancellor to fashion such relief as the facts of a given case may dictate we do not believe that any additional meaningful protection is afforded minority shareholders by the business purpose requirement of the trilogy of *Singer, Tanzer*,[10]

8. Under 8 Del.C. § 262(a), (d) & (e), a stockholder is required to act within certain time periods to perfect the right to an appraisal.

9. Weiss, The Law of Take Out Mergers: A Historical Perspective, 56 N.Y.U.L. Rev. 624, 671, n. 300 (1981).

10. Tanzer v. International General Industries, Inc., Del.Supr., 379 A.2d 1121,

Najjar,[11] and their progeny. Accordingly, such requirement shall no longer be of any force or effect.

The judgment of the Court of Chancery, finding both the circumstances of the merger and the price paid the minority shareholders to be fair, is reversed. The matter is remanded for further proceedings consistent herewith. Upon remand the plaintiff's post-trial motion to enlarge the class should be granted.

. . .

Reversed and Remanded.

(*l*) GOING PRIVATE

Insert the following note at p. 1560 of the unabridged edition, and p. 904 of the abridged edition, after the Note on Lynch v. Vickers Energy Corp.:

FURTHER NOTE ON LYNCH v. VICKERS ENERGY CORP.

Lynch v. Vickers Energy Corp., 402 A.2d 5 (Del.Ch.1979) was reversed by the Delaware Supreme Court, 429 A.2d 497 (1981). The Supreme Court held that the Chancery Court erroneously measured damages under an appraisal formula, whereas a claim founded on a breach of fiduciary duty permits accounting, rescission, or comparable remedies. Finding rescission to be impractible, the court held that Vickers was required to pay rescissory damages to plaintiffs, measured by the equivalent value of the TransOcean stock at the time of judgment. Two years later, the Delaware Supreme Court spoke to the issue again, in Weinberger v. UOP, supra.

(m) SHARE ACQUISITIONS AND TENDER OFFERS— TAKEOVER BIDS

---

(2) The Williams Act: Amendments to the Securities Exchange Act of 1934 Relating to Tender Offers and Takeovers

Insert the following material at p. 1571 of the unabridged edition, at the end of Chapter X, Section 1(m)(2):

SECURITIES EXCHANGE ACT

REGULATIONS 14D, 14E

14d–1 Scope of and Definitions Applicable to Regulations 14D and

1124–25 (1977).   Del.Supr., 407 A.2d 1032, 1036 (1979).

11.   Roland International Corp. v. Najjar,

14E

(a) *Scope.* Regulation 14D [Rules 14d–1 et seq.] shall apply to any tender offer which is subject to section 14(d)(1) of the Act, including, but not limited to, any tender offer for securities of a class described in that section which is made by an affiliate of the issuer of such class. Regulation 14E [Rules 14e–1 et seq.] shall apply to any tender offer for securities (other than exempted securities) unless otherwise noted therein.

(b) *Definitions.* Unless the context otherwise requires ... :

(1) The term "bidder" means any person who makes a tender offer or on whose behalf a tender offer is made: *Provided, however,* That the term does not include an issuer which makes a tender offer for securities of any class of which it is the issuer;

(2) The term "subject company" means any issuer of securities which are sought by a bidder pursuant to a tender offer ...

(7) The term "security position listing" means, with respect to securities of any issuer held by a registered clearing agency in the name of the clearing agency or its nominee, a list of those participants in the clearing agency on whose behalf the clearing agency holds the issuer's securities and of the participants' respective positions in such securities as of a specified date ...

14d–2 Date of Commencement of a Tender Offer ... *

[The provisions of Rule 14d–2(a)(1) through (3) are related to the methods by which tender offer materials may be disseminated under Rule 14d–4. ... [A] tender offer using long-form publication commences on the date of the newspaper publication. A tender offer disseminated by means of summary publication commences on the date the summary advertisement appears in the newspapers. ...

[Under Rule 14d–2(b) a bidder's public announcement through a press release, newspaper advertisement or public statement of certain material terms of a cash tender offer causes the bidder's tender offer to commence under Section 14(d) of the Exchange Act. In order to provide certainty to bidders, the information which will trigger Rule 14d–2(b) is set forth in Rule 14d–2(c). Generally, this information relates to: the identity of the bidder and the subject company; a statement of the class and amount of securities being sought; and disclosure of the price or range of prices being offered therefor. Safe harbor provisions for public announcements which will not trigger the operation of Rule 14d–2(b) are set forth in Rules 14d–2(d) and (e).**

---

* Bracketed material is adapted from Securities Act Release No. 6158 (1979). (Footnote by ed.)

** Rule 14–2(d) provides:

(d) *Announcements Not Resulting in Commencement.* A public announcement by a bidder through a press release, newspaper advertisement or public statement which only discloses the information in paragraphs (d)(1) through (d)(3) of this section concerning a tender offer in which the consideration consists solely of cash and/or securities exempt from registration under section 3 of the Securities Act of 1933 shall not be deemed to constitute

[Rule 14d–2(b) contains an exception clause which is designed to prevent the imposition of undue burdens on a bidder and to assure the availability of security holders' rights under Sections 14(d)(5) and 14(d)(6) and the rules promulgated thereunder. Under the exception clause, the tender offer would not be deemed to commence on the date of the public announcement if within five business days thereafter the bidder either: (1) issues a subsequent public announcement stating that the bidder has determined not to continue with the offer; or (2) complies with the filing requirements of Rule 14d–3(a) and disseminates the disclosure required by Rule 14d–6(a) to security holders pursuant to Rule 14d–4 or otherwise.

[If the bidder makes the subsequent announcement contemplated by the first option, the initial announcement will not be deemed to commence an offer. If the bidder complies with the filing, disclosure and dissemination requirements of the second option, the tender offer will commence on the date of such compliance, rather than the date of the earlier public announcement, except that Section 14(d)(7) will apply from the date of such earlier public announcement. If the bidder exercises neither option, the tender offer commences on the date of the initial announcement, resulting, however, in filing and disclosure violations. As a result, it is not anticipated that a bidder making such a public announcement will select the "do nothing" alternative.]

. . . [Rule 14d–2(b) is intended to prevent public announcements by a bidder of the material terms of its tender offer in advance of the offer's formal commencement. The Commission believes that this practice is detrimental to the interests of investors and results in many of the abuses the Williams Act was enacted to prevent. Such pre-commencement public announcements cause security holders to make investment decisions with respect to a tender offer on the basis of incomplete information and trigger market activity normally attendant to a tender offer, such as arbitrageur activity. Since they constitute the practical commencement of a tender offer, such pre-commencement public announcements cause the contest for control of the subject company to occur prior to the application of the Williams Act and therefore deny security holders the protections which that Act was intended by Congress to provide.

14d–3　Filing and Transmission of Tender Offer Statement

(a) *Filing and Transmittal.* No bidder shall make a tender offer if, after consummation thereof, such bidder would be the beneficial owner of more than 5 percent of the class of the subject company's securities

---

the commencement of a tender offer under paragraph (a)(5) of this section.

(1) The identity of the bidder;

(2) The identity of the subject company; and

(3) A statement that the bidder intends to make a tender offer in the future for a class of equity securities of the subject company which statement does not specify the amount of securities of such class to be sought or the consideration to be offered therefor.

(Footnote by ed.)

for which the tender offer is made, unless as soon as practicable on the date of the commencement of the tender offer such bidder:

(1) Files with the Commission ten copies of a Tender Offer Statement on Schedule 14D–1 ....

14d–4   Dissemination of Certain Tender Offers

(a) *Materials Deemed Published or Sent or Given.* A tender offer in which the consideration consists solely of cash and/or securities exempt from registration under section 3 of the Securities Act of 1933 shall be deemed "published or sent or given to security holders" within the meaning of section 14(d)(1) of the Act if the bidder complies with all of the requirements of any one of the following sub-paragraphs: *Provided, however,* That any such tender offers may be published or sent or given to security holders by other methods, but with respect to summary publication, and the use of stockholder lists and security position listings pursuant to Rule 14d–5, paragraphs (a)(2) and (a)(3) of this section are exclusive.

(1) *Long-form Publication.* The bidder makes adequate publication in a newspaper or newspapers of long-form publication of the tender offer.

(2) *Summary Publication.*

(i) ... [T]he bidder makes adequate publication in a newspaper or newspapers of a summary advertisement of the tender offer; and

(ii) Mails by first class mail or otherwise furnishes with reasonable promptness the bidder's tender offer materials to any security holder who requests such tender offer materials pursuant to the summary advertisement or otherwise.

(3) *Use of Stockholder Lists and Security Position Listings.* Any bidder using stockholder lists and security position listings pursuant to Rule 14d–5 shall comply with paragraphs (a)(1) or (a)(2) of this section on or prior to the date of the bidder's request for such lists or listing pursuant to Rule 14d–5(a). ...

14d–5   Dissemination of Certain Tender Offers by the Use of Stockholder Lists and Security Position Listings ...

[Rule 14d–5 gives bidders a Federal right to have their tender offer materials disseminated by means of the stockholder lists of the subject company and security position listings of clearing agencies. The subject company is able to elect whether to retain the stockholder lists, in which case the subject company will mail and transmit the bidder's tender offer materials, or to furnish the stockholder lists to the bidder, in which case the bidder will mail and transmit the tender offer materials. The option feature of Rule 14d–5 is patterned after Rule 14a–7 of the Proxy Rules.

[The principal paragraph relating to the requirements imposed on the subject company is Rule 14d–5(a). This provision is triggered by the subject company's receipt of a written request from a bidder for the use of stockholder lists and security position listings. Upon receipt, the subject company is required to notify promptly certain persons, including transfer agents, of the receipt of the request and to ascertain promptly whether the current stockholder list was prepared as of a date earlier than ten business days before the date of the bidder's request. If the list was prepared prior to the ten business day period, the subject company is required to prepare a stockholder list as of the most recent practicable date which shall not be earlier than ten business days before the day the bidder's request was received.

[While the name and address of record holders would be furnished to the bidder, the amount of securities held by such persons would not be disclosed.]

14d–6   Disclosure Requirements with Respect to Tender Offers

(a) *Information Required on Date of Commencement.*

(1) *Long-form Publication.* If a tender offer is published, sent or given to security holders on the date of commencement by means of long-[form] publication pursuant to Rule 14d–4(a)(1) ... such long-form publication shall include the information required by paragraph (e)(1) of this section.

(2) *Summary Publication.* If a tender offer is published, sent or given to security holders on the date of commencement by means of summary publication pursuant to Rule 14d–4(a)(2) ....,

(i) The summary advertisement shall contain and shall be limited to, the information required by paragraph (e)(2) of this section; and

(ii) The tender offer materials furnished by the bidder upon the request of any security holder shall include the information required by paragraph (c)(1) of this section.

(3) *Use of Stockholder Lists and Security Position Listings.* If a tender offer is published or sent or given to security holders on the date of commencement by the use of stockholder lists and security position listings pursuant to Rule 14d–4(a)(3) ....

(i) Either (A) the summary advertisement shall contain, and shall be limited to the information required by paragraph (e)(2) of this section, or (B) if long form publication of the tender offer is made, such long form publication shall include the information required by paragraph (e)(1) of this section; and

(ii) The tender offer materials transmitted to security holders pursuant to such lists and security position listings and furnished by the bidder upon the request of any security holder shall include the information required by paragraph (e)(1) of this section. ...

(e) *Information to Be Included.*

(1) *Long-form Publication and Tender Offer Materials.* The information required to be disclosed by paragraphs (a)(1), (a)(2)(ii), (a)(3)(i)(B) and (a)(4) of this section shall include the following:

(i) The identity of the holder;

(ii) The identity of the subject company;

(iii) The amount of [each] class of securities being sought and the type and amount of consideration being offered therefor;

(iv) The scheduled expiration date of the tender offer, whether the tender offer may be extended and, if so, the procedures for extension of the tender offer ...

(vi) If the tender offer is for less than all the outstanding securities of a class of equity securities and the bidder is not obligated to purchase all of the securities tendered, the period or periods ... during which the securities will be taken up pro rata pursuant to Section 14(d)(6) of the Act or Rule 14d–8 ... and the present intention or plan of the bidder with respect to the tender offer in the event of an oversubscription by security holders;

(vii) The disclosure required by Items 1(c); 2 ... ; 3; 4; 5; 6; 7; 8; and 10 of Schedule 14D–1 ... ;*

(viii) The disclosure required by Item 9 of Schedule 14D–1 or a fair and adequate summary thereof. ...

(2) *Summary Publication.* The information required to be disclosed by paragraphs (a)(2)(i) and (a)(3)(i)(A) of this section in a summary advertisement is as follows:

(i) The information required by paragraph (e)(1)(i) through (vi) of this section;

(ii) If the tender offer is for less than all the outstanding securities of a class of equity securities, a statement as to whether the purpose or one of the purposes of the tender offer is to acquire or influence control of the business of the subject company; ...

(iv) Appropriate instructions as to how security holders may obtain promptly, at the bidder's expense, the bidder's tender offer materials ....

14d–7 Additional Withdrawal Rights

(a) *Rights.* In addition to the provisions of section 14(d)(5) of the Act, any person who has deposited securities pursuant to a tender offer has the right to withdraw any such securities during the following periods:

(1) At any time until the expiration of fifteen business days from the date of commencement of such tender offer; and

(2) On the date and until the expiration of ten business days following the date of commencement of another bidder's tender offer other than pursuant to Rule 14d–2(b) for securities of the same class *provided that* ... withdrawal may only be effected with respect to securities which have not been accepted for payment in the manner

---

* See pp. 173–175, infra. (Footnote by ed.)

set forth in the bidder's tender offer prior to the date such other tender offer is first published, sent or given to security holders.   . . .

14d–8 [Pro Rata Requirement]

Notwithstanding the pro rata provisions of Section 14(d)(6) of the Act, if any person makes a tender offer or request or invitation for tenders, for less than all of the outstanding equity securities of a class, and if a greater number of securities are deposited pursuant thereto than such person is bound or willing to take up and pay for, the securities taken up and paid for shall be taken up and paid for as nearly as may be pro rata, disregarding fractions, according to the number of securities deposited by each depositor during the period such offer, request or invitation remains open.

14d–9 Solicitation/Recommendation Statements with Respect to Certain Tender Offers

(a) *Filing and Transmittal of Recommendation Statement.* No solicitation or recommendation to security holders shall be made by any person described in paragraph (d) of this section with respect to a tender offer for such securities unless as soon as practicable on the date such solicitation or recommendation is first published or sent or given to security holders such person complies with the following sub-paragraphs.

(1) Such person shall file with the Commission eight copies of a Tender Offer Solicitation/Recommendation Statement on Schedule 14D–9 . . . .*

(c) *Information Required in Solicitation or Recommendation.* Any solicitation or recommendation to holders of a class of securities referred to in section 14(d)(1) of the Act with respect to a tender offer for such securities shall include the name of the person making such solicitation or recommendation and the information required by Items 1, 2, 3(b), 4, 6, 7 and 8 of Schedule 14D–9 . . . or a fair and adequate summary thereof . . . .

(d) *Applicability.*

(1) Except as is provided in paragraphs (d)(2) and (e) of this section, this section shall only apply to the following persons:

(i) The subject company, any director, officer, employee, affiliate or subsidiary of the subject company . . . .

(e) *Stop-Look-and-Listen Communications.* This section shall not apply to the subject company with respect to a communication by the subject company to its security holders which only:

(1) Identifies the tender offer by the bidder;

(2) States that such tender offer is under consideration by the subject company's board of directors and/or management;

(3) States that on or before a specified date (which shall be no later than 10 business days from the date of commencement of such

* See pp. 175–176, infra. (Footnote by ed.)

tender offer) the subject company will advise such security holders of (i) whether the subject company recommends acceptance or rejection of such tender offer; expresses no opinion and remains neutral toward such tender offer; or is unable to take a position with respect to such tender offer and (ii) the reason(s) for the position taken by the subject company with respect to the tender offer (including the inability to take a position); and

(4) Requests such security holders to defer making determination whether to accept or reject such tender offer until they have been advised of the subject company's position with respect thereto pursuant to paragraph (e)(3) of this section.

(f) *Statement of Management's Position.* A statement by the subject company's of its position with respect to a tender offer which is required to be published or sent or given to security holders pursuant to Rule 14e–2 shall be deemed to constitute a solicitation or recommendation within the meaning of this section and section 14(d)(4) of the Act.

14e–1. Unlawful Tender Offer Practices

As a means reasonably designed to prevent fraudulent, deceptive or manipulative acts or practices within the meaning of section 14(e) of the Act, no person who makes a tender offer shall:

(a) Hold such tender offer open for less than twenty business days from the date such tender offer is first published or sent or given to security holders: *Provided, however,* That this paragraph shall not apply to a tender offer by the issuer of the class of securities being sought which is not made in anticipation of or in response to another person's tender offer for securities of the same class.

(b) Increase the offered consideration or the dealer's soliciting fee to be given in a tender offer unless such tender offer remains open for at least ten business days from the date that notice of such increase is first published, sent or given to security holders: *Provided, however,* That this paragraph shall not apply to a tender offer by the issuer of the class of securities being sought which is not made in anticipation of or in response to another person's tender offer for securities of the same class. ...

(d) Extend the length of a tender offer without issuing a notice of such extension by press release or other public announcement, which notice shall include disclosure of the approximate number of securities deposited to date. ...

14e–2. Position of Subject Company with Respect to a Tender Offer

(a) *Position of Subject Company.* As a means reasonably designed to prevent fraudulent, deceptive or manipulative acts or practices within the meaning of section 14(e) of the Act, the subject company, no later than 10 business days from the date the tender offer is first published or sent or given, shall publish, send or give to security holders a statement disclosing that the subject company:

(1) Recommends acceptance [or] rejection of the bidder's tender offer;

(2) Expresses no opinion and is remaining neutral toward the bidder's tender offer; or

(3) Is unable to take a position with respect to the bidder's tender offer.

Such statement shall also include the reason(s) for the position (including the inability to take a position) disclosed therein. ...

SECURITIES AND EXCHANGE COMMISSION
SCHEDULE 14D-1

. . .

Item 1. Security and Subject Company

(a) State the name of the subject company and the address of its principal executive offices;

(b) State the exact title and the number of shares outstanding of the class of equity securities being sought ..., the exact amount of such securities being sought and the consideration being offered therefor; and

(c) Identify the principal market in which such securities are traded and state the high and low sales prices for such securities in such principal market (or, in the absence thereof, the range of high and low bid quotations) for each quarterly period during the past two years.

Item 2. Identity and Background [of Persons Filing the Schedule]

. . .

Item 3. Past Contacts, Transactions or Negotiations [between Persons Filing the Schedule and] the Subject Company

. . .

Item 4. Source and Amount of Funds or Other Consideration

(a) State the source and the total amount of funds or other consideration for the purchase of the maximum number of securities for which the tender offer is being made.

(b) If all or any part of such funds or other consideration are or are expected to be, directly or indirectly, borrowed for the purpose of the tender offer:

(1) provide a summary of each loan agreement or arrangement containing the identity of the parties, the term, the collateral, the stated and effective interest rates, and other material terms or conditions relative to such loan agreement; and

(2) Briefly describe any plans or arrangements to finance or repay such borrowings, or if no such plans or arrangements have been made, make a statement to that effect. ...

Item 5.   Purpose of the Tender Offer and Plans or Proposals of the Bidder

State the purpose or purposes of the tender offer for the subject company's securities. Describe any plans or proposals which relate to or would result in:

(a) An extraordinary corporate transaction, such as a merger, reorganization or liquidation, involving the subject company or any of its subsidiaries;

(b) A sale or transfer of a material amount of assets of the subject company or any of its subsidiaries;

(c) Any change in the present board of directors or management of the subject company including, but not limited to, any plans or proposals to change the number or the term of directors or to fill any existing vacancies on the board;

(d) Any material change in the present capitalization or dividend policy of the subject company;

(e) Any other material change in the subject company's corporate structure or business ...;

(f) Causing a class of securities of the subject company to be delisted from a national securities exchange or to cease to be authorized to be quoted in an inter-dealer quotation system of a registered national securities association; or

(g) A class of equity securities of the subject company becoming eligible for termination of registration pursuant to section 12(g)(4) of the Act.

Item 6.   Interest in Securities of the Subject Company

(a) State the aggregate number and percentage of the class represented by ... shares ... beneficially owned (identifying those shares for which there is a right to acquire) by each person named in Item 2 of this schedule and by each associate and majority-owned subsidiary of such person. ...

Item 7.   Contracts, Arrangements, Understandings or Relationships with Respect to the Subject Company's Securities

Describe any contract, arrangement, understanding or relationship (whether or not legally enforceable) between the bidder ... and any person with respect to any securities of the subject company, (including, but not limited to, any contract, arrangement, understanding or relationship concerning the transfer or the voting of any of such securities, joint ventures, loan or option arrangements, puts or calls, guaranties of loans, guaranties against loss, or the giving or withholding of proxies) naming the persons with whom such contracts, arrangements, understandings or relationships have been entered into and giving the material provisions thereof. ...

Item 8. Persons Retained, Employed or to be Compensated

Identify all persons and classes of persons employed, retained or to be compensated by the bidder, or by any person on the bidder's behalf, to make solicitations or recommendations in connection with the tender offer and describe briefly the terms of such employment, retainer or arrangement for compensation.

Item 9. Financial Statements of Certain Bidders

Where the bidder is other than a natural person and the bidder's financial condition is material to a decision by a security holder of the subject company whether to sell, tender or hold securities being sought in the tender offer, furnish current, adequate financial information concerning the bidder *Provided* That if the bidder is controlled by another entity which is not a natural person and has been formed for the purpose of making the tender offer, furnish current, adequate financial information concerning such parent. ...

Item 10. Additional Information

If material to a decision by a security holder whether to sell, tender or hold securities being sought in the tender offer, furnish information as to the following:

(a) Any present or proposed material contracts, arrangements, understandings or relationships between the bidder or any of its executive officers, directors, controlling persons or subsidiaries and the subject company or any of its executive officers, directors, controlling persons or subsidiaries (other than any contract, arrangement or understanding required to be disclosed pursuant to Items 3 or 7 of this schedule);

(b) To the extent known by the bidder after reasonable investigation, the applicable regulatory requirements which must be complied with or approvals which must be obtained in connection with the tender offer;

(c) The applicability of anti-trust laws;

(d) The applicability of the margin requirements of section 7 of the Act and the regulations promulgated thereunder;

(e) Any material pending legal proceedings relating to the tender offer including the name and location of the court or agency in which the proceedings are pending, the date instituted, the principal parties thereto and a brief summary of the proceedings. ...

SECURITIES EXCHANGE ACT
SCHEDULE 14D-9

...

Item 4. The Solicitation or Recommendation

(a) State the nature of the solicitation or the recommendation. If this statement relates to a recommendation, state whether the person filing this statement is advising security holders of the securities being sought by the bidder to accept or reject the tender offer or to take other action with respect to the tender offer and, if so, furnish a description of such other action being recommended. If the person filing this statement is the subject company and a recommendation is not being made, state whether the subject company is either expressing no opinion and is remaining neutral toward the tender offer or is unable to take a position with respect to the tender offer.

(b) State the reason(s) for the position (including the inability to take a position) stated in (a) of this Item.

Instruction: Conclusory statements such as "The tender offer is in the best interest of shareholders," will not be considered sufficient disclosure in response to Item 4(b). ...

SECURITIES AND EXCHANGE COMMISSION
SECURITIES ACT RELEASE NO. 6158 (1979)
[TENDER OFFERS]

SUMMARY: The Commission announces the adoption of new rules ... pertaining to tender offers. ...

...

I. Overview of Application and Operation of Rules and Schedule

The rules are grouped into two regulations. The application of Regulations 14D and 14E depends on whether or not the tender offer is subject to Section 14(d)(1) of the Exchange Act. If the tender offer is subject to Section 14(d)(1), both regulations apply. If the tender offer is not subject to that sub-section, only Regulation 14E is applicable. The following discussion relates only to a tender offer in which both Regulations are applicable.

The rules regulating the person making the tender offer (the "bidder") may be divided into four categories: filing requirements; dissemination provisions; disclosure requirements; and substantive provisions. Before discussing these categories, it should be noted that the operation of these rules is triggered by the date of commencement of the tender offer, which is defined by Rule 14d–2 as essentially equivalent to the date the tender offer is first published or sent or given to security holders. ...

II. Synopsis of Rules and Schedule

A. Rule 14d–1 ....

... Section 14(d)(1) of the Exchange Act imposes certain requirements upon a bidder who makes a tender offer for a class of equity securities [6] described in that section if upon consummation of such tender offer the bidder would be the beneficial owner of more than five percent of such class. Rule 14d–1(a) limits the application of Regulation 14D to tender offers which are subject to Section 14(d)(1). Thus, tender offers by persons for securities of which they are the issuer are not subject to Regulation 14D. However, the rule specifically notes that tender offers by affiliates of such issuers are subject to Regulation 14D. Regulation 14E applies to any tender offer without regard to whether the class of securities being sought is described in Section 14(d)(1) or whether the person making the tender offer will upon consummation thereof be the beneficial owner of more than five percent of such class.[7] Therefore, issuer tender offers are subject to Regulation 14E unless a specific rule thereunder provides otherwise. However, Regulation 14E does not apply to any tender offer for "exempted securities" as that term is defined in Section 3(a)(12) of the Exchange Act. ...

Rule 14d–4 ....

Tender offers in which the consideration consists of securities registered under the Securities Act are disseminated pursuant to that Act. The former tender offer rules, however, did not provide specific guidance as to what constitutes adequate dissemination of a tender offer in which the consideration consists of cash and/or securities exempt from registration under Section 3 of the Securities Act. Rule 14d–4 provides such guidance and encourages the prompt and widespread dissemination of such tender offers by establishing standards whereby information disseminated in compliance with its provisions would be deemed "published or sent or given to security holders" for purposes of Section 14(d)(1) of the Exchange Act. This is accomplished by providing three alternative definitions of what constitutes dissemination: long-form publication; summary publication and use of stockholder lists and security position listings. ...

Rule 14d–6 ....

Rule 14d–6 establishes disclosure requirements for any tender offer which is subject to Section 14(d)(1) of the Exchange Act. ... The disclosure requirements ... depend on the method by which the tender offer is disseminated to security holders ....

... Rule 14d–6(e)(1) is applicable to tender offers which are published or sent or given to security holders other than by means of a summary advertisement. ...

Rule 14d–6(e)(2) specifies the limited disclosure to be made in a summary advertisement published, sent or given on the date of commencement pursuant to Rule 14d–6(a)(2) or (3). The inclusion of any

---

6. The classes are: any class of equity securities registered pursuant to Section 12 of the Exchange Act; any class of equity securities which would have been required to be registered pursuant to Section 12 except for the exemption provided in Section 12(g)(2)(G) of the Exchange Act; and any class of equity securities issued by a closed-end investment company registered under the Investment Company Act of 1940.

7. Section 14(e) applies to any tender offer, not only those subject to Section 14(d)(1). ...

... information in a summary advertisement [other than the limited information permitted under Rule 14d–6(e)(2)] will make this provision unavailable to the bidder and result in the necessity for publication of the information required by Rule 14d–6(e)(1). ... It should also be noted that summary advertisements are only a part of the method of summary publication. Bidders [who use the summary-advertisement option] are also required by Rule 14d–4(a)(2)(ii) to furnish tender offer materials containing the information required by Rule 14d–6(e)(1) to any security holder who requests such materials pursuant to the summary advertisement. ...

Rule 14d–7 ....

Rule 14d–7(a)(1) extends the statutory seven-day withdrawal right to fifteen business days from the date the tender offer commences. This affords security holders a longer period to reconsider their decision to deposit their shares. It also gives bidders a reasonable time prior to the expiration of the offer to ascertain the number of shares deposited and to determine whether to accept such securities for payment or to change the terms of the offer, such as extending the expiration date.

Certain commentators questioned the Commission's authority to extend the withdrawal period beyond that provided in Section 14(d)(5). The Commission notes, however that Section 14(d)(5) expressly grants the authority to vary the statutory periods "as necessary or appropriate in the public interest or for the protection of investors." In the Commission's view, the specific withdrawal rights contemplated by the rule serve the public interest and the protection of investors by providing effective means of withdrawal within the context of the minimum period for tender offers in Rule 14e–1(a).

Rule 14d–7(a)(2) establishes a conditional withdrawal right in competing tender offer situations under which shares can be withdrawn on the date and for ten business days following the commencement date of a competing tender offer by another bidder. ...

Rule 14e–1: Unlawful Tender Offer Practices.

With one exception Rule 14e–1(a) requires any tender offer to remain open for a minimum of twenty business days from the date it is first published or sent or given to security holders. The exception has been added to remove from the application of the rule tender offers by issuers for their own securities unless such offers are made in anticipation of or in response to another person's tender offer for securities of the same class. Requiring a minimum period of twenty business days for issuer tender offers that are made in anticipation of or in response to a third party tender offer will preserve the neutrality of the Williams Act. It should be noted, however, that tender offers by certain issuers which are not made in anticipation of or in response to another person's tender offer would be required by Rule 13e–4 [30] ... to remain open for fifteen

---

30. Rule 13e–4 applies to an issuer which has a class of equity security registered pursuant to section 12 of the Act, or which is required to file periodic reports

business days from the date the tender offer is first published or sent or given to security holders. The Commission believes that in the special context of such issuer tender offers the minimum period provided by Rule 13e–4 is adequate. ...

There are several purposes to be served by Rule 14e–1(a). Tender offers which do not stay open for a reasonable length of time increase the likelihood of hasty, ill-considered decision making on the basis of inadequate or incomplete information as well as the possibility for fraudulent, deceptive or manipulative acts or practices by a bidder and others. ...

Tender offers which do not remain open for a reasonable period may impede the effective operation of Regulation 14D. In particular, Rule 14d–4 contemplates methods of dissemination which require a considerable period of time to accomplish. Two of these methods, summary publication and the use of shareholder lists and security position listings, involve mailings to security holders. The latter method also requires transmittal to beneficial owners of the securities being sought of the bidder's tender offer materials through the facilities of brokers, banks and similar persons. Although these methods will provide improved dissemination of tender offer materials, mailing and transmittal will reduce the amount of time available to security holders to consider the tender offer materials. The Commission therefore believes a minimum period of twenty business days is necessary.

For similar reasons, the Commission is adopting Rule 14e–1(b) which requires that any tender offer must remain open for at least ten business days after the date of the notice of an increase in either the offered consideration or the dealer's soliciting fee. ...

Rule 14e–2: Position of Subject Company With Respect to a Tender Offer. ...

Rule 14e–2 [requires] the subject company to publish or send or give to security holders a statement disclosing its position with respect to the tender offer within ten business days of the commencement of a tender offer by a person other than the issuer. ...

... [A] statement of position pursuant to Rule 14e–2 with respect to a tender offer which is subject to Section 14(d)(1) of the Act is deemed by Rule 14d–9(f) to constitute a solicitation or recommendation within the meaning of Rule 14d–9 and Section 14(d)(4) of the Act. In such case, a subject company is required to comply with the requirements of Rule 14d–9. Thus, among other things, a subject company is required to file a Schedule 14D–9 with the Commission and include the information required by certain items thereof in the information disseminated to security holders. ...

SECURITIES EXCHANGE ACT
RULE 14e–3

pursuant to section 15(d) of the Act, or which is a closed-end investment company registered under the Investment Company Act of 1940.

14e–3. Transactions in Securities on the Basis of Material, Nonpublic Information in the Context of Tender Offers

(a) If any person has taken a substantial step or steps to commence, or has commenced, a tender offer (the "offering person"), it shall constitute a fraudulent, deceptive or manipulative act or practice within the meaning of section 14(e) of the Act for any other person who is in possession of material information relating to such tender offer which information he knows or has reason to know is nonpublic and which he knows or has reason to know has been acquired directly or indirectly from (1) the offering person, (2) the issuer of the securities sought or to be sought by such tender offer, or (3) any officer, director, partner or employee or any other person acting on behalf of the offering person or such issuer, to purchase or sell or cause to be purchased or sold any of such securities or any securities convertible into or exchangeable for any such securities or any option or right to obtain or to dispose of any of the foregoing securities, unless within a reasonable time prior to any purchase or sale such information and its source are publicly disclosed by press release or otherwise.

(b) A person other than a natural person shall not violate paragraph (a) of this section if such person shows that:

(1) The individual(s) making the investment decision on behalf of such person to purchase or sell any security described in paragraph (a) or to cause any such security to be purchased or sold by or on behalf of others did not know the material, nonpublic information; and

(2) Such person had implemented one or a combination of policies and procedures, reasonable under the circumstances, taking into consideration the nature of the person's business, to ensure that individual(s) making investment decision(s) would not violate paragraph (a), which policies and procedures may include, but are not limited to, (i) those which restrict any purchase, sale and causing any purchase and sale of any such security or (ii) those which prevent such individual(s) from knowing such information. ...

(d)(1) As a means reasonably designed to prevent fraudulent, deceptive or manipulative acts or practices within the meaning of section 14(e) of the Act, it shall be unlawful for any person described in paragraph (d)(2) of this section to communicate material, nonpublic information relating to a tender offer to any other person under circumstances in which it is reasonably foreseeable that such communication is likely to result in a violation of this section *except* that this paragraph shall not apply to a communication made in good faith,

(i) To the officers, directors, partners or employees of the offering person, to its advisors or to other persons, involved in the planning, financing, preparation or execution of such tender offer;

(ii) To the issuer whose securities are sought or to be sought by such tender offer, to its officers, directors, partners, employees or advisors or to other persons, involved in the planning, financing, preparation or execution of the activities of the issuer with respect to such tender offer; or

(iii) To any person pursuant to a requirement of any statute or rule or regulation promulgated thereunder.

(2) The persons referred to in paragraph (d)(1) of this section are:

(i) The offering person or its officers, directors, partners, employees or advisers;

(ii) The issuer of the securities sought or to be sought by such tender offer or its officers, directors, partners, employees or advisors;

(iii) Anyone acting on behalf of the persons in paragraph (d)(2)(i) or the issuer or persons in paragraph (d)(2)(ii); and

(iv) Any person in possession of material information relating to a tender offer which information he knows or has reason to know is nonpublic and which he knows or has reason to know has been acquired directly or indirectly from any of the above.

SECURITIES AND EXCHANGE COMMISSION
SECURITIES ACT RELEASE No. 6239 (1980)
[RULE 14e–3]

SUMMARY: The Commission announces the adoption of a new anti-fraud rule establishing a "disclose or abstain from trading rule" for any person who is in possession of material information that relates to a tender offer by another person which information he knows or has reason to know is nonpublic and was acquired, directly or indirectly, from that person or the issuer of the securities subject to the tender offer. The rule also contains exceptions pertaining to multi-service financial institutions and brokerage transactions. In addition, as a means reasonably designed to prevent fraudulent, deceptive, or manipulative acts or practices, the rule establishes an "anti-tipping" rule with respect to material, nonpublic information relating to a tender offer.[2]

. . .

II. Synopsis of Rule

A. *Rule 14e-3(a)*

2. The Commission had published for comment a proposed rule which would have prohibited the purchase of subject company securities by a bidder which had determined to make a tender offer therefor but had not yet publicly announced its intention to do so unless prior to any such purchase the bidder made a public announcement of certain information. See proposed rule 14e–2(c), Release No. 34–15548 (February 5, 1979) (44 FR 9956). As noted in Release No. 34–16384 (November 29, 1979) (44 FR 70326, 70338), the Commission continues to be concerned by such purchases by bidders and is still considering the wisdom of adopting such a rule. In any event, the adoption of Rule 14e–3 should not be construed as relating in any way to the Commission's authority to regulate the conduct of a bidder under Section 10(b) or Section 14(e) of the Exchange Act or as an indication that the Commission may not act to bar such purchases in the future.

... [Rule 14e–3(a)] establishes a specific duty to "disclose or abstain from trading" under Section 14(e). ...

... [T]he Commission does not believe that electing to make the public disclosure required by Rule 14e–3(a) prior to trading would be a defense for a breach of duty owed by such person under a contractual or fiduciary relationship with the offering person or the issuer. When such contractual or fiduciary relationships exist, abstention from trading may be the only alternative available to persons in possession of material, nonpublic information which will be both lawful and not in breach of the relationships.

1. *Operation of Rule 14e–3(a)*

The "disclose or abstain from trading" duty of Rule 14e–3(a) will arise if the following elements are present:

(a) If any person has taken a substantial step or steps to commence [33] or has commenced a tender offer and another person [34] is in possession of material information relating to such tender offer; [35]

(b) which information the other person knows or has reason to know is nonpublic;

(c) which information the other person knows or has reason to know has been acquired directly or indirectly from the offering person, from the issuer of the securities sought or to be sought in such tender offer or from an officer, director, partner or employee or any other person acting on behalf of the offering person or the issuer,[37] and

---

33. ... [T]he prohibition of Rule 14e–3(a) will apply to the period from the accomplishment by the offering person of a substantial step or steps to commence a tender offer to the termination of the tender offer. ...

The Commission believes that a substantial step or steps to commence a tender offer include, but are not limited to, voting on a resolution by the offering person's board of directors relating to the tender offer; the formulation of a plan or proposal to make a tender offer by the offering person or the person(s) acting on behalf of the offering person; or activities which substantially facilitate the tender offer such as: arranging financing for a tender offer; preparing or directing or authorizing the preparation of tender offer materials; or authorizing negotiations, negotiating or entering into agreements with any person to act as a dealer manager, soliciting dealer, forwarding agent or depository in connection with the tender offer.

34. This person is someone other than the offering person, or in the case of an issuer tender offer, the issuer.

35. ... Rule 14e–3(a) pertains to any material, nonpublic information relating to

a tender offer. Therefore, this element would include information prior to the commencement of a tender offer, such as the intention to make a tender offer, as well as such information during a tender offer such as the withdrawal of a tender offer or an increase in the consideration being offered to security holders.

37. ... Rule 14e–3(a) provides that the other person knows or has reason to know that he has directly or indirectly acquired the information. Thus, information received as well as information obtained by conversion, misappropriation and other means is included in the term "acquired", [T]he information may be acquired from the offering person, from the subject company or from an officer, director, employee or partner or any other person acting on behalf of the offering person or the issuer. ... [T]he response to a tender offer by the subject company, including its recommendation to accept or reject the tender offer, is within the purview of Rule 14e–3(a). One result ... is that, in circumstances where the subject company or its insiders are the source by which the information is acquired, the duty established by Rule 14e–

(d) the other person purchases or sells or causes the purchase or sale [38] of any security to be sought or sought in such tender offer, or any other security convertible into or exchangeable for such security or any option or right to obtain or to dispose of such securities. ...

In addition, Rule 14e–3(a) applies prior to the commencement of a tender offer as well as after an offer has commenced. Trading while in possession of material, nonpublic information prior to the commencement of a tender offer results in the same abuses and causes the same detrimental effects as trading during a tender offer. Since the scope of Section 14(e) applies to acts or practices "in connection with any tender offer," it was, in the Commission's judgment, intended that conduct prior to the date of commencement as well as during a tender offer be covered.

The operation of Rule 14e–3(a) may be illustrated by examples. It should be emphasized that these examples are not exclusive and do not constitute the only situations in which the duty under Rule 14e–3(a) would arise.[40]

(1) If an offering person tells another person that the offering person will make a tender offer which information is nonpublic, the other person has acquired material, nonpublic information directly from the offering person and has a duty under Rule 14e–3(a).

(2) If an offering person delegates the authority to determine whether such offering person should take a substantial step or steps to commence or should commence a tender offer to an officer, employee, director or partner and such person decides to implement the tender offer, such person will be deemed to have acquired information relating to the tender offer from the offering person and therefore will have a duty under Rule 14e–3(a) to disclose or abstain from trading.

(3) If the offering person sends a nonpublic letter to a subject company notifying the subject company of a proposed tender offer at a specified price and upon specified terms and the management of the subject company learns the contents of the letter, the management of the subject company has acquired material, nonpublic information directly from the offering person. An individual member of such management will violate Rule 14e–3(a) if he purchases or sells or causes the purchase or sale of the securities to be sought in the tender offer.

3(a) may overlap with a similar duty under Rule 10b–5. Thus, the subject company's response to the tender offer would be information from the subject company and would be covered by Sections 14(e) and 10(b) and Rule 10b–5. Since the information must come directly or indirectly from the offering person, from the subject company or from an officer, director, partner or employee or any other person acting on behalf of the offering person or the issuer, Rule 14e–3(a) would not apply if the information comes from an initial source other than such persons.

38. The meaning of the term "causes" in the context of this Rule includes a recommendation by one person to another person which results in a purchase or sale by the other person.

40. Also, these examples do not illustrate the operation of Rule 14e–3(d). ...

(4) If, under the facts in the preceding example, the management of the subject company also tells other persons not affiliated with management of the letter, then those other persons have acquired material, nonpublic information indirectly from the offering person and are under a duty to disclose or abstain from trading under Rule 14e–3(a).

(5) If a person receives material information from the subject company relating to its response to another person's tender offer for the subject company's securities, such person will be under a duty to disclose or abstain from trading provided that such person knows or has reason to know the information is nonpublic.

(6) If a person steals, converts or otherwise misappropriates material, nonpublic information relating to a tender offer from an offering person, such person will have acquired the information directly from the offering person and has a duty under Rule 14e–3(a).

(7) If an offering person tells another person of his intention to make a tender offer, and such other person subsequently tells a third person that a tender offer will be made and this third person knows or has reason to know that this non-public information came indirectly from the offering person, then this third person has a duty under Rule 14e–3(a). . . .

B. *Rule 14e–3(b)*

The abuse at which Rule 14e–3(a) is directed is the actual misuse of material, nonpublic information in connection with a sale or purchase. The Commission recognizes that the rule is capable of being applied to a person that is not a natural person even though the individuals making the investment decision on behalf of such person did not know the material, nonpublic information. This could occur, for example, where one department of a multi-service financial institution received material, nonpublic information relating to a tender offer while a separate and independent department of the same organization made the decision to purchase (or sell) securities of the subject company without any knowledge of such information. In the instance where the prohibition would be applicable to a person other than a natural person, and the individuals making the investment decision did not know the material, nonpublic information, there would be no actual misuse of the information, yet it could be said that the institution was in possession of the information and did purchase or sell in apparent violation of Rule 14e–3(a).

In recognition of this situation, the November proposal contained an exception from the prohibition on trading for a person, which is not a natural person, where the individuals making the investment decision on behalf of that person did not know and did not have access to such material, nonpublic information. The commentators supported the Commission's recognition that an exception was necessary and appropriate for such persons, typically multi-service financial institutions. Many, however, suggested certain changes in the formulation of the exception.

In response to the comments received and based on further analysis by the Commission, the exception provided in Rule 14e–3(b) has been revised.[41]

As adopted, Rule 14e–3(b) provides an exception to the prohibition of Rule 14e–3(a) where an institution or other non-natural person engaged in the securities business can show that the individual decision makers did not know the information and that the institution has implemented one or a combination of reasonable procedures to ensure that such individuals would not violate Rule 14e–3(a).

1. *Elements of the Exception*

In order to qualify for the exception in Rule 14e–3(b), a person who is not a natural person must carry the burden of proof for both elements of the exception. First, under Rule 14e–3(b)(1) such person must show that the individual decision maker(s) within the person did not know the information at the time the investment decision was made. Whenever the actual decision maker(s) know the information, the exception is not available whether or not the second element of the exception is satisfied. Second, Rule 14e–3(b)(2) requires that the person must show that it has implemented one or a combination of policies and procedures, reasonable under the circumstances to ensure that individual(s) making investment decision(s) would not violate paragraph (a). ...

Rule 14e–3(b)(2)(i) and (ii) specify certain types of policies and procedures, which are not exclusive. The first type of policies and procedures is the restricted list procedure and the second type refers to policies and procedures often called a "Chinese Wall." There are other informal procedures that some institutions employ when they receive material, nonpublic information, such as "watch lists." The "reasonable under the circumstances" standard may require one or a combination of these policies and procedures to ensure that actual investment decision maker(s) do not violate paragraph (a). ...

2. *Present Practices*

The Commission understands that policies and procedures to prevent the use of material, nonpublic information relating to a tender offer as well as other types of information are widely used by multi-service financial institutions. These present practices include the use of so-called "Chinese Walls" which are used to isolate the nonpublic flow of information from one department to the rest of the institution. Depending on the circumstances, it may be appropriate to advise customers of its use of the Chinese Wall, because the institution would not be using all information that it had received to the benefit of a particular customer.

---

41. Rule 14e–3(b) differs from proposed Rule 14e–3(b) in two respects. First, the proposed rule required the institution to prove that the individual making the investment decision did not know and did not have access to the material, nonpublic information. The separate requirement of proving lack of access was criticized by the commentators, based on the belief that it would be difficult, especially in smaller institutions, to prove that the investment decision maker did not have access to the information and because evidence concerning a lack of access really bears on the question of whether the investment decision maker had actual knowledge. ...

There is also a danger that the Chinese Wall may not be fully effective in all instances and that information may pass through the wall. In that regard, other informal procedures are often used in conjunction with and to supplement the Chinese Wall at times when the institution has material, nonpublic information but before the information is appropriate for public release or to cause placement of the security on a restricted list. This "watch list" procedure enables the institution to monitor trading activity to determine whether any leaks in the Chinese Wall have occurred.

Another type of procedure is the restricted list whereby an institution will prohibit recommendations relating to, solicitations of orders to purchase or sell, execution of unsolicited orders to purchase or sell a particular security or any combination of these prohibitions. Most firms are reluctant to place a security on a restricted list until the information is significant and ready to be publicly announced. This reluctance is based upon the perception that a restricted list often operates as a "tip-sheet" for the investment community—immediately signaling that the institution is in possession of material, nonpublic information about the issuer of the stock placed on restriction.

Depending upon the nature of the activities of a particular institution, it may use a Chinese Wall or a restricted list or a combination of these and other procedures. The specific policies and procedures selected by an institution will be those which will be most effective in preventing the misuse of material, nonpublic information. ...

D. *Rule 14e–3(d)* ...

1. *Operation of Rule 14e–3(d)(1)*

Rule 14e–3(d)(1) proscribes the selective communication of certain information by persons described in Rule 14e–3(d)(2). The proscription consists of two elements. First, such person must possess material, nonpublic information relating to a tender offer. Such person may create the information, e.g., the offering person or the subject company, or he may have acquired the information from the offering person or the subject company or from a person who is in a chain from the offering person or the subject company. Second, such person tips the information to another. The tipping occurs where it is reasonably foreseeable that the communication is likely to result in a violation of Rule 14e–3. The standard of reasonably foreseeable is premised on what a reasonable man would view as reasonably foreseeable. This formulation is reasonably related to the objective of preventing trading on the basis of material, nonpublic information because it operates to prohibit leaks which are the source of this information.

The rule is not intended to have an impact on casual and innocently motivated social discourse. The rule applies where the circumstances such as the identity, position, reputation or prior actions of the participants—or other relevant factors—make it reasonably foreseeable that a violation of Rule 14e–3 is likely to occur. Even beyond the reach of the rule, because of the disruptive effect of leaks of material, non-public information relating to tender offers, the Commission urges that persons in possession of such information exercise all due care in communications.

2. *Persons Subject to the Anti-tipping Rule*

Rule 14e–3(d)(2) specifies the persons subject to the proscription of Rule 14e–3(d)(1). These persons may be grouped into two categories. The first category consists of those persons who occupy a certain status such as the offering person, the subject company, or an officer, director, partner or employee or any other person acting on behalf of the offering person or the issuer. The second category consists of tippees of the persons in the status category. As a result, Rule 14e–3(d)(2) would reach intermediate level tippees, regardless of whether they trade on the basis of the information. For example, a person who receives such information from the offering person such as a broker dealer not involved in the tender offer will violate Rule 14e–3 if he communicates such information to another person under circumstances where it is reasonably foreseeable that such other person will trade on the basis of the information or such other person will tip someone else.

3. *Exception to Rule 14e–3(d)*

In order not to hinder tender offer practice and to allow both the offering person and the subject company to conduct their affairs without exposure to an unwarranted litigation hazard, the Commission believes that it is necessary to specify an exception to Rule 14e–3(d). On the basis of the exception, Rule 14e–3(d) will not apply to communications by the persons specified in Rule 14e–3(d)(2) to the persons enumerated in Rule 14e–3(d)(1)(i) through (iii), provided that they are made in good faith. The adoption of this exception responds to the concerns of several commentators that a safe harbor be added to assure that the offering person can communicate information to persons involved in the tender offer without violating the proposed rule.

The good faith standard is the critical concept to the availability of the exception and the person claiming the availability of the exception bears the burden of proof in establishing his good faith. If the person who communicates the information knows or has reason to know that the person enumerated in Rule 14e–3(d)(1)(i) through (iii) is going to violate Rule 14e–3, then the exception is not available. The communicator would be a tipper subject to the prohibition of Rule 14e–3(d) and the person who acquires and trades will violate rule 14e–3(a). ...

SECURITIES AND EXCHANGE COMMISSION
EXCHANGE ACT RELEASE NO. 18761 (1982)
[PROPOSING RULE 14d–8]

SUMMARY: The Commission is publishing for comment a proposed rule that would govern the acceptance of securities deposited in response to a partial tender offer if a greater number of securities are deposited than the bidder is bound or willing to purchase.

. . .

Over the past year, there has been an increasing number of partial tender offers that provided for the minimum ten calendar day proration period. This increase appears to be attributable to a number of factors, including the trend toward tender offers so large that often only partial offers are feasible, a concomitant increase in the number of competing partial tender offers involving a number of price increases, and, more recently, the growing use by bidders of "two-step" offers that combine a partial cash tender offer with an offer of the securities of the bidder, usually in a subsequent second or third step merger transaction. As a practical matter, security holders are compelled to make their investment decisions on these large and complex transactions within the ten calendar day proration period (which may be as few as six business days) or risk losing both the opportunity to sell into the market at prices reflecting the tender offer premium and the opportunity to participate in the cash (and frequently substantially higher priced) portion of the tender offer. . . .

The Commission recognizes that Section 14(d)(6) of the Exchange Act requires prorationing only during the first ten calendar days of a tender offer and for ten calendar days from the announcement of an increase in the consideration offered. However, the Commission believes that it has the authority to adopt proposed Rule 14d–8 pursuant to Section 14(e) of the Exchange Act. In 1970, two years after the enactment of the Williams Act, Section 14(e) was amended to give the Commission "full rulemaking authority" to "define and prescribe means reasonably designed to prevent . . . fraudulent, deceptive or manipulative" practices in connection with tender offers. The purpose of this additional grant of rulemaking authority was to give the Commission rulemaking powers to deal more effectively with rapidly evolving tender offer techniques that have the potential to injure investors. . . .

As used in recent partial tender offers, the minimum ten day proration period (1) fails to give some security holders an adequate opportunity to avail themselves of the minimum twenty business day tender offer period adopted pursuant to Section 14(e) of the Exchange Act and (2) leads to inordinately complex investment decisions.

. . . Even under the best circumstances, a ten calendar day period is insufficient for some security holders to obtain the requisite information about the tender offer, consider the information in view of personal circumstances, and, if the security holder decides to tender, physically deliver his letter of transmittal and share certificates (or a guarantee of delivery in lieu thereof) to the bidder's depository.

. . . [The] Commission in 1979 [required] that tender offers be kept open for at least twenty business days from the date of commencement and at least ten business days from the date of an increase in the offering price. However, the efficacy of these minimum time periods has been undermined in partial tender offers, where security holders faced with such offers have had to act within ten calendar days to protect their proration rights. It is anomalous that a security holder faced with a partial offer, that may include discussion of the issuance of the securities of the bidder in a second step transaction (in many cases worth significantly less than the cash paid in the first step), effectively has only ten calendar days in which to make his investment decision whereas a security holder faced with an "any and all" offer is assured at least twenty business days in which to make his decision.

The investment decision in an "any and all" offer is often far simpler than that in a partial offer. The security holder confronting a partial tender offer has a more complex task in assessing the risks of oversubscription and prorationing and the consequences of remaining a minority security holder of the subject company with the bidder now occupying a dominant role in the subject company's affairs. Moreover, proposed second step mergers, which frequently are part of the plan of takeover, tend to be significantly more complicated in the context of partial offers which typically involve the issuance of the bidder's securities, whereas in the any and all cash offer context the second step merger is more commonly for the same cash amount per share. . . .

SECURITIES AND EXCHANGE COMMISSION
EXCHANGE ACT RELEASE NO. 19336 (1982)
[ADOPTING RULE 14d–8]

. . .

Dissent by Chairman Shad:

On December 15th the Commission adopted Rule 14d–8 by a three-to-two vote. This rule extends the minimum proration period for the life of tender offers—from 10 calendar to 20 business days (26 to 28 calendar days). It is intended to reduce public shareholders' confusion and afford them more time to consider and act upon tender offers.

I share the majority's concerns for public shareholders, but dissented briefly for the following reasons.

I. Authority

The Commission's legal authority to extend the statutory proration period is not clear. . . . [W]hen Congress adopted Section 14(d)(6) of the Securities Exchange Act in 1968, it considered and explicitly rejected the proration scheme the new Rule 14d–8 implements. The Supreme Court has held that where the provisions of an Act are unambiguous and its directions specific, there is no power to amend it by regulation; and that if the passage of time indicates changes are needed in a congressionally established regulatory scheme, an agency must go to Congress, rather than implement change by regulation.

II. Merits

The minimum time periods of the old rule [Section 14(d)(6)] and the new Rule 14d–8 are as follows:

	Proration	Minimum Business (Calendar) Days Withdrawal	Termination
Old Rule	6–8(10)	15(19–21)	20(26–28)
New Rule	20 (26–28)	15(19–21)	20(26–28)

Changes in a tender offer and competitive offers may extend certain of the above time periods, which would compound the problems discussed below.

The new rule increases the proration uncertainty (i.e., risk) to all shareholders, bidder and target companies from 10 to 26–28 calendar days.

Under the old rule, after the 10th calendar day shareholders could redeploy the shares not accepted or sell them and reinvest the proceeds in more attractive securities. Under the new rule, they must wait 26–28 calendar days to learn the proration. Such a 16 to 18 day delay circumscribes shareholders' options.

Under the old rule, after the 15 business day withdrawal period, the bidder could purchase the shares tendered. Under the new rule, the bidder must wait an additional week, which increases the bidder's exposure to target defensive tactics, "white knights" and competitive bidders.

Under the old rule, shareholders had 9–11 calendar days after learning the proration to decide whether to withdraw all or any portion of their shares in order to: a) tender them to a competitive bidder; b) sell them and reinvest the proceeds in more attractive securities; or c) avoid an over-subscription. Under the new rule, the withdrawal period expires five business days *before* shareholders know the proration.

Extending the proration period five business days *beyond* the withdrawal period largely nullifies the benefit of the withdrawal period to shareholders. It also locks-in those who do not withdraw their shares by the 15th business day or who tender thereafter. Therefore, sophisticated shareholders will maximize their options by not tendering until the 20th business day, since there is no advantage in tendering earlier. Unsophisticated shareholders who tender earlier will be locked-in upon expiration of the withdrawal period. In addition, a large volume of last minute tenders will further compound the uncertainty for all shareholders, bidder and target companies.

The new rule does not address dilatory tactics by target companies in forwarding tender offer materials to their shareholders, nor so-called "golden parachutes", nor does it inhibit multiple tenders and proration pools, two-tier offers or legal and financial maneuvers by bidder and target companies, to the contrary, the longer proration period and last minute tenders will facilitate such activities and tend to compound unsophisticated investors' confusion, which will work to the advantage of sophisticated traders.

For example, the much longer proration period, greater uncertainty as to the ultimate proration, increased likelihood of a smaller percentage of the shares tendered being accepted and the increased risk of blocking legal actions by the participants can be expected to result in lower bids in the open market for the public's shares during the longer proration period (nearly a month). This will afford risk arbitrageurs over two extra weeks to accumulate more shares from the public in the open market at lower relative prices than heretofore. The net result may prove to be no greater (if not less) public shareholder participation in proration pools; and lower aggregate price realizations by public share-holders.

The longer proration period and greater uncertainty also increase the risks to first bidders. All other things being equal, this will result in fewer tender offers, to the detriment of public shareholders. Also, if first bidders raise or extend their offers, they will afford more time for competitive bidders and defensive tactics by target companies.

For the foregoing reasons, the new rule also increases potential [bidders'] incentive to accumulate more shares in the open market, prior to announcement of tender offers at higher prices.

III. Study

At the December 15th meeting, the Commission also unanimously approved a study of the foregoing and other aspects of tender offers. Such a study should help clarify these complex issues.

(6) Defensive Tactics

Insert the following three cases at p. 1597 of the unabridged edition, at the end of Section 1(m)(6):

PANTER v. MARSHALL FIELD & CO.

United States Court of Appeals, Seventh Circuit, 1981.
646 F.2d 271, cert. denied 454 U.S. 1092, 102 S.Ct. 658, 70 L.Ed.2d 631.

Before PELL and CUDAHY, CIRCUIT JUDGES, and DUMBAULD, SENIOR DISTRICT JUDGE *

PELL, CIRCUIT JUDGE. The nineteen named plaintiffs in these consolidated cases appeal from a judgment of the district court which granted the defendants' motion for a directed verdict at the close of the plaintiffs'

---

* Edward Dumbauld, Senior Judge of the   Pennsylvania, is sitting by designation.
United States District Court for Western

presentation of evidence to the jury. Panter v. Marshall Field & Co., 486 F.Supp. 1168 (N.D.Ill.1980). The plaintiffs, shareholders of Marshall Field & Company (Field's) sought to prove that the defendants, the company and its directors, had wrongfully deprived the plaintiffs of an opportunity to dispose of their shares at a substantial premium over market when the defendants successfully fended off a takeover attempt by Carter Hawley Hale (CHH), a national retail chain. The plaintiffs claimed relief under federal securities law and state corporation and tort law. The district court found the evidence insufficient to go to the jury [on] the federal law claims and, exercising its pendent jurisdiction, similarly found the evidence insufficient on the state law claims.

I. STATEMENT OF THE CASE

A thorough and accurate summary of the facts was presented in the opinion of the district court. However, because the posture of the case requires determination of whether the facts established by the plaintiffs provide a sufficient basis for a jury verdict, we review them in some detail here.

A. *The Parties.*

The named plaintiffs in the cases consolidated for trial were nineteen shareholders of Field's. On June 30, 1978, the plaintiffs were certified as class representatives of all persons who held Field's common stock at any time between December 12, 1977, and February 22, 1978. The plaintiff class was subdivided into four subclasses. Subclass I included all persons who held Field's stock on or before December 12, 1977, but disposed of it before February 22, 1978. Subclass II included all persons who acquired Field's stock after December 12, 1977, and disposed of it before February 22, 1978. Subclass III included all persons who acquired Field's stock after December 12, 1977, and did not dispose of it before February 22, 1978. Subclass IV included all persons who held Field's stock on or before December 12, 1977, and did not dispose of it before February 22, 1978.

Field's is a Delaware corporation with its principal office in Chicago, Illinois. The company has been engaged in the operation of retail department stores since 1852, and on December 12, 1977, it was the eighth largest department store chain in the United States, with thirty-one stores. Fifteen of the stores were located in the Chicago area: they included the State Street and Water Tower Place Stores in Chicago, the Oakbrook Store in west suburban Chicago, and the Old Orchard and Hawthorn Center Stores in north suburban Chicago. Other divisions included the Frederick & Nelson division in the state of Washington; the Halle Division of Halle Brothers Company in Ohio and Pennsylvania; and the Crescent Division of Halle with stores in Spokane, Washington.

The ten directors of Marshall Field & Company during the period from December 12, 1977 to February 22, 1978 are also named as defendants. Seven of the directors were not affiliated with Field's management; the remaining three were officers of Field's.

CHH is a California corporation engaged in the operation of retail department, specialty, and book stores. It was not a party here, although its efforts to acquire Field's gave rise to this litigation. CHH's Neiman-Marcus division operates retail stores in Texas and the southeastern United States. As of December 12, 1977, it had one store in Northbrook Court in north suburban Chicago. CHH also had acquired land on North Michigan Avenue, one block south of Field's Water Tower Place Store, and had expressed its intent to put a Neiman-Marcus Store there, although those plans were in abeyance during the relevant time period. CHH had also been attempting for some time to enter the Oakbrook Shopping Center in west suburban Chicago where Field's already had a store. Other divisions of CHH had department or specialty stores in the western United States. Its Walden Book division operated 433 book stores across the United States. In December 1977 Walden was the third or fourth largest bookseller in the Chicago market.

B. *The Pre-1977 Events.*

On several occasions in the late 1960's and continuing to the mid-1970's, Field's management was approached by would-be merger or takeover suitors. In 1969 Field's sought the help of Joseph H. Flom, an attorney with expertise in such matters, in determining how best to respond to the overtures of interested parties. Flom advised the board that the interest of the shareholders was the paramount concern, and that management should listen to such proposals, evaluate whether the proposal was serious, and whether the proposal raised questions of antitrust violations. He also advised Field's directors and management to invest the company's reserves and use its borrowing power to acquire other stores, if such acquisitions were in accord with the sound business judgment of the board, and in the best interest of the company and its shareholders. He counseled that such acquisitions were a legal way of coping with unfriendly takeover attempts.

Flom's advice was followed during this period in conjunction with a series of tentative approaches to Field's by or on behalf of potential acquirors. Thus, when in 1969 a third party interested in acting as a "catalyst" for a Field's-Associated Dry Goods merger approached the board, it considered the matter and rejected further exploration. While this offer was under consideration, Field's acquired Halle Brothers, a retailer with stores in communities in which Associated already had stores.

In 1975, investment bankers representing Federated Department Stores, then the nation's largest department store chain, approached Field's about a possible merger. Again, the Field's board considered the matter, but in light of advice of counsel that it would raise antitrust problems and damage the chances of a proposed Field's acquisition of the Wanamaker Company, the board determined not to pursue the contact.

Two approaches were initiated in 1976. In August, Dayton-Hudson, a large national department store, expressed interest in a possible merger. Field's management drew up a thorough list of options covering the advantages and disadvantages of such a merger. After reviewing that statement, Field's board decided that in light of their plans for future development and financial projections for 1977, a merger would not be advisable.

In September of 1976 Field's management received an inquiry from a third party asking whether Field's was interested in having Gamble-Skogmo, another national retailer, acquire a twenty percent block of Field's stock to "prevent a takeover by another party." Again the proposal was evaluated by Field's directors and turned down.

C. *The CHH Approach.*

In 1977 the Field's board decided to hire Angelo Arena, then head of CHH's Neiman-Marcus division, to commence employment with the company in 1977, work with its current president, Joseph Burnham, for two or three years, and then assume the presidency of Field's on Burnham's retirement. However, when Burnham died unexpectedly in October of 1977, the Field's board determined, in an emergency meeting held three days after Burnham's death, to elect Arena to the presidency immediately and ask him to come to Chicago earlier than originally planned. In the three day interval CHH made informal contacts with intermediaries and expressed an interest in merging with Field's. The board was informed of those contacts at the October 13 meeting and resolved at that time not to consider the merger.

CHH continued to press its attentions however, and on November 16, Arena asked Field's antitrust counsel, the Chicago law firm of Kirkland & Ellis, to investigate the antitrust aspects of such a merger. Field's board met the next day, and authorized Arena and George Rinder, another director and Field's executive, to meet with representatives of CHH. That meeting took place the next day. The CHH team expressed their reasons why a merger would be good for both companies, and noted that a foreign firm was likely to make a $60.00 tender offer for Field's at any time. Field's representatives conveyed the board's position that internal expansion would be best for Field's and expressed concern about antitrust problems of such a merger. CHH responded that their counsel had opined that there was no antitrust deterrent to the merger. Field's representatives agreed to report the discussions to the Field's board.

On December 2, Hammond Chaffetz of the Kirkland firm advised Field's management that in the opinion of Kirkland & Ellis the proposed combination would be illegal under the antitrust laws in light of (a) the existing competition between Field's stores and the Northbrook Neiman-Marcus store; (b) the potential competition between Field's Chicago stores and the Chicago stores Neiman-Marcus was planning to open; and (c) the existing competition between Field's stores (second in book sales in Chicago) and the stores operated by CHH's Walden division. Chaffetz' opinion was conveyed to Field's directors.

On December 10, Philip Hawley, the president and chief executive officer of CHH, called Arena and told him that unless Field's directors agreed to begin merger negotiations by the following Monday, December 12, he would make a public exchange proposal. He told Arena that CHH would propose beginning negotiations with an offer that for each share of Field's common stock CHH would exchange a number of its shares roughly equivalent to $36.00. Arena refused to enter such negotiations. Field's shares were trading on the market at around $22.00 per share on the Friday before Hawley delivered his ultimatum.

Arena construed Hawley's call as the beginning of an unfriendly takeover attempt by CHH. He contacted Flom, and arranged a meeting of key Field's directors, counsel, and investment bankers for the next day. At the meeting Arena reported the Kirkland & Ellis opinion. It was agreed to poll the absent directors for authorization to file a suit seeking resolution of the antitrust issues posed by the merger proposal. The group also determined to inform the New York Stock Exchange, and to call an emergency meeting of the Field's board for December 13.

On Monday, December 12, 1977, the CHH letter was received. Arena contacted all Field's directors but one by telephone, and they authorized the filing of the antitrust suit.

The special meeting of the board took place the next day with all members present. Also at the meeting were Field's attorneys and investment bankers. The lawyers, particularly Chaffetz, opined on the lack of legality of the merger, and the investment bankers evaluated the financial aspects of the merger. Field's management then made a report and projected that the company's future performance would be generally favorable. Many of the directors agreed with the investment bankers that a share of common stock would bring more than $36.00 in a sale of control of the company. After consideration of the above factors the directors voted unanimously to reject the proposal because in their judgment the merger as proposed would be "illegal, inadequate, and not in the best interests of Marshall Field & Company, its stockholders and the communities which it serves."

The directors also authorized issuance of a press release conveying their decision. On December 14, Field's issued the press release, which indicated that Field's directors and management had faith in the momentum of the company, and that "it would be in the best interests of our stockholders, customers and employees for us to take advantage of this momentum and continue to implement our growth plans as an independent company." Field's shares traded in the market in a range of $28.00 to $32.00 that day, and continued in approximately that range until January 31, 1978.

On December 20, 1977, Arena addressed a letter to Field's stockholders in which he spoke optimistically of the future and reviewed Field's immediate past performance. He pointed out that Field's had disposed of unprofitable ventures, and that "for the nine months ended October 31, income before ventures and taxes was up 24.4% and consolidated net income was up 13%." He referred to the CHH proposal for negotiation and to the advice of antitrust counsel "that a CHH-Marshall Field & Company merger would clearly violate the United States antitrust laws," and concluded that "[y]our Board of Directors believes the maximum benefits for Marshall Field & Company and its stockholders, employees, customers and the communities it serves will result from continuing to develop as an independent, publicly-owned Company."

On January 5, 1978, Field's issued another press release, announcing that it had amended its antitrust suit against CHH to include allegations of federal securities law violations. The release reiterated Field's confidence in its future, and stated "our management is continuing the implementation of our longstanding programs to further build and develop the business of Marshall Field & Company."

On January 19, 1978, Field's directors had their regular meeting. Two expansion proposals were on the agenda: one that the company expand into the Galleria, a Houston shopping mall where a planned Bonwit Teller store had failed to materialize, creating an attractive opening; the other that the company acquire a group of five Liberty House stores in the Pacific Northwest. The Galleria already contained a CHH Neiman-Marcus store. The board resolved to pursue both expansion programs. Field's executives and directors had long considered expansion into these two areas, and the company's interest in such expansion was well known to investment analysts in the department store field.

On February 1, CHH announced its intention to make an exchange offer of $42.00 in a combination of cash and CHH stock for each share of Field's stock tendered. The offer was conditioned on the fulfillment or non-occurrence of some twenty conditions. Appropriate documents for announcement of a tender offer were filed with the SEC. The market price of Field's stock rose to $34.00 per share, and stayed in the $30.00 to $34.00 range until February 22, 1978.

A special meeting of the Field's board was convened the next day to consider the new offer. The legal implications of the CHH filing were explained to the board by counsel, and Chaffetz brought the group up to date on the antitrust suit. There was no discussion of the adequacy of the offer in light of the board's determination that the proposed combination would clearly be illegal. The board also determined to go ahead with the Galleria plan, and approved the signing of a letter of agreement to enter the mall.

After the meeting Field's issued another press release reaffirming its opposition to the proposed merger. It concluded with a statement by Arena that "I assumed my position with Marshall Field & Company with the understanding that I would devote myself to making Marshall Field & Company a truly national retail business organization. We ... are determined not to be deterred from this course. Our recently announced agreement to acquire five Liberty House Stores in Tacoma, Washington and Portland, Oregon was one step in our program."

On February 8, another Field's press release announced that Field's had concluded negotiations for a department store to be opened in the Galleria. On February 22, CHH announced that it was withdrawing its proposed tender offer before it became effective, because "the expansion program announced by Marshall Field since February 1st has created sufficient doubt about Marshall Field's earning potential to make the offer no longer in the best interests of Carter Hawley Hale's shareholders." None of the events that conditioned CHH's tender offer had occurred since February 1. Following the announcement, the market price of Field's shares dropped to $19.00, lower than it had been on December 9, the last trading day prior to CHH's first proposed offer.
. . .

III. THE FEDERAL SECURITIES LAW CLAIMS

The plaintiffs allege violations of two broad antifraud provisions of the Securities Exchange Act of 1934. First, they claim the defendants violated § 14(e) of the Williams Act, . . . and second, they claim the defendants breached SEC Rule 10b–5 . . . .

A. *The Williams Act Claims.*

Section 14(e) of the Williams Act is a broad antifraud provision modeled after SEC Rule 10b–5, and is designed to insure that shareholders confronted with a tender offer have adequate and accurate information on which to base the decision whether or not to tender their shares.
. . .

Upon the announcement of a tender offer proposal a target company shareholder is presented with three options: he may retain his shares; he may tender them to the tender offeror if the offer becomes effective; or he may dispose of them in the securities market for his shares, which generally rises on the announcement of a tender offer. The plaintiffs have alleged that the defendants violated § 14(e) both by depriving them of their opportunity to tender their shares to CHH, the tender offeror, and by deceiving them as to the attractiveness of disposing of their shares in the rising market.

1. The Lost Tender Offer Opportunity.

By denying the plaintiffs the opportunity to tender their shares to CHH, the plaintiffs claim the defendants deprived them of the difference between $42.00, the amount of the CHH offer, and $19.76, the amount at which Field's shares traded in the market after withdrawal of the CHH proposal. Total damages under this theory would exceed $200,000,-000.00.

Because § 14(e) is intended to protect shareholders from making a tender offer decision on inaccurate or inadequate information, among the elements of § 14(e) plaintiff must establish is "that there was a misrep-

resentation upon which the target corporation shareholders relied.   ..."
Chris-Craft Industries, Inc. v. Piper Aircraft Corp., 480 F.2d 341, 373 (2d
Cir.), cert. denied, 414 U.S. 910, 94 S.Ct. 231, 38 L.Ed.2d 148 (1973).
Because the CHH tender offer was withdrawn before the plaintiffs had
the opportunity to decide whether or not to tender their shares, it was
impossible for the plaintiffs to rely on any alleged deception in making
the decision to tender or not.   Because the plaintiffs were never presented with that critical decision and therefore, never relied on the defendants' alleged misrepresentations, they fail to establish a vital element of
a § 14(e) claim as regards the CHH $42.00 offer.   ...

2.   The Plaintiffs' Decision Not to Sell in the Market.

The plaintiffs also contend that defendants' misrepresentations or
omissions of material fact caused the plaintiffs not to dispose of their
shares in the market, which was rising on the news of CHH's takeover
attempt.   Because we hold that a damages remedy for investors who
determine not to sell in the marketplace when no tender offer ever takes
place was not intended to be covered by § 14(e) of the statute, we are not
swayed by the surface appeal of this argument.   ...

...   Section 14(e) is applicable by its terms to conduct *"in connection with any tender offer* or request or invitation for tenders, or any
solicitation of security holders in opposition to or in favor of *any such
offer,* request or invitation."   15 U.S.C. § 78n(e) (1976) (emphasis added).
The language is not unambiguous, but it does seem to contemplate the
existence of an effective offer capable of acceptance by the shareholders.
The legislative history of the Act is replete with indications that Congress intended to protect an investor faced with the pressures generated
by the exigencies of the tender offer context, and that the sole purpose
of § 14(e) is protection of the investor faced with the decision to tender
or retain his shares   ....

...   In light of [the] trend to avoid unduly expansive interpretations
of the securities laws, and our finding that § 14(e) was not intended to
remedy the conduct complained of here, we hold that § 14(e) of the
Williams Act does not give a damages remedy for alleged misrepresentations or omissions of material fact when the proposed tender offer never
becomes effective.

The brief filed by the SEC as *amicus curiae* contends that failure to
afford investors a damages remedy under § 14(e) in situations where a
tender offer proposal is withdrawn before it becomes effective might
lead to abuses.   It poses the hypothetical situation "where a person
announces a proposed tender offer that he never intends to make in
order to dispose of securities of the subject company at artificially
inflated prices   ...."   We note that such conduct would fall within the
ambit of the prohibitions of Rule 10b–5   .... Cf. Zweig v. Hearst Corp.,
594 F.2d 1261 (9th Cir. 1979) (financial columnist purchased stock knowing he would recommend it in his column and sell on the resulting rise;
failure to disclose this scheme violated 10b–5).

The SEC also suggests that without such a remedy, persons could announce tender offers, again without intending to make them, to put pressure on management to consider merger proposals. Although the present case does not present such a situation, we believe that preliminary injunctive relief would be the appropriate remedy for such conduct.
. . .

[The court held that plaintiffs had also not established a Rule 10b–5 violation, because the alleged misstatements or omissions were either not material, or were "insulated from ... scrutiny" under Santa Fe Industries v. Green because they essentially involved claims of breach of fiduciary duty rather than deception or manipulation.]

IV. THE STATE LAW CLAIMS

The plaintiffs here have also sought to establish that the defendants committed two violations of state law. First, they contend, the defendants breached their fiduciary duty as directors to the corporation and its shareholders by adopting a secret policy to resist acquisition regardless of benefit to the shareholders or the corporation; by failing to disclose the existence of such a policy; by making defensive acquisitions; and by filing an antitrust suit against CHH. Second, they argue that the defendants interfered with the plaintiffs' prospective economic advantage when that allegedly wrongful behavior caused CHH to withdraw its proposed tender offer before it became effective.*

A. The Business Judgment Rule.

Under applicable Delaware corporate law, claims such as those made by the plaintiffs are analyzed under the "business judgment" rule. The trial court described this rule as establishing that

[d]irectors of corporations discharge their fiduciary duties when in good faith they exercise business judgment in making decisions regarding the corporation. When they act in good faith, they enjoy a presumption of sound business judgment, reposed in them as directors, which courts will not disturb if any rational business purpose can be attributed to their decisions. In the absence of fraud, bad faith, gross overreaching or abuse of discretion, courts will not interfere with the exercise of business judgment by corporate directors.

486 F.Supp. at 1194 (citations omitted). We find this an apt summary of appropriate Delaware law.[6] See GM Sub Corp. v. Liggett Group, Inc.,

---

* The portion of the opinion dealing with the second issue is omitted. (Footnote by ed.)

6. The trial court ... excluded the plaintiffs' proffered expert testimony on the ordinary standards against which the actions of boards of directors and investment bankers would be measured. The trial court ruled that such evidence would impinge on the function of the trial court, and furthermore, as to the investment bankers, was irrelevant to the issue of the directors' liability.

The standard of review in considering the admission of expert testimony is whether the trial court judge's exclusionary ruling was clearly erroneous. Karp v. Cooley, 493 F.2d 408, 424 (5th Cir. 1974). Viewing the

No. 6155, slip op. at 3 (Del.Ch. Apr. 25, 1980) (citing the district court opinion with approval). In the recent case of Johnson v. Trueblood, 629 F.2d 287 (3d Cir. 1980), the U.S. Court of Appeals for the Third Circuit had occasion to analyze the purpose of the Delaware business judgment rule in the context of a takeover attempt. The plaintiffs contended that an allegation of a purpose to retain control was enough to shift the burden to incumbent directors to show the rational business purpose of the disputed transaction. In rejecting that contention Chief Judge Seitz, formerly a Delaware Chancellor, stated:

> First, the purpose of the business judgment rule belies the plaintiffs' contention. It is frequently said that directors are fiduciaries. Although this statement is true in some senses, it is also obvious that if directors were held to the same standard as ordinary fiduciaries the corporation could not conduct business. For example, an ordinary fiduciary may not have the slightest conflict of interest in any transaction he undertakes on behalf of the trust. Yet by the very nature of corporate life a director has a certain amount of self-interest in everything he does. The very fact that the director wants to enhance corporate profits is in part attributable to his desire to keep shareholders satisfied so that they will not oust him.

> The business judgment rule seeks to alleviate this problem by validating certain situations that otherwise would involve a conflict of interest for the ordinary fiduciary. The rule achieves this purpose by postulating that if actions are arguably taken for the benefit of the corporation, then the directors are presumed to have been exercising their sound business judgment rather than responding to any personal motivations.

> Faced with the presumption raised by the rule, the question is what sort of showing the plaintiff must make to survive a motion for directed verdict. Because the rule presumes that business judgment was exercised, *the plaintiff must make a showing from which a factfinder might infer that impermissible motives predominated in the making of the decision in question.*

> The plaintiffs' theory that "a" motive to control is sufficient to rebut the rule is inconsistent with this purpose. Because the rule is designed to validate certain transactions despite conflicts of interest, the plaintiffs' rule would negate that purpose, at least in many cases. As already noted, control is always arguably "a" motive in any action

testimony in this light, we affirm the district court's ruling. In Marx & Co. v. Diners' Club, Inc., 550 F.2d 505, 509–10 (2d Cir.), cert. denied, 434 U.S. 861, 98 S.Ct. 188, 54 L.Ed.2d 134 (1977), the court cautioned against the danger of letting experts in a securities case usurp the function of the judge, stating, "It is not for witnesses to instruct the jury as to applicable principles of law, but the judge." The expert would have been able to add nothing to the formulation of the proper standards for evaluating the conduct of Field's directors enunciated by the trial court. We also agree with the trial court that testimony on how the investment bankers should have responded to the CHH proposal is irrelevant to this case, in which it is the conduct of the directors that is the issue.

taken by a director. Hence plaintiffs could always make this showing and thereby undercut the purpose of the rule.

Id. at 292–93 (emphasis added).

GM Sub Corp., supra, involved a shareholder's claim that the defendants, directors of a target company, divested the company of its most important asset in an attempt to make it less attractive to an ardent but unwelcome suitor. In analyzing this action under the Delaware business judgment rule, the court formulated the following test of the improper motive necessary to overcome the presumption of good faith:

[N]ot every action taken by a board of directors to thwart a tender offer is to be condemned. The test, loosely stated, is whether the board is fairly and reasonably exercising its business judgment to protect the corporation and its shareholders against injury likely to befall the corporation should the tender offer prove successful.

Slip op. at 3.

We also note that a majority of the directors of Field's were "independent": they derived no income from Field's other than normal directors' fees and the equivalent of an employee discount on merchandise. The presumption of good faith the business judgment rule affords is heightened when the majority of the board consists of independent outside directors. See, e.g., Warshaw v. Calhoun, 221 A.2d 487, 493 (Del.1966); Puma v. Marriott, 283 A.2d 693, 695 (Del.Ch.1971).

The plaintiffs suggest that director Blair's independence was called into question by the fact that his investment banking firm did work for Field's. In Maldonado v. Flynn, 485 F.Supp. 274 (S.D.N.Y.1980), the court dismissed such an implication as "a non sequitur and hardly worthy of comment." Id. at 283. We agree. Even less relevant was the plaintiffs' attempt to show that director Smith's independence was weakened because he owned a substantial share of a bank in which Field's deposited monies and had other accounts. That inference is so attenuated that the trial court properly excluded the evidence as irrelevant.

However, rather than proceeding under the business judgment rule, the plaintiffs here seek to apply a different test in the takeover context, and propose that the burden be placed upon the directors to establish the compelling business purpose of any transaction which would have the effect of consolidating or retaining the directors' control. In light of the overwhelming weight of authority to the contrary, we refuse to apply such a novel rule to this case. Crouse-Hinds Co. v. InterNorth, Inc., 634 F.2d 690, 701–03 (2d Cir. 1980); Treadway Cos. v. Care Corp., 638 F.2d 357, 381 (2d Cir. 1980); Johnson v. Trueblood, supra; Gimbel v. Signal Cos., 316 A.2d 599, 601, 609 (Del.1974); Sinclair Oil Corp. v. Levien, 280 A.2d 717, 720 (Del.1971); Warshaw v. Calhoun, 221 A.2d 487 (Del.1966); GM Sub Corp., supra; Kaplan v. Goldsamt, 380 A.2d 556, 568 (Del.Ch. 1977). To the extent that dicta in Klaus v. Hi-Shear Corp., 528 F.2d 225 (9th Cir. 1975), suggest a different result under the corporation law of California, we decline to follow that rule. ...

B. *The Breach of Fiduciary Duty.*

1. The Policy of Independence.

The plaintiffs contend that they have presented sufficient evidence to go to the jury on the existence of the secret policy, both circumstantially, from the history of prior rebuffs, and directly, from the testimony of two Field's directors.

On the resistance to prior approaches, we have established above that evaluation and response to such approaches is within the scope of the directors' duties. The plaintiffs have presented no evidence of self-dealing, fraud, overreaching or other bad conduct sufficient to give rise to any reasonable inference that impermissible motives predominated in the board's consideration of the approaches. The desire to build value within the company, and the belief that such value might be diminished by a given offer is a rational business purpose. The record reveals that appropriate consideration was given to each individual approach made to Marshall Field & Company.[8] The plaintiffs have failed to introduce evidence supporting a reasonable inference that any of the rejections of these approaches were made in bad faith. Therefore the presumption of good faith afforded by the business judgment rule applies, and the plaintiffs cannot survive the motion for directed verdict.

Having failed to establish the presence of an improper motive in any one of the defendants' responses to acquisition approaches, the plaintiffs seek to establish from the series of rejections the illogical inference that this reflects an invidious policy of independence regardless of benefit to the shareholders. All that the plaintiffs' evidence in this regard establishes is that Field's directors evaluated the merits of each approach made, and determined to implement their decisions as to each of the approaches by following the advice of counsel on how to respond to unwanted acquisition approaches.

---

8. The trial court judge limited admission of evidence on these pre-CHH takeover approaches to "documents that show statements made at the Board of Directors' meetings, [and] letters written by the defendants as to those." It excluded other evidence as to the transactions, stating, "to go through these individual transactions would require an inquiry into who made it, the circumstances of it being made, what were the economic circumstances at the time, what was the financial stability of those who made it, and what were the motives and purposes of those who made it. That will extend this record unnecessarily .... [T]o go into these individual transactions would go afield into all matters which would be totally collateral." Questions of admissibility of evidence of prior acts are peculiarly within the province of the trial court. See, e.g., United States v. Czarnecki, 552 F.2d 698, 702 (6th Cir.), cert. denied, 431 U.S. 939, 97 S.Ct. 2652, 53 L.Ed.2d 257 (1977). Particularly when admission of the challenged evidence is likely to be cumulative and confusing, we will not overturn the sound exercise of the trial court's discretion. Furthermore, the plaintiff was not prejudiced by this ruling because the trial court judge saw all the evidence in offers of proof before ruling that there was no issue of fact on which the jury could rule.

The court also excluded hypothetical questions based on the existence of a policy of resistance. Again, this determination was within the broad discretion of the trial court. When a hypothetical question is not supported by independent evidence it is subject to objection. Grand Island Grain Co. v. Roush Mobile Home Sales, Inc., 391 F.2d 35, 40–41 (8th Cir. 1968). Such a question is particularly harmful where it assumes that very wrongful conduct which is the central issue of the plaintiffs' case, and the trial court acted properly in excluding it.

The mere fact that two of the ten directors felt that the word "independence" reflected the board policy of trying to build value within the company rather than putting it up for sale, does not reveal an impermissible motive to reject all acquisition attempts regardless of merit. Furthermore, there is testimony by both directors who used the word "independent" that neither meant by it resistance at all costs, or against the best interests of the shareholders. We therefore affirm the district court's holding that the plaintiffs failed to raise a jury question on the issue of the alleged policy of independence.

The plaintiffs also contend that failure to reveal the prior rebuffs or the policy of independence amounted to a breach of fiduciary duty. None of the prior attempts ever rose to the level of a definite offer or merger proposal. Directors are under no duty to reveal every approach made by a would-be acquiror or merger partner. See Missouri Portland Cement Co. v. H.K. Porter Co., 535 F.2d 388, 398 (8th Cir. 1976); Berman v. Gerber Products, 454 F.Supp. 1310, 1318 (W.D.Mich.1978); Elgin National Industries, Inc. v. Chemetron Corp., 299 F.Supp. 367, 371 (D.Del.1969). Thus, there was no breach of fiduciary duty in the failure to disclose prior takeover attempts. Neither can there be liability for a failure to disclose the policy of resistance. Because we have found that it is not reasonable to infer that such a policy existed, there can be no liability for failure to disclose it. Vaughn v. Teledyne, 628 F.2d 1214, 1221 (9th Cir. 1980).

2. The Defensive Acquisitions.

The plaintiffs also contend that the "defensive" acquisitions of the five Liberty House stores and the Galleria were imprudent, and designed to make Field's less attractive as an acquisition, as well as to exacerbate any antitrust problems created by the CHH merger. It is precisely this sort of Monday-morning-quarterbacking that the business judgment rule was intended to prevent. Again, the plaintiffs have brought forth no evidence of bad faith, overreaching, self-dealing or any other fraud necessary to shift the burden of justifying the transactions to the defendants. On the contrary, there was uncontroverted evidence that such expansion was reasonable and natural. Thus even if the desire to fend off CHH was among the motives of the board in entering the transactions, because the plaintiffs have failed to establish that such a motive was the sole or primary purpose, as has been required by Delaware law since the leading case of Cheff v. Mathes, 41 Del.Ch. 494, 199 A.2d 548 (1964), the mere allegation, or even some proof, that a given transaction was made on "unfavorable" terms does not meet the fairly stringent burden the business judgment rules imposes on plaintiffs.[9]

9. It was therefore appropriate for the trial court to exclude as irrelevant evidence offered to show financial details of Field's negotiations with Homart Corporation re-

garding possible entry into Northbrook Court, and details of Field's leasing negotiations with the owners of the Galleria in Houston.

3.   The Antitrust Suit.

The plaintiffs also contend that the bringing of the antitrust suit
against CHH was a breach of the directors' fiduciary duty. Because it is
the duty of the directors to file an antitrust suit when in their business
judgment a proposed combination would be illegal or otherwise detrimental to the corporation, see Chemetron Corp. v. Crane Co., 1977–2 Trade
Cas. ¶ 61,717 at 72,933 (N.D.Ill.1977); Gulf & Western Industries, Inc. v.
Great A & P Tea Co., 476 F.2d 687, 698 (2d Cir. 1973), their decision to
file an antitrust suit is also within the scope of the business judgment
rule. There was substantial evidence before the court that the defendants were fairly and reasonably exercising their business judgment to
protect the corporation against the perceived damage an illegal merger
could cause, see Copperweld Corp. v. Imetal, 403 F.Supp. 579, 607
(W.D.Pa.1975) ("no doubt that [divestiture] would have a debilitating
effect on the acquired company ....").

Not only were the directors acting in good faith reliance on the advice
of experienced and knowledgeable antitrust counsel, which in itself
satisfies the requirements of the business judgment rule, Spirt v. Be-
chtel, 232 F.2d 241, 247 (2d Cir. 1956); Voege v. Magnavox Co., 439
F.Supp. 935, 942 (D.Del.1977), but one member of the board was an
experienced antitrust lawyer with a background of experience to evaluate the soundness of the legal claims. See Abramson v. Nytronics, Inc.,
312 F.Supp. 519, 531–32 (S.D.N.Y.1970) ("Boards of directors are deliber-
ately chosen from the ranks of businessmen, bankers, and lawyers
because of their expertise in evaluating the merits of precisely this sort
of proposal."). The plaintiffs have introduced no evidence that the suit
was brought in bad faith, but merely cite it as an example of the
defendants' desire to perpetuate their control. However, because the
bringing of the suit clearly served the rational business purpose of
protecting Field's from the damage forced divestiture would cause, it is
protected by the business judgment rule. Field's decision to resolve the
antitrust question through litigation in federal court rather than some
other method or in some other forum is a matter for the discretion of the
directors when it is exercised within the scope of the rule.

Because we find insufficient evidence on which a jury could base a
rational verdict that the defendants breached any fiduciary duty, neither
can any claim of concealment of bad faith activity give rise to a jury
question. We therefore affirm the district court's ruling on the state
law claims of breach of fiduciary duty. ...

CUDAHY, CIRCUIT JUDGE, concurring in part and dissenting in part:

Unfortunately, the majority here has moved one giant step closer to
shredding whatever constraints still remain upon the ability of corporate
directors to place self-interest before shareholder interest in resisting a
hostile tender offer for control of the corporation. There is abundant
evidence in this case to go to the jury on the state claims for breach of
fiduciary duty. I emphatically disagree that the business judgment rule
should clothe directors, battling blindly to fend off a threat to their

control, with an almost irrebuttable presumption of sound business judgment, prevailing over everything but the elusive hobgoblins of fraud, bad faith or abuse of discretion. I also disagree with the majority's view that misleading and deceptive representations about an offeror's proposal are immunized from the proscriptions of Section 14(e) if the offer is withdrawn before the shareholders have an opportunity to tender. ...

I.

Addressing first the state law claims of breach of fiduciary duty by the Board, the majority has adopted an approach which would virtually immunize a target company's board of directors against liability to shareholders, provided a sufficiently prestigious (and expensive) array of legal and financial talent were retained to furnish *post hoc* rationales for fixed and immutable policies of resistance to takeover. Relying on several recent decisions interpreting the Delaware business judgment rule, the majority fails to make the important distinction

> between the activity of a corporation in managing a business enterprise and its function as a vehicle for collecting and using capital and distributing profits and losses. The former involves corporate functioning in competitive business affairs in which judicial interference may be undesirable. *The latter involves only the corporation-shareholder relationship, in which the courts may more justifiably intervene to insist on equitable behavior.*

Note, Protection for Shareholder Interests in Recapitalizations of Publicly Held Companies, 58 Colum.L.Rev. 1030, 1066 (1958) (emphasis supplied).

The theoretical justification for the "hands off" precept of the business judgment rule is that courts should be reluctant to review the acts of directors in situations where the expertise of the directors is likely to be greater than that of the courts. But, where the directors are afflicted with a conflict of interest, relative expertise is no longer crucial. Instead, the great danger becomes the channeling of the directors' expertise along the lines of their personal advantage—sometimes at the expense of the corporation and its stockholders.[1] Here courts have no rational choice but to subject challenged conduct of directors and questioned corporate transactions to their own disinterested scrutiny. Of course, the self-protective bias of interested directors may be entirely devoid of corrupt motivation, but it may nonetheless constitute a serious

---

1. Hostile tender offers unavoidably create a conflict of interest .... Nearly all directors and managers are interested in maintaining their compensation and perquisites .... [A] hostile tender offer unavoidably involves forces tending to shape decisions that are not necessarily for the benefit of all shareholders. As a result a ... business judgment approach in hostile tender offer cases is inappropriate.

Gelfond and Sebastian, Reevaluating the Duties of Target Management in the Hostile Tender Offer, 60 B.U.L.Rev. 403, 435–37 (1980) (hereinafter "Gelfond and Sebastian").

threat to stockholder welfare. See Gelfond and Sebastian at 435–37 (footnotes omitted).

Despite this potential for abuse, the majority relies heavily on the business judgment rule's presumption of good faith in the exercise of corporate decision-making power and attaches special significance to the "independence" of Field's Board. . . .[2] The fact that Field's may have had a majority of non-management (independent) directors is hardly dispositive. The interaction between management and board may be very strong even where, as here, a relationship of symbiosis seems to prevail over the normal condition of "management domination." Whether the relationship is symbiotic or management "dominates," I do not think it necessary to rely primarily on such directly pecuniary relationships as one director's senior partnership in Field's investment banking firm (although this was admittedly a quite profitable arrangement) or another director's ownership of stock in a Field's depository bank (obviously a more attenuated interest) to establish a conflict of interest here. These factors deserve appropriate attention. But the very idea that, if we cannot trace with precision a mighty flow of dollars into the pockets of each of the outside directors, these directors are necessarily disinterested arbiters of the stockholders' destiny, is appallingly naive.

Directors of a New York Stock Exchange-listed company are, at the very least, "interested" in their own positions of power, prestige and prominence (and in their not inconsequential perquisites).[4] They are "interested" in defending against outside attack the management which they have, in fact, installed or maintained in power—"their" management (to which, in many cases, they owe their directorships). And they are "interested" in maintaining the public reputation of their own leadership and stewardship against the claims of "raiders" who say that they can do better. Thus, regardless of their technical "independence," directors of a target corporation are in a very special position, where the slavish application of the majority's version of the good faith presumption is particularly disturbing.

Under the business judgment rule, once a plaintiff demonstrates that a director had an interest in the transaction at issue, the burden of proof shifts to the director to prove that the transaction was fair and reasonable to the corporation. Treadway Companies v. Care Corp., 638 F.2d 357 at 382 (2d Cir. 1980). Accord, Crouse-Hinds Co. v. InterNorth, Inc., 634 F.2d 690 (2d Cir. 1980). There was more than sufficient evidence in the instant case to permit the jury to shift the burden of proof to Field's directors and to consider the reasonableness of the transactions. The

---

2. "In practice [and presumably regardless of its numerical composition], the American corporation's board of directors is largely dominated by the management of the corporation." Gelfond and Sebastian at 436. I recognize, however, that plaintiffs here have not sought to prove that management "controlled" the Board. Appellee's Br. at 78.

4. Apart, of course, from the very substantial salaries of the "inside" (management) directors and the benefits to certain outside directors, noted supra, all the outside directors had annual incomes from Field's which ranged from $11,200 to $16,-000 in 1977. Plaintiffs' Exhibit 437.

majority here, however, affirms a directed verdict which determines that the evidence was insufficient *as a matter of law* to establish that Field's directors were interested in this transaction. A brief examination of the majority's "overwhelming weight of authority" demonstrates that even these cases do not support its notion of the quantum of evidence necessary to create a jury question in this case.   ...

The majority   ...   relies on Johnson v. Trueblood, 629 F.2d 287 (3d Cir. 1980) and quotes from Chief Justice Seitz's opinion essentially to establish that self-interest must be the sole or primary motive underlying a director's challenged action rather than merely "a" motive when control is implicated. The issue arose in *Trueblood*, however, in the context of *how a jury was to be charged*, not whether the evidence should go to a jury at all. The *Trueblood* court concluded (and the majority here agrees) that to survive a motion for a directed verdict, the "plaintiff must make a showing from which a factfinder might infer that impermissible motives predominated in the making of the decision in question." Id. at 292–93. Regardless whether "a" self-interested motive is sufficient or whether a "primary" self-interested motive is requisite, there is sufficient evidence in the instant case to satisfy either standard. See pp. 304–310, infra. Nothing in *Trueblood* supports the view that the district court properly foreclosed jury consideration of the claims of Field's shareholders.

Beyond this, however, I believe that Judge Rosenn's dissent in *Trueblood* states the proper interpretation of the business judgment rule in control cases: "Once a plaintiff has shown that the desire to retain control was 'a' motive in the particular business decision under challenge, the burden is then on the defendant to move forward with the evidence justifying the transaction as primarily in the corporation's best interest." *Trueblood*, 629 F.2d at 301. This statement of the rule is compatible with both the Delaware case law [9] and the realities of corporate governance, and is by no means a minority position.   ...

Thus, the majority here has no basis for asserting that in "control" cases an interpretation of the business judgment rule which shifts the burden of proof to interested directors and requires them to establish a valid business purpose for their actions is a "novel" rule contrary to the "overwhelming weight of authority." [10]   In none of the cases cited by the

---

9. Nothing in Bennett [v. Propp, 41 Del.Ch. 14, 187 A.2d 405 (1962)] or Cheff [v. Mathes, 41 Del.Ch. 494, 199 A.2d 548 (1964)] suggests that the plaintiff must first prove that the sole or primary purpose of the transaction was the directors' desire to retain control over the corporation. Rather, the unequivocal thrust of *Bennett* is that once the record demonstrates that control is implicated in the transaction, a conflict of interest is *ipso facto* created. Once a conflict of interest is present, the burden of proof is shifted logically and pragmatically on the defendants 'to justify [the transaction] as one primarily in the

corporate interest.' *Bennett*, supra, 187 A.2d at 409.

   ...   Recent Delaware cases reveal a growing trend to impose obligations on management to justify control-related transactions. Cf. Singer v. Magnavox, 380 A.2d 969 (Del.1977)   ...   Sinclair Oil v. Levien, 280 A.2d 717, 720 (Del.1971)   ...   Petty v. Penntech Papers, Inc., 347 A.2d 140, 143 (Del.Ch.1975). *Trueblood*, 629 F.2d at 300–01 (Rosenn, J., dissenting).

10. Another case which figures prominently in the majority's discussion of the Delaware business judgment rule is GM

majority was the factfinder (whether judge or jury) precluded from evaluating the merits of the fiduciary duty claims. In the instant case, on the other hand, similar claims are buffered against jury examination by the *cordon sanitaire* of a distorted business judgment rule.

II.

The basic error of the majority in the instant case is in holding as a matter of law that there was insufficient evidence to go to the jury on the state claims of breach of fiduciary duty. In reviewing a directed verdict, this court must evaluate the evidence in a light most favorable to the appellant and determine "whether it is of sufficient probative value that members of the jury might fairly and impartially differ as to the inferences to be reasonably drawn therefrom." Hohmann v. Packard Instrument Co., 471 F.2d 815 (7th Cir. 1973). See also Chillicothe Sand & Gravel Co. v. Martin Marietta Corp., 615 F.2d 427 (7th Cir. 1980). There was abundant evidence from which a jury in this case could have concluded that Field's directors breached their fiduciary duties to the shareholders: 1) by pursuing a fixed, nondebatable and undisclosed policy of massive resistance to merger with, or acquisition by, a series of the nation's foremost retailers; 2) by making hasty and apparently imprudent defensive acquisitions to reduce Field's attractiveness as a takeover candidate and to force the withdrawal of the CHH offer; and 3) by hastily filing a major antitrust suit to further impair persistent acquisitive efforts of CHH.

Reviewing first the evidence on the existence of a policy of independence in a light most favorable to appellants, it is difficult to understand the basis for the majority's conclusion that jurors could not fairly and impartially differ as to the inferences to be drawn from the facts presented. See *Hohmann*, 471 F.2d at 820. Marshall Field's Board of Directors had long been aware of the fact that the company's "accumulated worth, strong balance sheet, large cash reserves and borrowing potential" made Field's vulnerable to an involuntary merger or takeover. Panter v. Marshall Field & Co., 486 F.Supp. 1168 (N.D.Ill.1980). In December 1969, at approximately the same time that Associated Dry Goods expressed an interest in acquiring Field's, the Board retained Joseph Flom of the New York law firm of Skadden, Arps, Slate, Meagher & Flom for advice on defeating takeover bids. Id. at 1175–76. Flom recommended the application of his "pyramid theory" which is based on the principle that the best way to remain independent is to acquire other enterprises.[11] In this way, Field's would either become too large to be

---

Sub Corp. v. Liggett Group, Inc., No. 6155 (Del.Ch. April 25, 1980). Except for the fact that this unpublished preliminary ruling by a Delaware trial court makes a passing reference to the district court opinion in the instant case, *GM Sub Corp.* has little relevance to the claims of Field's shareholders.

11. Flom testified that he advised every Field's Chief Executive from 1970 to 1977 that acquisitions were the best means to prevent takeover. *Panter*, 486 F.Supp. at 1176.

acquired or would have so much overlap that acquisition of Field's by another major retailer would inevitably create antitrust problems.

While the majority notes that Flom advised the Board to be interested and listen carefully to proposals from other retailers, the majority apparently overlooks the curious coincidence that Field's made a major acquisition and/or raised antitrust problems to fight off virtually every serious merger or takeover attempt after the company hired Flom. See maj. op. ante at 278. In response to the interest of Associated, a predominantly Ohio and Pennsylvania operation, Field's conveniently acquired the Cleveland and Erie retail operations of Halle Brothers. *Panter*, 486 F.Supp. at 1177. These stores have, however, been less than profitable for Field's in the decade since they were acquired. See Plaintiffs' Exhibits 370, 372.

Similarly, after a merger proposal from Federated Department Stores in 1975, Field's actively employed Flom's antitrust approach to prevent a takeover. Record at 2101–03. No major acquisition was necessary in this instance because Federated's Chicago Division of I. Magnin and the Chicago, Seattle, and Milwaukee-based Boston Stores (which Federated offered to divest [12]) created sufficient antitrust leverage for Field's to stave off the unwelcome opportunity. Again, in 1976, Field's was under siege by Dayton-Hudson, but sought to acquire overlapping stores in Portland, Oregon and Tacoma, Washington from Liberty House.[13] Although Field's Board vociferously contends that its fascination with the Pacific Northwest was part of a long-range plan to sustain growth and

---

12. Much of the documentary evidence relating to merger or tender offer proposals prior to the CHH offer was excluded by the district court on relevance grounds. Rule 401 of the Federal Rules of Evidence defines relevant evidence as anything which has a "tendency to make the existence of any fact that is of consequence to the determination of the action more probable or less probable than it would be without the evidence." Plaintiffs here sought to establish the existence of a fixed and pervasive policy of independence which prompted the board to actively resist any CHH proposal regardless of its merit. I believe Judge Will, who made several preliminary rulings in this case, correctly defined the parameters of relevant issues for trial when he said, "... the world didn't start on October 12, 1977 [the day CHH first expressed an interest in Field's]. The only way to interprete [sic] what happened from October 12, 1977 to February ... 22nd, when the [CHH] offer [was] withdrawn, is to look at what happened before." Hearing of 3/27/79, Record at 10–11 (emphasis added). Far from being irrelevant "collateral" material, much of the excluded evidence discloses facts which tend to make the existence of a policy of independence "more probable ... than it

would be without [that] evidence," and therefore was improperly withheld. Even in the absence of this evidence, however, I think the plaintiffs established a sufficient factual basis for a jury determination of the state claims.

13. When asked to examine the antitrust aspects of a Dayton-Hudson/Marshall Field's combination, William Blair & Co., Field's investment banker, could find no competitive overlap between the two retailers. However, in a letter dated August 5, 1976, a Blair representative commented:

... it could be that Marshall Field itself has acquisition thoughts which, if consummated, could result in direct overlap or conflict and conceivably could be the basis for anti-competitive considerations. We suggest that your management give careful review to any acquisition thoughts resulting in entry into new markets by Field's. To the extent that such expansion is a real possibility, it could at some point have a bearing on a consolidation with a company such as Dayton-Hudson.

Plaintiffs' Exhibit 61. This piece of evidence, however, was improperly excluded at trial. See note 12, supra.

profitability, the Board's interest in the Liberty House stores coincidentally subsided as Dayton-Hudson's interest in Field's waned. See *Panter*, 486 F.Supp. at 1177. Finally, it should surprise no one that Field's initial response to the CHH proposal was to raise antitrust questions and hastily seek to acquire retail operations which were adjacent to CHH operations. See pp. 306–312 infra.

The majority accepts the defendants' claim that the Board's responses were tailored to a "desire to build value within the company and the belief that such value might be diminished by a given offer." Maj. op. ante at 296.[14] But one man's desire to "build value" may be another man's desire to "keep control at all costs," and a jury must decide which characterization is most consistent with the facts. A properly charged jury could have fairly concluded that Field's carefully weighed each merger or takeover offer to determine stockholder interest, but they could have just as fairly concluded that Field's carefully built its defenses against each offer without regard to stockholder interest. A directed verdict on these claims is therefore indefensible.

The plaintiffs also presented extensive evidence to substantiate their claims that Field's Board gave the CHH merger proposal no bona fide consideration and instead engaged in classic anti-takeover maneuvers. Throughout the busy Christmas season, the Board hastily solicited and apparently imprudently consummated several defensive acquisitions to reduce the company's attractiveness as a takeover candidate, create additional antitrust problems and ultimately force the withdrawal of the CHH offer. The documentary and testimonial evidence presented at trial provided a sufficient basis from which a jury could conclude that Field's Board in this respect breached its fiduciary duty.

The Board first learned of the CHH interest at a meeting following the death of Field's then chief executive, Joseph Burnham, in October 1977. *Panter*, 486 F.Supp. at 1178. A resolution passed at that meeting announced the Board's swift and uncompromising response: "The proposed business combination *should not be considered* because the best interests of the company's shareholders would be served by ... continuing as an independent entity." Id. (emphasis added). When CHH presented a formal merger proposal to the Board on December 12, 1977, the directors received a limited review of the financial aspects of the merger,[15] heard conflicting reports on Marshall Field's future earnings,[16]

---

14. There seems to be a striking paucity of evidence on how value might have been "diminished by a given offer." For the most part, Field's managed to squelch these offers before their impact on value could be fully appreciated by its stockholders.

15. Field's investment bankers were never asked to evaluate the adequacy or the fairness of the CHH proposal or determine the range for an acceptable offer. Record at 2275–76. The record only shows that Mr. Flom asked whether "it [was] reasonable to assume that if the Marshall Field Board

chose to sell the company now, it could expect to attain a higher price than that proposed by CHH? The response was yes; [but] no price was specified." Plaintiffs' Exhibit 122.

16. The investment bankers' "best professional judgment" was that Field's future earnings would rise 15% in 1978 and 12% each year thereafter. Plaintiffs' Exhibit 122; Record as 2309–10. However, Field's President Angelo Arena, who had been on the job less than two months, presented a hastily prepared "five-year plan" which

and rejected the CHH proposal as "illegal, inadequate and not in the best interest of Marshall Field & Co., its stockholders and the community which it serves." Id. at 1181.

Less than two weeks later (and only four days before Christmas), a committee of Field's officers and investment bankers reviewed a list of candidates available for immediate acquisition by Field's. Record at 553. Within ten days of this meeting, committee members met with the principal stockholders of Dillard's, a southwestern retailer in direct competition with CHH's Neiman-Marcus division, to see if a deal could be struck.[17] Record at 555-57. Correspondence from one of Field's investment bankers established that the Board sought a speedy transaction which would not require shareholder approval.[18] Because there was no time for a full scale financial analysis, the banker relied on "the intuitive judgment [of a Field's officer] as to the business potential" of the acquisition. Plaintiffs' Exhibit 137. The deal ultimately fell through, however, when Dillard's was purchased by Dutch interests. Record at 578-79.

Shortly after the demise of the Dillard's deal, Field's Board considered a proposal to acquire five Liberty House stores in the Pacific Northwest.[19] In the absence of any historical operating data,[20] and

projected an earnings per share increase of 23% for 1978 and approximately 20% for each year thereafter. The plan also showed that Field's management expected the 1977 earnings (year ending January 31, 1978) would be down some 7% from the prior year, but anticipated a five year increase of up to 193% in Field's per share earnings despite the fact that in the prior five years, Field's per share earnings had declined by 20%. Plaintiffs' Exhibits 122, 413E. The Board rejected the bankers' estimates in favor of Arena's five-year plan. Plaintiffs' Exhibit 122; Record at 2314-17.

17. The December 21, 1977 Acquisition Status Report indicates that less than two weeks prior to the meeting with Dillard's shareholders, Field's officers did not even know whether Dillard's was a standard retailer or a discount operation. Plaintiffs' Exhibit 130.

18. The January 4, 1978, letter from a representative of William Blair & Co. to Field's Executive Vice-President stated:

The most important benefits to Marshall Field & Co. from an all cash transaction are as follows:

The speed of consummation, since the approach will not require the filing of a registration statement and, since it would be a friendly offer endorsed by Dillard management, it would not run afoul of anti-takeover laws *nor would there be a need for a stockholders meeting* by either company.

...

... The principal disadvantage of [a tax-free transaction] are the *time required to effect the total transaction* (registration and stockholders meetings) and the *risk of certain Field's stockholders throwing up roadblocks* to the transaction. ...

Plaintiffs' Exhibit 137 (emphasis supplied).

19. Defendants claim that the acquisition of these Liberty House stores was the fruit of a long-standing desire to expand its Seattle-based Frederick and Nelson division. They point to 1975 and 1976 visits to these locations as proof of their good intentions. They conveniently ignore two important facts, however: 1) in 1975 and 1976 when these visits were made, Field's was fighting off takeover attempts by Federated and Dayton-Hudson, respectively; and 2) a December 1, 1977, letter from John Nannes of Skadden, Arps to Joseph DeCoeur of Kirkland & Ellis suggests a Liberty House acquisition would bolster Field's potential competition theory:

Dear Joe:

The Wall Street Journal reported in November 25, 1977 (page 14, column 6), that Carter Hawley Hale acquired a Liberty House department store in San Jose, California from Amfac, Inc. I understand that there are a number of Liberty House department stores in the Pacific Northwest, and this may well bolster our potential competition theory.

despite reports from Field's Vice-President of Corporate Development that the estimated earnings potential of these stores was marginal,[21] the Board unanimously approved a $24 million agreement to purchase these operations. Record at 603. The acquisition was publicly announced the following day. Plaintiffs' Exhibit 154.

Field's Board supplemented its sudden interest in acquiring operating retail stores with a hasty investigation of opportunities for expansion in two major shopping centers. While members of the acquisition team were concentrating on Dillard's, Field's Vice-President in charge of real estate was assigned to negotiate with Homart Development Corporation, managers of Northbrook Court in Chicago's northern suburbs. Although the Board had rejected an earlier plan to develop a Field's store in this shopping center,[22] their renewed interest could be credited to the fact that Neiman-Marcus had a successful operation in the same location.[23] The center was designed to contain four anchor stores, and Homart had commitments from four major tenants. The Field's representative pressed for the creation of a fifth anchor, but the negotiations ultimately fell apart. Record at 391–92.

The Board was more successful in its efforts to acquire space in the Galleria, an exclusive shopping center in Houston, Texas (and, of course, the location of another Neiman-Marcus store). In less than a month, Field's Board received an initial presentation on the Galleria, authorized negotiations for a lease and approved a $17 million dollar commitment to establish the first Marshall Field's store outside the Chicago area. The letter of agreement between Field's and the Galleria management was signed one day after CHH made a formal tender offer to purchase Field's stock at $42 per share. The agreement was announced on February 8, 1978, and shortly thereafter, CHH withdrew its offer because Field's expansion program [27] had "created sufficient doubt about Marshall Field's earning potential to make the offer no longer in the best interest of CHH shareholders." Plaintiffs' Exhibit 345.

The majority reviewed this sequence of events and concluded that there was "uncontroverted evidence that such expansion was reasonable and natural." Maj. op. ante at 297. There was more than sufficient

---

Plaintiffs' Exhibit 109. This letter was written *before* CHH ever made a formal merger proposal which Field's Board could consider.

20. See Record at 668–69.

21. The figures prepared by Field's Vice-President of Corporate Development were rejected by Field's management and replaced with more optimistic estimates dated January 19, 1978, the day of the Board meeting at which the Liberty House acquisition was approved. Cf. Plaintiffs' Exhibit 148 (figures of Vice-President of Corporate Development) with Plaintiffs' Exhibit 151 (figures used in replacement report).

22. In 1975, Field's management decided not to move into Northbrook Court because

Field's already had stores nearby at the Old Orchard and Hawthorn shopping centers. Record at 3200–01.

23. The antitrust complaint filed by Field's relied heavily on the competitive overlap between the Neiman-Marcus Northbrook Court store and Field's Chicago stores. Plaintiffs' Exhibit 195B.

27. Field's also announced in February 1978 that it had commenced negotiations for a store in the North Park Mall in Dallas, Texas. Plaintiffs' Exhibit 169. Dallas is the headquarters of CHH's Neiman-Marcus division, and North Park Mall is the site of a Neiman-Marcus store.

evidence here, however, for a jury to conclude that it was not "reasonable and natural" for the directors of a major retailer to make expansion commitments totalling more than $40 million dollars during and shortly after a busy Christmas season in which their "top priority" was to help a new chief executive officer become familiar with Field's operation.[28] Particularly when considered with the evidence of a long-standing and uncompromising policy of independence, I am astonished that the business judgment rule under any guise could keep this case from the jury.

Finally, the plaintiffs presented sufficient evidence to survive a directed verdict on the claim that Field's directors breached their fiduciary duty to the shareholders by filing a major antitrust suit against CHH within hours of the receipt of CHH's first merger proposal. The majority here has concluded that the defendants were "fairly and reasonably exercising their business judgment to protect the corporation against the perceived damage an illegal merger could cause." Maj. op. ante at 297. Once again, however, the facts presented at trial could easily support a quite different conclusion.

CHH President Philip Hawley informed Field's President, Angelo Arena, on December 10th that CHH intended to make a formal merger proposal within two days unless Field's agreed to enter serious negotiations with CHH representatives. Record at 1341. Arena then hastily assembled one director, one officer and several of Field's investment bankers and lawyers in New York on Sunday, December 11th at an emergency meeting. *Panter*, 486 F.Supp. at 1180; Record at 457–59, 2861–62. Although Arena had privately solicited an opinion on the antitrust implications of a merger with CHH from Kirkland & Ellis, no Kirkland & Ellis representative attended the meeting. Record at 459. Arena reported, however, that he had received oral confirmation from a Kirkland attorney that the proposed merger was illegal. *Panter*, 486 F.Supp. at 1181. Two prominent law firms representing CHH had also reviewed the matter and believed an adequate agreement could be worked out to avoid any antitrust problems.[29] Id. at 1180. However, without written legal analysis and without further discussion, the emergency anti-takeover cabal agreed that Field's would file an antitrust suit against CHH and solicit investigatory action by the FTC,[30] the SEC and the Illinois Securities Commission[31] to help block the merger. Arena

---

28. At one point during the trial, Director William Blair testified that the Board's "top priority" was to help Arena in the transition period following Burnham's death "because without capable management at the top of the company as our Christmas season was starting, we would have been in trouble and the stockholders would have suffered." Record at 3021.

29. The CHH proposal received by the Board on December 12, 1977, stated, "Our counsel have considered the antitrust aspect of the combination. They believe that the proposed transaction would be lawful and

we will act on the basis of that advice." Plaintiffs' Exhibit 111.

30. Kirkland & Ellis initiated the FTC investigation, but no formal action or complaint was ever filed against CHH. Plaintiffs' Exhibit 441.

31. Kirkland & Ellis also asked the Illinois Securities Commission ("ISC") to file suit against CHH for violations of the state securities laws. Although Kirkland attorneys prepared a draft complaint and submitted it to the ISC, the Commission refused to take any action. Plaintiffs' Exhibits 196, 441.

then called each director not present at the meeting, briefly outlined the antitrust problem and obtained authorization to file the suit. Id. at 1181. The following day, the Board issued a press release announcing the merger proposal and stating that a suit had been filed. Plaintiffs' Exhibit 113.

A jury considering this evidence could have found that Field's Board failed to adequately review the legal aspects of the proposed merger with CHH. In addition to hastily approving a lawsuit arguably based on insubstantial antitrust claims (involving quite remediable problems), the Board made defensive acquisitions which bolstered those claims, drained Field's of cash and ultimately led to the withdrawal of the CHH offer. The jury could have concluded that the directors in a sense used Field's own assets against the shareholders to defeat the takeover proposal of a high quality retailer which essentially doubled the market price of Field's stock.[32] With these findings, a jury charged even under the defendants' version of the business judgment rule could have decided the case for plaintiffs.

One may, of course, argue that what the directors did here was merely to make the normal reflexive response of incumbent management to efforts by outsiders to take over control of a corporation. In fact, applicable federal and state takeover legislation suggests that incumbent management—protective of its own powers and perquisites—may almost automatically attempt to defeat hostile tender offers, whatever their merits.[33] These assumptions may reflect a realistic view of human and corporate nature, and perhaps the law should simply excuse directors for thinking of themselves first and stockholders second in the event of a threatened takeover. In that regard I do not perceive the actions of Field's directors here as necessarily more egregious than many others in like circumstances. But under the legal norms which now must guide us (and no matter who has the burden of proof), there is no good reason to take this unfortunately too typical, but nonetheless important and substantial, case from the jury. ...

---

32. The fair market value of Marshall Field & Co. stock in the period December 1977—February 1978 was $18–20 per share. The actual price of Field's stock on the New York Stock Exchange increased from about $19–20 per share in September 1977 to just under $23 on December 9, 1977. On December 14, 1977, when trading resumed after being suspended in light of the CHH $36 merger announcement, the price of Field's stock jumped to about $32. In the next six weeks the price ranged from the high $20's to the low $30's. After the February 1, 1978, $42 tender offer announcement, the price of Field's stock increased to a high of over $35 and stayed in the high $20's and low $30's until February 22, 1978 when the price plunged to $19⅞ with the announcement of the withdrawal of CHH's offer. Plaintiffs' Exhibit 510.

33. In the debate on the Senate floor leading to enactment of the federal takeover disclosure statute, Senator Harrison Williams (its author) said:

> I have taken extreme care with this legislation to balance the scales equally to protect the legitimate interests of the corporation, management, and shareholders without unduly impeding cash takeover bids. Every effort has been made to avoid tipping the balance of regulatory burden in favor of management or in favor of the offeror. The purpose of this bill is to require full and fair disclosure for the benefit of stockholders while at the same time providing the offeror and management equal opportunity to fairly present their case.

113 Cong.Rec. 854–55 (1967), *quoted in Mite*, 633 F.2d at 496 n. 22.

MOBIL CORP. v. MARATHON OIL CO.

United States Court of Appeal, Sixth Circuit, 1981.
669 F.2d 366.

ENGEL, CIRCUIT JUDGE. On October 30, 1981, Mobil Corporation ("Mobil") announced its intention to purchase up to 40 million outstanding common shares of stock in Marathon Oil Company ("Marathon") for $85 per share in cash. Mobil conditioned that purchase upon receipt of at least 30 million shares, just over one-half of the outstanding shares. It further stated its intention to acquire the balance of Marathon by merger following its purchase of those shares.

Marathon directors were concerned about the effects of a merger with Mobil, and they immediately held a board meeting. The directors determined that, together with consideration of other alternatives, they would seek a "white knight"—a more attractive candidate for merger.

On November 1, 1981, Marathon filed an antitrust suit against Mobil in the United States District Court for the Northern District of Ohio, claiming that a merger between Marathon and Mobil would violate section 7 of the Clayton Act, 15 U.S.C. § 18. Marathon Oil Co. v. Mobil Corporation, 530 F.Supp. 315 (N.D.Ohio). The district court initially granted Marathon's request for a temporary restraining order, which allowed Mobil to receive tenders but precluded it from purchasing shares pending resolution of Marathon's application for a preliminary injunction. The court invited Marathon to continue its search for a white knight.

Negotiations developed between Marathon and several companies. Allied Industries sought to offer to purchase shares on the condition that Marathon buy certain Allied property to finance Allied's subsequent tender offer. Gulf Oil considered making an offer conditioned on a stock option for ten million shares. United States Steel Corporation ("U.S. Steel") indicated its interest, and on November 18, 1981, offered what it termed a "final proposal" to be acted upon that day. By that proposal U.S. Steel offered $125 per share for 30 million shares of Marathon stock, with a plan for a follow up merger with its subsidiary, U.S.S. Corporation ("USS").

The Marathon directors voted to recommend the U.S. Steel offer to the shareholders on November 18, 1981. Marathon, U.S. Steel and USS executed a formal merger agreement on that day. USS made its tender offer on November 19, 1981. Both USS and Marathon filed the appropriate documents with the Securities Exchange Commission.

The USS offer, and subsequently the merger agreement, had two significant conditions. First, they required a present, irrevocable option to purchase ten million authorized but unissued shares of Marathon common stock for $90 per share ("stock option"). These shares equalled approximately 17% of Marathon's outstanding shares. Next, they required an option to purchase Marathon's 48% interest in oil and mineral rights in the Yates Field for $2.8 billion. ("Yates Field option"). The latter option could be exercised only if USS's offer did not succeed and if a third party gained control of Marathon. Thus, in effect, a potential competing tender offeror could not acquire Yates Field upon a merger with Marathon.

The value of Yates Field to Marathon and to potential buyers is significant; Marathon has referred to the field as its "crown jewel." As Judge Kinneary [the trial court judge] has indicated, it is viewed as an enormous resource .... Judge Kinneary observed the unique characteristics of the Yates Field:

> [E]ven though the Yates Field has been producing oil for more than fifty years, petroleum engineers consider the field to be in the intermediate state of depletion, that is, they expect the field to continue producing oil for ninety years; in that there are between 3 and 3.5 billion barrels of oil still in place, the Yates Field holds the promise of providing additional reserves of oil that could be recovered; and cumulative production, as of the date of the report, accounted for only 39 percent of the conservatively estimated recoverable reserves of 2.0 billion barrels.
>
> . . .
>
> [One expert] estimated total recoverable reserves of 565 million barrels ... [although 150 million barrels] were potential reserves and their recovery might not occur.

Mobil Corp. v. Marathon Co., C–2–81–1402 at 27–28.

The importance of Yates to a potential tender offeror is illustrated by the fact that both Gulf Oil and Allied indicated that they would propose a tender offer only upon assurances that they would have an option to buy Marathon's interest in the Yates Field. Such requests are a recent but recurring phenomenon in connection with tender offers. See, e.g., Conoco, Inc. v. Mobil Oil Corp., No. 81–4787 (S.D.N.Y. Aug. 4, 1981).

Following this agreement, Mobil filed suit in the United States District Court for the Southern District of Ohio, seeking to enjoin the exercise of the options and any purchase of shares in accordance with the tender offer. Named as defendants were Marathon, its directors, and USS. Mobil alleged that the options granted to USS served as a "lock-up" arrangement to defeat any competitive offers of Mobil or third parties, thereby constituting a "manipulative" practice "in connection with a tender offer," in violation of section 14(e) of the Williams Act, 15 U.S.C. § 78n(e). It claimed further that Marathon failed to disclose material information regarding the purpose of the options to its shareholders, also in violation of section 14(e). It also complained of various violations of state law: Marathon acted in breach of its fiduciary duties; it violated Ohio Rev.Code § 1701.76 by selling "all or substantially all" of its assets without shareholder approval; and it effected transactions outside the scope of any legitimate corporate purpose.

On November 24, 1981, Judge Kinneary granted in part Mobil's motion for a temporary restraining order, prohibiting Marathon and USS from taking any action in connection with the tender offer or the Yates

Field option agreement. Mobil announced a new tender offer on November 25, 1981, offering to purchase at least 30 million common shares of Marathon at $126 per share in cash. This offer was conditioned on a finding that the USS stock option and the Yates Field option were invalid. Mobil reserved a right to waive these conditions and thereafter limit its purchase to less than fifty percent of the shares outstanding. Mobil again indicated its intention to merge with Marathon if the tender offer were successful, proposing to purchase remaining shares with Mobil debentures having a value of $90 in cash.

Following that offer, Judge Kinneary considered Mobil's application for a preliminary injunction. In an opinion dated December 7, 1981, he denied a preliminary injunction on the grounds that the test enunciated in Mason County Medical Ass'n v. Knebel, 563 F.2d 256 (6th Cir. 1977), had not been satisfied. This appeal followed. Because there appears to be a substantial likelihood that Mobil will succeed on its claim that execution of the Yates Field and stock options are "manipulative acts or practices, in connection with [a] tender offer" in violation of section 14(e), 15 U.S.C. § 78n(e) [3], we conclude that a consideration of the *Mason County* criteria required the grant of preliminary injunctive relief, and accordingly, we reverse.

I.

As Judge Kinneary stated, the factors to consider in evaluating whether a preliminary injunction will issue have been outlined in Mason County Medical Ass'n v. Knebel, 563 F.2d 256, 261 (6th Cir. 1977):

1. Whether the plaintiff has shown a strong or substantial likelihood or probability of success on the merits;

2. Whether the plaintiff has shown irreparable injury;

3. Whether the issuance of a preliminary injunction would cause substantial harm to others;

4. Whether the public interest would be served by issuing the preliminary injunction.

Judge Kinneary found that Mobil made a showing with regard to the last three factors. ...

Judge Kinneary nonetheless denied the motion for preliminary injunction because he determined that Mobil had not demonstrated a "substantial likelihood of success on the merits." He found that the disclosures were in accord with section 14(e) requirements. He found further that the state law claims were not substantial in light of Marathon's good faith in connection with the tender offer negotiations. Judge Kinneary also rejected the argument that execution of the Yates Field and stock options could be manipulative acts in violation of section 14(e). We

---

3. Our holding makes unnecessary for purposes of this appeal any consideration of whether Marathon acted in violation of state law or violated disclosure requirements of section 14 of the Williams Act, 15 U.S.C. § 78n(e).

disagree with his finding, and we now turn to a consideration of that question.

II.

Although the issue has not been raised by either party, out of an abundance of caution we believe it necessary to determine whether Mobil has a private cause of action for injunctive relief under section 14(e) of the Williams Act. ... In Piper v. Chris-Craft, Inc., 430 U.S. 1, 97 S.Ct. 926, 51 L.Ed.2d 124 (1977), the Supreme Court in an opinion by Chief Justice Burger held that a defeated tender offeror (Chris-Craft) did not have a private cause of action for damages against the successful bidder (Bangor Punta) and the target company (Piper). The Court, however, carefully limited its consideration to whether money damages could be recovered. It expressly reserved the question of "whether as a general proposition a suit in equity for injunctive relief ... would lie in favor of a tender offeror under ... § 14(e) ...." Id. at 47 n. 33, 97 S.Ct. at 952 n. 33. This open question has not been resolved by the Supreme Court or by this circuit, although other courts faced with the issue have found that such a cause of action exists.[4] After an examination of the *Piper* analysis, a consideration of the distinctions between damage actions and injunctive actions, and a recognition of the special problems associated with the dynamics of tender offer battles, we agree with these courts and hold that a tender offeror has an implied cause of action under the Williams Act to obtain timely injunctive relief for violations of section 14(e). ...

Whether Congress intended a cause of action to be implied from legislation is a question of statutory construction. ... In *Piper*, the Court examined the statutory scheme and legislative history in order to identify the legislative purpose of the Williams Act and concluded that "the sole purpose of the Williams Act was the protection of investors who are confronted with a tender offeror." *Piper*, supra, 430 U.S. at 35, 97 S.Ct. at 946. With that purpose in mind, the Court proceeded to evaluate the Williams Act under the four-part test set forth in Cort v. Ash, 422 U.S. 66, 95 S.Ct. 2080, 45 L.Ed.2d 26 (1975). Therefore, in the instant case, we must also examine the *Cort* factors to determine whether Congress in the Williams Act intended to grant an implied cause of action for injunctive relief to a tender offeror.

The first *Cort* factor is whether the plaintiff is "one of the class for whose *especial* benefit the statute was enacted." Id. at 78, 95 S.Ct. at 2087 (emphasis in original). As a tender offeror, Mobil would not appear to be the intended beneficiary of the Act. We believe, however, that we can look to the practical realities of this type of action and determine

---

4. See Weeks Dredging & Contracting, Inc. v. American Dredging Co., 451 F.Supp. 468 (E.D.Pa.1978); Humana, Inc. v. American Medicorp, Inc., 445 F.Supp. 613 (S.D.N.Y.1977). Cf. Crane Co. v. Harsco Corp., 511 F.Supp. 294 (D.Del.1981) (a tender offeror has an implied cause of action for an injunction under section 14(e) of the Williams Act.)

that a cause of action is necessary to aid the shareholders of Marathon and to prevent violations of the Williams Act. A preliminary injunction against manipulative practices would be the only means of preserving the free, informed choice of shareholders that the Williams Act was designed to protect. As the Supreme Court acknowledged in *Piper*, "in corporate control contests the stage of preliminary injunctive relief, rather than post-contest lawsuits, 'is the time when relief can best be given.' " Piper v. Chris-Craft, supra, 430 U.S. at 42, 97 S.Ct. at 949. In a tender offer battle, events occur with explosive speed and require immediate response by a party seeking to enjoin the unlawful conduct. Issues such as incomplete disclosure and manipulative practices can only be effectively spotted and argued by parties with complete knowledge of the target, its business, and others in the industry. The tender offeror has frequently made intensive investigations before deciding to commence its offer, and may often be the only party with enough knowledge and awareness to identify nondisclosure or manipulative practices in time to obtain a preliminary injunction.

The second factor in *Cort* is whether there was "any indication of legislative intent, explicit or implicit, either to create such a remedy or to deny one." Cort v. Ash, supra, 422 U.S. at 78, 95 S.Ct. at 2087. In *Piper*, the Court concluded that the legislative history of the Williams Act showed:

> [T]he narrow intent to curb the unregulated activities of tender offerors. The expression of this purpose, which pervades the legislative history, negates the claim that tender offerors were intended to have additional weapons in the form of an implied cause of action *for damages*, particularly if a *private damages claim* confers no advantage on the expressly protected class of shareholder-offerees, a matter we discuss later.

Piper v. Chris-Craft, 430 U.S. at 38, 97 S.Ct. at 947 (emphasis added).

On the other hand, an injunctive action by a tender offeror has significantly different effects than a damage action. First, clear benefit is derived by the shareholders of the target. An injunction would protect the Marathon shareholders from making their decisions whether to sell without full information. As such, it furthers the purpose of the Williams Act. Second, an injunctive action does not tip the balance in favor of one tender offeror. This type of action serves merely to prevent the manipulative practices at which the Williams Act was aimed without deterring management or competing offerors from engaging in the battle.

The third *Cort* factor requires a determination that the existence of a private remedy is "consistent with the underlying purpose of the legislative scheme." Cort v. Ash, supra, 422 U.S. at 78, 95 S.Ct. at 2087. In *Piper*, the Court concluded:

> . . . The class sought to be protected by the Williams Act are the shareholders of the *target* corporation; hence it can hardly be said

> that their interests as a class are served by a judgment in favor of
> Chris-Craft and against Bangor Punta.

Piper v. Chris-Craft, supra, 430 U.S. at 39, 97 S.Ct. at 948 (emphasis in
original). The injunctive action in the instant case, however, would have
very different effects. It would protect *all* Marathon shareholders by
preventing management or competing tender offerors from failing to
disclose fully or from using manipulative tactics. Because of the unique
ability of Mobil to act quickly while armed with information necessary to
prove any section 14(e) violations, this injunctive action may often be the
only means to provide adequate assurance that Marathon's shareholders
have a fully informed, free choice. Moreover, because no monetary loss
is threatened for one who inadvertently violates the Williams Act, an
action for an injunction does not pose the danger of deterring future
offers.

In the fourth and final *Cort* factor, we must determine whether "the
cause of action [is] one traditionally relegated to state law." Cort v.
Ash, supra, 422 U.S. at 78, 95 S.Ct. at 2087. In *Piper*, the Supreme
Court found that a tender offeror had a common law cause of action for
damages under principles of interference with a prospective commercial
advantage. Piper v. Chris-Craft, supra, 430 U.S. at 40–41, 97 S.Ct. at
948–949. While such an action may be an effective common law alternative for a damage action, we do not believe that the common law has
traditionally provided an injunctive remedy that would effectively protect
Marathon shareholders from nondisclosure or manipulation by the parties in the bidding. ...

Thus, we conclude after an examination of the four factors of Cort v.
Ash that Mobil has an implied cause of action under section 14(e) to
obtain an injunction against Marathon and USS for failure to make
proper disclosure and employment of manipulative practices. ...

III.

Having determined that Mobil has an implied cause of action under
the Williams Act, we now consider Mobil's claim that the Yates Field and
stock options granted by Marathon to USS, the wholly owned subsidiary
of U.S. Steel, constitute a "manipulative act or practice" in connection
with the USS tender offer of November 19, 1981, in violation of section
14(e). ... The district court found no substantial likelihood of success
by Mobil on the merits of this claim, holding that it "amounts to no more
than a claim that the Marathon directors acted unfairly and breached
their fiduciary [duty] to Marathon and its shareholders," and as such
fails to state a cause of action under section 14(e). The district court
relied on Santa Fe Industries, Inc. v. Green ... [which] held that a
mere allegation of unfair treatment of minority shareholders, corporate
mismanagement, or breach of corporate fiduciary duty by majority
shareholders or corporate directors does not state a cause of action
under section 10(b), and particularly that such conduct, standing alone,

does not constitute a "manipulative device or contrivance" under the statute. 430 U.S. at 474–77, 97 S.Ct. at 1301.

Although Mobil alleges a breach of fiduciary duty by the Marathon directors as one of its pendent state law claims, this claim is not the only basis upon which it complains. We offer no opinion regarding the merits of the fiduciary duty claim, but we conclude that the Yates Field option and the stock option individually and together are "manipulative" as that term is used in section 14(e).

The term "manipulative" is not defined in either the Securities Exchange Act or the Williams Act. See, e.g., 15 U.S.C. § 78c. "Manipulation" in securities markets can take many forms, see, e.g., 15 U.S.C. §§ 78i, 78j (proscribing certain forms of manipulation), but the Supreme Court has recently indicated that manipulation is an affecting of the market for, or price of, securities by *artificial* means, i.e., means unrelated to the natural forces of supply and demand.

> Use of the word "manipulative" is especially significant. It is and was virtually a term of art when used in connection with securities markets. It connotes intentional or willful conduct designed to deceive or defraud investors by controlling or artificially affecting the price of securities.

Ernst & Ernst v. Hochfelder, 425 U.S. 185, 199, 96 S.Ct. 1375, 1383, 47 L.Ed.2d 668 (1976) ....

In our view, it is difficult to conceive of a more effective and manipulative device than the "lock-up" options employed here, options which not only artificially affect, but for all practical purposes completely block, normal healthy market activity and, in fact, could be construed as expressly designed solely for that purpose. ...

... The Yates Field option which USS demanded and received in connection with its tender offer of $125 per share greatly dampens the demand by Mobil and other potential bidders in the tender offer market, because a successful takeover by any bidder other than USS will give USS the right to exercise its option and purchase the Yates Field interest for $2.8 billion. This presents a significant threat to other bidders that even if they gain control of Marathon they will lose the Yates Field oil reserves.

The district court found that the $2.8 billion which Marathon would receive from USS in exchange for the Yates Field oil reserves is a fair price, but there was evidence that the field might be worth as much as $3.639 billion. We point this out not to disturb the district court's finding, but to illustrate that potential tender offerors may value the Yates Field reserves at a higher figure than $2.8 billion, especially in today's world of ever-depleting oil supplies and the volatile, unpredictable nature of oil prices over the long term. Oil companies and other companies like USS seeking to invest in the oil industry may believe that long-term oil reserves, not cash or other assets, will best ensure long-term profits. As a result, we cannot say that Mobil and other potential bidders for control of Marathon would not be willing to make tender offers reflecting a Yates Field valuation far greater than $2.8 billion, were it not for the Yates Field option which USS possesses. Only the open market contemplated by the Act provides a means to measure its value.

The Yates Field option is exercisable if, and only if, control of Marathon is obtained by a third party. The only effect of this option can be to deter Mobil and any other potential tender offerors from competing with USS in an auction for control of Marathon. Others cannot compete on a par with USS; its bid of $125 per share thus amounts to an artificial ceiling on the value Marathon shareholders can receive for their shares. Therefore, there is a substantial likelihood that the option is manipulative under section 14(e) of the Williams Act.

The particular facts before us also indicate that the stock option that USS demanded and received in connection with its tender offer prevents all others from competing on a par with USS for control of Marathon. In our opinion, the stock option was large enough in this takeover contest to serve as an artificial and significant deterrent to competitive bidding for a controlling block of Marathon shares.

The stock option gave USS the right to purchase 10 million authorized but unissued shares of Marathon for $90 per share. USS could exercise its option at any time during the takeover contest and acquire 10 million newly issued shares; presently there are 58,685,906 Marathon common shares outstanding. The original Mobil tender offer was for 40 million shares at a price of $85 per share. The USS tender offer was for 30 million shares at $125 per share. An estimate prepared by the First Boston Corporation, Marathon's investment banker, calculated that because of the stock option, it would cost Mobil (or any other outside bidder seeking 40 million shares of Marathon) 1.1 to 1.2 billion additional dollars to match the USS tender offer. A chart contained in page six of the first Boston report discloses that every dollar raise in the bid by USS would cost USS $30 million, while each such dollar raise would cost Mobil $47 million. App. 718. Harold D. Hoopman, president and chief executive officer of Marathon, testified about the stock option and the First Boston chart, which the Marathon directors had before them when they decided to grant the stock option to USS on November 18, 1981, as follows:

Q. That would be 1.2 billion of additional cost to Mobil if they attempted to match US Steel, isn't that true?

A. That's true.

Q. Would you agree that the fact as it relates to Mobil, or a third party, of giving this option in terms of these costs would mean that any third party or Mobil would have to put up a very significant additional amount of money in order to make a tender offer?

A. That's correct.

Q. Was that discussed at the meeting?

A. Yes.

Q. It was discussed, I assume, on the basis that if we can make this fly, this is one way to make it much more expensive for Mobil to come to the same price; isn't that true?

A. That's true.

Q. Further, you discussed this would be a deterrent not only to Mobil, but to other third parties, wouldn't it?

A. That's right.

App. 201–202.

The size and price of the stock option, together with the fact that it was granted to USS, a tender offeror, prevented all others from competing on a par with USS for a controlling block of Marathon shares, and tipped the scales decidedly in favor of USS. In our opinion, the stock option artificially and significantly discouraged competitive bidding for the Marathon stock.

The Yates Field option and the stock option, both individually and in combination, have the effect of circumventing the natural forces of market demand in this tender offer contest. Were this contest a straight price-per-share auction, tender offers well in excess of the USS offer of $125 per share may have been forthcoming. Of course, Mobil itself has offered $126 per share, conditional on the judicial removal of the options. Our task under the Williams Act is not to speculate about what price the Marathon shareholders might have been offered if the natural market forces existed in this tender offer contest, but rather to enforce the mandate of section 14(e) against manipulation of the market. The purpose of the Williams Act, protection of the target shareholders, requires that Mobil and any other interested bidder be permitted an equal opportunity to compete in the marketplace and persuade the Marathon shareholders to sell their shares to them.

The defendants argue that section 14(e) requires full disclosure and nothing more. They point to the following language in the Supreme Court's opinion in *Santa Fe*, concerning section 10(b):

[T]he Court repeatedly has described the "fundamental purpose" of the [Securities Exchange] Act as implementing a "philosophy of full disclosure"; once full and fair disclosure has occurred, the fairness of the terms of the transaction is at most a tangential concern of the statute.

430 U.S. at 477–78, 97 S.Ct. at 1302–03. The defendants read too much into this language. *Santa Fe* held that mere allegations of unfairness and breach of fiduciary duty by majority shareholders to the minority did not violate section 10(b). It did not find that nondisclosure was the only ground upon which to base a 10(b) claim. Instead, the Court expressly made a factual determination that "the conduct ... alleged in the complaint was not 'manipulative' ..." 430 U.S. at 476, 97 S.Ct. at 1302. *Santa Fe* thus cannot be taken to mean that conduct that falls within the special meaning of the term "manipulation" is legal so long as it is fully disclosed. "[N]ondisclosure is usually essential to the success of a

manipulative scheme," id. at 477, 97 S.Ct. at 1302, but this case illustrates that disclosure alone does not always mean that there is no manipulation. It may be that the Marathon shareholders in this case have now been fully informed that their management granted USS the Yates Field option and the stock option. They may now understand fully how these options deter any tender offers higher than $125 per share. Yet, they have had no real alternative to accepting the USS offer, because Mobil's offer of $126 is conditional upon the invalidity of the options, and there is and could be no other comparable tender offer as long as the "lock-up" options remain in effect. The artificial ceiling on the price of their shares at $125 is manipulation to which they must submit whether it is disclosed to them or not, since in not tendering their shares to USS they risk being relegated to the "back end" of USS's takeover proposal and receiving only $90 per share.

In short, to find compliance with section 14(e) solely by the full disclosure of a manipulative device as a *fait accompli* would be to read the "manipulative acts and practices" language completely out of the Williams Act.

The district court found that the Marathon directors' decision on November 18, 1981 to accept USS's proposed merger agreement, including the Yates Field and stock options, was not a breach of fiduciary duty. The district court's holding was based in part on its finding that the Marathon ... directors were faced with a non-negotiable package proposal from USS which had to be accepted or rejected in less than a day, and which they accepted because they felt it was the only way they could get the USS $125 bid for their shareholders. (Mobil's bid at that time was $85.) In holding today that the option agreements were manipulative under section 14(e) of the Williams Act, we need not disturb the district court's finding of good faith and loyalty by the Marathon directors. Section 14(e) prohibits manipulation by *"any* person", and thereby covers the conduct of USS in demanding and obtaining the options, as well as any manipulative conduct by the Marathon directors. The Williams Act protects the target shareholders regardless of who did the manipulating.

In conclusion, it is apparent to us that the particular options granted to USS by Marathon under the circumstances of this tender offer contest constitute "manipulative acts" in connection with the tender offer, violative of section 14(e) of the Williams Act. In so ruling, we do not purport to define a rule of decision for all claims of manipulation under the Williams Act, or indeed for all forms of options which might be claimed to "lock up" takeover battles or otherwise discourage competing tender offers. We leave these issues to developing law in this new and difficult area of securities regulation.

RELIEF

By the terms of its tender offer, USS gave Marathon shareholders a time in which to tender their shares and in turn promised that it would not withdraw its tender offer before that time. These dates have been extended. It is apparent from the record that a substantial majority of shareholders have agreed with the trial judge that the tender offer was reasonable and that they desired to accept it. It would be anomalous, indeed, if after our holding that USS had engaged in manipulative practices under § 14(e), it was by the very illegality of its conduct able to gain an unjustified benefit by the untimely withdrawal of the offer after its conduct may have dissuaded others from entering into the field as competing tender offerors. In this respect, the fashioning of appropriate equitable relief requires, and we so order, that the tender offer of USS of $125 per share be kept open for a reasonable time but free of the inhibiting and unlawful impact of the two options which it extracted from the Marathon board as a condition of its agreement.[6] Therefore, considerations of equity require that there be a time sufficient for adequate notice to Marathon shareholders under the Williams Act and to give shareholders an opportunity to withdraw their tenders of stock already made. The period of time likewise should be sufficient to permit the acceptance of any competing tender offers by Marathon from others who may now have an interest in bidding, uninhibited by the coercive impact of the two options which have been declared violative of § 14(e).

Reversed and remanded to the District Court for further proceedings consistent with this opinion. The mandate shall issue forthwith.

MERRITT, CIRCUIT JUDGE, dissenting.

Although I do not disagree that some defensive moves by a tender offeror may be found to be manipulative acts under the Williams Act, my view is that Mobil's Williams Act case is moot in light of our disposition of the antitrust case. ...[†]

DATA PROBE ACQUISITION CORP. v. DATATAB, INC.

United States Court of Appeals, Second Circuit, 1983.
722 F.2d 1, cert. denied ___ U.S. ___, 104 S.Ct. 1326, 79 L.Ed.2d 722 (1984).

Before KEARSE, CARDAMONE and WINTER, Circuit Judges.

WINTER, Circuit Judge:

Plaintiffs Data Probe, Inc. and its wholly owned subsidiary Data Probe Acquisition Corp. (collectively "Data Probe") brought this action to enjoin the merger of defendants CRC Acquisition Corp., a wholly owned subsidiary of defendant CRC Information Systems, Inc. (collectively "CRC"), and Datatab, Inc. ("Datatab"). CRC and Datatab had entered into an Agreement and Plan of Merger (the "Merger Agree-

---

6. By this order we do not deprive USS of any benefit of its proposed bargain, except the illegal option advantages. These, of course, do not diminish the value of Marathon to USS—if USS proves to be the successful bidder.

[†] In Marathon Oil Co. v. Mobil Corp., 699 F.2d 378 (6th Cir. 1981), the Sixth Circuit affirmed an order preliminarily enjoining Mobil from acquiring Marathon on antitrust grounds. (Footnote by ed.)

ment") under which Datatab would become a wholly owned subsidiary of CRC. In its complaint, Data Probe, which itself was attempting to gain control of Datatab through a tender offer, alleged that Datatab and CRC had committed various violations of federal securities laws and regulations. After an expedited trial, the district court, 568 F.Supp. 1538, found that an option to purchase Datatab stock acquired by CRC was a "manipulative" device proscribed by Section 14(e) of the Securities Exchange Act of 1934 (the "Act"), 15 U.S.C. § 78n(e) (1976). It also found that a letter written by Datatab to its shareholders failed to satisfy the disclosure requirements established by Section 14(e) of the Act and by Securities and Exchange Commission ("SEC") Rule 14e–2, 17 C.F.R. § 240.14e–2 (1983). For these two reasons the district court enjoined exercise of the option by CRC, thus preventing the merger as well. This expedited appeal followed.

We reverse on both grounds.

BACKGROUND

In December, 1982, the management of Datatab, a publicly traded New York corporation engaged in the market research business, approached the management of CRC, a privately held New York corporation in the same field, to discuss the possibility of CRC's acquiring Datatab. The decision to approach CRC was prompted by the deteriorating financial condition of Datatab, which had been experiencing mounting losses. Negotiations ensued, and on April 29, 1983, the two companies announced the Merger Agreement, which provided that a wholly owned CRC subsidiary would be merged into Datatab and that holders of Datatab common stock would then receive $1.00 per share in cash, leaving Datatab a wholly owned subsidiary of CRC.

Applicable New York law required the approval of two-thirds of Datatab's shareholders and Datatab's Board scheduled a special meeting of shareholders to be held on June 23, 1983. On May 26, proxy materials announcing the meeting and describing the merger were sent to Datatab shareholders. Among the conditions of the merger described in the proxy materials was an undertaking by CRC to enter into employment agreements with Sanford Adams, Lee Gallaher and John Lobel, who were officers of Datatab or a subsidiary and who comprised Datatab's Board of Directors. Each was to receive a three-year contract. It is undisputed that the proxy materials, including the disclosure of the employment agreements, conformed to the requirements of applicable state and federal law.

On June 21, 1983, two days before the shareholders' meeting, Data Probe, a New York corporation also engaged in the market research business, announced a cash tender offer for any and all shares of Datatab stock at $1.25 per share. The offer, which was apparently not discussed with the management of Datatab or CRC, was contingent on the failure of Datatab shareholders to approve the proposed merger between Datatab and CRC. Its announcement caused Datatab's Board to adjourn the special shareholders' meeting.

On the evening of June 21, Yitzhak Bachana, president and majority shareholder of Data Probe, met over dinner with Sanford Adams of Datatab to discuss Data Probe's interest in Datatab.[1] The two men took up the subject of the future of current Datatab employees in the event Data Probe's tender offer was successful. Adams's notes from the meeting indicate that Bachana thought that discussion of the employment contracts of Adams, Lobel, and Gallaher was "premature." Bachana testified at the hearing that he indicated to Adams that "he could not made any promises" with respect to the future of current Datatab management.

Further negotiations between Datatab and CRC were held and, on July 1, the two firms concluded a revised merger agreement (the "July 1 Agreement") under which Datatab shareholders would receive $1.40 per share. As a part of the July 1 Agreement, Datatab granted CRC a one-year irrevocable option to purchase 1,407,674 authorized but unissued Datatab shares at $1.40 per share. Since Datatab had only 703,836 shares of common stock outstanding, the practical effect was to guarantee that CRC could acquire Datatab by exercising the option, no matter how many of the outstanding shares were tendered to Data Probe. It could then vote its resulting two-thirds interest in Datatab for the merger with its subsidiary.

In a letter to its shareholders also dated July 1 (the "July 1 shareholders' letter") the Datatab Board announced its response to the still outstanding Data Probe tender offer. The letter was sent to conform with the duty imposed by SEC Rule 14e–2, 17 C.F.R. § 240.14e–2 (1983), which requires that within ten business days of the making of a tender offer the subject company must inform its shareholders of its position with respect to the offer and of the reasons supporting its position. The letter advised that "[i]n view of the new $1.40 per share merger offer from CRC, the Board recommends that [shareholders] *not* tender ... shares for the $1.25 price ... offered by Data Probe." (Emphasis in the original). The letter described the CRC option to purchase Datatab shares, but it drew no explicit connection between the grant of the option and the likely outcome of the struggle for control of Datatab.

On July 14, Data Probe increased its offer to $1.55 per share, conditioned upon termination of the CRC option or a judicial determination of the option's invalidity. At the same time it commenced this action by filing a complaint that alleged, among other things, that the option was a "manipulative act or practice" committed in connection with a tender offer in violation of Section 14(e) of the Act. The complaint alleged no violations of state law. The relief sought was, *inter alia*, an injunction barring exercise of the option.

---

1. Also attending this meeting were James Sheridan of Data Probe and defend- ant John Lobel of Datatab.

After a hearing, Judge Sofaer announced his findings and conclusions and rendered final judgment in favor of plaintiff Data Probe. He held that Section 14(e), by forbidding "manipulative ... practices in connection with any tender offer," proscribed acts that "unduly obstruct the exercise of informed shareholder choice." Because CRC's option to purchase the unissued Datatab shares effectively nullified Data Probe's tender offer, Judge Sofaer concluded that the option was proscribed by Section 14(e). He also found that the July 1 shareholders' letter was materially misleading in that it did not state as a reason for the Board's position the fact that, unlike Data Probe, CRC had guaranteed employment to Adams, Lobel and Gallaher, and in that it drew no connection between the grant of the option and the outcome of the contest for control of Datatab. Judge Sofaer enjoined exercise of the option.

Following the district court's decision Data Probe went forward with its $1.55 per share tender offer. As of August 9, 1983, more than 60 percent of Datatab's outstanding stock had been tendered to Data Probe.

This appeal, also expedited, followed.

DISCUSSION

1. *Manipulative Devices Under Section 14(e)*

Congress added Section 14(e) to the Act in 1968 by passing the Williams Act, Pub.L. No. 90–439, 82 Stat. 454 (codified at 15 U.S.C. §§ 78m(d)–(e), 78n(d)(f) (1976)). Section 14(e) provides in pertinent part that "[i]t shall be unlawful for any person ... to engage in any fraudulent, deceptive, or manipulative acts or practices ... in connection with any tender offer." [2] Relying exclusively on this language for authority and assuming the option's validity under the New York State Corporation Law, the district court held the CRC option invalid. Since we must also assume the option's validity under state law, the question presented on appeal is whether Section 14(e) authorizes federal courts to review the substantive validity of corporate actions undertaken during the course of a tender offer. We conclude that it does not.

Viewing the CRC option solely as a self-serving barrier created by Datatab's management to prevent its shareholders from choosing the Data Probe offer, the gravamen of the wrong alleged is a breach of fiduciary duty which we are not free to condemn under existing federal legislation. In Santa Fe Industries, Inc. v. Green, 430 U.S. 462, 97 S.Ct. 1292, 51 L.Ed.2d 480 (1977), the Supreme Court explicitly refused to

---

2. Whether Section 14(e) implicitly creates a private cause of action under which a tender offeror may seek injunctive relief against the target company, its management, and other rivals in the takeover contest has not been decided by this court. The Supreme Court explicitly reserved this question in Piper v. Chris-Craft Industries, 430 U.S. 1, 47 n. 33, 97 S.Ct. 926, 952 n. 33, 51 L.Ed.2d 124 (1977). The defendants argued in the district court that Section 14(e) does not create such a cause of action but abandoned this contention on appeal, explicitly declining to argue it at oral argument. Lacking the benefit of briefs and argument on this major issue and noting that it does not affect the outcome, we will assume such a cause of action exists for purposes of this decision.

extend the prohibition against "manipulative ... devices," SEC Rule 10b–5, 17 C.F.R. § 240.10b–5 (1983), to "instances of corporate mismanagement ... in which the essence of the complaint is that shareholders were treated unfairly by a fiduciary." Id. at 477, 97 S.Ct. at 1302. The Court construed the term "manipulative" in a "technical sense of artificially affecting market activity in order to mislead investors." 430 U.S. at 476, 97 S.Ct. at 1302. We have held this construction applicable to Section 14(e). Billard v. Rockwell Intern. Corp., 683 F.2d 51, 56 (2d Cir.1982). A complaint which alleges only that management has for self-serving reasons acted so as to deprive shareholders of a favorable financial opportunity does not state a valid claim under Section 14(e), therefor. *Billard* explicitly held that the fairness or unfairness to shareholders of a transaction engaged in by a control group is irrelevant under Section 14(e), id. at 55, even where that transaction prevents shareholders from an opportunity to sell their shares at a higher price to a "White Knight." Misrepresentation is thus an essential element of a cause of an action under Section 14(e). Lewis v. McGraw, 619 F.2d 192, 195 (2d Cir.), cert. denied, 449 U.S. 951, 101 S.Ct. 354, 66 L.Ed.2d 214 (1980).

In *Santa Fe*, the Supreme Court also stated that "[a]bsent a clear indication of congressional intent," it was "reluctant to federalize the substantial portion of the law of corporations that deals with transactions in securities, particularly where established state policies of corporate regulation would be overridden." Id. 430 U.S. at 479, 97 S.Ct. at 1304. The gravamen of the claim advanced here is a breach of management's fiduciary duty to shareholders, a matter traditionally committed to state law, which, if entertained, would unquestionably embark us on a course leading to a federal common law of fiduciary obligations. We decline to embark on such a course under Section 14(e).

In Edgar v. Mite Corp., 457 U.S. 624, 102 S.Ct. 2629, 73 L.Ed.2d 269 (1982), a majority of the Court held that the Illinois Takeover Act imposed an impermissible burden on interstate commerce, a rationale inapplicable to the present dispute which involves private acts. A plurality of the Court found that the statute was preempted by the Williams Act on at least three grounds: (1) the Illinois statute required that an offeror inform both the Secretary of State and the target of its intentions twenty business days before the offer; (2) tender offerors were forbidden to proceed until after a hearing before the Secretary of State; and (3) the Secretary could block an offer if he or she found its terms unfair. Id. 102 S.Ct. at 2637–40. Our decision is consistent with the plurality opinion in *Mite*, written by Justice White, the author of *Santa Fe*. The *Mite* plurality addresses the extent to which states may regulate the process of tender offers through timing requirements, mandatory hearings on fairness, and the like in light of the provisions of the Williams Act. Language in the plurality opinion suggesting that neither management nor bidders should have an "unfair advantage," 102 S.Ct. at 2636, means that states may not seek to provide such an advantage through legislative regulation of the tender offer process, including administrative review of the fairness or unfairness of the offer. States are forbidden to impose such burdens on the process, not because the Williams Act imposes similar burdens, but because it was intended to be the outer limit of the positive regulatory role of government.[3]

We disagree, therefore, with Mobil Corp. v. Marathon Oil Co., 669 F.2d 366 (6th Cir.1981) to the extent that *Marathon* creates judge made substantive obligations imposed upon offerors or the management of offerees engaged in a tender offer contest and repeat our conviction that it is "an unwarranted extension of the Williams Act." Buffalo Forge Co. v. Ogden Corp., 717 F.2d 757 at 760, slip op. at 6662 (2d Cir.1983).

2. *Disclosure*

The district court also found that the July 1 shareholders' letter was materially misleading in that it did not disclose that Datatab management preferred the CRC offer because of the employment guarantees and in that it failed to discuss the effect on the takeover contest of the CRC option.

This holding misinterprets management's obligation of disclosure. By referring to the Merger Agreement, the July 1 letter incorporated the proxy materials sent to Datatab shareholders which described the guarantees of employment negotiated by Adams, Gallaher and Lobel and thus disclosed their conflict of interest. We see no additional informational benefit accruing to shareholders by requiring the beneficiaries of such contracts to announce that they regard them favorably. In our view, Rule 14e–2, read in light of the Williams Act's purpose of insuring that "public shareholders who are confronted by a cash tender offer for their stock will not be required to respond without adequate information," Rondeau v. Mosinee Paper Corp., 422 U.S. 49, 58, 95 S.Ct. 2069, 2075, 45 L.Ed.2d 12 (1975), calls for a statement of why the shareholders should accept or reject a tender offer, based upon objective factual material. The highly subjective inquiry pursued by the district court assumes that boards of directors have monolithic viewpoints and threatens to burden the tender offer process with judicial oversight which yields little in the way of useful or new information but subjects tender offers to the delay inherent in judicial dockets. So long as any personal stake of any member of management is fully disclosed, the Rule 14e–2 disclosure may be limited to objective, non-misleading factual material.

As for the failure to state that the option, if valid, brought the takeover contest to an end, that conclusion is obvious to anyone conversant with elementary mathematics. We are also not inclined to subject every tender offer to a nit-picking judicial scrutiny which will in the long run injure shareholders by preventing them from taking advantage of favorable offers.

The disclosure required by the Act is not a rite of confession or exercise in common law pleading. What is required is the disclosure of

---

3. *Mite*, of course, did not involve the application of fiduciary obligations of a con-   tractual nature imposed by state law.

material objective factual matters. That was fulfilled by disclosure of the employment guarantees contained in the terms of the merger negotiated by Datatab's management and of the terms of the CRC option.

CONCLUSION

For the foregoing reasons, the order of the district court is reversed.

---

(9) Policy Questions and State Takeover Laws

Insert the following material at p. 1604 of the unabridged edition, at the end of Chapter X, Section 1(m)(9):

EDGAR v. MITE CORP.

Supreme Court of the United States, 1982.
457 U.S. 624, 102 S.Ct. 2629, 73 L.Ed.2d 269.

JUSTICE WHITE delivered an opinion, Parts I, II, and V–B of which are the opinion of the Court.[*]

The issue in this case is whether the Illinois Business Take-Over Act, Ill.Rev.Stat., ch. 121½, ¶ 137.51, et seq. (1979), is unconstitutional under the Supremacy and Commerce Clauses of the Federal Constitution.

I

Appellee MITE Corporation and its wholly-owned subsidiary, MITE Holdings, Inc., are corporations organized under the laws of Delaware with their principal executive offices in Connecticut. Appellant James Edgar is the Secretary of State of Illinois and is charged with the administration and enforcement of the Illinois Act. Under the Illinois Act any takeover offer[1] for the shares of a target company must be registered with the Secretary of State. Ill.Rev.Stat., ch. 121½, ¶ 137.-54.A (1979). A target company is defined as a corporation or other issuer of securities of which shareholders located in Illinois own 10% of the class of equity securities subject to the offer, or for which any two of the following three conditions are met: the corporation has its principal executive office in Illinois, is organized under the laws of Illinois, or has

---

[*] The Chief Justice and Justices White, Blackmun (except for Part V–B), Powell (except for Part II), Stevens and O'Connor join Parts I, II, and V–B of the opinion. [Footnote by the court.]

1. The Illinois Act defines "take-over offer" as "the offer to acquire or the acquisition of any equity security of a target company, pursuant to a tender offer. ..." Ill.Rev.Stat., ch. 121½, ¶ 137.52-9 (1979). "A tender offer has been conventionally understood to be a publicly made invitation addressed to all shareholders of a corporation to tender their shares for sale at a specified price." Note, The Developing Meaning of "Tender Offer" Under the Securities Exchange Act of 1934, 86 Harv.L.Rev. 1250, 1251 (1973). The terms "tender offer" and "takeover offer" are often used interchangeably.

at least 10% of its stated capital and paid-in surplus represented within the state. Id., at ¶ 137.52–10. An offer becomes registered 20 days after a registration statement is filed with the Secretary unless the Secretary calls a hearing. Id., at ¶ 137.54.E. The Secretary may call a hearing at any time during the 20-day waiting period to adjudicate the substantive fairness of the offer if he believes it is necessary to protect the shareholders of the target company, and a hearing must be held if requested by a majority of a target company's outside directors or by Illinois shareholders who own 10% of the class of securities subject to the offer. Id., at ¶ 137.57.A. If the Secretary does hold a hearing, he is directed by the statute to deny registration to a tender offer if he finds that it "fails to provide full and fair disclosure to the offerees of all material information concerning the takeover offer, or that the take-over offer is inequitable or would work or tend to work a fraud or deceit upon the offerees. ..." Id., at ¶ 137.57.E.

On January 19, 1979, MITE initiated a cash tender offer for all outstanding shares of Chicago Rivet and Machine Co., a publicly held Illinois corporation, by filing a Schedule 14D–1 with the Securities and Exchange Commission in order to comply with the Williams Act. The Schedule 14D–1 indicated that MITE was willing to pay $28.00 per share for any and all outstanding shares of Chicago Rivet, a premium of approximately $4.00 over the then-prevailing market price. MITE did not comply with the Illinois Act, however, and commenced this litigation on the same day by filing an action in the United States District Court for the Northern District of Illinois. The complaint asked for a declaratory judgment that the Illinois Act was preempted by the Williams Act and violated the Commerce Clause. In addition, MITE sought a temporary restraining order and preliminary and permanent injunctions prohibiting the Illinois Secretary of State from enforcing the Illinois Act.

Chicago Rivet responded three days later by bringing suit in Pennsylvania, where it conducted most of its business, seeking to enjoin MITE from proceeding with its proposed tender offer on the ground that the offer violated the Pennsylvania Takeover Disclosure Law, 70 Pa.Cons. Stat. § 71 et seq. (Supp.1978). After Chicago Rivet's efforts to obtain relief in Pennsylvania proved unsuccessful,[3] both Chicago Rivet and the Illinois Secretary of State took steps to invoke the Illinois Act. On February 1, 1979, the Secretary of State notified MITE that he intended to issue an order requiring it to cease and desist further efforts to make a tender offer for Chicago Rivet. On February 2, 1979 Chicago Rivet notified MITE by letter that it would file suit in Illinois state court to enjoin the proposed tender offer. MITE renewed its request for injunctive relief in the District Court and on February 2 the District Court

---

3. In addition to filing suit in state court, Chicago Rivet filed a complaint with the Pennsylvania Securities Commission requesting the Commission to enforce the Pennsylvania Act against MITE. On January 31, 1979 the Pennsylvania Securities Commission decided that it would not invoke the Pennsylvania Takeover Disclosure Law. The next day, the United States District Court for the Western District of Pennsylvania, to which MITE had removed the state court action, denied Chicago Rivet's motion for a temporary restraining order.

issued a preliminary injunction prohibiting the Secretary of State from enforcing the Illinois Act against MITE's tender offer for Chicago Rivet.

MITE then published its tender offer in the February 5 edition of the Wall Street Journal. The offer was made to all shareholders of Chicago Rivet residing throughout the United States. The outstanding stock was worth over $23 million at the offering price. On the same day Chicago Rivet made an offer for approximately 40% of its own shares at $30.00 per share.[4] The District Court entered final judgment on February 9, declaring that the Illinois Act was preempted by the Williams Act and that it violated the Commerce Clause. Accordingly, the District Court permanently enjoined enforcement of the Illinois statute against MITE. Shortly after final judgment was entered, MITE and Chicago Rivet entered into an agreement whereby both tender offers were withdrawn and MITE was given 30 days to examine the books and records of Chicago Rivet. Under the agreement MITE was either to make a tender offer of $31.00 per share before March 12, 1979, which Chicago Rivet agreed not to oppose, or decide not to acquire Chicago Rivet's shares or assets. App. to Brief for Appellees 1a–4a. On March 2, 1979, MITE announced its decision not to make a tender offer.

The United States Court of Appeals for the Seventh Circuit affirmed sub nom. MITE Corp. v. Dixon, 633 F.2d 486 (7th Cir. 1980). It agreed with the District Court that several provisions of the Illinois Act are preempted by the Williams Act and that the Illinois Act unduly burdens interstate commerce in violation of the Commerce Clause. We noted probable jurisdiction, 451 U.S. 968, 101 S.Ct. 2043, 68 L.Ed.2d 347 (1981), and now affirm.

II

The Court of Appeals specifically found that this case was not moot, 633 F.2d, at 490, reasoning that because the Secretary has indicated he intends to enforce the Act against MITE, a reversal of the judgment of the District Court would expose MITE to civil and criminal liability[5] for making the February 5, 1979 offer in violation of the Illinois Act. We agree. It is urged that the preliminary injunction issued by the District Court is a complete defense to civil or criminal penalties. While, as Justice Stevens' concurrence indicates, that is not a frivolous question by any means, it is an issue to be decided when and if the Secretary of State initiates an action. That action would be foreclosed if we agree with the Court of Appeals that the Illinois Act is unconstitutional. Accordingly, the case is not moot.

III

4. Chicago Rivet's offer for its own shares was exempt from the requirements of the Illinois Act pursuant to Ill.Rev.Stat., ch. 121½, ¶ 137.52–9.(4) (1979).

5. The Secretary of State may bring an action for civil penalties for violations of the Illinois Act., Ill.Rev.Stat. ch. 121½, ¶ 137.65 (1979), and a person who willfully violates the Act is subject to criminal prosecution. Id., at ¶ 137.63.

We first address the holding that the Illinois Takeover Act is uncon-stitutional under the Supremacy Clause. We note at the outset that in passing the Williams Act, which is an amendment to the Securities and Exchange Act of 1934, Congress did not also amend § 28(a) of the 1934 Act, 15 U.S.C. § 78bb(a).[6] In pertinent part, § 28(a) provides as follows:

> "Nothing in this chapter shall affect the jurisdiction of the securities commission (or any agency or officer performing like functions) of any state over any security or any person insofar as it does not conflict with the provisions of this chapter or the rules and regula-tions thereunder."

Thus Congress did not explicitly prohibit states from regulating take-overs; it left the determination whether the Illinois statute conflicts with the Williams Act to the courts. Of course, a state statute is void to the extent that it actually conflicts with a valid federal statute; and,

> "[a] conflict will be found 'where compliance with both federal and state regulations is a physical impossibility ...,' Florida Lime & Avocado Growers, Inc. v. Paul, 373 U.S. 132, 142–143 [83 S.Ct. 1210, 1217, 10 L.Ed.2d 248] (1963), or where the state 'law stands as an obstacle to the accomplishment and execution of the full purposes and objectives of Congress.' ...

Our inquiry is further narrowed in this case since there is no contention that it would be impossible to comply with both the provisions of the Williams Act and the more burdensome requirements of the Illinois law. The issue thus is, as it was in the Court of Appeals, whether the Illinois Act frustrates the objectives of the Williams Act in some substantial way.

The Williams Act, passed in 1968, was the congressional response to the increased use of cash tender offers in corporate acquisitions, a device that had "removed a substantial number of corporate control contests from the reach of existing disclosure requirements of the federal securi-ties laws." Piper v. Chris-Craft Industries, 430 U.S. 1, 22 [97 S.Ct. 926, 939, 51 L.Ed.2d 124] (1977). The Williams Act filled this regulatory gap. ...

There is no question that in [adopting the Williams Act], Congress intended to protect investors. Piper v. Chris-Craft Industries, supra, at 35, 97 S.Ct. at 946; Rondeau v. Mosinee Paper Corp., 422 U.S. 49, 58, 95 S.Ct. 2069, 2075, 45 L.Ed.2d 12 (1975); S.Rep. No. 550, 90th Cong., 1st Sess. 3–4 (1967) ("Senate Report"). But it is also crystal clear that a major aspect of the effort to protect the investor was to avoid favoring either management or the takeover bidder. As we noted in *Piper*, the

---

6. There is no evidence in the legislative history that Congress was aware of state takeover laws when it enacted the Williams Act. When the Williams Act was enacted in 1968, only Virginia had a takeover stat-ute. The Virginia statute, Va.Code § 131–528, became effective March 5, 1968; the Williams Act was enacted several months later on July 19, 1968. Takeover statutes are now in effect in 37 states. Sargent, On the Validity of State Takeover Regulation: State Responses to *MITE* and *Kidwell*, 42 Ohio St.L.J. 689, 690 n. 7 (1981).

disclosure provisions originally embodied in S.2731 "were avowedly pro-management in the target company's efforts to defeat takeover bids." 430 U.S., at 30, 97 S.Ct., at 943. But Congress became convinced "that takeover bids should not be discouraged because they serve a useful purpose in providing a check on entrenched but inefficient management." Senate Report at 3.[9] It also became apparent that entrenched manage-ment was often successful in defeating takeover attempts. As the legislation evolved, therefore, Congress disclaimed any "intention to provide a weapon for management to discourage takeover bids ..." Rondeau v. Mosinee Paper Corp., supra, 422 U.S., at 58, 95 S.Ct., at 2075, and expressly embraced a policy of neutrality. As Senator Williams explained, "We have taken extreme care to avoid tipping the scales either in favor of management or in favor of the persons making the takeover bids." 113 Cong.Rec. 24664 (1967). This policy of "evenhand-edness," Piper v. Chris-Craft Industries, supra, 430 U.S. at 31, 97 S.Ct., at 944, represented a conviction that neither side in the contest should be extended additional advantages vis-a-vis the investor, who if furnished with adequate information would be in a position to make his own informed choice. We, therefore, agree with the Court of Appeals that Congress sought to protect the investor not only by furnishing him with the necessary information but also by withholding from management or the bidder any undue advantage that could frustrate the exercise of an informed choice. 633 F.2d, at 496.

To implement this policy of investor protection while maintaining the balance between management and the bidder, Congress required the latter to file with the Commission and furnish the company and the investor with all information adequate to the occasion. With that filing, the offer could go forward, stock could be tendered and purchased, but a stockholder was free within a specified time to withdraw his tendered shares. He was also protected if the offer was increased. Looking at this history as a whole, it appears to us, as it did to the Court of Appeals, that Congress intended to strike a balance between the investor, manage-ment and the takeover bidder. The bidder was to furnish the investor and the target company with adequate information but there was no "intention to do ... more than give incumbent management an oppor-tunity to express and explain its position." Rondeau v. Mosinee Paper Corp., supra, 422 U.S., at 58, 95 S.Ct., at 2075. Once that opportunity was extended, Congress anticipated that the investor, if he so chose, and the takeover bidder should be free to move forward within the time-frame provided by Congress.

IV

The Court of Appeals identified three provisions of the Illinois Act that upset the careful balance struck by Congress and which therefore

---

9. Congress also did not want to deny shareholders "the opportunities which re-sult from the competitive bidding for a block of stock of a given company," namely the opportunity to sell shares for a premi-um over their market price. 113 Cong.Rec. 24666 (1967) (remarks of Sen. Javits).

stand as obstacles to the accomplishment and execution of the full purposes and objectives of Congress. We agree with the Court of Appeals in all essential respects.

A

The Illinois Act requires a tender offeror to notify the Secretary of State and the target company of its intent to make a tender offer and the material terms of the offer 20 business days before the offer becomes effective. Ill.Rev.Stat., ch. 121½, ¶¶ 137.54.E, 137.54.B (1979). During that time, the offeror may not communicate its offer to the shareholders. Id., at ¶ 137.54.A. Meanwhile, the target company is free to disseminate information to its shareholders concerning the impending offer. The contrast with the Williams Act is apparent. Under that Act, there is no pre-commencement notification requirement; the critical date is the date a tender offer is "first published or sent or given to security holders." 15 U.S.C. § 78n(d)(1). See also 17 CFR § 240.14d–2 (1981).

We agree with the Court of Appeals that by providing the target company with additional time within which to take steps to combat the offer, the precommencement notification provisions furnish incumbent management with a powerful tool to combat tender offers, perhaps to the detriment of the stockholders who will not have an offer before them during this period.[10] These consequences are precisely what Congress determined should be avoided, and for this reason, the precommencement notification provision frustrates the objectives of the Williams Act.

It is important to note in this respect that in the course of events leading to the adoption of the Williams Act, Congress several times refused to impose a precommencement disclosure requirement. In October 1965, Senator Williams introduced S.2731, a bill which would have required a bidder to notify the target company and file a public statement with the Securities and Exchange Commission at least 20 days before commencement of a cash tender offer for more than five per cent of a class of the target company's securities. 111 Cong.Rec. 28259 (1965). The Commission commented on the bill and stated that "the requirement of a 20-day advance note to the issuer and the Commission is unnecessary for the protection of security holders ..." 112 Cong. Rec. 19005 (1966). Senator Williams introduced a new bill in 1967, S.510, which provided for a confidential filing by the tender offeror with the Commission five days prior to the commencement of the offer. S.510 was enacted as the Williams Act after elimination of the advance disclosure requirement. As the Senate Report explained,

> "At the hearings it was urged that this prior review was not necessary and in some cases might delay the offer when time was of the essence. In view of the authority and responsibility of the Securities and Exchange Commission to take appropriate action in the event that inadequate or misleading information is disseminated to the

10. See note 11 and accompanying text,   infra.

public to solicit acceptance of a tender offer, the bill as approved by the committee requires only that the statement be on file with the Securities and Exchange Commission at the time the tender offer is first made to the public." Senate Report at 4.

Congress rejected another pre-commencement notification proposal during deliberations on the 1970 amendments to the Williams Act.[11]

B

For similar reasons, we agree with the Court of Appeals that the hearing provisions of the Illinois Act frustrate the congressional purpose by introducing extended delay into the tender offer process. The Illinois Act allows the Secretary of State to call a hearing with respect to any tender offer subject to the Act, and the offer may not proceed until the hearing is completed. Ill.Rev.Stat., ch. 121½, ¶¶ 137.57.A and B (1979) The Secretary may call a hearing at any time prior to the commencement of the offer, and there is no deadline for the completion of the hearing. Id., at ¶¶ 137.57.C and D. Although the Secretary is to render a decision within 15 days after the conclusion of the hearing, that period may be extended without limitation. Not only does the Secretary of State have the power to delay a tender offer indefinitely, but incumbent management may also use the hearing provisions of the Illinois Act to delay a tender offer. The Secretary is required to call a hearing if requested to do so by, among other persons, those who are located in Illinois "as determined by post office address as shown on the records of the target company and who hold of record or beneficially, or both, at least 10% of the outstanding shares of any class of equity securities which is the subject of the take-over offer." Id., at ¶ 137.57.A. Since incumbent management in many cases will control, either directly or indirectly, 10% of the target company's shares, this provision allows management to delay the commencement of an offer by insisting on a hearing. As the Court of Appeals observed, these provisions potentially afford management a "powerful weapon to stymie indefinitely a takeover." 633 F.2d, at 494.[12] In enacting the Williams Act, Congress itself "recognized that delay can seriously impede a tender offer" and sought to avoid it. Great

---

11. H.R.4285, 91st Cong., 2d Sess. (1970). The bill was not reported out of the subcommittee. Instead, the Senate amendments to the Williams Act, which did not contain pre-commencement notification provisions, were adopted. Pub.L. No. 91–567, 84 Stat. 1497.

The Securities and Exchange Commission has promulgated detailed rules governing the conduct of tender offers. Rule 14d–2(b), 17 CFR § 240.14d–2(b) (1981), requires that a tender offeror make its offer effective within five days of publicly announcing the material terms of the offer by disseminating specified information to shareholders

and filing the requisite documents with the Commission. Otherwise the offeror must announce that it is withdrawing its offer. The events in this litigation took place prior to the effective date of Rule 14d–2(b), and because Rule 14d–2(b) operates prospectively only, see 44 Fed.Reg. 70326 (1979), it is not at issue in this case.

12. Delay has been characterized as "the most potent weapon in a tender offer fight." Langevoort, State Tender-Offer Legislation: Interests, Effects, and Political Competency, 62 Cornell L.Rev. 213, 238 (1977). ...

Western United Corp. v. Kidwell, 577 F.2d 1256, 1277 (CA5 1978); Senate Report at 4.[13]

Congress reemphasized the consequences of delay when it enacted the Hart-Scott-Rodino Antitrust Improvements Act, Pub.L. No. 94–435, 90 Stat. 1383, 15 U.S.C. 12, et seq.

"[I]t is clear that this short waiting period [the ten-day period for proration provided for by § 14(d)(6) of the Securities Exchange Act, which applies only after a tender offer is commenced] was founded on congressional concern that a longer delay might unduly favor the target firm's incumbent management, and permit them to frustrate many pro-competitive cash tenders. This ten-day waiting period thus underscores the basic purpose of the Williams Act—to maintain a neutral policy towards cash tender offers, by avoiding lengthy delays that might discourage their chances for success." H.R. Rep. No. 94–1373, 94th Cong., 2d Sess. 12 (1976).[14]

As we have said, Congress anticipated investors and the takeover offeror be free to go forward without unreasonable delay. The potential for delay provided by the hearing provisions upset the balance struck by Congress by favoring management at the expense of stockholders. We therefore agree with the Court of Appeals that these hearing provisions conflict with the Williams Act.

C

The Court of Appeals also concluded that the Illinois Act is pre-empted by the Williams Act insofar as it allows the Secretary of State of

---

13. According to the Securities and Exchange Commission, delay enables a target company to:

"(1) repurchase its own securities;

"(2) announce dividend increases or stock splits;

"(3) issue additional shares of stock;

"(4) acquire other companies to produce an antitrust violation should the tender offer succeed;

"(5) arrange a defensive merger;

"(6) enter into restrictive loan agreements;

"(7) institute litigation challenging the tender offer." Brief for the Securities and Exchange Commission as *amicus curiae* 10, n. 8.

14. Representative Rodino set out the consequences of delay in greater detail when he described the relationship between the Hart-Scott-Rodino Act and the Williams Act:

"In the case of cash tender offers, more so than in other mergers, the equities include time and the danger of undue delay. This bill in no way intends to repeal or reverse the congressional purpose underlying the 1968 Williams Act, or the 1970 amendments to that act. ... Lengthier delays will give the target firm plenty of time to defeat the offer, by abolishing cumulative voting, arranging a speedy defense merger, quickly incorporating in a State with an antitakeover statute, or negotiating costly lifetime employment contracts for incumbent management. And the longer the waiting period, the more the target's stock may be bid up in the market, making the offer more costly—and less successful. Should this happen, it will mean that shareholders of the target firm will be effectively deprived of the choice that cash tenders give to them: Either accept the offer and thereby gain the tendered premium, or reject the offer. Generally, the courts have construed the Williams Act so as to maintain these two options for the target company's shareholders, and the House Conferees contemplate that the courts will continue to do so." 122 Cong.Rec. 30877 (1976).

Illinois to pass on the substantive fairness of a tender offer. Under ¶ 137.57.E of the Illinois law, the Secretary is required to deny registration of a takeover offer if he finds that the offer "fails to provide full and fair disclosure to the offerees ... *or that the take-over offer is inequitable.* ..." (Emphasis added).[15] The Court of Appeals understood the Williams Act and its legislative history to indicate that Congress intended for investors to be free to make their own decisions. We agree. Both the House and Senate Reports observed that the Act was "designed to make the relevant facts known so that shareholders have a fair opportunity to make their decision." H.R. Rep. No. 1711, 90th Cong., 2d Sess. 3 (1968); Senate Report at 3. Thus, as the Court of Appeals said, "[t]he state thus offers investor protection at the expense of investor autonomy—an approach quite in conflict with that adopted by Congress." 633 F.2d, at 494.

V

The Commerce Clause provides that "Congress shall have Power ... [t]o regulate Commerce ... among the several states." U.S. Const., Art. 1, § 8, cl. 3. "[A]t least since Cooley v. Board of Wardens, 53 U.S. (12 How.) 299, 13 L.Ed. 996 (1852), it has been clear that 'the Commerce Clause. ... even without implementing legislation by Congress is a limitation upon the power of the States.' " Great Atlantic & Pacific Tea Co. v. Cottrell, 424 U.S. 366, 370–371, 96 S.Ct. 923, 927, 47 L.Ed.2d 55 (1976), quoting Freeman v. Hewitt, 329 U.S. 249, 252, 67 S.Ct. 274, 276, 91 L.Ed. 265 (1946). See also Lewis v. BT Investment Managers, Inc., 447 U.S. 27, 35, 100 S.Ct. 2009, 2014, 64 L.Ed.2d 702 (1980). Not every exercise of state power with some impact on interstate commerce is invalid. A state statute must be upheld if it "regulates even-handedly to effectuate a legitimate local public interest, and its effects on interstate commerce are only incidental ... unless the burden imposed on such commerce is clearly excessive in relation to the putative local benefits." Pike v. Bruce Church, Inc., 397 U.S. 137, 142, 90 S.Ct. 844, 847, 25 L.Ed.2d 174 (1970), citing Huron Cement Co. v. Detroit, 362 U.S. 440, 443, 80 S.Ct. 813, 815, 4 L.Ed.2d 852 (1960). The Commerce Clause, however, permits only *incidental* regulation of interstate commerce by the states; direct regulation is prohibited. Shafer v. Farmers Grain Co., 268 U.S. 189, 199, 45 S.Ct. 481, 485, 69 L.Ed. 909 (1925). See also Pike v. Bruce Church, Inc., supra, 397 U.S., at 142, 90 S.Ct., at 847. The Illinois Act violates these principles for two reasons. First, it directly regulates and prevents, unless its terms are satisfied, interstate tender offers which in turn would generate interstate transactions. Second, the burden the Act imposes on interstate commerce is excessive in light of the local interests the Act purports to further.

---

15. Appellant argues that the Illinois Act does not permit him to adjudicate the substantive fairness of a tender offer. Brief for Appellant 21–22. On this state-law issue, however, we follow the view of the Court of Appeals that ¶ 137.57.E allows the Secretary of State "to pass upon the substantive fairness of a tender offer. ..." 633 F.2d, at 493.

A

States have traditionally regulated intrastate securities transactions,[16] and this Court has upheld the authority of states to enact "blue-sky" laws against Commerce Clause challenges on several occasions. Hall v. Geiger-Jones Co., 242 U.S. 539, 37 S.Ct. 217, 61 L.Ed. 480 (1917); Caldwell v. Sioux Falls Stock Yards Co., 242 U.S. 559, 37 S.Ct. 224, 61 L.Ed. 493 (1917); Merrick v. N.W. Halsey & Co., 242 U.S. 568, 37 S.Ct. 227, 61 L.Ed. 498 (1917). The Court's rationale for upholding blue-sky laws was that they only regulated transactions occurring within the regulating states. "The provisions of the law ... apply to dispositions of securities *within* the State and while information of those issued in other States and foreign countries is required to be filed ... they are only affected by the requirement of a license of one who deals with them *within* the State. ... Such regulations affect interstate commerce in securities only incidentally." Hall v. Geiger-Jones Co., supra, 242 U.S., at 557–558, 37 S.Ct., at 223 (cites omitted). Congress has also recognized the validity of such laws governing intrastate securities transactions in § 28a of the Securities Exchange Act, 15 U.S.C. § 78bb(a), a provision "designed to save state blue-sky laws from preemption." Leroy v. Great Western United Corp., 443 U.S. 173, 182, n. 13, 99 S.Ct. 2710, 2716, n. 13, 61 L.Ed.2d 464 (1979).

The Illinois Act differs substantially from state blue-sky laws in that it directly regulates transactions which take place across state lines, even if wholly outside the State of Illinois. A tender offer for securities of a publicly-held corporation is ordinarily communicated by the use of the mails or other means of interstate commerce to shareholders across the country and abroad. Securities are tendered and transactions closed by similar means. Thus, in this case, MITE Corporation, the tender offeror, is a Delaware corporation with principal offices in Connecticut. Chicago Rivet is a publicly-held Illinois corporation with shareholders scattered around the country, 27% of whom live in Illinois. Mite's offer to Chicago Rivet's shareholders, including those in Illinois, necessarily employed interstate facilities in communicating its offer, which, if accepted, would result in transactions occurring across state lines. These transactions would themselves be interstate commerce. Yet the Illinois law, unless complied with, sought to prevent Mite from making its offer and concluding interstate transactions not only with Chicago Rivet's stockholders living in Illinois, but also with those living in other states and having no connection with Illinois. Indeed, the Illinois law on its face would apply even if not a single one of Chicago Rivet's shareholders were a resident of Illinois, since the Act applies to every tender offer for a corporation meeting two of the following conditions: the corporation has its principal executive office in Illinois, is organized under Illinois laws, or has at

16. For example, the Illinois Blue Sky Law, Ill.Rev.Stat. ch. 121½, § 137.1, et seq. (Supp.1980), provides that securities subject to the law must be registered "prior to sale in this State. ..." Id., at § 137.5.

least 10% of its stated capital and paid-in surplus represented in Illinois. Ill.Rev.Stat., ch. 121½, ¶ 137.52–10.(2) (1979). Thus the Act could be applied to regulate a tender offer which would not affect a single Illinois shareholder.

It is therefore apparent that the Illinois statute is a direct restraint on interstate commerce and that it has a sweeping extraterritorial effect. Furthermore, if Illinois may impose such regulations, so may other states; and interstate commerce in securities transactions generated by tender offers would be thoroughly stifled. In Shafer v. Farmers Grain Co., 268 U.S., at 199, 45 S.Ct., at 485, the Court held that "a state statute which by its necessary operation directly interferes with or burdens . . . [interstate] commerce is a prohibited regulation and invalid, regardless of the purpose with which it was enacted." See also Hughes v. Alexandria Scrap Corp., 426 U.S. 794, 806, 96 S.Ct. 2488, 2496, 49 L.Ed.2d 220 (1976). The Commerce Clause also precludes the application of a state statute to commerce that takes place wholly outside of the state's borders, whether or not the commerce has effects within the state. In Southern Pacific Co. v. Arizona, 325 U.S. 761, 775, 65 S.Ct. 1515, 1523, 89 L.Ed. 1915 (1945), the Court struck down on Commerce Clause grounds a state law where the "practical effect of such regulation is to control . . . [conduct] beyond the boundaries of the state. . . ." The limits on a state's power to enact substantive legislation are similar to the limits on the jurisdiction of state courts. In either case, "any attempt 'directly' to assert extraterritorial jurisdiction over persons or property would offend sister States and exceed the inherent limits of the State's power." Shafer v. Heitner, 433 U.S. 186, 197, 97 S.Ct. 2569, 2576, 53 L.Ed.2d 683 (1977).

Because the Illinois Act purports to regulate directly and to interdict interstate commerce, including commerce wholly outside the state, it must be held invalid as were the laws at issue in *Shafer* and *Southern Pacific*.

B

The Illinois Act is also unconstitutional under the test of Pike v. Bruce Church, Inc., 397 U.S., at 142, 90 S.Ct., at 847, for even when a state statute regulates interstate commerce indirectly, the burden imposed on that commerce must not be excessive in relation to the local interests served by the statute. The most obvious burden the Illinois Act imposes on interstate commerce arises from the statute's previously-described nationwide reach which purports to give Illinois the power to determine whether a tender offer may proceed anywhere.

The effects of allowing the Illinois Secretary of State to block a nationwide tender offer are substantial. Shareholders are deprived of the opportunity to sell their shares at a premium. The reallocation of economic resources to their highest-valued use, a process which can improve efficiency and competition, is hindered. The incentive the tender offer mechanism provides incumbent management to perform well so that stock prices remain high is reduced. See Easterbrook and Fischel, The Proper Rule of a Target's Management in Responding to a Tender Offer, 94 Harv.L.Rev. 1161, 1173–1174 (1981); Fischel, Efficient Capital Market Theory, the Market for Corporate Control, and the Regulation of Cash Tender Offers, 57 Tex.L.Rev. 1, 5, 27–28, 45 (1978); H.R. Rep. No. 94–1373, 94th Cong., 2d Sess. 12 (1976).

Appellant claims the Illinois Act furthers two legitimate local interests. He argues that Illinois seeks to protect resident security holders and that the Act merely regulates the internal affairs of companies incorporated under Illinois law. We agree with the Court of Appeals that these asserted interests are insufficient to outweigh the burdens Illinois imposes on interstate commerce.

While protecting local investors is plainly a legitimate state objective, the state has no legitimate interest in protecting non-resident shareholders. Insofar as the Illinois law burdens out-of-state transactions, there is nothing to be weighed in the balance to sustain the law. We note, furthermore, that the Act completely exempts from coverage a corporation's acquisition of its own shares. Ill.Rev.Stat., ch. 121½, ¶ 137.52.09.-(4). Thus Chicago Rivet was able to make a competing tender offer for its own stock without complying with the Illinois Act, leaving Chicago Rivet's shareholders to depend only on the protections afforded them by federal securities law, protections which Illinois views as inadequate to protect investors in other contexts. This distinction is at variance with Illinois' asserted legislative purpose, and tends to undermine appellant's justification for the burdens the statute imposes on interstate commerce.

We are also unconvinced that the Illinois Act substantially enhances the shareholders' position. The Illinois Act seeks to protect shareholders of a company subject to a tender offer by requiring disclosures regarding the offer, assuring that shareholders have adequate time to decide whether to tender their shares, and according shareholders withdrawal, proration and equal consideration rights. However, the Williams Act provides these same substantive protections, compare Ill.Rev.Stat., ch. 121½, ¶¶ 137.59.C, D, and E (1979) (withdrawal, proration, and equal consideration rights) with 15 U.S.C. § 78n(d)(5), (6) and (7) and 17 CFR § 240.14d–7 (1981) (same). As the Court of Appeals noted, the disclosures required by the Illinois Act which go beyond those mandated by the Williams Act and the regulations pursuant to it may not substantially enhance the shareholders' ability to make informed decisions. 633 F.2d, at 500. It also was of the view that the possible benefits of the potential delays required by the Act may be outweighed by the increased risk that the tender offer will fail due to defensive tactics employed by incumbent management. We are unprepared to disagree with the Court of Appeals in these respects, and conclude that the protections the Illinois Act affords resident security holders are, for the most part, speculative.

Appellant also contends that Illinois has an interest in regulating the internal affairs of a corporation incorporated under its laws. The internal affairs doctrine is a conflict of laws principle which recognizes that only one state should have the authority to regulate a corporation's internal affairs—matters peculiar to the relationships among or between the corporation and its current officers, directors, and shareholders—because otherwise a corporation could be faced with conflicting demands. See Restatement (Second) of Conflict of Laws, § 302, Comment b at 307–308 (1971). That doctrine is of little use to the state in this context. Tender offers contemplate transfers of stock by stockholders to a third party and do not themselves implicate the internal affairs of the target company. Great Western United Corp. v. Kidwell, 577 F.2d, at 1280, n. 53; Restatement, supra, § 302, comment e at 310. Furthermore, the proposed justification is somewhat incredible since the Illinois Act applies to tender offers for any corporation for which 10% of the outstanding shares are held by Illinois residents, Ill.Rev.Stat., ch. 121½, ¶ 137.52–10 (1979). The Act thus applies to corporations that are not incorporated in Illinois and have their principal place of business in other states. Illinois has no interest in regulating the internal affairs of foreign corporations.

We conclude with the Court of Appeals that the Illinois Act imposes a substantial burden on interstate commerce which outweighs its putative local benefits. It is accordingly invalid under the Commerce Clause.

The judgment of the Court of Appeals is affirmed.

JUSTICE POWELL, concurring in part.

I agree with Justice Marshall that this case is moot. In view, however, of the decision of a majority of the Court to reach the merits, I join Parts I and V–B of the Court's opinion.

I join Part V–B because its Commerce Clause reasoning leaves some room for state regulation of tender offers. This period in our history is marked by conglomerate corporate formations essentially unrestricted by the antitrust laws. Often the offeror possesses resources, in terms of professional personnel experienced in takeovers as well as of capital, that vastly exceed those of the takeover target. This disparity in resources may seriously disadvantage a relatively small or regional target corporation. Inevitably there are certain adverse consequences in terms of general public interest when corporate headquarters are moved away from a city and State.*

The Williams Act provisions, implementing a policy of neutrality, seem to assume corporate entities of substantially equal resources. I agree with Justice Stevens that the Williams Act's neutrality policy does not necessarily imply a congressional intent to prohibit state legislation designed to assure—at least in some circumstances—greater protection to interests that include but often are broader than those of incumbent management.

---

* The corporate headquarters of the great national and multinational corporations tend to be located in the large cities of a few States. When corporate headquarters are transferred out of a city and State into one of these metropolitan centers, the State and locality from which the transfer is made inevitably suffer significantly. Management personnel—many of whom have provided community leadership—may move to the new corporate headquarters. Contributions to cultural, charitable, and educational life—both in terms of leadership and financial support—also tend to diminish when there is a move of corporate headquarters. [Footnote by the Court.]

JUSTICE STEVENS, concurring in part and concurring in the judgment.

. . . I agree with the Court that the Illinois Take-Over Act is invalid because it burdens interstate commerce. I therefore join Part V of its opinion. I am not persuaded, however, that Congress' decision to follow a policy of neutrality in its own legislation is tantamount to a federal prohibition against state legislation designed to provide special protection for incumbent management. Accordingly, although I agree with the Court's assessment of the impact of the Illinois statute, I do not join its preemption holding.

JUSTICE O'CONNOR, concurring in part.

I agree with the Court that the case is not moot, and that portions of the Illinois Business Take-Over Act, Ill.Rev.Stat., ch. 121½, ¶ 137.51 et seq. (1979), are invalid under the Commerce Clause. Because it is not necessary to reach the preemption issue, I join only Parts I, II and V of the Court's opinion, and would affirm the judgment of the Court of Appeals on that basis.

[JUSTICES MARSHALL, BRENNAN, and REHNQUIST dissented on the ground that the case was moot.] **

OHIO REV. CODE ANN. §§ 1701.01, 1701.831

§ 1701.01 Definitions.

. . .

(Y) "Issuing public corporation" means a domestic corporation with fifty or more shareholders that has its principal place of business, principal executive offices, or substantial assets within this state. . . .

(Z)(1) "Control share acquisition" means the acquisition, directly or indirectly, by any person . . . of shares of an issuing public corporation that, when added to all other shares of the issuing public corporation in respect of which such person may exercise or direct the exercise of voting power as provided in this division (Z)(1), would entitle such person, immediately after such acquisition, directly or indirectly, alone or with others, to exercise or direct the exercise of the voting power of the issuing public corporation in the election of directors within any of the following ranges of such voting power:

** Since the *MITE* decision a number of cases have invalidated state takeover statutes, or certain provisions or applications of those statutes. See, e.g., Martin-Marietta Corp. v. Bendix Corp., 690 F.2d 558, 565–68 (6th Cir. 1982) (Michigan statute); Telvest, Inc. v. Bradshaw, 697 F.2d 576 (4th Cir. 1983) (portion of Virginia statute); National City Lines, Inc. v. LLC Corp., 687 F.2d 1122, 1128–1133 (8th Cir. 1982) (Missouri statute); Bendix Corp. v. Martin Marietta Corp., 547 F.Supp. 522, 524–532 (D.C.Md.1982) (Maryland statute); Occidental Petroleum Corp. v. Cities Service Co., CCH Fed. Sec. Law Rptr. ¶ 99,063 (W.D.Okla. 12/20/82) (provisions of Oklahoma statute). But see Agency Rent-A-Car, Inc. v. Connolly, 686 F.2d 1029, 1033–1040 (1st Cir. 1982) (Mass. statute's one-year ban on subsequent purchases of target securities by bidders who have violated the statute's disclosure provision is not pre-empted by Williams Act; case remanded on the Commerce Clause issue). (Footnote by ed.)

(a) One-fifth or more but less than one-third of such voting power;

(b) One-third or more but less than a majority of such voting power;

(c) A majority or more of such voting power. . . .

(AA) "Acquiring person" means any person, . . . who has delivered an acquiring person statement to an issuing public corporation pursuant to section 1701.831 . . . .

(BB) "Acquiring person statement" means a written statement that complies with division (B) of section 1701.831 . . . .

(CC) "Interested shares" means the shares of an issuing public corporation in respect of which any of the following persons may exercise or direct the exercise of the voting power of the corporation in the election of directors:

(1) An acquiring person;

(2) Any officer of the issuing public corporation elected or appointed by the directors of the issuing public corporation;

(3) Any employee of the issuing public corporation who is also a director of such corporation. . . .

§ 1701.11   Regulations adopted by shareholders . . . .

(A) Regulations for the government of a corporation, the conduct of its affairs, and the management of its property, consistent with law and the articles, may be adopted by the shareholders at a meeting held for such purpose, by the affirmative vote of the holders of shares entitling them to exercise a majority of the voting power of the corporation on such proposal . . . .

(B) Without limiting the generality of such authority, the regulations may include provisions with respect to . . . .

(8) The manner in which and conditions upon which certificates for shares, and the shares represented thereby, may be transferred, restrictions on the right to transfer the same, and reservations of liens thereon. The regulations may include restrictions on the transfer and the right to transfer shares of an issuing public corporation to any person in a control share acquisition, including requirements and procedures for consent to such acquisition by directors based on a determination by the directors of the best interests of the issuing public corporation and its shareholders, consent to such acquisition by shareholders, and reasonable sanctions for a violation of such requirements, including the right of the issuing public corporation to refuse to transfer, to redeem, or to deny voting or other shareholder rights appurtenant to shares acquired in such an acquisition. . . .

§ 1701.831   [Procedure for control share acquisitions.]

(A) Unless the articles or the regulations of the issuing public corporation provide that this section does not apply to control share acquisitions of shares of such corporation, any control share acquisition of an issuing public corporation shall be made only with the prior authorization of the shareholders of such corporation in accordance with this section.

(B) Any person who proposes to make a control share acquisition shall deliver an acquiring person statement to the issuing public corporation at the issuing public corporation's principal executive offices. Such acquiring person statement shall set forth all of the following:

(1) The identity of the acquiring person;

(2) A statement that the acquiring person statement is given pursuant to this section;

(3) The number of shares of the issuing public corporation owned, directly or indirectly, by the acquiring person;

(4) The range of voting power, described in division (Z)(1)(a), (b), or (c) of section 1701.01 of the Revised Code, under which the proposed control share acquisition would, if consummated, fall;

(5) A description in reasonable detail of the terms of the proposed control share acquisition;

(6) Representations of the acquiring person, together with a statement in reasonable detail of the facts upon which they are based, that the proposed control share acquisition, if consummated, will not be contrary to law, and that the acquiring person has the financial capacity to make the proposed control share acquisition.

(C) Within ten days after receipt of an acquiring person statement that complies with division (B) of this section, the directors of the issuing public corporation shall call a special meeting of shareholders of the issuing public corporation for the purpose of voting on the proposed control share acquisition. ... Unless the acquiring person agrees in writing to another date, such special meeting of shareholders shall be held within fifty days after receipt by the issuing public corporation of the acquiring person statement. If the acquiring person so requests in writing at the time of delivery of the acquiring person statement, such special meeting shall not be held sooner than thirty days after receipt by the issuing public corporation of the acquiring person statement.

(D) Notice of the special meeting ... shall include or be accompanied by both of the following:

(1) A copy of the acquiring person statement delivered to the issuing public corporation pursuant to this section;

(2) A statement by the issuing public corporation, authorized by its directors, of its position or recommendation, or that it is taking no position or making no recommendation, with respect to the proposed control share acquisition.

(E) The acquiring person may make the proposed control share acquisition if both of the following occur:

(1) The shareholders of the issuing public corporation who hold shares of such corporation entitling them to vote in the election of directors authorize such acquisition at the special meeting held for

that purpose at which a quorum is present by an affirmative vote of a majority of the voting power of such corporation in the election of directors represented at such meeting in person or by proxy, and a majority of the portion of such voting power excluding the voting power of interested shares. A quorum shall be deemed to be present at such special meeting if at least a majority of the voting power of the issuing public corporation in the election of directors, and a majority of the portion of such voting power excluding the voting power of interested shares is represented at such meeting in person or by proxy.

(2) Such acquisition is consummated, in accordance with the terms so authorized, not later than three hundred sixty days following shareholder authorization of the control share acquisition. ...

REPORT OF THE SECURITIES AND EXCHANGE COMMISSION ADVISORY COMMITTEE ON TENDER OFFERS

xvi-xxii, 34–46 (1983)

EXECUTIVE SUMMARY

Since the Williams Act was adopted in 1968, acquisition practices have undergone fundamental changes, many in response to significant developments in the environment—financial, technological, social and legal—in which such acquisitions have taken place. These changes have been highlighted in recent years as the introduction of the "billion dollar takeover bid", complex and creative bidding strategies, and equally inventive defensive responses, have made tender offers front page news.

In light of these developments and the fundamental issues they have raised, the Commission has undertaken a reexamination of the takeover process and a reevaluation of the laws that govern it. As the first step, the Chairman of the Commission established the Advisory Committee on February 25, 1983 to review the techniques for acquisition of control of public companies and the laws applicable to such transactions. The 18 individuals appointed to the Advisory Committee included prominent members of the business and financial community, academia and the legal and accounting professions, who have been actively involved in numerous tender offers as institutional investors, bidders, targets, arbitrageurs, investment and commercial bankers, attorneys, accountants and recognized authorities. The Committee's mandate was to consider the process in terms of the best interests of all shareholders, i.e. shareholders of all corporations, whether potential acquirors, target companies or bystanders, and to propose specific legislative and regulatory improvements for the benefit of all shareholders.

There follows a brief summary of the principal conclusions and recommendations of the Committee.

Economics of Takeovers and their Regulation

After considerable study, discussion and consideration of commentators' views, the Committee finds that there is insufficient basis for concluding that takeovers are either per se beneficial or detrimental to the economy or the securities markets in general, or to issuers or their shareholders, specifically. While in certain cases takeovers may have served as a discipline on inefficient management, in other cases there is little to suggest that the quality of management of the target company was at issue. Similarly, while the threat of takeover may cause certain managements to emphasize short term profits over long term growth, there is little evidence that this is generally true. Nor has the Committee found a basis for concluding that the method of acquisition is a major factor in determining whether an acquisition proves successful. As with other capital transactions, the fact that some takeovers prove beneficial while others prove disappointing is attributable less to the method of acquisition than it is to the business judgment reflected in combining the specific enterprises involved. Therefore, the Committee concluded that the regulatory scheme should be designed neither to promote nor to deter takeovers. Such transactions and related activities are a valid method of capital allocation, so long as they are conducted in accordance with the laws deemed necessary to protect the interests of shareholders and the integrity and efficiency of the capital markets.

As part of its study of the economic consequences of takeovers, the Committee specifically addressed the issue of the effect of the takeover process on the availability of credit and its allocation in the market. On the basis of its deliberations, including discussion with Federal Reserve Board Chairman Paul Volcker and members of his staff, the Committee believes that there is no material distortion in the credit markets resulting from acquisition of control transactions, and that no regulatory initiative should be undertaken to limit or to allocate the availability of credit in such transactions.

Objectives of Federal Regulation of Takeovers

The Committee recommends the following premises as the bases for the regulation of takeovers:

Neutrality and Protection of Shareholders. Takeover regulation should not favor either the acquiror or the target company, but should aim to achieve a reasonable balance while at the same time protecting the interests of shareholders and the integrity and efficiency of the markets.

National Market. Regulation of takeovers should recognize that such transactions take place in a national securities market.

Elimination of the Present Bias Against Exchange Offers. Cash and securities tender offers should be placed on an equal regulatory footing so that bidders, the market and shareholders, and not regulation, decide between the two.

Innovation. Regulation of takeovers should not unduly restrict innovations in techniques. These techniques should be able to evolve in relationship to changes in the market and the economy.

Scope of Regulation. Even though regulation may restrict innovations in takeover techniques, it is desirable to have sufficient regulation to insure the integrity of the markets and to protect shareholders and market participants against fraud, non-disclosure of material information and the creation of situations in which a significant number of reasonably diligent small shareholders may be at a disadvantage to market professionals.

Restriction of Periodic Abuses. The evolution of the market and innovation in takeover techniques may from time to time produce abuses. The regulatory framework should be flexible enough to allow the Commission to deal with such abuses as soon as they appear.

Relationship to Other Legislative Objectives.

a. *State Takeover Law.* State regulation of takeovers should be confined to local companies.

b. *State Corporation Law.* Except to the extent necessary to eliminate abuses or interference with the intended functioning of federal takeover regulation, federal takeover regulation should not preempt or override state corporation law. Essentially the business judgment rule should continue to govern most such activity.

c. *State Regulation of Public Interest Businesses.* Federal takeover regulation should not preempt substantive state regulation of banks, utilities, insurance companies and similar businesses, where the change of control provisions of such state regulation are justified in relation to the overall objectives of the industry being regulated, do not conflict with the procedural provisions of federal takeover regulation and relate to a significant portion of the issuer's business.

d. *Federal Regulation.* Federal takeover regulation should not override the regulation of particular industries such as banks, broadcast licensees, railroads, ship operators, nuclear licensees, etc.

e. *Relationship with Other Federal Laws.* Federal takeover regulation should not be used to achieve antitrust, labor, tax, use of credit and similar objectives. Those objectives should be achieved by separate legislation or regulation.

Regulation of Acquirors of Corporate Control

The Committee identified four major concerns with respect to the current regulation of acquirors of corporate control: (1) the substantial disincentives to undertake an exchange offer; (2) the use of open market accumulation programs and other methods to acquire control of issuers that deny all shareholders the opportunity to share in the premium paid for control of an issuer; (3) the potentially coercive effects on shareholders of a partial or two-tier offer; and (4) the need to provide equal opportunity to participate in an offer.

1. *Exchange Offers.* Because of the need to register securities to be offered in exchange for those of another company and the delay inherent in preparing the registration statement and having it processed by the Commission, the Committee found that the regulations applicable to exchange offers under the Securities Act of 1933 are a major disincentive to using securities as consideration in a tender offer. The Committee believes that such regulatory disincentives can be remedied without affecting investor protection and that the deterrence of exchange offers is not in the best interests of shareholders. If such regulatory disincentives were minimized, the Committee expects there would be greater use of securities in single step transactions. Therefore, the Committee recommends that the concept of integration of disclosure under the Securities Act of 1933 and the Securities Exchange Act of 1934, previously effected by the Commission in securities offerings for cash, be extended to exchange offers. The Committee also recommends that exchange offers be permitted to commence upon the filing of the registration statement relating to the exchange offer, rather than upon effectiveness of such registration statement.

2. *Limitations on Acquisition of Securities*

a. *Schedule 13D.* The Committee found that the current rules under section 13(d) of the Exchange Act, which require reporting of the acquisition of more than 5% of certain classes of an issuer's securities, have failed to give adequate notice to shareholders and the market of potential acquisitions of control. Currently, the acquiror may continue to purchase securities after passing the reporting threshold and prior to the date the report is required to be filed, i.e. the tenth day after reaching the threshold. This ten-day window presents substantial opportunity for abuse as the acquiror "dashes" to buy as many shares as it can before disclosure of its investment and its intentions. The Committee therefore recommends that the ten-day window be closed by prohibiting any acquisition that would result in a person's having beneficial ownership of more that 5% of the specified classes of securities prior to the expiration of 48 hours from filing of a Schedule 13D with the Commission.

b. *Shareholders' Access to Control Premium.* Concluding that "control" is essentially a corporate asset and that shareholders should have equal opportunity to share in any premium paid for such asset, the Committee recommends that the law prohibit any acquisition of voting securities of an issuer, if immediately following such acquisition, such person would own more than 20% of the voting power of the issuer. Excepted from such prohibition would be acquisitions made (1) from the issuer, or (2) pursuant to a tender offer. To deal with situations not within the purpose of this provision, the Committee recommends that the Commission retain broad exemptive power with respect to this prohibition.

3. *Partial Offers and Two-Tier Bids.* The Committee is concerned with the potentially coercive nature of partial and two-tier bids. However, given that partial offers can serve valid business purposes and that two-tier bids generally have proved more favorable to shareholders than partial offers with no second step, the Committee is not prepared to recommend that such bids be prohibited. The Committee recommends instead, as a regulatory disincentive for partial and two-tier offers, the adoption of a minimum offering period for the partial bid that is approximately two weeks longer than that required for a full bid.

4. *Equal Opportunity.* A fundamental premise of the Committee's recommendations is that all target company shareholders should have an equal opportunity to participate in a tender offer. Essential to providing such opportunity is a minimum offering period sufficient to permit a reasonably diligent shareholder (individual or institution) to receive the offering materials and to make an informed investment decision. The Committee concluded that the appropriate period for an initial bid for a particular target is 30 calendar days. Given the "alerting" of the market and target shareholders by the initial bid, the Committee believes that the minimum offering period for subsequent competing bids need only be 20 calendar days, except that generally a subsequent competing bid would not be permitted to expire prior to the initial bid. As noted above, in either case, if the bid is a partial offer, the minimum offering period will be increased by approximately two weeks. The Committee also recommends that the minimum offering period and prorationing period remain open for five calendar days from the announcement of an increase in price or number of shares sought.

A major change in the timing provisions applicable to tender offers recommended by the Committee is the elimination of the extension of withdrawal rights upon the commencement of another bid. The Committee believes that the ability of another bidder to effect changes in the terms of an existing bidder's offer results in confusion and "game playing", presents opportunities for abuse and tips the balance in favor of the second bidder.

Regulation of Opposition to Acquisitions of Control

[This portion of the executive summary is omitted. See the text of Chapter IV of the Report, infra.]

Regulation of Market Participants

The recommendations of the Committee regarding the activities of market participants are directed principally to strengthening Rule 10b–4's prohibition of short tendering and to including specifically within its prohibitions hedged tendering and multiple tendering. Such practices, in the Committee's judgment, give market professionals such an advantage in the takeover process as to jeopardize public confidence in the fairness and integrity of the capital markets. ...

. . .

CHAPTER IV

REGULATION OF OPPOSITION TO ACQUISITIONS OF CONTROL

A. General Policy Regarding State and Federal Regulation of Takeovers

While the activities of bidders are largely regulated by federal law,
the response of the target company generally has been governed by
state law, statutory and common. A principal issue defined by the
Committee is the extent to which federal regulation should intrude into
this area. Resolution of the issue requires a balancing of two competing
interests: minimal preemption of traditional state corporate law and
maintenance of the integrity of the national securities market in which
tender offers take place. As to the first interest, the Committee concludes as follows:

Recommendation 33

The Committee supports a system of state corporation laws and the
business judgment rule. No reform should undermine that system.
Broadly speaking, the Committee believes that the business judgment
rule should be the principal governor of decisions made by corporate
management including decisions that may alter the likelihood of a
takeover.

While the Committee supports a system of state corporation law,
however, it concluded that provisions generally restricting the transfer
of control of an issuer, whether contained in state statutes or included in
an issuer's charter or by-laws, improperly interfere with the conduct of
takeovers in the national market place. Courts have invalidated state
tender offer statutes that interfere with the bidder's conduct of a tender
offer under federal rules and burden tender offers in interstate commerce. Newly developed state statutes which, through regulation of
target companies, have substantially similar effects on the ability to
conduct a tender offer should not be permitted regardless of the form in
which they are drafted. This category would include not only provisions
incorporated into state corporation law but also broad policy enactments
such as environmental quality legislation. Similarly, the Committee does
not believe a company should be permitted to adopt charter or by-law
provisions that erect high barriers to change of control and accomplish
the very results that the Committee recommends be prohibited under
state statutes. ...

B. *Specific Defensive Measures and Federal Regulation*

1. *Charter and By-law Provisions*

Until such provisions are prohibited, the Committee recommends that
companies be required to adopt supermajority provisions by the same
vote percentage as that contained in the provisions and to have the
provisions ratified periodically.

Recommendation 36

To the extent not prohibited or otherwise restricted, companies should be permitted to adopt provisions requiring supermajority approval for change of control transactions only where the ability to achieve such a level of support is demonstrable.

a. Any company seeking approval of a charter or by-law provision that requires, or could under certain circumstances require, the affirmative vote of more than the minimum specified by state law should be required to obtain that same level of approval in passing the provision initially. Ratification should be required every three years.

b. Where a charter or by-law provision provides a formula for the required level of approval, which level cannot be determined until the circumstances of the merger are known, the formula shall be limited by law so as to require a vote no higher than the percentage of votes actually ratifying the charter or by-law provision. Ratification should be required every three years.

c. For a nationally traded company that has adopted a supermajority provision prior to the date of enactment of this recommendation, and for a local company with a supermajority provision which becomes nationally traded at a later date, shareholders must ratify the supermajority provision within three years after such date, and continue to ratify such provision every three years thereafter. ...

2. Advisory Votes

The Committee found that there were other actions taken by management with respect to takeovers that, while not appearing to interfere substantially with the national securities market, called for additional disclosure to shareholders and the opportunity for shareholders to express their opinions on the appropriateness of such actions. The Committee thus recommends that change of control related policies and compensation be required to be disclosed annually in an issuer's proxy statement and submitted to an advisory vote.

Recommendation 37

The Commission should designate certain change of control related policies of corporations as "advisory vote matters" for review at each annual stockholders' meeting for the election of directors and for disclosure in the proxy statement.

a. *Matters Covered.* Advisory vote matters should include:

i. *Supermajority provisions.* To the extent not prohibited or otherwise restricted, charter provisions requiring more than the statutorily imposed minimum vote requirement to accomplish a merger, including provisions requiring supermajority approval under special conditions (e.g., "fair value" and "majority of the disinterested shareholders" provisions);

ii. *Disenfranchisement.* Charter provisions (other than cumulative voting and class voting) that abandon the one-share, one-vote rule based on the concentration of ownership within a class (e.g., formulas diluting voting strength of 10% shareholders, and "majority of the disinterested shareholders" approval requirements);

iii. *Standstill agreements.* Current agreements with remaining lives longer than one year that restrict or prohibit purchases or sales of the company's stock by a party to the agreement; and

iv. *Change of control compensation.* Arrangements that provide change of control related compensation to company managers or employees. (See Recommendation 38).

b. *Proxy Statement Disclosure.* Companies should be required to disclose all advisory vote matters in a "Change of Control" section of the proxy statement.

c. *Vote.* Shareholders should be requested to vote on an advisory basis as to whether they are or continue to be in favor of the company's policy with respect to the advisory vote matters disclosed in the proxy statement. The board would not be bound by the results of the advisory vote but could, in its own judgment, decide whether company policy should be changed on the advisory vote matters. The outcome of an advisory vote would have no legal effect on an existing agreement.

The recommendation for advisory votes was one that evoked substantial debate. A number of Committee members strongly objected to the process of advisory votes as a substantial and unwarranted interference in the internal affairs of a corporation better left to state corporation law. Questions also were raised as to the need for anything more than disclosure of control-related matters in the proxy statement. Some thought was expressed that advisory voting did not go far enough and that target company management should obtain shareholder approval before adopting any change of control policy.

3. *Change of Control Compensation*

Based on private surveys as well as filings with the Commission, it appears that contracts with change of control compensation are increasingly prevalent. Justifications articulated for contracts that became operative only in the event of a change of control are based on the issuer's interests in attracting and retaining high quality management, in keeping management's attention on running the business, and in aligning management's interests more closely with those of shareholders when an offer for the company is at hand. In general, the Committee does not believe that arrangements for change of control compensation in fact deter takeovers, as they are a small fraction of an acquisition price. Nevertheless, the Committee shares the public concern that such forms of compensation, particularly when adopted following the commencement of a tender offer, can present the appearance of self-dealing on the part of management at a moment of corporate vulnerability and a failure to place the interests of shareholders foremost. The Committee believes this perception is significant enough to warrant regulation.

The Committee's proposal is designed to strike a balance between the competing views on the issues raised by change of control compensation. On the one hand, the Committee recommendation avoids a direct restriction of free bargaining of management employment agreements by federal regulation. On the other hand, it eliminates an element of the practice that raises doubts as to the propriety of the takeover process and provides annual disclosure and the opportunity for shareholders to express their views on such arrangements.

Recommendation 38

a. *Change of Control Compensation During a Tender Offer.* The board of directors shall not adopt contracts or other arrangements with change of control compensation once a tender offer for the company has commenced.

b. *Change of Control Compensation Prior to a Tender Offer.*

i. *Disclosure.* The issuer should disclose the terms and parties to contracts or other arrangements that provide for change of control compensation in the Change of Control section of the annual proxy statement.

ii. *Advisory Vote.* At each annual meeting, shareholders should be requested to vote, on an advisory basis, as to whether the company should continue to provide change of control compensation to its management and employees. The board would not be obligated by the results of the vote to take any specific steps, and the outcome of the vote would have no legal effect on any existing employment agreement.

4. *Self-Tenders*

Although there may be a perception that a self-tender will decapitalize the target company, the Committee does not view the practice as one that is substantively invalid. The self-tender may provide means of getting more value to shareholders. In some cases a self-tender can provide a favorable alternative to the second step of a front-end loaded deal. In view of the legitimate business purposes that can be served by a self-tender, the Committee believes that regulation of the mechanism generally should be governed by the business judgment rule and, if abused, principles of fiduciary duty under state law. ...

5. *Counter Tender Offers*

The use of a counter tender offer as a defensive measure, the so-called "Pac-Man" defense, has evoked significant criticism. Given the circumstances where a counter tender offer can be used for the benefit of target company shareholders, the Committee is reluctant to recommend a total prohibition of such transactions, except in the instance where the bidder company has made a cash tender offer for 100% of the target company.

The counter tender offer is a defensive action whereby the target company makes a tender offer for the shares of the bidding company. In mounting such a defense, the target company implicitly acknowledges the appropriateness of a combination between itself and the bidder, but may contest the ultimate management control and capital structure of the combined enterprise, as well as the terms of the exchange. The counter tender offer may be necessary to protect the interests of target company shareholders who will remain shareholders in the combined enterprise. Where, however, the bidder is offering cash for 100% of the target company, the counter tender offer is not appropriate because there will be no remaining shareholders on whose behalf target company management is acting.

The Committee believes principles of business judgment and fiduciary obligations under state law generally should provide adequate protection to shareholders against abuse of the technique.

6. *Stock and Asset Transactions with Friendly Acquirors*

Arrangements or options to sell stock or assets to a preferred acquiror (generally referred to as "leg-ups" or "lock-ups") have been criticized as providing an unfair advantage to one bidder over another and as possibly reducing the value received by shareholders by stifling competition. In the Committee's experience, however, such arrangements frequently are necessary to induce a second bidder into a takeover contest. Rather than stifling competition, such action may enhance the potential for an auction.

Nonetheless, above a certain level, the contract to issue stock becomes less supportable in that in may foreclose competition altogether. Therefore, the Committee recommends that the issuance of stock representing more than 15% of the fully diluted shares outstanding after issuance should be approved by shareholders. This recommendation extends the basic concept of the New York Stock Exchange rule that requires shareholder approval for the issuance of more than 18.5% of a company's shares where such shares are to be listed. ...

7. *Third Party Asset Sales*

Although the sale of significant assets ("crown jewels") by a target company during the course of a tender offer may appear to alter the value of a company to its shareholders should the bidder retract its offer, the Committee believes that asset dispositions may be a legitimate part of a plan to realize value for shareholders in excess of a proposed bid. When tested against the business judgment rule, the company must be satisfied that full value is being received for the assets disposed. Transactions of this sort should be allowed because, in many cases, value for a company can only be maximized by selling different components in different markets. There may, in fact, be no preferred acquiror for the entire company.

Recommendation 42

The sale of significant assets, even when undertaken during the course of a tender offer, should continue to be tested against the business judgment rule.

8. *Use of Employee Benefit Plans*

A target company may attempt to use an employee benefit plan to defend against a takeover bid in two ways. First, the company may instruct the retirement plan managers not to tender company shares held by the plan to an unapproved bidder. Second, the target company may instruct the plan managers to purchase company stock with a view to defeating a hostile tender offer. It may be that in either case such instructions constitute economically unsound investment practice and result in substantial risks to plan beneficiaries. The Committee believes, nevertheless, that the substantial issues raised by the use of employee benefit plans during a tender offer are, and should be, governed by regulations other than under the federal securities laws. Traditional principles of fiduciary duty as well as existing pension regulations appear to prohibit observance of "no sale" instructions or instructions to purchase company stock for the purpose of defeating a tender offer.

9. *Block Repurchases at a Premium*

The Committee is particularly concerned with a target company's repurchase of its stock at a premium to market from a dissident shareholder. Under current law, the ability of a company to repurchase shares from dissident shareholders at a premium has created incentives for investors to accumulate blocks with the intention to sell them back to the issuer at a profit. Not only does such a transaction generally serve little business purpose outside the takeover context but also it constitutes a practice whereby a control premium may be distributed selectively and not shared equally by all shareholders. Moreover, the Committee is concerned about the doubt that such a transaction casts on the integrity of the takeover process. The Committee recommends prohibiting the repurchase at a premium of a block of stock held for less than two years without shareholder approval.

Recommendation 43

Repurchase of a company's shares at a premium to market from a particular holder or group that has held such shares for less than two years should require shareholder approval. This rule would not apply to offers made to all holders of a class of securities.

†